Captain's Diary 2007

Captain's Diary 2007

Ricky Ponting

HarperSports
An imprint of HarperCollinsPublishers

Harper*Sports*

An imprint of HarperCollins*Publishers* Australia

First published in Australia in 2007
by HarperCollins*Publishers* Australia Pty Limited
ABN 36 009 913 517
www.harpercollins.com.au

HarperCollins*Publishers*
25 Ryde Road, Pymble, Sydney, NSW 2073, Australia
31 View Road, Glenfield, Auckland 10, New Zealand
77–85 Fulham Palace Road, London, W6 8JB, United Kingdom
2 Bloor Street East, 20th floor, Toronto, Ontario M4W 1A8, Canada
10 East 53rd Street, New York NY 10022, USA

Ponting, Ricky.
    Ricky Ponting's captain's diary : from reclaiming the Ashes
    to conquering the World Cup.
    ISBN 978 0 7322 8490 9 (pbk.).
    1. Ponting, Ricky. 2. Cricket captains – Australia –
    Biography. 3. Cricket players – Australia – Biography.
    4. Cricket – Australia. I. Armstrong, Geoff. II. Title.
796.358092

Cover photographs courtesy of Getty Images
Cover design by Matt Stanton
Internal design adapted from original by Chrisabella Designs
Typeset in 11/17 Sabon by Kirby Jones
Printed and bound in Australia by Griffin Press
79gsm Bulky Paperback used by HarperCollins*Publishers* is a natural,
recyclable product made from wood grown in a combination of sustainable
plantation and regrowth forests. It also contains up to a 20% portion of
recycled fibre. The manufacturing processes conform to the environmental
regulations in Tasmania, the place of manufacture.

5 4 3 2   07 08 09 10

For Rianna … I could never have made it through such a long and intense season of cricket without your constant love, support and understanding.

It's no coincidence that my best days as a cricketer have occurred since I met you.

GEOFF ARMSTRONG

Ricky Ponting's co-author on *Captain's Diary 2007*, Geoff Armstrong, has worked — as writer, editor or publisher — on more than 70 books on sport, more than 30 of them on cricket. Between 1993 and 2005, he collaborated with Steve Waugh on each of Steve's 12 best-selling books, including all of his diaries and the former Australian captain's autobiography *Out of My Comfort Zone*. Geoff is the author of *A Century of Summers*, the centenary history of the Sheffield Shield (featuring an epilogue by Sir Donald Bradman), *ESPN's Legends of Cricket*, which profiles 25 of the game's greatest players, *The 100 Greatest Cricketers*, and the co-author, with Mark Gately, of *The People's Game*, a history of Australia in one-day international cricket. He has worked as co-author on books by David Boon, Ian Healy, Mike Whitney, Bob Simpson and Michael Bevan, and with Ian Russell produced *Top 10s of Australian Test Cricket*, a study of Australian cricket statistics.

Geoff is also the co-author, with Peter Thompson, of *Phar Lap*, the definitive biography of the legendary racehorse, and *Melbourne Cup 1930*, the story of the most remarkable of Phar Lap's many big-race victories.

ACKNOWLEDGMENTS

Our thanks go to Sam Halvorsen, Ricky's long-time manager, for his strong backing of the project. We are also grateful for the help received from Peter Young and Philip Pope at Cricket Australia, and from everyone at HarperCollins, especially Alison Urqhuart, Belinda Yuille, Natalie Costa Bir, Matt Stanton and the legendary Graeme Jones, who were brilliant throughout. Thanks, too, to Alexia Pettenon, Stella Tarakson, Mike Coward and Steve Keipert for their help with getting the manuscript in order.

STATISTICS

The statistics, scores and averages that appear through the pages and at the end of this book were derived from a variety of sources, including three websites — *Cricinfo Australia* (www.baggygreen.com.au), *Howstat.com: the cricket statisticians* (www.howstat.com.au) and *CricketArchive* (www.cricketarchive.com) — plus *Wisden* and the *Sydney Morning Herald*.

CONTENTS

THE INCOMPARABLES VERSUS THE INVINCIBLES

By Geoff Armstrong

IN THE AFTERMATH OF Australia's 5–0 Ashes triumph in 2006–07, the renowned cricket writer Mike Coward wrote, 'The greatness of this Australian team is indisputable. If need be, Ricky Ponting and his men can be called "The Incomparables"'

Coward's tribute was just one of a multitude of plaudits the team received in the wake of their epic victory, yet — no matter how many matches this current Australian side wins — you can still find a number of old cricketers and commentators willing to shout, 'They were better in my day!' Neil Harvey was at it before the second Ashes Test, arguing that Shane Warne was the only current-day Australian player who would have got a game with Bradman's 'Invincibles'.

Of course, this is impossible to prove. But what if the question was turned around? How many of the 1948 Australians would get into Ricky Ponting's team that regained the Ashes? It's a subtle tack, but an interesting one.

Quickly, the two sides ...

Fifth Test, 1948: Arthur Morris, Sid Barnes, Don Bradman (captain), Lindsay Hassett, Keith Miller, Neil Harvey, Sam Loxton, Ray Lindwall, Don Tallon, Bill Johnston, Doug Ring.

Fifth Test, 2006–07: Matthew Hayden, Justin Langer, Ricky Ponting (captain), Michael Hussey, Michael Clarke, Andrew Symonds, Adam Gilchrist, Shane Warne, Brett Lee, Stuart Clark, Glenn McGrath.

Let's work down the batting order. Hayden and Langer were fantastic as a duo for five years, averaging 51.41 per opening stand in 113 Test innings, and Hayden is the only Australian opening batsman in Test history to play 30 innings and average more than 50. Langer averaged 45.27 in 105 Tests, which is comparable with Morris' 46.49 from 46 Tests. However, a case can be made that Morris' career figures are inflated by the fact that he faced inferior bowling for the first half of his Test career. In his first four series, straight after World War II when the attacks that bowled to him were mediocre, Morris averaged 67.78. After that, in his final 27 Tests, he averaged only 34.76. Maybe those latter Tests against better bowlers are a fairer guide to his ability. Barnes did average 63.06 in Test cricket, but he only played in 13 matches, most of them against those same ordinary bowlers Morris flayed.

No doubt, Morris and Barnes were fine players, but did they do enough in Test cricket to eclipse Hayden and Langer? At best, it's line-ball. In such a situation, involving four excellent players and with the current Aussie team winning so often, the selectors should stay with the status quo.

Bradman at No. 3 and Ponting (more than 6000 Test runs since the start of 2002, at an average of nearly 72 with 24 hundreds, is a hard record to argue with) at No. 4 pick themselves, as does Miller as the allrounder at No. 6. We'll leave the five spot for last.

Gilchrist or Tallon? Plenty of people want to tell you Tallon was the greatest wicketkeeper Australia has ever had, but why then does he have the worst byes-per-100 balls ratio of any Aussie keeper to play in 10 or more Tests? 'I have never seen a stumper to equal Tallon in speed,' wrote Jack Fingleton in his book of the 1948 Ashes tour, *Brightly Fades the Don*, '[but] he missed a number of chances ...'

Tallon took 12 catches in four Tests on the Invincibles tour, a couple of them fabulous, but he did have ordinary days, most notably when he spilt three straightforward chances in England's first innings of the third Test. Gilchrist is closing in on 400 Test dismissals, and he's arguably the most damaging No. 7 batsman of all time. He wins over Tallon every time.

Lindwall and McGrath (taker of more Test wickets than any other pace bowler, at a miserly average of 21.64) are certain picks to lead the pace attack, and Warne, of course, is the spinner. The final bowling spot comes down to one of Johnston, Lee and Clark, though Ernie Toshack from the 1948 squad and Stuart MacGill, taker of 198 wickets in 40 Tests, are also worthy of consideration.

Given that Miller is also in the side, it is hard to resist the left-handed Johnston, who might just be one of the most underrated bowlers in cricket history.

While England's bowling attack straight after the war might have been weak, her batting — featuring Len Hutton, Denis

Compton, Bill Edrich and Cyril Washbrook — was not. The West Indies side that came to Australia in 1951–52 included the famous three Ws: Everton Weekes, Clyde Walcott and Frank Worrell. Johnston was superb against all these accomplished players. At the end of that Windies series, he'd taken 111 wickets in 24 Tests at just 19.23. To put these figures in perspective, only one Australian bowler in Test history, Charlie 'The Terror' Turner, has taken 100 career wickets at an average less than 20.

From 1952 on, injuries hampered Johnston, but what he did in his first 24 Tests was enough to confirm his great quality. As good as Lee and Clark are, Bill Johnston was better.

This leaves us with the following team: Hayden, Langer, Bradman, Ponting, Miller, Gilchrist, Lindwall, Warne, Johnston, McGrath, plus the No. 5.

The choice for this last batting spot comes down to Neil Harvey or Mike Hussey. Lindsay Hassett was an outstanding Test batsman, good enough to average 46.56 in 43 Tests, but few critics would put him ahead of Harvey, who was Australia's best batsman throughout the 1950s. There are at least a couple of parallels between Harvey and Hussey: both are left-handed, and both got off to extraordinary starts to their Test careers.

Hussey has averaged 79.85 with the bat in his first 16 Tests, up to the end of 2006–07 Ashes series, with four centuries, but Harvey's own record is hardly shabby. After his first 16 Tests, the youngest member of the Invincibles was averaging 64.59. After nine Tests, he had been averaging an astonishing 106.56, with six centuries. He was still above 60 after 40 Tests, and finished with an average of 48.42 from 79 Tests.

The selectors could argue that Harvey's superb career record should get him the final spot, but they could also mount a strong case for retaining the man known as Mr Cricket. After all he's done in the early stages of his Test career, you couldn't really drop

Hussey, could you? He's a crucial part of a special team. Some selectors would stick with him, even ahead of the great Neil Harvey.

SUGGESTING THAT ONLY FOUR of the Invincibles would find places in the 2006–07 Australian Ashes team would be seen as sacrilegious by many fans of the 'good old days'. After all, Sir Donald Bradman's famous side is generally considered to be one of the greatest of all cricket combinations. Its effort in going through the 1948 English summer undefeated ranks among the game's most notable achievements, even if Great Britain was still recovering from the damage inflicted on it during World War II.

Almost six decades later, Ricky Ponting's Test and one-day sides won the Ashes 5–0 and the World Cup without losing a match. The only other Australian team to clean sweep a five-Test Ashes series was Warwick Armstrong's side of 1920–21, so the achievement of Ponting's Test team was not quite unprecedented. How the Incomparables and the Invincibles line up is really a matter for individual opinion, but what is beyond question is that the manner in which the Australian one-day side totally dominated the 2007 World Cup was phenomenal:

- Australia's winning margins in its 11 games were 203 runs, 229 runs, 83 runs, 103 runs, 10 wickets, seven wickets, nine wickets, seven wickets, 215 runs, seven wickets and 53 runs.
- Australia lost only 43 wickets in the tournament while scoring 2851 runs, at an average of 66.30 per wicket.
- Five of the top 10 batting averages in the tournament belonged to Australians: Shane Watson (145.00), Michael Clarke (87.20), Brad Hodge (76.00), Matthew Hayden (73.22) and Ricky Ponting (67.38). Andrew Symonds, who averaged 63.00, was 13th.

- Only nine Australians batted in the tournament. Of these nine, Brad Hogg was not out on each of the three occasions he batted and Shane Watson was dismissed once.
- Four of the seven bowlers to take 15 or more wickets in the tournament were Australian: Glenn McGrath (26 wickets), Shaun Tait (23), Brad Hogg (21) and Nathan Bracken (16). Sri Lanka's Muttiah Muralitharan (23) was the only non-Australian to take more than 20 wickets.
- The team stretched their unbeaten run in World Cup matches to 29, going back to 1999 (including the tie against South Africa in the 1999 semi-final).

Because the World Cup was played in the Caribbean, which meant much of the action took place when Australian fans back home were sleeping, and also because the tournament itself received plenty of bad media for being too long and inadequately organised, the Australian team's performance has not received the kudos it deserves. However, a strong case can be put that, based on what the scoreboard tells us, it was the most dominant team performance by a side representing Australia in sporting history.

Australian teams have remained unbeaten through a tournament and they have also been dominant throughout a competition, but never before has a side wearing the green and gold in the highest profile competition of a major sport won *all* of its matches, including matches against high-ranking opponents, so emphatically. The Invincibles might have lost the third Test in 1948 but for rain, and then were behind in the fourth Test until Bradman and Morris performed a batting miracle on the final day. The Australian women's hockey team that won Olympic gold in 1996 and 2000 was held to one draw at each Games. The Australian rugby league teams of 1982 and 1986 were undefeated throughout Kangaroo tours, but sadly in the '80s international league was hardly competitive. The Australian Davis Cup team of 1973, featuring Rod Laver, John Newcombe and Ken Rosewall, beat the USA 5–0 in the final; having lost only two of 14 matches to get there, but there were a few dramatic five-set victories along the way, including the first two matches in the final. Similarly, the successful 1955 Davis Cup team of Rosewall, Lew Hoad and Rex Hartwig won 23 of 24 matches, including all five matches against the United States, but the Challenge Round contests with the Americans were much closer than the final scoreline suggests. Australian swimming teams have dominated Commonwealth Games, but never world championships or an Olympics; the closest would be the Melbourne Games of 1956 when they won all seven freestyle gold medals on offer, but only one gold in other strokes.

Of course, comparisons across eras and sports are always difficult, many would argue impossible. What is important, surely, is that Ricky Ponting's team gets due credit for its fantastic achievement in the 2007 World Cup. The Australian Test XI of 2006–07 received due recognition from most observers for its Ashes clean sweep, praise boosted further because of the retirements of a trio of champions, Shane Warne, Glenn McGrath and Justin Langer, and also because of the win in the second Test, at Adelaide, a victory acclaimed as one of the best Ashes Test comebacks of them all. In its own way, however, the World Cup triumph was something else again.

HOPEFULLY, THIS BOOK CAN help give that daylight-ran-second conquest the status it deserves. This must not belittle at all the Ashes win, though, because that was remarkable, too, especially given the hype that had followed the 2005 series in England and that led to one of the longest and most enthusiastic build-ups to a cricket series ever seen in this country. And, don't forget, Australia won the Champions Trophy, too, and the DLF Cup.

The book came together in much the same way as Ricky's 2006 diary. The captain kept notes throughout the season, and afterwards we went through those notes and also through mountains of newspaper and internet reports, to come up with this story of the 2006–07 season. The events are recorded in a diary format — not a day-by-day account; rather, a few days at a time — a method that allowed us to concentrate on the major issues and the unforgettable performances, to show why certain decisions were made, and to identify when, how and why the big matches were won. Complementing this story, Ricky looks back on the careers of Warne, McGrath, Langer, Damien Martyn, and John Buchanan, five men who were a part of the Australian cricket team for so many years, and who all contributed to the side's success during their 'farewell' summer.

It was a long season, a unique season and for Aussie fans one to cherish. For everyone inside and outside the Australian set-up, it was a time to remember ...

THE ROAD TO REDEMPTION

By Ricky Ponting

redemption *n.* **1. IMPROVING OF SOMETHING** the saving or improving of something that has declined into a poor state **2. REDEEMED STATE** the improved state of somebody or something saved from apparently irreversible decline ...

revenge *n.* **1. RETALIATORY PUNISHMENT** the punishing of somebody in retaliation for harm done **2. SOMETHING DONE IN REVENGE** something done to get even with somebody else who has caused harm **3. DESIRE FOR REVENGE** the desire or urge to get even with somebody ...

— *Encarta World English Dictionary*

FOR THE AUSTRALIAN CRICKET team, regaining the Ashes in 2006–07 was never about *revenge*. It was about *redemption*. There wasn't one team meeting where I, as captain, implored the players to get even with England. We wanted more than that. It was about us — as individuals and as a unit — improving ourselves to the point where we could perform at the highest level we believed we could play. As captain, I wanted everyone in the squad to take responsibility for making that happen; from the day we accepted that challenge, we were on a mission to prove to ourselves and show the rest of the cricket world that there is a big gap between Australia and England as far as Test-match cricket is concerned.

We took the same attitude into the World Cup that followed the Ashes series, only this time it was the one-day squad wanting to demonstrate that there is a significant difference between Australia and the other cricket-playing nations.

It was a process that began almost straight after we arrived home after that Ashes defeat. Victories in 2005–06 over the ICC World XI, the West Indies, South Africa and Bangladesh were all part of the process. For things to fall into place the way they ultimately did, we had to find the right attitude, plan our preparation, and work hard. No short cuts. A lot of things had to happen before we even started thinking about achieving the right results. As a team, we had to work out what was the most effective way for us to play our cricket; and within that framework the individuals who made up the team had to work out the best way for them to play. Once that had been determined, it was about us turning words into actions. If we did that, the results would come.

Maybe it is possible to learn more about life from losing than from winning. Our inability to retain the Ashes in 2005 forced each member of the Aussie team to look closely at how he and his mates were going about his and their sport. It wasn't until we lost that we stopped to recognise flaws that might have been obvious to others for a while. We'd kept winning despite making mistakes — it's amazing how far confidence and a 'winning environment' can take you, even when you're doing plenty wrong. It's a bit like a horse trainer who won't change the way he's preparing a horse on a winning streak, even if the winning margin is getting less every race. But once the favourite loses, that's when things change.

That Ashes setback taught me more about myself and the guys around me — how I and they work — than any of the wins we'd enjoyed in my previous 18 months as Test captain. I learned, for example, that I trusted everybody too much. I thought that everyone in the team knew the way I wanted them to play and train, so if I observed that things were not happening exactly as I wanted, I didn't react because I thought the guys had the wherewithal to ensure the problem would get fixed. A genuine leader can't risk that assumption. From October 2005, if I saw that something was not right then I was on it immediately. If things weren't exactly as I wanted them to be, I wasn't going to rely on others to put things right.

We came to label the flaws we'd exhibited in England as 'handbrakes'. During that tour, we didn't have many games between the Test matches, which in itself wasn't a factor, but it meant that our preparation for the big games became ultra important. Yet as a team we didn't practice smart enough or hard enough.

Part of this came from an ill-conceived plan to reduce the length of training sessions, on the basis that there were times when guys were standing around, waiting for their turn in the nets, so that if time was allocated better maybe practice could be reduced from four hours to two. It was a good idea, but it resulted in a lot of little 'team stuff' — such as helping mates out during 'down' time or completing fielding drills in a group — being lost. The competitive edge disappeared, especially from fielding practice. When I first came into the side, the thing I used to enjoy most about Australian cricket team training was the all-together fielding sessions we used to do — because I wanted to pit myself against everybody else. I wanted to be better than Mark Waugh, who was the best fielder and catcher in the squad. The intensity of those sessions was fantastic, but in England in 2005 they were a memory.

As I had with my captaincy style, we sought to correct this flaw immediately after the Ashes were lost. The training sessions before the Super Series at the beginning of the 2005–06 season were so much better than what had happened in England I get goose bumps just thinking about them. That was when the search for redemption began.

The beauty of our performances during the Ashes series and in the World Cup was that we never took success for granted. Occasionally during the World Cup, in a few different games, we took a moment or two lightly, where a fieldsman might not have tried 100 per cent to save a run along the boundary, or maybe a bowler didn't show total respect to a tail-end batsmen, but whenever that happened I cracked the whip and things were immediately back on track. One run can make a difference, something that was reinforced for us at Edgbaston in 2005 when we lost a Test (and, as it turned out, the series) by a solitary single.

WHILE I HAVE BECOME a more assertive captain, I don't think I've changed too much as a person. During the Ashes series, people kept talking about a 'steely determination in my eyes' as if it was something new, but I would think that's been part of my make-up every time I've gone out to bat. I've always had a strong will to win, always been very determined to be the best that I can be, and I sought to lead by example before I was appointed captain. I try to be the first to arrive at practice, for instance, and the last to leave, and if others can take something away from such an attitude and apply it to their own preparation, then I've achieved something.

From the end of the 2005 Ashes series to the last of the 2006–07 Tests, I averaged almost 20 runs per innings more in Test cricket than I had from the start of my career to the end of our ill-fated '05 campaign. I believe that would have happened regardless of whether we won that series in England rather than lost it. I would have prepared the same way for each innings, and sought to make the most of each opportunity, as I've always done. Though my game hasn't changed too much, a little more maturity and a bit more cricket know-how has helped me to play at my best for the last couple of years.

I don't think I was any more disappointed than anyone else in the Australian dressing room after the final Test of the '05 series, at the Oval, but there is no doubt that from the moment I walked out of that room I was filled with a burning desire to be the best player I could be. The two years since have been extremely productive, but I'm still a long way from satisfied. When I'm satisfied with what I've done in cricket, that'll be the time to finish. I remember Steve Waugh said that when he was retiring, and I think Shane Warne, Glenn McGrath and Justin Langer echoed Stephen when they announced their retirements during the Ashes summer. The reason these great players went for as long as they did is because every day they got up and went to training with the thought that they could make themselves better players. When the day arrived when they weren't sure they could keep doing that, they pulled up stumps.

Justin Langer likes to tell the story of my talk to the team before we took the final wicket of the Perth Test in '06–07, of how I asked the team to be 'humble' in victory. England were nine wickets down in their second innings at lunch on the final day, which meant we were one dismissal away from regaining the

Ashes. I probably wouldn't have said that to the team before '05. The break for lunch gave me the chance to sit back and think about how I wanted the team to be remembered, and also that I needed the boys to appreciate that victory never comes cheap. I also felt it was important to get the point across that if we wanted to achieve our ultimate quest for excellence then we had to win the series 5–0. Building a three-Test advantage was simply one stop in a longer journey.

As captain, I've always sought to be honest with everyone, and John Buchanan, who retired as Australian coach after the World Cup, is cut from the same cloth. Asking ourselves if we could have done anything better became a constant theme of meetings, to the point that we very rarely ever worried about the things we'd done well, being more concerned with errors made or inadequacies revealed. Once we'd identified where we needed to improve, then we set out to use the time before the next game to get things right. I don't know if other teams look at their performances in that way, but in 2006–07 it worked for us.

With guys such as Warne, McGrath, Langer and Damien Martyn now missing from the Australian line-up, many are wondering what the future holds for the Australian team. I am extremely confident we'll continue to be successful, so long as everyone in the squad is following the same game plan, wants to keep improving and is never happy with what they and the team have achieved. The responsibility for the senior guys in the group is to pass on this work ethic to the younger players, in the way it has been handed down by past masters during my time in the Australian team. It's an exciting time for me, as captain, to not just have younger guys around but to learn about them, the way they play on the field and operate off it.

I've never been one to try to force my way of thinking on young cricketers. The way I'll handle new guys coming into the team will be to sit back and observe the way they go about things, and wait for them to come to me. This might sound to be in conflict with my earlier claim that I am now a more assertive leader, but the key, I believe, is for me and the new coach, Tim Nielsen, to create a working environment within the team that makes it easier for newcomers to come and talk to me about their cricket or their lives. I feel this approach worked well in 2006–07 with Michael Clarke, Shane Watson and Mitchell Johnson. I know that when you're a young bloke coming into a side, you are trying hard to impress everybody, and the last thing you need is a line of experts tapping you on the shoulder, insisting that you should be doing it this way or playing that way.

With a bit of luck, the rise of the next generation will go smoothly. Stuart Clark, Mitchell Johnson and Shaun Tait are ready to fill the gap left by Glenn McGrath. Phil Jacques, Chris Rogers or Shane Watson could open the batting. In the final three Ashes Tests, Andrew Symonds was quite dynamic as he came in for Damien Martyn. Only Warney, the greatest spin bowler who ever lived, is irreplaceable, yet we have Stuart MacGill (who actually has a better strike rate in Test cricket) available to bowl the leg breaks.

In the 13-and-a-half years since Allan Border retired, someone has always stepped up to replace a departing champion. Think of the great players who have retired since 'AB' — Craig McDermott, Mark Taylor, Ian Healy, the Waughs — somehow the team has kept winning. I think it can happen again.

FROM A CRICKET PERSPECTIVE our 2006–07 season commenced in mid-September with the DLF Cup, a one-day tournament played in Malaysia that also featured India and the West Indies. But in reality our 'summer' began in August, when all members of the Test and one-day squads, and our support staff, participated in a 'boot camp' that took place in the forests and mountains of the Sunshine Coast hinterland. Right from the time we were dropped off in the bush with just a few rations, a scrap of clothing, our wits and our mateship (a rare adventure I'll soon be describing in chapter one), the team's planning was always about three prizes: the Champions Trophy, the Ashes and the World Cup. This trifecta had been a long-term target since October 2005, not least because whenever we thought about the Ashes — which was often — we knew that the big Test series had a major one-day competition scheduled on either side of it. Whenever we mapped out our long-term goals, a favourite pastime of our coach, John Buchanan made sure to include the Champions Trophy in the pre-Ashes planning, and never forgot to emphasise that the World Cup was on our immediate post-Ashes agenda.

The boot camp ended in late August, the Champions Trophy won in early November, the Ashes regained in the first week of 2007. Now it was April 27, the day before the ninth World Cup final. We had been conducting our pre-match team meetings slightly differently during the Cup, in a way that I felt was more effective than we'd ever done before. Within the team, we'd established a 'fast-bowling group' (Stuart Clark, Nathan Bracken, Mitchell Johnson, Glenn McGrath, Shaun Tait and Shane Watson), a 'spin-bowling group' (Michael Clarke, Brad Hodge, Brad Hogg and Andrew Symonds), and a 'batting group' (Michael Clarke, Adam Gilchrist, Brad Haddin, Matt Hayden, Brad Hodge, Brad Hogg, Mike Hussey, Andrew Symonds, Shane Watson and me), and it was the responsibility of these groups to meet at some time during the day before the evening meeting, to discuss how our opponents were going to approach the upcoming game. At the team meeting, one representative of each group would present the thoughts of him and his colleagues, for the entire team to digest.

The Australian teams for the 2006–07 season featured the following players:

Ricky Ponting (captain) — *Punter*

Adam Gilchrist (vice captain) — *Gilly*

Nathan Bracken — *Bracks* or *Andy G*

Mark Cosgrove — *Cossie*

Stuart Clark — *Sarfraz* or *Sarf*

Michael Clarke — *Pup*

Dan Cullen — *DC*

Brad Haddin — *BJ* or *Hadds*

Shane Harwood — *Stickers*

Matthew Hayden — *Haydos*

Ben Hilfenhaus — *Hilfy*

Brad Hodge — *Hodgey*

Brad Hogg — *Hoggy* or *George*

Michael Hussey — *Huss* or *Mr Cricket*

Phil Jaques — *Pro* or *Jaquesy*

Mitchell Johnson — *Mitch* or *Notch*

Simon Katich — *Kato*

Justin Langer — *Lang* or *Alfie*

Brett Lee — *Bing*

Glenn McGrath — *Pigeon* or *Pidge*

Damien Martyn — *Marto*

Andrew Symonds — *Symmo* or *Roy*

Shaun Tait — *Taity*

Adam Voges — *Kenny*

Shane Warne — *Warney*

Shane Watson — *Watto*

Cameron White — *Bear*

In one sense, how we did this came back to a method adopted at the boot camp — each group had a leader, who was the guy who made the presentation, and each group also had a second-in-command who had been assigned the task of scheduling the group's meeting and making sure everyone knew where and when it was on. These group meetings weren't long, usually no more than 15 or 20 minutes, and the presentation to the team meeting only lasted two or three minutes, but as a prelude to the main team meeting, and as a way of getting everyone involved and thinking about the game ahead, this process had proved invaluable.

The batting-group meeting before the Cup final was staged at the hotel where we were staying, the Barbados Hilton. We spent a little time identifying the strengths of their danger bowlers —

Muttiah Muralitharan, Chaminda Vaas and Lasith Malinga — but we knew about these guys from previous encounters; mainly it was about what we would do to combat their approach in the conditions we would see the following day. At different times in the tournament, Vaas and Malinga had both taken early wickets, Vaas through swing and changes of pace, Malinga with sheer speed, so we stressed the need to try to get through the early overs without losing a wicket. If we could keep wickets in hand, then we could be a lot more aggressive, a lot more positive, in the middle overs. We knew we'd need to have established batsmen at the crease when Murali came on; over the years we have played the champion off-spinner very well in one-day cricket, and we have come to the conclusion that — great bowler that he undoubtedly is — we're probably the last team he'd like to bowl at in either form of the game. If we had wickets in hand, we could attack him even if he was bowling well, and hopefully take the momentum out of his game.

Our overall batting plan against Sri Lanka has always been to keep wickets in hand for that middle period, because their bowlers always try to take the pace off the ball. The main reason they beat us in the 1996 World Cup final at Lahore was that their spinners controlled the 'middle' overs of our innings, and little had changed in their strategy in the 11 years since. New batsmen at the crease always find it hard to start working the ball around in these circumstances.

At the evening team meeting, after the three groups had reported, John Buchanan invited me to ask the guys how they were feeling on the eve of the final. Buck remembered how, back in 2003 before that year's final in Johannesburg, I had called an extra meeting before the final, because I had sensed that there were plenty of nerves floating around the whole group in our final training session before the big game. I looked at the cream of Australian cricket gathered in the room and asked how they were feeling — because I've always believed that when you talk about a difficult situation, it serves as an outlet for much of the nervousness. It's comforting, too, to get stress out into the open, and to realise that your comrades are also on edge. In 2007, contrasting with four years earlier, most of the guys said that they were reasonably relaxed and looking forward to the final.

As the boys put words to their feelings, a recurring comment was that because we had trained so well, prepared so thoroughly, there was a strong desire to get the big show on the road. When I first asked the question there was no looking around at each other waiting for someone else to comment first. We were ready to go.

I have always been conscious — especially when big games come around and even more especially when things are going smoothly — of saying less rather than more in team meetings. Never talk just for the sake of it. My speech before the 2007 World Cup final was one of my shortest of our long 2006–07 campaign, and much of it was taken up by a concept I had spoken about quite a few times in the recent past. I wanted us to carry a real *presence* throughout the game. I'm a big believer that the way you carry yourself, if it truly reflects what you believe, can have an impact on your opponent. The Sri Lankans fear us, which is why, I believe, they left some of their best players out of the team that played us in the Super Eights, earlier in the World Cup, I felt it was because they were scared we'd beat their strongest team so easily they'd be mortally wounded as a result. Instead, they rested some blokes and had an alibi when they lost. By striding confidently onto the field and expressing our confidence through positive words and body language, I felt we could accentuate their worries. But you can't fake *presence*; if we weren't as well-prepared as we were, if we hadn't done all the hard work over the preceding 19 months, my words would have been cheap.

FIVE MONTHS BEFORE, I'D been thinking along the same lines in the lead-up to the first Ashes Test, at the Gabba in Brisbane. In the lead-up to the game, I told all the guys that I was sure this English team would be extremely nervous. A lot had been made about how 'friendly' we had been with them in 2005 — that we had been smiling too much on the field, Warney was too matey with Kevin Pietersen, all that sort of stuff. 'This time,' I said to the boys, 'we've got to try to impose ourselves on these guys at every opportunity.'

Again, the way we could do this was through our *presence* — on and off the field. I was well aware of the stories of Allan Border telling his Australian team not to talk to their opponents during the 1989 Ashes series, to play it as hard as they could, how that had played a part in Australia's 4–0 victory. This time, I didn't think we needed to try to bully Flintoff's team, but I did want to impress on them that for us this Ashes series was serious business — that we'd raised the bar and it was up to them to match us. We could do this in many ways: our enthusiasm and professionalism at training, the way we talked to them about the cricket, the manner in which we celebrated each other's successes, even how we ran on and off the field at the beginning or end of a session of play.

In recent years, a lot has been made of the aura of the Australia cricket team. Some people argued that we lost it in 2005, but I don't think we did. Misplaced it, maybe, for a couple of Tests, but it wasn't gone. The cricket we played in 2005–06 demonstrated how we'd rediscovered it, and I wanted the Poms to be aware of it from the jump. I liked the idea of them thinking about us and what we going to do next, rather than them worrying about their own games. That could only happen if we'd improved a great deal from the previous time we played them.

I've always thought that you can tell when you've got the better of a team when you are doing your warm-ups and all they are doing is looking at everything you do. By the end of the Ashes series, that was all the Englishmen were doing. The Sri Lankans were doing the same before the World Cup final. When I saw that, I knew our redemption was complete.

CHAPTER 1

BOOT CAMP

Tuesday, August 29

THE BOOT CAMP WAS John Buchanan's idea. We were first told about it last April, when we were at Chittagong, in Bangladesh, when Buck conducted a meeting in a very small room at the hotel where we were staying. Our coach had his butcher's paper out, and had written down a schedule of the things we would be doing over the following few months. Between the start of May and early September there was plenty of down time, except for a period in late-August when he had programmed a 'boot camp' that, he explained, would be physically and mentally demanding. There were a few strange looks around the room, mainly because of the timing: *this was going to break into our break time.*

For the guys who were only playing Test cricket, the camp would take place three months before their next game of international cricket. For those signed with English counties, it would involve a flight back to Australia, time in camp, then a return flight to England. But Buck didn't care about that. He wanted this to be start of our preparation for what he called the 'Big Three': the Champions Trophy (which Australia has never won), the fight for the Ashes (the prize we desperately want to regain) and the World Cup (which we will be trying to win for an unprecedented third time in a row).

From that meeting in Chittagong, I had some idea about what this 'boot camp' would involve. I knew it was designed to see how we'd operate when we are taken out of the lifestyle and training regime we were familiar with. I felt there was still plenty I could learn about some of my team-mates — how they respond to responsibility and react under pressure — and this would offer that opportunity. The more Buck talked about it, the more enthusiastic I became. The hard-work side of it appealed to me; the boy in me was looking forward to getting away and sleeping out under the stars with a few of my best mates.

RIGHT UP TO AUGUST 22, the day we landed in Brisbane (it seems so much more than a mere week ago), there was a fair amount of secrecy surrounding the operation, with Cricket Australia keeping most of the details quiet — from the players as well as the media. The boot camp concept had been devised by an ex-member of the SAS and a former tactical operations instructor with the Queensland police force, a couple of tough men, and its development was supported by a group of around 15 instructors, who all have military or police experience. I knew we were going to be spending a couple of days and nights traipsing around the Sunshine Coast hinterland before heading up to the Border Ranges, but not too much more.

The rough plan, as it was explained to me, was that over the first two days they'd try to 'break' us: we'd be deprived of all luxuries, sleep, food and water; numbers would replace names and titles; and we'd be divided into groups of six and asked to perform a series of activities while under pressure. Feedback and encouragement from the instructors would be limited, to exacerbate our stress. The idea, I was told, is to remove pre-conceived ideas about what participants can and can't do, to make us work together to get through, to survive.

As we sat in the bus on the way to the first activity, I read and re-read a story in the *Australian*. This would be the last piece of reading material I'd see for a few days. 'The guys will be pushed to their breaking point and, from there, we want to see which personalities bubble to the surface,' one of the camp organisers was quoted as saying. 'We want to see how each player responds to being taken out of their comfort zone and forced to rely on the blokes beside them.'

This fellow went on: 'The program we have planned out for them will really test them physically and mentally, because the exercises they will be asked to perform will demand input from everyone within the group or things will simply collapse. No-one will get a free ride, no-one will get to ride on the coat-tail of the bloke beside him …

'When things are performed successfully, they can share and enjoy that success, but, conversely, there will be ramifications for failure.'

We were certainly tested, but everybody came through. Afterwards, the organisers told us that they'd had the Brisbane Broncos rugby league team up for the camp the previous year, but the manner in which we went about the tasks and got into them was significantly better than the way the footballers had performed. They admitted they were surprised that a bunch of cricketers could work together as we did to get things done.

WE'D BEEN TOLD THAT the initial bus trip up the freeway would be a two-hour drive to some rustic location out in the bush. I was reading the paper, others were lounging around or making last-minute calls (we'd been told that we'd be out of contact with the world while we were away), when, well before the two hours were up, the bus pulled over and parked beside a big warehouse on the side of the road, and a posse of 'special forces' style commandos jumped on board. TURN OFF YOUR PHONES. GRAB YOUR BAGS. OFF THE BUS. SINGLE FILE. ONE. TWO. THREE. That's when it started. No more talking. Get your trendy gear off, grab your backpack. We were allowed two pairs of trousers, two shirts, two pairs of undies, two pairs of socks, one pair of shoes, one water bottle. We were assigned a number. No longer could you be referred to by your name, your nickname or even as 'mate'. You were a number.

I was number seven. We were split into groups, each of six or seven guys —Australia's best cricketers and some of our key support staff. Quickly, we were marched back on to the bus, and driven out into the bush. I'd call the mood 'intense'; I don't think it's too much of an exaggeration to say that some of the guys were in a state of mild shock.

Yet, I enjoyed the experience from just about the start. Once I got into it and started to realise what it was all about, *everything* was good. The first drill we had, after we arrived, was to help one of the country fire services out. We were told there was a big fire on the top of that hill over there, and first up we had to lug 20-litre jerry cans full of water to a location where we could ascertain exactly where the fire was. We were on a time limit, and the groups set off at specific intervals — if the group behind got too close, or the one in front too far away, then the blokes running the drill (now I'd call them 'facilitators'; under my breath I wasn't always so kind) ordered us to drop everything, get down and do 20 bloody push-ups. That was on all the way up the hill. If anyone dropped off at the back of our team, we were all in trouble. Fielding coach Mike Young and team manager Steve Bernard were part of our group, and they couldn't even pick the jerry cans up, so Simon Katich and I had to each haul two cans up the hill at a fair pace. For all of us, it was about finding ways and means of helping out your mates.

I liked the fact the support staff were with us. If we wanted to win, there were certain standards *everyone* in the squad had to adhere to right through the summer. It wasn't just about how we were going to play and train; it was also about how we were going to be organised. I think they would have wanted to be a part of it anyway. I know 'Youngy' did.

I reckon we walked/ran 30 to 35 kilometres on that first day, carrying our packs and at different times those jerry cans, or compasses and maps as we tried to find our way through the bush. After sunset, camp was set up next to a creek bed. We each had a little piece of reputedly waterproof plastic, which we lay on the ground; we put our sleeping bags on top of them, and the tents on top of the sleeping bags. Then they brought dinner out, which on the first night consisted of three tins of soup and a loaf of bread per group. You can imagine how hungry we were, yet we each were allocated half a can of cold chunky soup and two bites of bread.

Soon it was time to try to sleep. There were mosquitoes everywhere, I'm a light sleeper by nature, so there was no way I was getting any kip, especially with Mike Young beside me, snoring his head off. I couldn't move, wasn't allowed to anyway, so all I could do was lie on my back, eyes wide open. Then ... it was about one o'clock, I reckon ... I heard a noise over on the nearby road. Then I sensed a ghost run past ... and another ... and I thought to myself, *there is something going on ...*

Sure enough, next minute, a couple of explosions went off right next to our camp, and the facilitators were in among us, shouting, 'Right, you've got three minutes, pack your things, we're moving.' It was pitch black, and we had to roll up our sleeping bags and plastic, rediscover the branch on which we'd hung our clothes, and get ourselves lined up on the road, all in 180 seconds. If we missed that deadline, it was more bloody push-ups. While we stood there, they pored over the ground with their torches, scouring for anything we'd left behind — a scrap of bread, a tent peg, anything — and when they returned everyone, not just the guilty parties, did more bloody push-ups.

We trudged in the dark for about five kilometres and then set up camp again. I didn't have a clue where we were. No one did. I managed some kip this time, but when I woke up and looked around through weary eyes and couldn't see Kato anywhere. I was sure he'd been there in his sleeping bag when I finally fell asleep, but now he was missing. I sat bolt upright, momentarily alarmed, but there he was, not too far from my feet, in a long, narrow hole that might have been a drain. He'd slept there, snugly, for the previous few hours.

Stuart MacGill had hurt his knee when he tripped over a hole in the dark, so he wasn't happy, and I don't think our other leg-spinner was enjoying himself too much either, but the rest of us had embraced the adventure. We quickly realised that we weren't going to discover the benefits of the exercise until it was over, and had come to appreciate, rather than dislike, the military way the operation was run. At one point, while we were climbing up a mountain, we were ordered to stop and one of the staff began asking questions that made us think about what we were about and how we would respond, as individuals and as a group, in a variety of situations. This former military man started the process by telling us about the stresses of his marriage break-up, and how he coped with not being able to see his kids. The way our young blokes responded, sometimes baring a little of their soul as they recalled awkward situations they'd had to confront, was revealing, even courageous.

This was what I liked most about the boot camp. It's never a bad thing to be surrounded by good mates, blokes you can rely on. I came away thinking more than ever that being part of the Australian cricket team is like being in an extended family. I have always strived to be totally honest and open with people, and in the past 12 months have done everything I could to build a team environment in which everyone else felt they could do the same. The camp helped this process, no doubt about it.

THE CAMP CONTINUED FOR two more days and one night. At one point, we were told, using a map and a compass, to find some vans that had been parked (or should that be hidden?) in the middle of the bush. Eventually, we located them, and assumed we'd then jump and drive them to wherever our next task would begin. Not quite. The vehicles had broken down and we had to push and drag them to the next location. We did get there, somehow. Then it was more jerry cans ... exhausting, relentless work ... all of it done not to make us fitter or physically tougher, but to put us in positions where we had to use our initiative and make key decisions while totally fatigued, and had to work as a unit. At another time, we found ourselves on the same track a ranger named Bernard O'Reilly famously used to get to the wreck of the Stinson plane that had crashed in these mountains in 1937. There was abseiling, which some guys found a little tough, not so much when we descended looking at the cliff face, but when we were asked to drop down face out. What was fantastic was that, if a bloke hesitated before descending, his mates below were encouraging him, saying 'you can do it', rather than putting the boot in or having a snigger.

At other times, if one guy couldn't do something there were plenty of team-mates ready there to assist him or do it for him, to help get the job done. As an example, at one point on the second day, we were required to walk up a narrow track on a ridge, where the ground fell away quickly on both sides. One of the blokes didn't fancy heights at the best of times, and at one point, where the path was really narrow, all he could do was get down on his hands and knees, and crawl. So Haydos put himself on one side of the track and I got on the other, with one foot each on the path and the other on the ground that angled away, and we helped our comrade through. It wasn't just these 'physical' tasks either where we helped each other out; blokes were cleaning up after each other, partly to dodge the bloody push-ups, partly, too, because that's what good mates do.

The way the boot camp finished was quite funny. We finally returned to the base where we'd started, and the facilitators ordered us into line one last time. And then one of them told us how impressed he was with our efforts. The chief facilitator said his piece, and then he invited me to step forward and offer a few words. Before these speeches, our final exercise had been a general clean-up, and during that activity Justin Langer had discovered one of the staff's sunglasses, which had apparently been left behind. So after I thanked everyone for their support, and gave the camp and all involved a wrap, I explained that Lang was keen to say something. Which he did beautifully, beginning by emphasising once more a point that had been reinforced often during the previous three days: if you make a mistake you've got to own up to it and take responsibility for it.

Lang then pulled the sunglasses out of his pocket, looked sternly at the line of staff in front of us, and asked defiantly, 'Whose are these?'

No one put a hand up. We knew whose sunglasses they were, but that didn't stop Lang from asking each of the guys individually, 'Are they yours ... or yours ... or yours?' There was no alternative: all of them had to do bloody push-ups, and plenty of them. We were putting our foot on their backsides and holding them down. We didn't let up.

One night during the camp, one of the boys had been called out because he referred to one of the staff as 'mate'. He might have said, 'Sorry, mate.' Or, 'Good on you, mate.' Of course, this misdemeanour resulted in all the members of his group having to do bloody push-ups, in front of everyone. While this punishment was being served, the staff leader came in and asked why the rest of us were just watching. 'Is that how you blokes do it?' he asked. 'You just stand back and laugh at your mates! Righto, everyone down.'

It was bloody push-ups for all … to which someone at the back mumbled under their breath something like, 'These blokes aren't our mates any more.' But he was overheard, and we were ordered to not only do our bloody push-ups but also to stand between each one and say, 'You are not our mates.'

Now, while dishing out our revenge over those misplaced sunglasses, we made the staff boys chant, while they were trying to do their push-ups, 'You are now our mates … you are now our mates!' It was a good fun way to finish everything off. I doubt I'll ever forget those blokes, their boot camp or the good things it taught me and my best mates.

CHAPTER 2

DLF CUP

Sunday, September 10

WE ARRIVED HERE IN Kuala Lumpur three days back, after a hectic 48 hours in which I was involved in the launch, at the Sydney Cricket Ground, of the new state-of-the-art bottle-green uniforms we'll be wearing in the new year during the one-day series in Australia, flew to Brisbane to meet up with all the boys, and then took off for my 31st tour as an Australian international cricketer (dating back to a tour to New Zealand for four one-day internationals in early 1995), but my first in five months.

In that time since our last on-field action, I had enjoyed a total break from batting until just a couple of weeks ago. However, we had been asked to adhere to extensive individual fitness plans that had been mapped out for us and I know in my case that this approach has paid dividends. The Australian team's former fitness adviser, Jock Campbell, worked with Michael Clarke, Stuart Clark, Glenn McGrath, Phil Jaques and me around Cronulla, south of Sydney, throughout the off-season, and I've never felt as sharp physically at the start of a summer as I do right now.

Normally, I would have said that taking 18 players was too many for a short tour such as this journey to Malaysia to compete for the DLF Cup, a three-team competition involving India, West Indies and Australia, but there were a few things to consider, two of them highly significant in my opinion. One, this tournament represents the start of a long season, and while we've had a long break from international cricket, the workload from here will be grueling, so we need to be realistic when it comes to players' workloads. That's why Adam Gilchrist isn't here; we want our great keeper-batsman to be as fresh as can be at the end of the season, not just at the start. And two, there are plenty of guys in consideration for places in our one-day squad, and we'd like to give some of them a go in genuine one-day internationals. This doesn't mean we won't be trying to win — one characteristic of Australian one-day teams in the last seven or eight years has been that we try to prevail in every game — but at the same time we're going to give everyone at least a couple of games, to the point that the selectors have mapped out teams for the qualifying games. Further, some blokes will only stay for the first part of the event. The only man who will play in all our matches will be Brad Haddin, the one keeper in the squad.

Of particular interest to me was the return to the Australian squad of two senior men: Matthew Hayden and Glenn McGrath. Haydos was back for his first one-day internationals since 2005, in part because no one — notably Simon Katich, Phil Jaques or Mark Cosgrove — had nailed the second opening-bat spot, while Pigeon had missed our tour to South Africa and Bangladesh to be with his wife Jane as she recovered from illness. I was thrilled to see both of them back in our one-day set-up.

The full Australia squad is: Ricky Ponting (captain), Michael Hussey (vice-captain), Nathan Bracken, Stuart Clark, Michael Clarke, Mark Cosgrove, Dan Cullen, Brad Haddin, Matthew

Hayden, Brad Hogg, Phil Jaques, Mitchell Johnson, Simon Katich, Brett Lee, Damien Martyn, Glenn McGrath, Andrew Symonds, Shane Watson.

Glenn had celebrated his 36th birthday during his time away from the side, which made him pretty old for an international paceman, so it was only natural that some critics were questioning his comeback. I know he'll be okay, but I do wonder if he will be able to return to his absolute best form, which concerns me mainly because how he performs will have an impact on the make-up of our final line-up, especially our Test XI. If Glenn and the other front-line bowlers are in total control of their games, then our need for a fifth bowler will dissipate, meaning that Michael Clarke's chances of beating Shane Watson to the Test No. 6 spot will improve. But if Glenn struggles a little, we'll need Watto's overs. The one thing I don't want is a repeat of 2005, when Glenn missed two Tests, England attacked Jason Gillespie, Michael Kasprowicz and Shaun Tait, none of whom was bowling well, and as a consequence our other two bowlers, Brett Lee and Shane Warne, had to bowl more defensive overs than we'd have liked them to.

Some critics wondered whether we would have been better leaving Glenn in Australia to prepare for the Ashes series by bowling in the Pura Cup. As things stand, unless we fail to reach the semi-finals of the Champions Trophy, the members of the Australian one-day squad will only get to play in one four-day match before the opening Test. But as I explained to *AAP*: 'I don't think one-day form as such counts for a lot as far as Test form goes, but if you're out in the middle, hitting balls and scoring runs — or taking wickets and bowling the ball where you want to — it doesn't matter what form of the game you are playing. You can feel like you've got your game in pretty good order.' We had spent a fair amount of time talking about what might be the best way to go with Pidge and in the end he said that he wanted to play as many games for Australia as he could in the one-day format before the his season started at home. He knows his body and the way he is bowling better than anybody, so we were basically happy to leave it to him. Interestingly, every time he has been to the subcontinent in September–October for Tests or one-dayers, he has returned home and bowled extremely well.

As the journos kept speculating about our team for the first Ashes Test and our squad for the World Cup, it was interesting how I received a lot of questions about our 24-year-old left-arm fast bowler Mitchell Johnson, a 'veteran' of no Tests and five one-day internationals. It seems they've looked at the different bowlers competing for the third fast-bowling spot behind Lee and McGrath and decided that Notch is the one. Stuart Clark's bowling style, they reason, despite all his success in South Africa just a few months ago, is too much like Pigeon's. Gillespie, they believe, despite the fact he topped the bowling averages (and scored an unbeaten double century) in our most recent series, against Bangladesh, is past his best. Tait and Kasprowicz are under injury clouds. Johnson, they reckon, has moved past Nathan Bracken, at least as far as the competition for the Test team is concerned.

I can see where they're coming from, because Notch is making an impact with me every time he bowls — a young left-armer who can bowl fast and swing the ball is an appealing prospect.

Wednesday, September 13

DLF Cup Game 1, at Kuala Lumpur (September 12): Australia 9–279 (50 overs: MJ Clarke 81, RT Ponting 56; JE Taylor 3–59) beat West Indies 201 (34.3 overs: S Chanderpaul 92, CH Gayle 58; SR Watson 4–43) by 78 runs

IT'S BEEN AN INTERESTING 24 hours. We beat the Windies in pretty remarkable fashion, taking their last nine wickets for 29 runs. I was busted my entire match fee for breaching the ICC Code of Conduct after a 'run-in' with umpire Asad Rauf. And Andrew Flintoff has been named England's captain for the Ashes series, a decision that hasn't met with universal approval. I have read stories on the internet suggesting that while their chairman of selectors David Graveney wanted Flintoff, coach Duncan Fletcher preferred Andrew Strauss.

I must confess I had expected them to go for Strauss, mainly because I assumed they'd be wary of giving their star all-rounder too much to do, especially as he's coming back from a serious ankle injury. He's got a big enough job without the captaincy, bowling as much as he does and being one of their top-six batsmen.

Furthermore, I know the captains in the upcoming Ashes series are going to have a lot on their plates. There was plenty of off-field work to be done and conjecture to be countered in 2005, and I'm sure it's going to be magnified this time, given the interest that keeps growing. In Flintoff's case, there is also all the physical work he is going to have to do because he's coming back from that ankle problem, and all the on-field pressure that comes with being your team's No. 1 player. Maybe if he wasn't such a laid-back character, he'd be up for it, but in his case this pressure might work against him.

I think the main reason Flintoff has been appointed is that the English authorities want an imposing identity at the helm, rather than someone who is more reserved. I must confess that I find it hard to picture Freddie as a tactician in the Mike Brearley mould, but I only have to recall some of his grandest days in 2005 to know that if he gets on a roll in the Ashes series, then he might be able to take his whole team along for the ride.

I THOUGHT WE DID a pretty fair job to get as many runs as we did in our first game of the new season, because the conditions here aren't that conducive to aggressive batting. Or at least that's what we thought until Shivnarine Chanderpaul came out and smashed the ball around the way he did, finishing with 10 fours and four sixes in 83 balls. Maybe that was the best way to play on what is a slow, gripping sort of pitch — to just back yourself and try to make use of the 'powerplays'. Hard as it was when we batted, though, we always thought that it would be even more difficult batting second, because in the prevailing humid atmosphere it is always going to seam around a bit more at night. Once we finally found a couple of wickets, the ball did duck around, we got on a roll and it turned into a decent fightback.

Glenn McGrath was frustrated early on. He was actually swinging it, which is very unlike him, and he bowled too many wides, so I advised him halfway through his first spell not to worry about swinging the ball, to just to focus on landing them in the right area: short of a length on or about off stump. He was excellent in the second spell, when he came back to take a wicket and keep things tight. The most encouraging thing was that we saw the early signs that he'll get better the more he bowls. That's why he's here: to get some bowling miles in his engine.

I guess some people might find it surprising that I, a specialist batsman, would dare to tell the great Glenn McGrath how to bowl, rather than let him work it out for himself. Most of the time I will leave Pidge alone, but here in Malaysia, with him working his way back to his best, I'm keen to help. More generally, say it's a Test match and I'm standing in the slips with cricket brains such as Gilly and Warney, and they agree with my analysis, then I'll throw in my two bob's worth. It's the same for all the bowlers; I see it as part of my role as captain. Maybe Glenn's not conceding any runs and he feels like he is bowling well, but we feel that if he pitches it up half a metre, that length will draw the batsman forward a little bit more and give us a better chance of getting a wicket. In such circumstances, I'm thinking, *if I was the batsman facing him, that's what I'd least like him to do*. I think it would be negligent of me not to put this idea in his head. It's his call whether he heeds my advice. To me, that is very different to *telling* him how to bowl.

Even if you've got a bowler of McGrath's skill and experience, it can be really hard for the fielding team when the opposition is blazing away as Chanderpaul and Chris Gayle did. No matter which bowler you turn to or what fields you set, when the batsmen are on such a roll, as captain you feel almost helpless, as if all you can do is wait for them to burn themselves out. But then, once they do get a wicket or two, the conditions can suddenly seem a lot different, and that's what happened last night. A smashing innings can have an inspiring effect on the batsmen that follow, or it can be another mountain to climb. I've often found it hard batting three in one-day cricket after an Adam Gilchrist special, because I've felt an obligation to keep scoring not just rapidly but spectacularly, too. And when you can't you have to fight the feeling that you're somehow not good enough — just because you can't score at eight-an-over!

After 30 overs, the Windies were 4–195, with Ramnaresh Sarwan and Wavell Hinds at the crease. They needed 85 from 20 overs, and I said to my vice-captain, 'Huss, I reckon Cossie can win us the game here. Let's bring him on, give him a couple of overs. I reckon he can get us a couple of wickets.' Now I would describe Mark Cosgrove's bowling as 'steady' medium pace, but he's got a good yorker, nips it around a bit, and on that wicket, at that stage of the game, I thought he'd be hard to get away. Sure enough, he had Hinds caught behind second ball of the over. He would have kept going, too, but he hurt himself and had to come straight off with figures of 1–1 from one over. But he'd done the job for us, and from that moment I was always sure we'd win.

I CAME AWAY FROM this game wondering just how significant the use of the powerplays might be during the next seven months. For the first 10 overs of each 50-over innings in a modern one-day international cricket match, the fielding team must have two men in catching positions and can only have two men working outside the 'circle'. For another 10 overs of the innings the fielding team can only have two men outside the circle, and when that happens is the prerogative of the fielding captain. It's up to him as to when he wants to bowl those overs, in two lots of five. These five-over spells are the powerplays.

Since the powerplay was first introduced to one-day international cricket, captains have tended to bowl them at the time when it will cost them the least amount of runs. In other words, they've adopted a defensive mindset — let's get them over and done with before they damage us too much. Many is the time when a captain has used their powerplays as soon as possible: by the end of the 20th over.

In recent times I have come to the view that is not always the right way to go. Maybe a powerplay can be looked upon as an attacking option, as a means of changing mood of the game. There's got to be more to life than just stopping boundaries. The key to using a powerplay as a weapon is to pick the right moment in the right conditions … and to have the right bowlers.

First impressions would be that you don't bowl spinners during a powerplay, on the basis that they need the protection of 'boundary riders' or they'll cost you. But if your spinner has immaculate control, why not get him on and put the pressure on the batsmen to meet the run-scoring expectations that come with the field being up? I'm especially thinking of a Warne or a Murali here, but in the right conditions, where the pitch is turning or maybe the pitch is slow, many international-class spinners can be hard to get away. In different circumstances, if the ball is going to reverse swing from the 25-over mark, and you have an excellent proponent of that art, why not hold a powerplay back? If one of your bowlers is an exceptional yorker bowler, why not schedule a powerplay to suit him, rather than to fit a standard defensive formula?

In Australia, it's less inviting to keep a powerplay back because the ball doesn't reverse swing and the pitches rarely turn as they might on the subcontinent or in the Caribbean. But here in Asia and later in the season, during the World Cup, I believe there will be chances to do things differently. By the end of this long summer, we might be looking upon powerplays in a whole new light.

I also wonder if the appeal of powerplays would increase if one of them was handed to the batting team. Let's say to the batsmen, 'It's your turn. For five overs, at any time between the 10th and 40th over, you can ask for the fielding team to bring all but two of their men up into the circle.' The tactics and machinations this might introduce to a one-day game could be fascinating, as the fielding captain will have to plan the use of his bowlers and the implementation of his own powerplay with the knowledge that the batsmen are holding a joker of their own.

THE BIG NEGATIVE TO come out of the West Indies game for me was that incident where I found myself in trouble with the match referee again. Having lost a quarter of my match fee after an incident in the Test at Chittagong last April, when I questioned the on-field umpires about their use of the TV official my crime this time became a 'level 2' offence. 'A captain should set the example for his players to follow,' referee Chris Broad explained in a statement, 'and it is not acceptable for any player, let alone a captain, to question an umpire's decision.'

Shane Watson had bowled a delivery to Sarwan that flicked the batsman's leg, bounced twice on the leg-side, and was gathered by keeper Brad Haddin, who picked it up and threw it to me as I came running in from mid-wicket. Just as I caught the ball the umpire called wide, and my immediate reaction was to say, 'How can that be a wide — you didn't hear it?' ('It' being the ball catching the pad.) Then I added, 'If you can't hear things like that you shouldn't be standing out here.' I regret saying that, but that wasn't why I was reported — I had to defend the charge that I had approached the umpire when I shouldn't have, which I thought was unfair given that I'd been running in anyway. It looked worse than what it was.

There was never a chance that I'd be suspended over this incident, but I knew that I'd be in trouble if I 'offended' again, which did worry me. No one likes such a stigma hanging over his head. Yet I was frustrated that both here and at Chittagong I'd got into trouble over little things that shouldn't have happened. In Bangladesh I'd been reported for 'influencing the umpires' decision' when all I'd done was insist they get their communication with the third umpire right, and the consequence of our discussion was that they got a decision right instead of wrong. I don't see how when the umpires make mistakes I should be the only one tarnished as the bad guy. Yet at the same time I had to acknowledge that I'd made a mistake, that the way I'd communicated with the umpires in both instances was unacceptable. For that reason, I made a point of apologising to my team-mates. I've got to make sure it doesn't happen again.

Sunday, September 17

DLF Cup Game 2, at Kuala Lumpur (September 14): India 5–309
(50 overs: SR Tendulkar 141*, IK Pathan 64; JE Taylor 3–64) lost to West Indies
2–141 (20 overs: CH Gayle 45) by 29 runs (D/L method)

DLF Cup Game 3, at Kuala Lumpur (September 16): Australia 244
(49.2 overs: SR Watson 79, MJ Clarke 64; MM Patel 3–53) versus India 5–35
(8 overs: MG Johnson 4–11) — match abandoned

THE WEATHER HAD A major impact on both our game yesterday
and the West Indies-India game two days earlier, but it wasn't the
action on the field or the rain that received the most attention.
Instead, it was a book launch on the other side of the world that
prompted most of the questions I've received in the last 24 hours.

Over in England, following the release of his latest book,
Shane Warne has been quoted in the papers apparently
lampooning John Buchanan. Among the quotes I read in internet
reports were:

> *'John Buchanan sometimes over-complicates issues and he
> has lacked commonsense ... I'm a big believer that the
> coach is something you travel in to get to and from the
> game ...*
>
> *'You need some sort of team manager more than a
> coach, like we have at Hampshire where the captain runs
> the team and the manager sorts out everything else ...*
>
> *'International players know how to play. You don't
> need a coach getting too technical. You can forget that you
> just need to bowl the ball ...'*

Inevitably, the media started getting excited about a rift in the
Australian camp. My first reaction was that I wished Shane had

kept his mouth shut, and I needed to know exactly what he'd said, and whether there really is a problem. It is common knowledge that the great coach and the great leg-spinner are not close and we are also fully aware that Shane was not a keen fan of the boot camp, but in my view over the past seven years they've worked extremely well together and the fact we've won a lot more than we've lost during Buck's time as coach supports this. First, I sent Shane a text message, then I spoke to his manager (who was at the book launch) and eventually we had a one-on-one chat, and he convinced me that while he did say the things that were reported, they weren't meant to be malicious and to a degree they had been taken out of context. It is certainly true that the positive things that were said in the same interview have hardly rated a mention. 'He has lots of good points,' Warney said of Buck at that very same book launch. 'I think, tactically, he looks at things in a different way and thinks outside the box. He's very good on those regards.' But those comments were left behind as the negative stuff was turned into headlines.

As he said again during our conversation, Shane has his views on coaching that don't match mine and they don't always match the ways of John Buchanan either. But the one thing we all share is that sense of team that has typified the Aussie squad in recent seasons, and in this regard nothing has changed. Shane has always given his all for the Australian team and he always will.

HERE IN MALAYSIA, WE were happy with the way a few of the young blokes batted against India, especially Shane Watson, Phil Jaques and Michael Clarke. It was very important for us that Watto batted the way he did at the top of our innings, for two reasons: one, because it gave us an excellent chance of winning the game; and two, because it was exactly what we've been looking for from him. Watto has a good technique for batting against the new ball and, as he showed against the Indians, he can play good and aggressive strokes when the ball is new and field is up. One day he might even open the batting for Australia in a Test match. He's got the talent to do that. He is a strong guy who can hit the ball cleanly over the off-side field, which is an important attribute in the early overs of a limited-over game when the field is up and the bowlers' line is predominantly on or just outside the off stump. If he continues to produce performances like this, it'll be difficult to move him back down the order.

As good as Watto batted, the undoubted highlight for us came when Mitchell Johnson grabbed four wickets in just seven balls. It was a stunning and exhilarating period of cricket, featuring a sequence of extraordinary deliveries that began when Notch had Rahul Dravid caught by Damien Martyn at backward point. He then bowled Irfan Pathan first ball with an absolute beauty that swung, straightened and hit the top of off stump, and then — after Virender Sehwag was run out during Glenn McGrath's fourth over — Sachin Tendulkar was caught behind and Yuvraj Singh caught in the slip cordon. It was simply classic left-arm *fast* bowling. Notch is learning more about himself and feeling more confident about playing at the highest level, and now all the talk is about Notch making the first Test team. I think everyone now is aware of how much talent he has, and what a great athlete he is.

But while Notch dominated the scorebook, Rahul Dravid seemed keener to talk about how well McGrath bowled. 'He was fantastic,' Dravid said at the post-game media conference. 'It was a great lesson for a lot of our young seamers. To see him bowl after six months and pitch the ball exactly where he wanted to was awesome. It's not always fun batting against him, but it's nice to watch a great craftsman at work.' What the Indian captain's praise showed to me was that whether Pigeon is bowling at his best or not, he is still inside the minds of most of the great batsmen around the world. I'm not sure if Rahul has ever felt fully comfortable when confronted by Pidge's nagging line and length. Ironically, we feel Glenn is going okay, but that's all. His pace isn't quite there, and his line is not as relentless as it's been in the past.

Unfortunately, we were locked into the plan that involved Notch being one of the guys, with Mark Cosgrove and Phil Jaques, to head back home following this game. Of course, this was hardly the best way to exploit his brilliant performance, but this strategy had been decided well in advance and Notch knew it was going to happen. He'll still take a lot of confidence away from his dynamic performance here, and from knocking over Brian Lara and then Sachin Tendulkar in successive games.

Saturday, September 23

DLF Cup Game 4, at Kuala Lumpur (September 18): Australia 6–272 (50 overs: MEK Hussey 109*, BJ Haddin 70, ML Hayden 49) lost to West Indies 7–273 (47.2 overs; BC Lara 87, CH Gayle 79) beat by three wickets

DLF Cup Game 5, at Kuala Lumpur (September 20): India 162 (39.3 overs: SR Tendulkar 65: DR Smith 4–31) defeated West Indies 146 (41 overs: BC Lara 40*, Harbhajan 3–35) by 16 runs

DLF Cup Game Six, at Kuala Lumpur (September 22): Australia 213 (48.1 overs: ML Hayden 54, BJ Haddin 46) defeated India 195 (43.5 overs: D Mongia 63*; B Lee 5–38) by 18 runs

I WAS RESTED FROM our third game, the return bout with the West Indies, which gave Mike Hussey the chance to captain his country, but it proved to be a frustrating leadership debut for him, as Chris Gayle and Brian Lara both batted beautifully and the Windies successfully chased 273, winning with 16 balls to spare.

Stuart Clark was smashed for 87 in seven overs, bowling figures so bad you just have to forget about them, and while I was happy to leave Huss alone as he led the side, I did speak to Sarf a couple of times. I had my colours on and was running the drinks on the boundary, and when I spoke to him from behind the rope at fine leg he told me it felt as if he had never bowled before. He had no rhythm, couldn't get his run-up right and bowled a lot of no balls. If it had been the middle of the World Cup I would have been worried, but at this stage of our preparation he just needs to bowl. I doubt he'll be out of kilter in this way during the Champions Trophy.

After the game, I pondered the thought that Sarf might have been thrown a bit by the fact that so many blokes were in the original squad. He had to share opportunities, and pressures had been created as blokes felt they had to perform immediately or lose their place. In his case, Mitchell Johnson had set the bar high by his sensational effort against India. I've wondered if this sort of competition for places *within a squad* can be counter-productive since the 2001-02 season, Steve Waugh's last season as one-day captain, when the selectors responded to Matty Hayden's superb Test-match form that year by adding him to the one-day squad. Having one extra batsmen travelling with the squad had everyone concerned about their place, fearful about having a game off, and the mood within the team deteriorated. There's usually enough pressure on anyway without extra factors being introduced.

In this instance, Sarf came back in our fourth game, the return match with India, to take 2–36 from eight overs. It says something about the bloke that he was able to turn things around so quickly.

After that India game, I was asked if I was 'relieved' to have prevailed, and I think most of the journos were expecting me to say, 'Yeah, absolutely.' Instead, though, I said I was 'proud'. We've mixed and matched our teams, so to make the final under those circumstances is very satisfying. Against India last night, it was important that we kept our nerve in what was a 'crunch' game and we did that. As a rehearsal for the big games ahead, this was a fantastic result.

While 213 is not a great total, in the conditions it wasn't too bad, provided we bowled and fielded well. We captured four wickets in the first 13 overs for only 50 runs, and given that they had a fairly long tail and we had bowlers such as Lee, McGrath and Clark left with plenty of overs, I was pretty confident. Brett was terrific; it is so reassuring for me to know that during the middle of the innings I can go back to a bowler of his pace and wicket-taking ability. It is always going to be difficult for new batsman at the crease to be positive against him as they start their innings.

Afterwards, and not for the first time, I proudly described Bing as 'the best one-day bowler in the world'. I've felt he has deserved this high rating for a couple of years, essentially because during that time he has consistently dismissed the best top-order batsmen in the world with the new ball. In this encounter, he dismissed Chris Gayle first ball with a yorker that hit the Windies' explosive opener right on the toe — exactly how Brett said he was going to get him out. I'm not going to come out and make statements about a guy being the best in the business unless they've done it for a long period of time — that's one of the things that for me defines greatness. I have no doubt Brett is a great one-day bowler.

Another bloke who was having a good tournament for us was Brad Hogg, who scored a crucial 38 in our innings and then took two key wickets, breaking partnerships for the fifth and seventh wickets that could have taken the game away from us. Hoggy has been unlucky over the years, in that, whenever the selectors have decided to make a change, more often than not he's been the one to miss out. Yet he's always rebounded, always done the job when called upon. Of course, there are times in one-day cricket when the conditions compel us to go with the quicks plus Andrew Symonds, but the reassuring thing for us is that we have never doubted Hoggy's ability to deliver when we need him to. There are certain locations across the cricket world, primarily when the pitches are slow and turn a little, when he becomes a key member of the team, because his wrist spinners can be difficult to get away in such conditions, he's a smart No. 7 or No. 8 batsman, and he's an excellent fieldsman. Always, he's a brilliant team man. With the Champions Trophy being played in India and the World Cup in the Caribbean, where many of the pitches are slow and suit the spinners, I believe he'll be an important man for us.

The two Brads, Hogg and Haddin, had rescued our innings, after we sank to 6–117 in the 32nd over, with a partnership that reflected the fact that both are tough, pragmatic cricketers. BJ is a very good gloveman, and at the batting crease is a great striker of the ball and very quick between the wickets. He assesses situations and adapts to situations really well, and he's a strong character, a real fighter. He receives little acclaim in his role as Adam Gilchrist's 'shadow', because Gilly never gets injured, so he is left with the 'crumbs', an unfortunate situation for a bloke who could easily be a Test and one-day regular. Here in Malaysia, he's responded to obtaining a regular role by being our best batsman through the qualifying matches.

Eleven hot and humid days ago, I scored 54 in our opening game of this competition, but have failed after that, scoring 19 and 4 in the two matches against India. To be honest, it's a little hard to judge whether I'm in form or not because I've received a couple of balls that have kept very low, and as the training facilities here aren't that flash the reason why I'm struggling a little to find the middle of the bat is impossible to gauge. I actually felt really good in the opener against the Windies until a ball from Ian Bradshaw ran along the ground and trapped me lbw, and since then I've only faced 30 balls. Because I didn't have a terrific one-day series in Bangladesh, I'm hearing references to the fact that I'm averaging less than 20 in my last five one-day innings, which to some means I'm in a slump. Maybe I should respond by saying I'm feeling terrific, but the truth is that if you don't get time in the middle then you always feel like you are a little out of touch.

One episode that really did annoy me occurred in the game against India, when Sachin Tendulkar was given out but then the umpires changed their minds, and one reporter wrote a story suggesting I'd got myself in trouble again for disputing the decision. That bloke didn't know what he was writing about.

Sachin went for a pull shot, the ball nicked him on the shoulder and he was given out caught behind. We were all in a group celebrating, and the batsman was halfway off the field, when the umpire, Mark Benson, called me out of the huddle to tell me that he was calling Sachin back. This scene was interpreted by the bloke in the pressbox as me approaching the ump demanding an explanation, which was completely wrong. In fact, I was highly impressed that Benson had the guts to do what he did. Much better to 'fess up to a mistake and get things right than let the error run.

Monday, September 25

DLF Cup Final, at Kuala Lumpur (September 24): Australia 6–240
(50 overs: DR Martyn 52, A Symonds 52) defeated West Indies 113 (34.2 overs:
Lee 4–24, NM Bracken 3–16) by 127 runs

IT WAS HARD FOR us to be over-confident going into the final,
given that the West Indies had beaten us in our third game and
could have won the opening match as well. In that game we lost,
which featured a big, match-defining stand between Chris Gayle
and Brian Lara when they were chasing 272, we nearly pegged
them back, which suggested to us that they might be a bit shaky
chasing, especially under the pressure of a final. The West Indies
do rely on two or three batsmen, though when those bats do
start firing, as they did the second time we played them here,
they're a very dangerous side. Our aim was to win the toss, then
put a decent total on the board and go from there.

And in the end, that strategy proved a successful one. Given
that we were coming off a five-month spell, I think we can be
pretty satisfied with the way we claimed the DLF Cup. We might
not have been at the top of our games, but given the manner in
which the slow pitches made it hard to hit through the line with
any confidence and how the bounce was sometimes unreliable, it's
been hard to get a true measure as to how we are going, especially
the form of the batsmen. However, we managed a few decent
batting partnerships and a number of excellent bowling ones, we
won when it mattered, and we did all this while experimenting
with our line-up, so I think we're entitled to be happy.

I was disappointed to be asked questions about whether the
Windies had 'surrendered' in the final. Sides that reach finals
don't give up. What happened was that Brett Lee, Glenn
McGrath and especially Nathan Bracken bowled very well early

on, and by knocking over their key batsmen we took a decisive advantage.

Maybe even more so than earlier in the competition, in the final the pitch was never an easy one to bat on, one of those pitches where because there was no pace in it you never felt you were truly 'in', and it often seemed that the batsmen were struggling to rotate the strike. That's why I was so impressed by the way Damien Martyn and Andrew Symonds batted, as they both compiled half-centuries. Marto seemed to hit everything in the middle of the bat, and was able to put the ball into gaps in the field, while Symmo was close to his bludgeoning best. He's one of those dangerous batsmen who can explode out of a form slump with a brilliant innings, which he did here, as he'd only scored 10 runs in the DLF Cup before he strode out to bat in the final. Everyone talks about Symmo's incomparable fielding, and how when combined with his batting and the overs he can contribute, he becomes a *complete* one-day cricketer, but what is also important is that, in the modern one-day game, he is one of those batsmen who can adapt to various situations. He can bat at three or four and take advantage of powerplays or he can come in late in an innings and hit at eight or 10 an over.

It was interesting to compare the performances of Brett Lee and Glenn McGrath in the tournament. Bing was named the player of the series, after taking 12 wickets at nine, an effort crowned by his first-ball dismissal of Chris Gayle in the final. Pigeon, in contrast, finished with one wicket for 71 from 26 overs, but he bowled better than that. It is true that he has a few things to work on, and I know he isn't thrilled with the way he's going, but in the final he bowled six overs for six runs, just 12 days after he bowled six wides in his first game of the new season. The cynics have their poison pens ready, but I'm sure he just needs to get a few more overs under his belt.

So now we can direct our attention to the Champions Trophy. It's the second biggest one-day tournament we play, and we've never won it, but I know we have the players to challenge seriously this time. And there is not a shred of doubt in our minds about playing in Indian conditions, as there were with Australian teams in the past. Over the past few years — probably since the one-dayers we played in India in 1998 and definitely since we won the Test series in 2004 — we've buried that bogey big time.

CHAPTER 3

ICC CHAMPIONS TROPHY

Wednesday, October 4

A LOT HAS BEEN made about the fact that Australia has never won the Champions Trophy. The journos like to ask us about the one we haven't won and why we can't win it? Do we treat it seriously? Is there is something different about it? The fact is there are many reasons why we haven't played our best cricket in any of the Champions Trophy tournaments to date. Maybe on this occasion it is scheduled a little close to next year's World Cup, but it's still the second biggest event in the one-day calendar. For us, this time, it matters a lot. To not try our utmost to win would go against that commitment to excellence we adopted at the start of the 2005–06 summer.

In the first two editions, 1998 and 2000, when the competition was a straight knockout known as the 'mini-World Cup', Australia were knocked out at the earliest opportunity. In 2002 and 2004, we lost in the semi-finals, both times by fair margins, so the event has hardly been good for us. This time, our approach is not too different to if it *was* the World Cup; our biggest fear being that because it is coming at the start of our season and — DLF Cup not withstanding — because we are coming off a long break, we might be a little 'underdone'. But we've worked our backsides off in the lead-up, to the point that I will never forget the way the guys really got stuck in from the moment we landed here in India. On the back of that hard work, we're going into the event reasonably confident.

Winning the event is important. So, too, is the fact that it is a key stepping stone on our road to the World Cup. Because the pitches we'll be playing on here in India should be similar to those we'll see in the Caribbean during the Cup, there is an opportunity for players to make a lasting impression. There is also a chance to experiment with different tactics, such as who should take the new ball in circumstances where the ball will only swing right at the start of the innings, and when might be the best time to use powerplays, but at the same time we are wary of offering our rivals too much of a preview of the strategies and plans we're likely to implement when we get to the Caribbean in February. But given that we are here to win, there'll undoubtedly be times where we need to show at least part of our hand in order to prevail.

In one sense, we come into the competition at a little bit of a disadvantage, and confronted by something of a conundrum. Our first match will be against a team that's been forced to qualify because of its low international ranking, but that means, most likely, we'll be playing either the West Indies, defending champions, or Sri Lanka, whom I rate as one of the best teams in the one-day game. Either side will be coming off a series of competitive games, which can only help them. But the quality of our squad is reflected by the names of the men who have not been chosen. Of the 18 players we took to Malaysia for the DLF Cup, Mark Cosgrove, Dan Cullen, Brad Haddin, Matthew Hayden and Phil Jaques were missing from the original selection for the Champions Trophy, with Adam Gilchrist coming back as vice-captain. However, just a few days before we were due to depart for India, Stuart Clark had to withdraw after tearing his quadriceps muscle playing grade cricket in Sydney (fortunately, we've been assured he'll be fully recovered in plenty of time for the start of the Ashes series), and DC was called into the touring party as his replacement. Our squad is: Ricky Ponting (captain), Adam Gilchrist (vice-captain), Nathan Bracken, Michael Clarke, Dan Cullen, Brad Hogg, Michael Hussey, Mitchell Johnson, Simon Katich, Brett Lee, Glenn McGrath, Damien Martyn, Andrew Symonds and Shane Watson.

Something the Test players in our one-day squad will have to do over the next four weeks is concentrate on the present and resist the temptation to worry about the upcoming Ashes series. With the Tests edging closer and the questions being asked about them increasing by the day, this will be harder than it was in Malaysia, and it will be a credit to our professionalism if we can stay on track. Some are questioning if a month-long limited-over tournament in India is the right preparation immediately before the most eagerly awaited Test series in recent memory, but I reckon we just have to be pragmatic about it — it is the way the program has been laid out, so rather than moan about it we have to get as much out of our situation as we possibly can. England are in the same boat, India provides a good environment in which we can train hard, and maybe being away from the glare of the Ashes publicity that keeps building back home will actually be good for us.

Monday, October 9

ON THE SAME DAY, two former Australian captains, Ian Chappell and Kim Hughes, decided to have a shot at various aspects of the current Australia team. Criticism from Ian Chappell is something I've become used to, and because it comes so regularly these days I pretty much ignore it. In one sense, this is a shame, because there is no doubt he has some good ideas, but in my view his comments rarely seem constructive and there is a consistent negativity about most of them. Hughes had a go at Shane Warne, suggesting Warney's recent comments about Buck will damage our team spirit. Of course, Hughes was entitled to say this (though I don't agree with him), but I wondered why he felt the need to add: 'He (Shane) would have been an embarrassment if he had captained our country.' We'll probably never know how Warney would have gone as Australian skipper, but he wouldn't have embarrassed anyone.

Hughes went on to say we had been too 'matey' with the England players during the 2005 series, and highlighted Shane's friendship with his Hampshire team-mate, Kevin Pietersen. He is not alone in believing this, as I know that Mark Waugh and Allan Border (among others) have made similar comments. I've gone on the record as saying I don't agree with this — if anyone thought we were too chummy on the first morning of the Ashes series last time I'd be pretty surprised — but maybe it is true that against the Poms we did lose a little of the 'aura' that had come to characterise the Australian team of the past few years. If that was the case, we need to let *all* our opponents know that we've got it back. I know the South Africans respected us when we played them last season, and I want Andrew Flintoff's team to look at us in a similar light.

Having finished with Warney, Hughes then moved on to question Flintoff's appointment as England captain. He described 'Freddie' as a 'fantastic bloke', but said that he wouldn't have made him captain, because he feared that the total workload would be too great. I know as much as anyone just how demanding the captaincy can be. It takes more than being a talented player to just *play* cricket for Australia these days. International sport has changed; we know we're role models and accept that reality. Some blokes from the good old days, when the press weren't sweating on your every mistake, would have to change their ways if they played today or they wouldn't survive. The money that's come into big-time sport, which has been brought about by sponsors and wall-to-wall media coverage, has forced this evolution.

Most of the time, I don't mind the pressure of setting a good example, and get dirty on myself if I ever fall short.

Tuesday, October 17

Practice match at Wankhede Stadium, Mumbai (October 12): Australians 7–297 (50 overs: A Symonds 78, SR Watson 70; DR Martyn 42) defeated Maharashtra Cricket Association XI 7–194 (50 overs: YV Takawale 50) by 103 runs

Practice match at Bandra, Mumbai (October 15): Mumbai Cricket Association President's XI 8–218 (50 overs: AM Nayar 40*, WA Mota 41*; SR Watson 3–42) defeated Australians 292 (50 overs: AC Gilchrist 61, RT Ponting 55, DR Martyn 54; NM Kulkarni 5–43) by seven runs (target revised to 300)

Group A match, at Jaipur (October 15): England 125 (37 overs: MM Patel 3–18, RR Powar 3–24) lost to India 6–126 (29.3 overs) by four wickets

Group B match, at Brabourne Stadium, Mumbai (October 16): New Zealand 195 (45.4 overs: SP Fleming 89; JH Kallis 3–28) defeated South Africa 108 (34.1 overs: GC Smith 42; JS Patel 3–11, KD Mills 3–18, JDP Oram 3–26) by 87 runs

THE CRICKET WE PLAYED while rehearsing for the Champions Trophy did nothing to alter our conviction that Shane Watson is the right man to open the batting with Adam Gilchrist during the tournament. Playing Watto as an opener gives us more flexibility, which is something that is always handy, especially in Indian conditions, when the wickets often — but not always — suit spinners and slow seamers. In the past, if we played a bowling all-rounder such as Shane, Ian Harvey or James Hopes and batted him at No. 7 that meant we had to omit Brad Hogg from our line-up, but on wickets that are likely to take spin, Hoggy can be an important option for us. Batting Shane at the top of the order allows us to cover more bases.

For all that, at this stage I can't be sure exactly how much bowling Shane will do in our opening encounter. It is almost certain that the pitch at the Brabourne Stadium, the venue for our opening game tomorrow against the West Indies, will be slow and awkward, with the likelihood that it will get tougher to bat on the longer the game goes. (The Wankhede Stadium, the regular venue for international cricket here in Mumbai, is currently out of action for big matches.) The two Champions Trophy games already played at the ground — which hadn't hosted a ODI in more than a decade and hasn't seen a Test match since 1973 — have created some heartache, as the square appears to be sub-standard. First, the West Indies were bowled out for 80 batting second in their qualifying game against Sri Lanka (which means we'll be facing Brian Lara's team in our opening game), and yesterday South Africa were dismissed for just 108 chasing 195 against New Zealand. The way the wicket deteriorated over the course of the two encounters was alarming, with a number of deliveries breaking the pitch surface and catching batsmen out as they tried to drive. Balls were often failing to carry through to the wicketkeepers.

Without trying to sound too narky about the wickets, I hope tomorrow's pitch is not as slow and responsive to spin as the track we played on last Sunday, at Bandra in the Mumbai suburbs. The scorecard for this game looks a bit weird, but what happened was that we fielded first against a 16-man opposition (any 11 of that 16 could bat, any 11 to field), and then our target was bumped up to 300 to make the game more competitive, our hit more productive, and the run-chase more entertaining for the people perched in the temporary stands that had been put up in a venue not used to spectators. It was all a bit contrived, but it made the day more worthwhile for everyone.

Wednesday, October 18

Group B match, at Jaipur (October 17): Sri Lanka 253 (49.2 overs: ST Jayasuriya 48; Abdul Razzaq 4–50) lost to Pakistan 6–255 (48.1 overs: Imran Farhat 53, Mohammad Yousuf 49, Shoaib Malik 46*) by four wickets

Group A match, at Brabourne Stadium, Mumbai (October 18): West Indies 6–234 (50 overs: RS Morton 90*, BC Lara 71) defeated Australia 9–224 (50 overs: AC Gilchrist 92 MJ Clarke 47; JE Taylor 4–49) by 10 runs

OUR CHAMPIONS TROPHY CAMPAIGN has got off to a disappointing start, simply because the West Indies were too good for us. Paceman Jerome Taylor's hat-trick in the last over of the game put the seal on what for them must have been a very satisfying performance. Earlier, Taylor had knocked me over for 1, and then, with the final two balls of the 48th over and the first of the 50th, he dismissed Mike Hussey, Brett Lee and Brad Hogg.

Apart from a good partnership between Michael Clarke and Adam Gilchrist that ended when Gilly was run out in the 42nd over, triggering a collapse that saw our last five wickets fall for 37, our batting was ill-disciplined, and our bowling wasn't much better. We bowled too many 'four balls' through the middle of their innings; which means our blokes didn't bowl the right line or to their fields. We had talked beforehand about not giving Brian Lara a chance to hit square of the wicket, especially on the off-side, yet here he was hitting boundaries between backward and cover point. That gave them a momentum that meant they scored 234 when we could have kept them around 200. With the bat, we talked about the importance of consolidation at the top of the innings and we've stressed many times, whatever kind of cricket we're playing, how important partnerships are. Yet we lost wickets in the third, fourth and 11th overs.

At the same time, Lara and Runako Morton batted superbly, Taylor bowled extremely well, the much-criticised wicket held together reasonably well, so we must give due credit to our opponents. The Windies were missing Corey Collymore and Shivnarine Chanderpaul; if anyone was entitled to use excuses, it was them. This defeat was Australia's fifth in nine Champions Trophy matches going back to our first game in 1998. Back then, the tournament was a straight knock out; fortunately, these days we get a second chance.

The last time we'd seen Morton was in the final of the DLF Cup, when he managed to score exactly no runs from 31 deliveries. This time he played really well, finishing with 90 not out at almost a run a ball, and Lara was in excellent form, but the Australian captain helped them by spilling a skied catch when Morton was on 41. I did have to run about 20 metres to my right from cover to get to the catch, but I arrived there in plenty of time but didn't get my face right under the ball and though it struck a fair bit of my hands it went straight through. I'll always contend that there is no worse feeling in the game than dropping a catch. Lara, who kept himself down the order at No. 6, played Brad Hogg really well and made us use our bowlers in a different way to how I would have liked. Yet part of me couldn't help thinking that it isn't right the way he keeps himself away from the quicks — and especially away from Bing, who I don't think he fancies — at the start of the innings.

If that strategy suggests he's past his best, the Windies captain remains the best manipulator of fields I've ever tried to set a field against, especially when the spinners are on. At one point, Hoggy was pitching outside off stump with two fieldsman placed behind point because Lara loves to use that area to deflect and glide cheap ones and twos. So Lara just walked out and across and swept the ball against the spin on the 45-degree angle backward of square-leg. Hoggy and I decided that he'd bowl a straighter line, with one of the off-side fieldsmen moved to short fine leg, so Lara gave himself room and cut the ball precisely into the area that had just been vacated. In this form, you can only admire him; he ends up batting to the fields he wants to bat to, rather than anything you might prefer to put in place.

The decision to go back to the strategy we used in the early matches at the DLF Cup — to open the bowling with Lee and Bracken and bowl Glenn McGrath first change — was not the 'relegation' some people perceived it to be. It was the same tactical move we'd adopted in Kuala Lumpur, made again because we believed (correctly as it turned out) that the ball would only swing for a few overs at the start of the innings, and swing bowling is more part of Bracks' armoury than McGrath's best asset. Fortunately, there isn't any 'ego' in the Australian team when it comes to making these kind of decisions. If Glenn was feeling any angst at not getting the new ball he certainly didn't make it known. I was particularly keen to have our left-armer swinging them at their left-handers at the top of the order, and the strategy worked okay, with Wavell Hinds falling in Bracks' second over and the Windies sinking to 4–63 after 15 overs. But then Morton and Lara took over. When Glenn did bowl, I thought he went pretty well, though he did go for a few runs at the end of the innings.

We were under plenty of pressure throughout our run-chase, though we did get to a point where we needed 29 runs off 23 balls, with Huss still there, so we could have won. But then, emphatically, Taylor had the last word. Near the end of our innings, as the game drew to a potentially thrilling climax, Chris Gayle appeared to walk the length of the pitch at the conclusion of an over and then brush shoulders with Michael Clarke while Pup was trying to talk with his batting partner, Adam Gilchrist. From the dressing-room it sure looked pretty animated, and all a bit weird because the two protagonists are actually good mates who have known each other since the time, six or seven years back, when Gayle spent some time at the Australian Cricket Academy as an overseas scholarship holder. I think what started as a bit of fun kept building over by over. I must confess to being surprised that no one has been reported. Having been busted myself a couple of times in recent months, I reckon it's important there is some consistency when it comes to these types of incidents.

WE KNOW THE PLAYING conditions in the northern Indian city of Jaipur will be very different to what we've seen in Mumbai. The way our program has fallen, we only have two 'free' days between our first two group matches, time for just one net session in our new surroundings (in comparison, Flintoff's side will have been in Jaipur for more than a week when we play them, and have already played a game there). Then there will be an *eight-day* gap between games two and three. The Australian team's philosophy is that we take what we're given and try to make the best of it. We'll concentrate on the England game — which because of the upcoming Ashes series has special significance — and then we'll put the machine in neutral for a couple of days before commencing our preparation for what could be a crucial game against India at Mohali.

Friday, October 20

Group B match, at Brabourne Stadium, Mumbai (October 20):
New Zealand 165 (49.2 overs: NJ Astle 42, DL Vettori 46; M Muralitharan 4–23) lost to Sri Lanka 3–166 (36 overs: WU Tharanga 56, DPMD Jayawardene 48) by seven wickets

TWO DAYS BACK, I wrote that I was surprised that Chris Gayle wasn't reported after our opening group game, after he seemed to be the aggressor in his spat with Michael Clarke. However, the following morning, things were set straight when he was fined 30 per cent of his match fee for conduct contrary to the 'spirit of cricket'. The authorities, it turned out, had decided to sleep on the matter before issuing any reports. Pup was also charged but found not guilty, which I'm sure was the correct verdict. In my view, he should be congratulated for the way he handled the whole affair. There's no doubt he had a few words to say, but Gayle was the man at fault, the one who was invading someone else's personal space. My understanding is that two of them had a yarn after the match, and everything's fine.

The annual Diwali, the festival of light, one of the biggest and most important festivals of the Hindu year, is in full swing in Jaipur. We've been told that fireworks will dominate the city's skyline during our game against England tomorrow, and that there will be a smoky haze about. 'We've just got to hope,' I laughed when questioned today, 'that we'll still be able to see the ball.'

It was a light-hearted remark, born in part out of a lack of awareness on my part as to exactly what the celebrations are about. I appreciate that the festival means a great deal to the locals, and part of me wants to dive out into the street to find out more about the culture, and experience the buzz that was everywhere. But the fact that if we go anywhere we need to be accompanied by security guards, especially here where the streets are full and rowdy, is a go-slow in itself. Furthermore, except when it comes to getting the absolute best of my cricket, I'm usually a bloke happy to stay where I'm most comfortable.

We are only here in Jaipur for three nights. Our opening match was played in Mumbai last Wednesday, and yesterday was a travel day. We trained today, and with the game now less than 24 hours away, I preferred to occupy my spare time with a relaxing swim and a massage at our hotel, and to think about what we need to do to keep our Champions Trophy chances alive.

It is possible for us to sneak into the semi-finals with just one win from three group games, but that would need a lot of results to go our way. So this clash against the Poms is not quite a knockout game, but it's close enough that we have to think that way. No doubt, they'll lift against us — it's the first time Australia and England have met since that last Ashes series. There is a lot riding on the game just as far as this competition is concerned, even before we start thinking about any psychological advantages to be gained for the battles ahead.

Sunday, October 22

Group A match, at Jaipur (October 21): England 169 (45 overs: AJ Strauss 56, IR Bell 43; MJ Johnson 3–40, SR Watson 3–16) lost to Australia 4–170 (36.5 overs: DR Martyn 78) by six wickets

WE WERE LOOKING FORWARD to the England game from the moment we saw the tournament draw, not least because of a comment their coach Duncan Fletcher had made about the Poms' semi-final victory over us in the Champions Trophy in 2004. Fletcher has claimed that they used that win as a real fillip leading into the 2005 Ashes series, as though that one victory had given them a significant psychological advantage. In my view, this was bunkum, but it made me think that if we could beat them decisively here, and then remind them of their coach's opinions in regards to the importance of Champions Trophy matches, then *this defeat* might really stay with them. We had read, too, of analysis from English journalists that this was a one-day game and as such not much of a precursor to the Ashes, but when I looked at the England team for this game — which included among others Andrew Flintoff, Andrew Strauss, Ian Bell, Kevin Pietersen, Paul Collingwood and Steve Harmison, all of whom played in the '05 Test series — there seemed to be enough guys there who'd be lining up against us in Brisbane in 33 days time.

The game actually began well for them, as they reached 0–83 in the 19th over and were going pretty easily, but from the fall of the first wicket most of the momentum flowed in our direction. Interestingly, when Glenn McGrath came on first change Strauss and Bell tried to smash him, taking eight from his first over, and 27 from his opening four-over spell, as if this was their chance to make some sort of statement, but the premeditated ploy backfired somewhat when Pidge came back to take two wickets for nine runs from his last five overs. Shane Watson got the first wicket, and then Mitchell Johnson produced a fantastic two-ball sequence to Pietersen, who came out at No. 3.

Notch was at the top of his mark, ready to start his fourth over, when I said to him, 'Mate, give him a good one first ball. Sit him on his arse.' He promptly bowled the perfect bouncer, which hit him on the glove and then lobbed up in the air. Pietersen reacted as if he'd never seen a short ball before. The follow-up was beautiful — a rapid, well-pitched up delivery that needed a classic forward defence. But the rattled batsman wasn't quite there, the ball nipped away off the seam and he was caught behind. Notch finished with 3–40, having in recent games taken the key wickets of Lara, Tendulkar and Pietersen, each time with a memorable delivery.

England lost 10 wickets for 86, and in reply we were a bit shaky at 3–34 before Damien Martyn and Michael Hussey came together to build a smooth road home. This was one of Marto's best innings, proof again that he is at his best when needed most, while Huss made me look good by the way he responded to being moved up the order ahead of Michael Clarke. This was a touchy move from Pup's perspective, as he is one of those batsmen who hates being moved around the batting order, however the innings evolves, but I knew Huss is in career-best form, and I thought his experience as an opening batsmen would work best against the swinging ball. Having a left-hander in there with the right-handed Marto wasn't a bad thing either. We needed someone to occupy the crease, and Huss did that superbly, deflecting and nudging an unbeaten 32 from 85 balls.

A couple of well-timed risers delivered in the England innings were interpreted as being the first chapter in a bowling plan we've come up with for Pietersen and Andrew Flintoff. But it really wasn't that. The short balls bowled at them straightaway were more a statement than a scheme, and the fact that in both cases they led to wickets was a bonus. In Flintoff's case, he was pinged on the helmet by a bouncer from Watto, and then caught at deep square-leg two balls later. We'll follow up with more short balls for the two of them in future weeks, but I don't think that is necessarily the best way to get them out. If it makes them think, though, that can't be a bad thing.

Marto, on his 35th birthday, made his own statement against Steve Harmison. As firecrackers lit up the night sky, Flintoff called a powerplay, beckoned his No. 1 quick, to the bowling crease, and watched helpless as some ordinary deliveries were belted away for five fours. It was brilliant batting, an instance of a top batsman seeing an opportunity and grabbing it. If any of the Englishmen bowl that way in Australia we'll be looking to do exactly the same thing, and I'm sure they know that.

Friday, October 27

Group B match, at Motera, Ahmedabad (October 24): South Africa 9–219 (50 overs: AB de Villiers 54*, JH Kallis 43; SL Malinga 4–53) defeated Sri Lanka 141 (39.1 overs: A Nel 3–41) by 78 runs

Group B match, at Mohali, Chandigarh (October 25): New Zealand 7–274 (50 overs: SB Styris 86, SP Fleming 80) defeated Pakistan 223 (46.3 overs: Mohammad Yousuf 71, Shoaib Malik 52; SE Bond 3–45) by 51 runs

Group A match, at Motera, Ahmedabad (October 26): India 9–223 (50 overs: MS Dhoni 51, R Dravid 49; IDR Bradshaw 3–30) lost to West Indies 7–224 (49.4 overs: RR Sarwan 53, S Chanderpaul 51, RS Morton 45) by three wickets

WE HAD A PRETTY scary moment three days back, when Shane Watson was rushed to hospital in Chandigarh with chest and stomach pains. We'd held a team meeting that morning and an hour later Watto was a crumpled mess on the floor of his hotel room, fearful he was having a heart attack. Fortunately, the tests for serious ailments were all clear — the diagnosis was gastritis (which can cause heartburn and chest pain) — and now we're hopeful he'll be right for our game against India at Mohali in two days time

Watto isn't the only one who is or has been crook, with Glenn McGrath suffering a stomach ailment and Michael Clarke still missing training due to a bout of tonsillitis. No matter how hard you try, and our support staff are always conscious of keeping the risk of catching something to an absolute minimum, sometimes these things occur.

ONE OF THE THINGS we have talked about in team meetings is the concept of treating every one-dayer we play as a knockout game. The attraction of doing this is twofold: one, it will help us understand what playing under pressure is all about; and two, at some stage in important tournaments we will find ourselves in sudden-death situations, so testing ourselves in similar circumstances can only be beneficial.

I must confess I wasn't expecting to be at the knockout stage quite as early as we found ourselves here in India. We came through the England game okay, but now we face another do-or-die encounter. The equation is simple: win, and we're through to the semi-finals, possibly topping the group; lose, and we'll be getting more practice for the Ashes Tests by appearing in the Pura Cup earlier than expected.

The build-up to the game against India is typically intense and exciting. Everywhere, it is hoped that we will play well, but not too well, with the overwhelming dream being that Sachin will score plenty of runs, that Sehwag will score plenty of runs, and that India will win. There is plenty of pressure on us, but this is child's play compared to the attention being given to the Indian team and their coach, Greg Chappell. The local media and supporters want so much out of their cricketers, a fervour that would work as a spur if they were playing well, but in times like now, when a few of their key men (including Tendulkar and Sehwag) aren't going too well and Chappell's every move and motive is being questioned, these stresses can choke the enthusiasm out of the team.

I'm sure we'll enjoy the 'must-win' aspect to the upcoming game; I doubt our opponents will welcome it.

MUCH HAS BEEN MADE of the impact of the heavy evening dew on day-night matches being played in northern India. This moisture can make things more difficult for the team bowling second, and not just because the ball gets slippery. The dampness on the surface of the wicket means that if your bowlers pitch the ball up, it skids on to the bat which makes it safer for the batsmen to swing through the line, and if a batsman hits the ball hard into the ground on the edge of the wicket, it can scoot off through the infield significantly faster than would otherwise be the case. In effect, the dew can quicken up a wicket, rather than the wicket losing pace as the game progresses, which is what happened in Mumbai.

I don't think batting second was much of an advantage in our game against England at Jaipur, but it didn't hurt, and it could be that the dew will have even more of an impact at Mohali. We took a close look at the New Zealand v Pakistan game at that venue two nights back, and the atmosphere got very dewy and the ground very wet during the evening. We've been practising bowling with wet balls, in case we had to bowl second, and I've spoken to New Zealand coach, John Bracewell, and he said that during the night session it was as if it had been raining for an hour, and the ball did bounce a lot and moved around a fair bit off the pitch. The Black Caps' strategy was to pitch the ball fairly short and not give the Pakistani batsmen an opportunity to stroke it around. If we bowl second, we'll try to do much the same thing.

THE MEMBERS OF THE Australian cricket team have resolved in recent times not to use these sorts of unusual or unfavourable conditions as an alibi for sub-standard performance. Sometimes you've got to take what you're given, make the best effort to acclimatise, plan well in advance and take nothing for granted.

As an example, in order to have a reasonable guide to how the pitch in Jaipur would play, in the lead up to the England game we studied at some length the way the wicket had behaved in the Champions Trophy games that had already been played here, by going through the videos of those matches. Long gone are the days when we arrived for the 1996 World Cup final in Lahore with little idea of how the pitch and ground conditions would play. This is an example of one aspect of Richard McInnes' contribution to our cause. Since we landed in India, Richard, the team's 'performance analyst', has spent a fair amount of time sitting in his hotel room capturing every ball that's been bowled in the tournament, and then tagged it for future reference and added it to the vast collection of footage that weighs down his lap top.

Because of Richard's efforts, we can study on video a vast assortment of things — how opposition bowlers go about their business, how a pitch has been playing, how we've batted or bowled against certain teams in the past. You can see past dismissals, hundreds, plays-and-misses, anything. And because it's so well catalogued, we can see it quickly. The whole package helps us enormously in our quest to be as well prepared as possible for every single game.

The scale of Richard's database is quite remarkable. If Binger wants to see video of his bowling at certain times or in specific conditions, or he wants to see how his upcoming opponents are playing, Richard can make him a DVD that he can study on his laptop. I'm actually exploring the idea of taking this concept one step further, by getting hold of some portable Playstations for our contracted players, on to which Richard could download a stack of easily accessible content. My idea is that if the guys each had one of these PSPs in their backpack, they could easily use their down time waiting at the airport, on the bus or in the hotel foyer, going through any aspect of their game they might need checking.

From the moment they learned that there would be an eight-day gap between our game against England at Jaipur, and the next match, versus India at Mohali, near Chandigarh, our coaching staff was proactive, doing the groundwork for what wasn't too far short of a second 'pre-season' camp. They booked a venue that featured a centre wicket, three sets of nets, plenty of net bowlers, and after a couple of quiet days, we took full advantage of their forward thinking. I don't know if other teams train as enthusiastically or prepare as diligently as we do, but I do feel we get full value for the hard work everyone puts in.

Because of the long break between the England and India matches, we opted to go low-key for the first couple of days here in Chandigarh. Nothing was compulsory; everyone could go down to the ground and do their own individual sessions. Those who wanted to bat for an hour or bowl for as long as they preferred were able to; their team-mates who wanted to take it easy could do that. In the last couple of days, we've enjoyed some excellent centre-wicket practice, attempting to replicate match conditions as closely as possible.

I was one who opted for some extra work, though not too much. The whispers about my batting form have started to grow louder, to the point that our assistant coach, Dene Hills, who knows my game pretty well, asked me after one net session just how I was going. I had spent the previous half hour hitting everything in the middle of the bat (which I bet Dene was aware of), so I was able to say with some confidence, 'I think a score is just around the corner.' Against the West Indies, I chopped on a half-tracker that didn't bounce, always an unlucky way to get out, and then against England I got an excellent one from Sajid Mahmood — good pace, bit of outswing — and I didn't get forward enough and nicked it to slip. The lack of runs was more disappointing than a worry for me, because I'd been getting out in circumstances when the ball was hard and swinging and the team needed its No. 3 to make a contribution. These are usually the times when I love to bat the most. In all, I've scored two from nine balls in this tournament; what I need to do is get in, get set, and go from there.

There have been a couple of times during my career — in the first half of 1998–99 and then in India and England in 2001 — when I did have extended runs of unproductive form, but I'm not sure that would happen to me now. One thing I've developed as my career has unfolded is an understanding of my game and what I need to do to get things back on track if something is not quite right. In the old days, if runs weren't coming, I would be in the nets all the time hitting thousands and thousands of balls and before I knew it there were thousands of conflicting thoughts and theories in my head. I was thinking about all the different things I'd decided I needed to be doing, and I became mentally stale, almost fried. I reckon one of the biggest challenges for anyone to do in any walk of life is to work out for themselves what are the things that work really well for *them* and what doesn't. In my mid 20s, I didn't really know what was right for me, but I think I do now. That's the best way I can explain the fact that I haven't gone too many games without a decent score in recent years.

IT HAS NEVER STOPPED amazing me just how big the Ashes series is right now, even though the first Test is still a month away and we are currently in the middle of the second biggest one-day tournament in world cricket. It feels like every time I do a media conference or interview, the conversation turns to the upcoming Tests. It was the same today. For the Indian population, our game tomorrow is all that matters, but still the questions about the old urn kept coming from English and Australian reporters. All I can do is keep answering them. How much of a driving force, I was asked, is the memory of those two Test-match losses in 2005?

'I've never been a dweller on things that have gone. You can't afford to be. But I'm sure a few of our guys have been getting up at six in the morning for their training with that in the back of their mind and to make sure they're right for the Ashes. That's how much it stung us last time.

'We will be a better team this time. We've looked at ourselves closer than before the last Ashes. We've identified what might have held us back last time.

'I don't think there's going to be too much drastic change. We just made a lot of mistakes last time. The no-balls we bowled, we put a lot of catches down. When we had partnerships going, we managed to make a mistake that got England back into the game, or Andrew Flintoff came on and got a wicket.

'They're things we won't allow to happen again ...'

Tuesday, October 31

Group B match, at Mohali, Chandigarh (October 27): South Africa 8–213 (50 overs: MV Boucher 69, JM Kemp 64; Umar Gul 3–36) defeated Pakistan 89 (25 overs: M Ntini 5–21) by 124 runs

Group A match, at Motera, Ahmedabad (October 28): West Indies 4–272 (50 overs: DJ Bravo 112, CH Gayle 101) lost to England 7–276 (48.3 overs: KP Pietersen 90*, AJ Strauss 50, IR Bell 50; CH Gayle 3–31) by three wickets

Group A match, at Mohali, Chandigarh (October 29): India 8–249 (50 overs: V Sehwag 75, R Dravid 52) lost to Australia 4–252 (45.4 overs: DR Martyn 73*, RT Ponting 58, SR Watson 50) by six wickets

THE QUESTIONING OF Glenn McGrath's future has continued unabated throughout the Champions Trophy to date, with the usual suspects in the media claiming he is a spent force while we've been reasonably happy with his progress. No one in our camp has claimed that he is near his best, but at the same time only the narky could claim he's finished, and in this game against India he demonstrated one of the reasons he's been a great bowler for so long.

The pitch didn't play as we expected, not as bouncy, but whereas we read the signs pretty quickly the Indians made the mistake of pitching too short for too long. The key spell was McGrath's, as he conceded just 12 runs from his first six overs, a performance that also featured the wicket of Tendulkar — always a vital moment in India because it takes the enthusiasm out of the home crowd. We'd given Glenn the new ball specifically because he loves the one-on-one battle with Sachin, and he responded by getting the edge that led to Adam Gilchrist's world-record 400th dismissal in ODI cricket. Brett Lee conceded a few too many early on, but came back admirably at the death, slowing the run rate and bowling quick, smart and scary all at the same time. In between, we managed to take wickets at regular intervals, which meant India couldn't get on a roll.

As we'd expected, it was probably better to bat during the wet night session than during the dryness of the day. The ground authorities knew the dew was coming, and consequently the interval between innings was abbreviated and there was a long drinks break during our innings so the groundstaff could try to dry the ground a little. That shortened gap between innings didn't help Shane Watson, who cramped up severely when he opened our innings, having fielded (and bowled nine overs) during India's 50 overs. Fortunately, our embattled opener fought through to an impressive 50 from 46 balls, I was happy with the way I hit them, and then Marto batted beautifully again, to steer us into the semis and send all of India into mourning.

It is true that the home team's inexperienced attack didn't bowl well, but I was still very happy with the professional way we went about getting the required runs. Given the fact we were playing India on their turf, in a match both teams had to win, and our victory was pretty clinical, I'd have to rate this as one of our better one-day victories of recent times. Going into the finals of this tournament, and with the World Cup just a few months away, our squad is starting to look really good — lots of flexibility, plenty of experience, a bit of youth to keep us older blokes in line, and a few guys just outside the team who'll keep the pressure on and who could step in if required.

WE GO INTO THE semi-finals as confident as we can be. We have a full list of players to choose from and because of the way the results have fallen we have been able to stay in Chandigarh, to play on a pitch we like and which we've had some success on.

Furthermore, we are playing a team, New Zealand, against whom we have an excellent record (15 wins from our past 17 ODIs). Yet the memory of our experience in the Chappell–Hadlee Trophy games last season, where they beat us once and could have won the series, is a reminder that they are an ultra-competitive side with a shrewd captain and some very good, versatile players. And, of course, they always seem to lift when they're playing Australia — it's part of the All Black psyche.

However, we are also very keen to win and therefore go further in the tournament than any Australian team has ever gone before.

Thursday, November 2

First semi-final, at Mohali, Chandigarh (November 1): Australia 9–240 (50 overs: RT Ponting 58, A Symonds 58; KD Mills 4–38) defeated New Zealand 206 (46 overs: DL Vettori 79, JDP Oram 43; GD McGrath 3–22) by 34 runs

AN INTERESTING STATISTIC I read after this game involved Andrew Symonds, who was the batting star of our semi-final against New Zealand, scoring his first half-century of the tournament: a run-a-ball 58. It was his 20th fifty in 152 one-day international, and the 19th time he'd scored a half-century in an Australian victory, which strongly suggests that if Symmo fires with the bat we're likely to win. (Sadly, it doesn't always work this way; my first three ODI centuries, for example, all came in Australian losses.) It is true that this current Aussie ODI team does have a high success-rate, but even so the conclusion that has to be drawn from this stat is that he is a very important part of our line-up. Having him batting at No. 5 or No. 6 gives us a priceless advantage. On this occasion, he came to the crease with our score at 4–123 in the 29th over and turned what looked like it was going to be a good total on the Mohali wicket into an imposing one.

Soon, it was an impossible target, because for the second straight game Glenn McGrath was outstanding. He was able to swing and seam the new ball as he liked, bowling 10 overs straight for 3–22, and New Zealand were reduced to 6–35 in the 15th over. From there they limped to 206 all out, but if Huss hadn't dropped Daniel Vettori — a sitter to first slip when the batsman was five and the score was 6–47 — they might not have made many more than 60.

In the post-match media conference, McGrath commented, 'I came over here and also in Kuala Lumpur to improve each game I played. I have done that and I will keep doing that. By playing in this series and at Kuala Lumpur, I have put a piece of the puzzle together.'

It was never the intention that making Glenn bowl first change would prod him into action — there was logic in opening with Bing and Bracks that went beyond where Pidge was with his form and fitness. For me, seeing Pidge rise to the occasion in this important game and also against Sachin Tendulkar in the final group game underlined a reality that I've been aware of for some time: senior players in big tournaments are crucial. Major contests are often won by people who have experienced the pressure before. If you look back to our previous World Cup victories, we had a really good mix of experience and youth around the squad. That's why we could withstand setbacks such as our poor early form in 1999 and Shane Warne's failed drug test in 2003. Last night, the oldest player on the park came out and was man of the match. Glenn knew exactly what he had to do, and he is still good enough to do it.

Before I leave the semi-final, I'll bring up a favourite gripe of mine one last time. Another instance arose in this game of a disputed catch that could have been sent to the video umpire. I've just about given up trying to promote the issue, but for the record the way Michael Clarke handled this one — he dived forward and might have (but probably didn't) catch Jacob Oram — was exactly the way I believe these matters should be handled. Ninety-nine times out of a 100, the players involved will have a better idea than the bloke in front of the TV screen, but people want to argue that it should be left to that bloke in front of the TV screen. Here, Pup said he wasn't sure he'd caught it, and in those circumstances the decision has to be not out. If players are honest, it doesn't need to go any further than that. If any fieldsman wants to exploit that scenario, then rub 'em out.

Saturday, November 4

Second semi-final, at Jaipur (November 2): South Africa 8–258 (50 overs: HH Gibbs 77, AB de Villiers 46) lost to West Indies 4–262 (44 overs: CH Gayle 133*, S Chanderpaul 57) by six wickets

ICC AWARD WINNERS

Player of the Year: Ricky Ponting (Australia)
Test Player of the Year: Ricky Ponting (Australia)
ODI Player of the Year: Michael Hussey (Australia)
Women's Player of the Year: Karen Rolton (Australia)
Emerging Player of the Year: Ian Bell (England)
Captain of the Year: Mahela Jayawardene (Sri Lanka)
Spirit of Cricket Award: England
Umpire of the Year: Simon Taufel

World Test Team of the Year (in batting order): Matthew
   Hayden (Australia), Michael Hussey (Australia), Ricky
   Ponting (Australia), Rahul Dravid (India, captain),
   Mohammad Yousuf (Pakistan), Kumar Sangakkara (Sri
   Lanka, wicketkeeper), Andrew Flintoff (England), Shane
   Warne (Australia), Makhaya Ntini (South Africa),
   Muttiah Muralitharan (Sri Lanka), Glenn McGrath
   (Australia), 12th man: Brett Lee (Australia)
World ODI Team of the Year (in batting order): Adam
   Gilchrist (Australia, wicketkeeper), MS Dhoni (India),
   Ricky Ponting (Australia), Mahela Jayawardene (Sri
   Lanka, captain), Yuvraj Singh (India), Michael Hussey
   (Australia), Andrew Flintoff (England), Irfan Pathan
   (India), Brett Lee (Australia), Shane Bond (New Zealand),
   Muttiah Muralitharan (Sri Lanka); 12th man: Andrew
   Symonds (Australia)

I'M NOT SURE IF the annual ICC awards night — a black-tie
function attended by all the members of the Australian squad —
was an ideal inclusion in our program leading up to the
Champions Trophy final, but I can see its value and why it was
staged when it was. The fact it took place two days before the final
at a venue located an hour from our hotel was a little frustrating,
as that meant we didn't get to sleep until well after midnight. But
what really annoyed us was that apart from their coach Bennett
King, the West Indies team — who we'll be playing in the final —
didn't turn up. We'd been told we *had* to go, and did what was
required of us, but they didn't, and I was happy to let the media
know I wasn't impressed. In the Windies players' defense, their
semi-final against South Africa was played a day after ours, which
meant they'd travelled from Jaipur to Mumbai and were then
being asked to get to the function that same evening.

What has been stranger than the Windies' no show is the nature of most of the questions I was asked by media at that awards night and everywhere in the lead-up to the Champions Trophy final. It was all about the Ashes. Stranger still, here we were, the home team for the upcoming Test series, in Mumbai preparing for a major one-day final, while the away team, the Englishmen, were already in Australia. Stranger even than that, we have been reading reports that the English team's preparations are rushed, they will struggle to acclimatise and they might be underdone going into the first Test. Where does that leave us? The truth is we all knew the schedule from many months ago and it was up to each team to get its house in order. If the Poms are struggling they have only themselves to blame.

With all the talk about the Ashes, it has become something of a challenge for the guys likely to play in the Tests to stay committed to the Champions Trophy. But it is important we do so — not least because not everyone here in India will be playing against England. For a few of the guys, this is their biggest moment before the World Cup. Inevitably, as captain, most of the responsibility for answering questions about the Ashes campaign fell to me, but if that meant my team-mates could concentrate on the task at hand then I was fine with that.

As I fielded all the media enquiries, I became frustrated with the negativity surrounding any questions relating to the Champions Trophy. Maybe that was why I had a jab at Brian Lara, specifically about the way the great left-hander has been batting down the order. I want there to be an 'edge' about the big game. 'If Brian happens to bat up the order, where he should be batting, then hopefully our quicks can get to him and get him out of there pretty quickly,' I said a little provocatively. 'I've always been a huge believer in the best batsman batting as high up the order as you can possibly get him. I don't know why he's batting where he is, but the only thing I can think of is that he is trying to stabilise their innings.'

The fact that the Windies were in the final was in itself some justification for the way Lara had been setting up his batting order, and given his propensity for toying with the spinners on slow wickets in the middle overs, I could see some sense in his tactics. And the Brabourne Stadium track for the final will be on the slow side, to the point that we'll be playing Brad Hogg instead of Mitchell Johnson. But as I've said before, whether having your captain and best batsman batting at No. 6 sends the right signals, I'm not sure.

Wednesday, November 8

Champions Trophy Final, at Brabourne Stadium, Mumbai
(November 5): West Indies 138 (30. 4 overs: NW Bracken 3–22) lost to Australia 2–116 (28. 1 overs: SR Watson 57*, DR Martyn 47*) by eight wickets (D/L method)

I WAS AS NERVOUS as I am for any game before the final, which is always a good thing. When I'm not getting nervous about batting or cricket will be the time to start worrying.

There was much to be concerned about. This has been a good tournament for a number of the West Indies players — especially Chris Gayle, but also Ramnaresh Sarwan, Shiv Chanderpaul and Dwayne Bravo — and they were the defending champions. Gayle, who had been the batsman of the competition, having made hundreds against Bangladesh, England and South Africa, is a 'Sehwag type' player, a guy who relies on his great eye, doesn't worry about getting his foot near the pitch of the ball, and can be so destructive. Once he gets into a rhythm of hitting the ball everywhere, he just doesn't stop and over the past month it has been a case of if you don't get him early on, look out.

Back in the DLF Cup final, Brett Lee had trapped him lbw, first ball of the innings, with a big inswinging yorker that struck him on the toe. Gayle, a left-hander, had always used a conventional batting stance that had the toes of both feet aiming towards point, which we felt — because he doesn't use his feet much — always left him susceptible to a quick one that ducks in. In the opening Group A game here we'd tried that tactic, but he'd still been good enough to make 58 off 46 balls; now, he came out and used a much more open stance, and started charging from ball one. But Chanderpaul, his opening partner, outblasted him, hitting 27 from 18 balls before he was dismissed by the first ball of the sixth over, after an opening stand of 49. In Bing's second over, Chanderpaul tried to front-foot pull a quick delivery over mid-wicket, and top-edged it over third man's head for six. But just when I thought it was going to be another of Gayle's golden days, Nathan Bracken stepped up, getting Chanderpaul to chop one on and Sarwan to hit a tame catch to Brad Hogg at mid-on. Then he bowled Gayle with an absolute beauty that crashed into the off stump. I guess we got him fairly early, as we'd hoped, but the score was 3–80 in the 10th over. Finally, my nerves could start to fade away.

McGrath's first two overs had gone for 22, all but one of them conceded when he was bowling to Gayle, but now he came back to get Lara and Morton and concede just two runs from his final five overs. The Windies lost their last eight wickets for 58 and the game was as good as over. Not even the Mumbai rain could stop us, though it got a bit laughable during our innings, when it started raining and the possibility of the game dragging into a second day became a real possibility. We had all been away from home for long enough, but the groundstaff didn't seem to be in any hurry to get moving, so I geed up everyone connected with our team — players, coaches, whoever we could find — and we went out and put the covers on and dragged them off, and did anything else we could do to get the game going.

Brian Lara seemed happy enough to wait until tomorrow, but he didn't have an Ashes series to play. He also, I conceded, would be disadvantaged if the game did continue that night, as we would be chasing a smaller total under the Duckworth-Lewis method used to calculate run-chases when play has been delayed, but the reality was that our bowlers had produced such a commanding performance that the result was beyond doubt. Shane Watson and Damien Martyn sealed the win with an unconquered 103-run partnership.

THE LACK OF URGENCY that pervaded the groundstaff's work carried over to the presentation ceremony, which dragged on and then degenerated into an unfortunate incident that took a little of the gloss off our victory. As we crowded around the trophy on stage for the stock-standard celebration photograph, Marto gave Sharad Pawar, the BCCI president and an Indian government minister, a nudge. It didn't look good and it wasn't good (I base this comment on a replay of the incident I saw after we arrived back home), though Mr Pawar hadn't helped things by the way he refused to let go of the trophy after he was supposed to hand it to me. Maybe he wanted to get his picture taken with the winning team, I'm not sure, but had he stepped to one side in the way presenters usually do, none of the kerfuffle that followed would have occurred.

At the time, I didn't know that Marto had done anything wrong, and I doubt that Marto did either. It wasn't until we were about to board the flight for Sydney that I was told there was a story in one of the Indian papers about the episode. By the time the plane landed it was an international incident, and I resolved to ring Mr Pawar personally to apologise and explain that we meant no offence. When I did speak to him he seemed happy to accept my apology. I guess a few people will use the episode to tag us as 'ugly Australians', and we'll have to live with that, but I'm not going to let it get to me. There's now only 15 days to the first ball of the first Ashes Test. It's been on our minds every day for the past 14 months, yet somehow it seems to have arrived quicker than I expected.

International cricket in the 21st century can be like that.

CHAPTER 4

ASHES LEAD-UP

Thursday, November 9

WE ARRIVED HOME FROM India on Tuesday, Melbourne Cup Day, and that same afternoon I was at a function at Woolloomooloo Wharf in Sydney with my wife Rianna. Of course, the quality of a Cup-Day function is always judged by whether you nailed the winner of the great race, and my day was almost spot on. The prominent radio broadcaster Alan Jones tipped me into the Japanese horse Pop Rock, ridden by Damien Oliver, but it missed out narrowly, going down in an exciting photo finish to another 'raider' from Japan, Delta Blues.

Missing out on the Cup winner by a half-head was disappointing, but nothing compared to the frustration I felt the following day, at the launch of my *Captain's Diary 2006*, when I was once again asked questions concerning negative comments about the current Australian team made by a former Australian player. The book is about a year of cricket that was littered with outstanding performances and some memorable cricket, about a season in which the Australian team won 11 of 12 Test matches. Yet, just three days after we won the Champions Trophy, I was being asked to react to comments that suggested the team was in decline. What made this particular situation a little different was that one of my team-mates has already responded. The episode began when Dennis Lillee came out with the old line that the Aussie team is an aging one, as if that hadn't been said before. This time, though, Damien Martyn returned fire, suggesting that maybe Lillee needs to think about the fact that as well as being a newspaper columnist he is also the President of the Western Australian Cricket Association. In Marto's view, the WACA needs the national team to be successful, but it hardly helps having one of his state's senior administrators taking aim at the side. You've got to admit, it's a fair argument. Prominent cricket officials should be building the team up, highlighting our successes, rather than searching for negatives.

Had Lillee not been one of cricket's greatest ever fast bowlers, his unkind words would probably have been lost in the flood of media comment that reflects the unprecedented interest in the upcoming Test matches. As I have described, I was often surprised in India by the way I kept being asked about the Ashes, but now that we're home I've been blown away by the scale of the build-up. The Tests had been sold out for months, reporters are queuing up to ask any number of questions about what transpired in 2005 and what might happen now, even cricket history has become trendy again as the Ashes urn is undertaking a celebrity tour of Australia. I can't help thinking how fortunate we are as a team that we are well prepared for the first Test, how valuable it was that in early October last year we made that commitment to excellence that has allowed us to play so well in the past 12 months. My best guess is that our opponents are not quite on the same page. As has been highly publicised, injuries mean they will be without their captain from '05, Michael Vaughan, and also Simon Jones, whose bowling in the first four Tests, especially the way he got the ball to reverse swing, played a significant part in their victory. Flintoff, of course, has been under an injury cloud, and there are those doubts about his leadership credentials. I guess there is still a slight question about Glenn McGrath's readiness for a five-day Test, but otherwise we are travelling nicely.

Friday, November 10

Tour match, at Canberra (November 10): Prime Minister's XI 5–347 (50 overs: PA Jaques 112, SE Marsh 78, TR Birt 40) defeated England XI 181 (38.4 overs: AJ Strauss 67; SW Tait 3–21) by 166 runs

THE NEWS FROM MANUKA Oval in Canberra, where the Englishmen played their first match in Australia, was all good. It wasn't just that the tourists lost; they were thrashed, with a couple of blokes on the fringe of the Australian line-up having a real day out. Compared to the colts in the PM's XI, the Englishmen looked ponderous. Phil Jaques scored a slashing century, while Shaun Tait added his name to the growing list of fast bowlers seeking a place in the first Test squad with some blistering deliveries that had commentators recalling the days of Lillee and Thommo. His three wickets weren't mugs either: Marcus Trescothick, Andrew Strauss and Andrew Flintoff. I'm as big a fan as anyone of getting express bowlers into your team, and I know from painful experience in the nets how quick Shaun can be, so to see him back to full pace was fantastic.

Tuesday, November 14

Tour match, at Sydney (November 12–14): NSW 9–355 dec (PA Jaques 107, SM Katich 68, MJ Clarke 50) and 6–194 (MJ Clarke 68, SM Katich 55) drew with England XI 349 (KP Pietersen 122, A Flintoff 62, AN Cook 59, AJ Strauss 50)

Ford Ranger Cup match, at Melbourne (November 12): Victoria 200 (49.3 overs: CL White 50; AR Griffith 3–45) defeated Tasmania 145 (43.1 overs: TD Paine 56; ML Lewis 3–32) by 55 runs.

TWO DAYS AFTER THE massacre at Manuka, Phil Jaques followed up with another hundred in the game against the Poms in Sydney, as the touring bowlers again looked a little short of a gallop. Yet for all the NSW left-hander's runs, and despite the simmering debate about the age of Australia's team, I couldn't see the selectors making any change at the top of the Australian batting order. This wasn't just blind loyalty — as the long-time No. 3, I appreciate more than anyone what Langer and Hayden have meant to the Aussie XI over the past five years. It's not just their runs, but also their relentless desire and commitment that has meant so much to our success, and I for one would be loathe to give any of that up even one game too quickly.

As Jaquesy continued on his run-making way at the SCG, I was in Melbourne being caught down the leg-side for 10 during Tasmania's Ford Ranger Cup loss to Victoria. While I wasn't really concerned about missing out again, I was just beginning to get frustrated by my inability to put together a long innings, especially given that there was not a lot of time available before the first Ashes Test to get reacclimatised to Australian conditions. Consequently, I see the Pura Cup game against the Victorians which began today as being important for me. Even though the Victorians made a good start, Brad Hodge and Cameron White making hundreds on what is a very flat deck, it should also be an enjoyable experience — a chance for me to play for Tassie at a time when the team is going really well, having won their two opening Pura Cup games, in Brisbane and Perth.

Back in Sydney, the Englishmen finally had a good day or two, with Kevin Pietersen scoring his first century of the summer.

Two images from the 'boot camp' that launched our 2006–07 season. Note the matching uniforms, numbers of the T-shirts, and our ever-present 'mates' (in dark shirts) who made sure we did everything exactly as *they* wanted.

The celebration team photo after our first win of the season: the DLF Cup. Back row (left to right): Brad Haddin (obscured), Simon Katich, Glenn McGrath, Matthew Hayden. Middle: Brad Hogg (wearing white cap), Nathan Bracken, Shane Watson, Stuart Clark, Dan Cullen, Brett Lee. Front: Damien Martyn, me, Mike Hussey, Andrew Symonds, Michael Clarke.

The Champions Trophy in India offered us not only the opportunity to play in the second biggest one-day tournament in world cricket, but also an excellent chance to prepare for the upcoming Ashes series. Above left: centre-wicket practice at Chandigarh. Above right: Glenn McGrath with the local net bowlers at Mumbai.

Mike Hussey, Andrew Symonds and Shane Watson sharpen up with some touch footy at the Brabourne Stadium.

Above left: Mitchell Johnson gets excited after claiming the key wicket of Kevin Pietersen at Jaipur.

Above right: Michael Clarke has just trapped Ramnaresh Sarwan lbw at Mumbai.

Left: Damien Martyn during his match-winning 73 not out against India at Mohali.

Damien Martyn (left) and Shane Watson steered us to victory in the final.

Two images of the Champions Trophy. Left: Smiles all round after the presentation. Below: At the media conference in Sydney after we arrived home on Melbourne Cup Day.

Left: Caught behind for 10 during the Tasmania–Victoria Ford Ranger Cup game at the MCG on November 12.

Left: The toss that launched the most eagerly anticipated Ashes series in history. Andrew Flintoff called incorrectly and we were batting.

Justin Langer during his opening session assault at the Gabba that set the tone for the entire series.

Four images from one of the most satisfying hundreds of my life, scored in the first Test.

Justin Langer, me, Shane Warne, Matthew Hayden and Glenn McGrath after we'd gone one-up in the series.

Justin Langer at the Adelaide Oval, being reminded how fair dinkum our net sessions have become.

Images from the first two-and-a-bit days of the second Test.

Above: Paul Collingwood (left) and Kevin Pietersen during their big partnership that stretched over the first two days of the game.

Below: Andrew Flintoff after dismissing Justin Langer late on the second afternoon.

Above: Matthew Hoggard bemoans Ashley Giles' critical dropped catch early on day three.

Apparently, he did so with some style. There is no doubting Pietersen's enormous talent, and I will be stunned if he doesn't play at least a couple of major innings during the series, but what was more encouraging for the Poms was that their bowlers enjoyed a little bit of success in NSW's second innings. Jimmy Anderson took three wickets, which probably means he'll be in the first Test side, but I also noticed that Andrew Flintoff only bowled four overs — an indication, perhaps, that he's not travelling as well as he'd like to be.

We will be targeting Flintoff during the series, on the basis that if we can find a chink in his armour it could discourage his team-mates. The great West Indies sides of the 1980s made an art form out of pressuring the opposing captain, and the Australian captains of the '90s who played against them — Allan Border, Mark Taylor and Steve Waugh — made sure future Aussie teams never forgot the strategy. I'm not so concerned with putting him under pressure as a captain, but as a player, because we've seen in the past how dynamic he can be with bat and ball, and also how he can inspire his colleagues. If we can keep him pinned down, a few of his mates might not be so keen to step into the ring.

Friday, November 17

Pura Cup match, at Melbourne (November 14–17): Victoria 6–429 dec (BJ Hodge 153, CL White 150*) and 1–192 (N Jewell 100*, BJ Hodge 66*) drew with Tasmania 518 (MJ Di Venuto 129, GJ Bailey 101, DJ Marsh 95, RT Ponting 51; J Moss 4–70)

THERE WAS SIGNIFICANT INTEREST in the Tasmania–Victoria Pura Cup game, not least because one of the Victorian bowlers I'd be facing was Shane Warne. Unfortunately, the pitch the

MCG ground crew gave us was too flat for its own good, and consequently from a public relations point of view the game was something of an opportunity lost. Wickets were at a premium — Michael Di Venuto, George Bailey and Nick Jewell joined Brad Hodge and Cameron White as century-makers and only 17 wickets fell in four days — but even if the conditions were in my favour, I still came away encouraged by my hour and a half at the batting crease. It took me a couple of overs to get used to the bounce and pace of the wicket, but after that I felt like I hit everything pretty much in the middle. I'm not trying to be critical of one-day cricket, but there is something nice about not feeling obliged to get things moving right from the start. I might have pushed a bit hard at the ball a couple of times early on, and a couple of deliveries from Gerard Denton didn't go quite where I wanted them to, but once I got in the groove things went along nicely.

Shane finished with 3–159 from 46.3 overs and afterwards I was asked if he seemed up for the contest. 'He's never *not* up for it,' I replied. Warney is the most competitive person I've ever seen on a cricket ground, but in this game our guys played him really well. There was nothing in the track for him, yet he still beat me when I was in the 40s with an evil ball that seemed from my vantage point to be akin to the legendary 'Gatting ball': pitching just outside the leg stump and fizzing past my bat's outside edge and the off bail. How he did it, on that pitch, I have no idea.

Throughout my knock, I wanted to be aggressive against him. I've seen enough batsmen who just try to stand there, hoping to survive, letting him dictate terms, to know that is *not* the way to play him. I was keen to use my feet whenever I could, and I would never sweep him. I don't sweep much, full stop, but if I tried he would get me out with the one out the front of the hand that skids straight on. I always try to use my feet against spin bowlers, whether to hit them over the top, past mid-on or through the covers. On this occasion, with the pitch so docile, there were times when Shane tried too hard to get some decent turn and dropped the delivery too short, and as a consequence there were chances to hit some boundaries. It was really good fun, but then Cameron White got me out at the other end with a half-tracker that I bottom-edged back on to my stumps. I could hardly believe it! The number of times I've told others never to take anything for granted, and I fell for it.

Especially on the final day, the cricket at the MCG became somewhat tedious, as the benign pitch took all the life out of what could have been a good contest. About the only positive I could see to come out of the day was the bowling of Tassie's Ben Hilfenhaus, who stuck at it all day and bowled with real pace, further underlining the fact that there are some exciting young quicks emerging around the country. Australian cricket's future in the post-McGrath era will never be the same, but it certainly won't be dull or unproductive.

INEVITABLY, THE QUESTIONS OVER who would make the Australian team for the first Test continued right up until the naming of the squad last Wednesday. The things I will remember most about that conjecture are the debate over Justin Langer's place and who should bat at No. 6, and the surprise when 13 names were announced, five of them belonging to fast bowlers.

For a month leading up to the day the team was selected, Lang was on a very sharp knife's edge. It got worse when Phil Jaques started scoring all those runs against England in Canberra and Sydney, as members of the Sydney press corp started arguing that a revamp at the top of the Australian batting order was imminent. The clamour for change grew so loud that I took it upon myself to ring Lang during WA's Pura Cup game against

Queensland in Perth last weekend, to try to set his mind at ease. As far as I am concerned — though I must stress that I am not a selector — Lang is crucial to our chances. A lot of people will be feverishly counting down the days to the first Test, but now that he's safely in the team, few will be doing so as loudly as Justin Langer.

Lang wasn't the only bloke I rang in the days before the team was picked. A few days back, Allan Border, who had until recently been on the selection committee, went on TV and named the team he would have picked, and Michael Clarke wasn't in it. There was no real surprise there — I think the balance of opinion probably favoured Shane Watson — but AB was so strident as he explained why he wouldn't have picked Pup, I felt there was a need to reassure the best young batsman in the country that he is very much part of our plans. I told Pup he has the talent to score so many runs the selectors have to notice him, and I wanted him to know that I believed in him. I knew how hard Pup has worked on his game during the off-season; I'm not sure AB does.

Of course, I always have to be careful when I have these conversations. I'm not a selector, so I can't say to any player that he is going to be chosen. I also can't tell them that if I was a selector, I'd pick them. That's the worse thing I can say, because the immediate implication is that, if they're left out, there'll be someone in the team who I don't think should be, and it would never be fair or productive if that opinion entered the public domain. Once that happens, people start looking over their shoulder and splits within the unit can occur. For me, this gets hardest when I've got to talk to a player after he's been dropped — I might not necessarily agree with the selectors' thinking but it is the selectors' thinking that I have to pass on. I know this is part of my job, but it doesn't mean I have to enjoy doing it. It is true that there were a number of our blokes not totally sure of their places in the starting XI — Lang, Marto, Watto, Sarf, even Pigeon — so I guess there could be a couple of tough post-selection conversations to be had before the summer is through.

I like the idea of the five fast men — Glenn McGrath, Brett Lee, Stuart Clark, Mitchell Johnson and Shaun Tait — working with the squad in the lead-up to the start of the series, and not just because it will also keep the Englishmen guessing for a little longer. I can picture centre-wicket practice being somewhat lively, as the quicks compete with each other to impress the people that matter. I can just imagine them queuing up to bowl at the captain, on the basis that a couple of quick risers into my thigh or ribcage might get them noticed. Probably the best example of this occurring in the past came in the 1999-2000 season, when Brett Lee was first brought into the squad at the WACA back in the days when the Perth pitches were quick and bouncy. The young punk was very excited about impressing the people who mattered, and was unbelievably quick. Here in Brisbane, I'm probably not supposed to be looking forward to a similar experience, but I am. Highly competitive practice has become something of a trademark of this Australian team, to the point that every time it happens, it brings a satisfied smile to my face.

IN THE VISITORS' CAMP, Middlesex opener Ed Joyce has been called up to replace Marcus Trescothick, who has had to return home, opening up the chance for Paul Collingwood to come into their middle order. My only reaction when I heard Trescothick was still struggling with depression was to hope he recovers as quickly as possible. He is a good bloke and a good cricketer, who deserves every chance to get his life back in order.

Sunday, November 19

Tour match, at Adelaide (November 17–19): South Australia 7–247 dec (DS Lehmann 99, CJ Borgas 73) and 2–164 (DJ Harris 71*, MTG Elliott 55) drew with England XI 415 (IR Bell 132, PD Collingwood 80)

BEFORE HE JOINED UP with us in Brisbane, Shaun Tait renewed acquaintances with the Englishmen in Adelaide. Apparently, his first ball of the England XI's first innings, late on day one, was so wide it scared the life out of first slip but then a couple of deliveries later he beat Andrew Strauss for pace and trapped him lbw. Nightwatchman Matthew Hoggard was the new batsman, and South Australia skipper Darren Lehmann greeted him with an eight-man slip cordon. Alastair Cook had to wear a Tait bouncer on the body, and at stumps the Poms were 1–24 in replay to SA's 7–247 declared. The contrast between Tait and Steve Harmison, who dropped out just before the start of the game because of an ailment of some kind, was stark.

Not that we were free from injury concerns, as Shane Watson has limped back into Brisbane carrying a strained hamstring suffered while playing for Queensland against WA in Perth. I first heard about his injury last Friday night, and though I was a bit worried, my fears were calmed somewhat by the television reports of the moment he hurt himself — I looked for the reaction on Shane's face and it wasn't that grimace of sharp pain that normally accompanies a major hamstring tear. My guess is he'll be okay, but Michael Clarke has come up to Brisbane as his 'shadow', and will bat at No. 6 if Watto is ruled out.

The second and third days of the tour game in Adelaide actually went pretty well for the English batsmen, with Ian Bell making a hundred and Paul Collingwood (the likely substitute for Marcus Trescothick in their Test XI) scoring 80. Allied to the hundred Kevin Pietersen hit in Sydney and the fact that Andrew Flintoff has also made a couple of handy scores, it seems the tourists' batting isn't going too badly, though their bowling still appears rusty.

ELSEWHERE, I WAS GIVEN a lesson in how the media can offer a wide variety of opinion on the same subject. Just a couple of days after Richie Benaud named me as captain of his best Australian Ashes team from the past 30 years, I received a call this morning from my mate Brady Rawlings of the Kangaroos AFL team, suggesting I shouldn't read today's *Sunday Age* because Darren Berry, the former Victorian wicketkeeper, has taken a shot at me. Apparently, Berry believes that most of the success that I'd enjoyed as a captain had come about because I've been in charge of a great team and often playing opposition that compared poorly with teams from days gone by. I've never felt it was my job to publicly analyse my leadership skills, but I am often intrigued at how different experts can look at the same storyline and come up with very different endings.

Throughout my cricket career, I have always tried to not get too disappointed or carried away with negative remarks about me or too excited by accolades. It can be different when the team or a colleague is being unfairly criticised, but I'm sure that if I had listened too carefully to public comments about my ability, going right back to the time when I was 15 years old and Rod Marsh went public with his opinion of my ability, I definitely wouldn't be the Australian captain today. All the self-congratulation, worry and angst would have distracted me from what I really needed to concentrate on. Over the years, I think I've learned well to take away only what I need from the positive and negative things that are being said about me.

AS THE AUSSIE SQUAD settled into our hotel in Brisbane over the weekend, I was struck by a sense of freshness that has engulfed the group. Maybe in my mind we were resuming too quickly after the fortnight in Malaysia and four weeks in India. It's funny how, just a decade ago, people were predicting gloom and doom over the concept of separate Test and one-day squads. It was predicted that such a division would ruin team harmony, but what has happened is that the changeover in personnel that occurs when we switch from one form of the game to the other eliminates any sense of production-line sameness in blokes such as me who play both one-day and five-day matches. This is especially true in situations such as now, where we've had six weeks of limited-over cricket away from home but the men coming into the squad are individuals of the calibre of Justin Langer, Matthew Hayden and Shane Warne. In the cases of Lang and Warney, they haven't played international cricket for six months or more (Matty, you might remember, was in Kuala Lumpur for the DLF Cup), and after this series there is no more Test cricket for Australia until next season, so it's little wonder they're as keen as can be. Their enthusiasm is contagious.

The three are completely different characters, something you can tell just by observing the way they go about their preparation. Justin will hit a thousand balls in the lead-up to the Test, always be the first man to arrive at the nets, and be the last to leave. The other two walk with a fraction less intensity, but more bravado. They all know their games well. Haydos will wander over to the nets when he feels like it, then stand around, maybe have a short hit, or just go and sit out in the middle on the Test pitch with his shoes and socks off. When Warney, the extrovert, is not bowling, he will have his music up loud in the dressing room, revving us up like we're a footy team. A common link between the three is that they are all champions who have seen every situation you can be confronted with in a Test match and know how to fight their way out of tough positions and get in front from there.

Tuesday, November 21

SHANE WATSON RAN LIGHTLY for about an hour at yesterday's session at our training base for the week, Brisbane Grammar School, after which he had further scans done on his troublesome leg. These were taken to try to gauge just how much the injury has improved. I'm no doctor, but I must confess that based on what I saw at training, I now doubt that he'll be right. Watto walked and then jogged lightly with team physio Alex Kountouris before making a brief appearance in the nets, where he couldn't disguise a slight limp as he bowled off three or four paces. The contrast as the rest of us went through a vigorous two-hour session was massive, and couldn't have left our all-rounder feeling too good about his chances of being right for Thursday's start.

The set up at the Grammar School is brilliant. It is 30 or 40 minutes drive from our hotel, but we're lucky it is available, because the Allan Border Field, where we would normally have worked, had been sold out to corporate sponsors. On one of the playing fields, batsmen enjoyed centre-wicket practice against the quicks, all of whom had a new ball in their hand. At nearby nets, batsmen could fine-tune their game against a range of net bowlers, and also the world's greatest leg-spinner. As well, a bowling machine had been set up, mounted on a platform to try to replicate the delivery angle of the tall English pacemen, Steve Harmison and Andrew Flintoff. Away from the nets, assistant coaches conducted a series of fielding drills, which provided opportunities to rehearse a range of manoeuvres, including ground fielding, overarm and underarm throwing, and outfield, close-to-the-wicket and slips catching. Gully specialist Matthew Hayden teamed up with a different bowling machine that shot balls at a wooden table that had been perched at an angle, so that the resulting rebounds mimicked balls slicing off a thick outside edge.

As I expected, the competitiveness throughout our training sessions before the first Test has to be fun and fantastic. I will never forget one centre-wicket practice, when I had Brett Lee, Stuey Clark and Mitch Johnson running in off their full run and kept thinking to myself: *this is the best preparation I can possibly have*. Binger would bounce me, then Notch would bounce me, then Stuey would deliver a good outswinger that pitched just outside off stump. Brett would fire in a yorker, Mitch an inswinger, then Stuey would get his bouncer in. I loved it. Everyone had been waiting so long for the series to get underway, it was inevitable that the energy and the anticipation would be as enormous as the first-day crowd.

THE WAY THE GUYS were bowling in practice reflected the impact our new bowling coach had made. The story of Troy Cooley is not that well known. A former Tasmanian Sheffield Shield bowler, his career was cut down by injury, after which he managed a gym, which is when he became interested in the physiology of fitness and, specifically, of bowling. 'I wanted to know why I had been injured so often and what I could do to prevent other bowlers from suffering in the same way,' he explained to the *Observer* in 2005. 'I used to have a regular problem with no-balling, so that was something else where I thought I could draw on my own experiences to help bowlers.'

At the same time, Troy earned his Australian coaching badges and worked with some junior rep bowlers. In 2000, he won a role at the Australian Cricket Academy, working under Rod Marsh, where, as he puts it, 'I had the opportunity to treat bowling not just as an art, but as a science; I had time to work with individual bowlers and devise training programmes that were right for them and their lifestyle.' His association with the England team commenced in 2003, and two years later he was considered to have played an important role in the Poms' Ashes win. We 'poached' him back last May, and he has brought plenty of expertise into the group that had not been available before — an understanding of the mechanics that make a bowling action work or disassemble.

I've known Troy for most of my life, having played all my club cricket and some of my state cricket with him, so I appreciate more than most that with his deep knowledge of the art of bowling comes a genuineness that allows him to communicate well with his charges. He is a bit of a 'softie', too, which appeals to all fast bowlers. I chuckled the day he told me that if he knew about bowling now what he did when he was playing he would have been a superstar. It might be true, too, because he could bowl.

I think Troy is at his best as a coach when he works with a bowler 'one on one'. He makes a point of getting to know the blokes he's working with, letting them know that he *really* cares, that he wants to know about them as people and cricketers, as well as about their techniques. I understand that when he was the England bowling coach he actually went and stayed with Steve Harmison at the paceman's house for a while, because that's what he thought would get the best of him.

One of the greatest disappointments of my cricket career was going through England in 2005 with Jason Gillespie and Michael

Kasprowicz a long way from their best and there being no expertise in the touring party to help them. That won't happen now.

Troy is keen for his bowlers to work as a unit, for them to 'hunt as a pack' as he likes to put it. For me, this is just an extension of something Buck and I have always stressed: that cricket is all about partnerships. It's not about Warney bowling 10 overs for 20 at one end while the batsmen are taking eight an over from the other. Bowling partnerships are as important as batting partnerships. The other thing that needs to be acknowledged — and Troy is big on this — is that it is not as simple as watching how Glenn does it, or how Shane does it, and that's the way everyone else must do it. If there were plenty of bowlers out there like Pigeon then he wouldn't be special. How many times have I sat in team meetings in the past and heard how all the bowlers are going to attack a certain batsman in the same way?

It's all right telling Glenn, who can bowl at 135k on the same line and length, to try to tie down say, Virender Sehwag, and give him nothing to attack, but you can't say that to Brett Lee or Mitchell Johnson because they don't bowl that way. Bing and Notch's bowling plans have to be developed with due consideration for what they're good at, not what Pigeon does so expertly. Everyone needs to know their roles within the team set-up and their roles have to be shaped to their skills. I imagine this is how most businesses should work, but I'm not sure all of them do.

TROY, OF COURSE, IS a Tasmanian, as is Jamie Cox, who has become the fourth member of the Australian team selection panel, joining Andrew Hilditch, David Boon and Merv Hughes. This is just further proof of the growing domination of world cricket by Tasmanians! Test captain, bowling coach, two selectors ... even the head of the Marylebone Cricket Club in London, Keith Bradshaw, is from Tassie. You need good people in important positions, and I reckon Jamie is the perfect man for the selectors' role. He's a terrific bloke, has a vast knowledge of the game, was unlucky not to play for Australia, played plenty of Pura Cup cricket and county cricket, and is pretty forthright with his views. Having the boys from Tassie around, who I know well and who know me well, is for me a good thing. Their state of origin is not the reason any of them have been appointed, but it definitely makes my life easier.

Wednesday, November 22

OVER THE PAST FEW days, I have made a point of observing how the guys have gone about their business. I was looking for flaws, for someone not being as enthusiastic as the rest of us, but there was no one out of 'sync'. The coaches had left nothing to chance, and throughout our net sessions and centre-wicket practices, always with new red balls, we've been keen and sharp. In days long gone, after a few weeks on the subcontinent, we might have been forgiven for being a little lax. Not this time. If we were a Formula One car, you'd say we were primed to charge into the first corner.

Our opponents, on the other hand, have more than a whiff of caution about them. We are in no doubt that they'll play Geraint Jones as their wicketkeeper instead of Chris Read and Ashley Giles as their spinner rather than Monty Panesar. Unless we've totally misjudged Duncan Fletcher's conservative nature, that is the way they'll go, and Troy Cooley keeps reminding us that Fletcher is always keen to have as much depth in his batting order as he can muster, to the point that at times he'll go for the better lower-order batsman even if that player isn't as proficient at what he is actually in the team to do. I'm sure choosing Giles and Jones is a mistake — neither, after all, is going to win a Test for them — but still we can't underrate either of them, as they both did a job for their team in 2005 and Giles especially is one of those dependable cricketers every coach likes to have around.

SHAUN TAIT WAS RELEASED from our squad this morning, as the odds firmed that Stuart Clark would get the third quick's guernsey. For me, the memory of Sarf's bowling in South Africa remains strong, and with Watto now ruled out it is important that our four bowlers are all capable of handling long spells. For this reason, Sarf's greater experience counts for plenty, because, as gifted as Mitchell Johnson is, there is always the possibility of a young player 'blowing up' on the game's biggest stage. In Notch's case, I doubt that would happen, and it is true that in England in 2005 it was two experienced guys, Michael Kasprowicz and Jason Gillespie, who were unable to deliver, but the odds are still in Stuey's favour, because as well as giving us a real wicket-taking option he is almost guaranteed to be able to deliver the long, tight spells that we might need. Some critics have complained that he is too similar to McGrath, but I can't see that as a negative — surely having two Glenn McGraths in your team can be no bad thing.

I must confess it's a strange feeling I'm having trying to come to terms with Watto dropping out. On the one hand, I'm extremely disappointed, because as everyone knows I am a huge believer in balance in the cricket team and in Watto I'm sure we have a bloke who can deliver that to us. At the same time, I am also a huge believer in Michael Clarke as a Test batsman. I see plenty of me as a young cricketer in Pup, I know how gifted he is and I also know — because I've seen it in the Australian camp and in private training sessions — how determined and dedicated he is. In the time he has been out of the Test XI, he might have worked harder on his technique, his batting and his body than anyone else I have ever played with. When his elevation to the starting XI was confirmed, my mind immediately shifted to a scenario down the track where Watto would be fit and Pup would be firing. I wouldn't want to be a selector when that happens.

From even before he knew he was playing Pup has been buzzing around like a kid about to play in his first grand final. Players, supporters, commentators, everyone is so happy to be here. Last night, I was involved in a live Channel Nine cricket show at the Queensland Performing Arts Centre that tried to create a similar atmosphere to what you see on the network's *Footy Shows*, and while I'm not sure if they pulled it off there was no doubting the enthusiasm of all the cricket fans, Australian and English, in the audience. You can smell it in the street, around the Gabba, at our hotel; I've never felt quite like *this much* of a celebrity in Australia. Constantly over the last few days, I have stressed the need for us to keep a lid on all the excitement and expectations that started building the day after we lost the Ashes 14 months ago, and have become almost irresistible in the last few days. That was the main message I gave to the boys tonight — that it is vital we not get carried away and try to make things happen too quickly.

I have always used our preparation for the 2003 World Cup, when we stayed at Potchefstroom, a fair distance from Johannesburg, away from the buzz of the tournament, as the best example of how you can insulate yourself from such a frenzied build-up. This time, because our team hotel is in Brisbane, it was so much harder, but in its own way Brisbane Grammar has been like a sanctuary for us. Perhaps it was a good thing Queensland cricket gave Allan Border Field to the corporates! There was still a stack of media around, but the facilities were so good and expansive when we needed space it did feel as if there was a divide between us and the world outside. As captain, I was happy to absorb as much of the attention as I could, to let the other guys do what they had to do to get ready. That's what they did.

A constant theme in the questions I've been receiving has concerned McGrath. It was like that in Malaysia, in India and all of this week. I sense that some reporters have already prepared obituaries, refusing to believe that at age 36 he can bowl at anything like the ultra-high standard he has reached so often in the past. I'm sure they're wrong. 'Glenn knows his body and knows himself better than anybody else,' I told Peter Lalor from the *Australian* today. 'He's not going to take himself into a game if he thinks he's not 100 per cent prepared. You have to show a lot of trust in these sort of players. I've got no concerns on him.'

And then I returned to a theme I have been hammering the guys with since the time last October when we sat down to analyse why the Ashes were no longer in Australian hands:

'We have to play at a higher standard for longer periods of time than we did last time. We had moments of very good cricket through the last Ashes series, and moments of really poor cricket, with lots of mistakes — no-balls, dropped catches — we don't normally make. That was the difference in the last series …'

CHAPTER 5

FIRST TEST

Tuesday, November 28

First Ashes Test, at Brisbane (November 23–27): Australia 9–602 dec
(RT Ponting 196, MEK Hussey 86, JL Langer 82, MJ Clarke 56; A Flintoff 4–99)
and 1–202 dec (JL Langer 100*, RT Ponting 60*) defeated England 157
(IR Bell 50; GD McGrath 6–50) and 370 (PD Collingwood 96, KP Pietersen 92;
SR Clark 4–72, SK Warne 4–124) by 277 runs

AS JUSTIN LANGER AND Matthew Hayden prepared to go out to
bat on the opening morning of the first Ashes Test, I was going
through my usual routine in the dressing room. From outside, I
could hear the buzz of the big crowd, and everywhere, the sense
of great anticipation was palpable. As I gathered my helmet,
gloves and a bottle of water (which I always have next to me
when I'm waiting to bat), Lang took guard out in the middle,
while Steve Harmison walked to his mark, ready to bowl the
series' opening delivery. I found a seat in the viewing area just in
time, 10.03am, as Harmison began his run to the wicket. At that
precise moment, Troy Cooley, sitting just near me, commented to
those around him:

'Watch this. It'll go straight to second slip ...'

Which is exactly where the ball went. At that moment, I wasn't sure quite what to think. My memory of the frenzied start of the 2005 Ashes series was so strong; as I've said many times, it was the most intense period of cricket I have ever been involved with. This was so different, almost slapstick. Harmison looked forlorn, the English fieldsmen embarrassed, the spectators were now a strange mix of shocked, excited and bemused. Then Troy spoke again:

'This second one will be a massive over correction. It'll go miles down the leg-side.'

Our bowling coach knew his man, how much the nerves of this huge occasion would impinge on his mindset. Sure enough, the second delivery barely touched the pitch surface as it speared down the leg-side.

So astounded were we at what was happening on the field and Troy's Nostradamus impersonation, it was a good two or three minutes before we really realised the series was underway. My mind was awash with thoughts: *If these blokes are that nervous out there ... no Michael Vaughan ... no Marcus Trescothick ... no Simon Jones ... don't forget the controversy over leaving out Panesar and Read ... they're a long way from home ... no Troy Cooley as their bowling coach ... these blokes are vulnerable, we've got to jump all over them.* In these circumstances, the manner in which Lang and Haydos went about their opening partnership was perfect. Whenever we 'had' them in 2005, we'd promptly made a mistake — lost two or three wickets in a row, missed a vital catch, lost the momentum. There was none of that here ...

FOR ME, BRISBANE AND Boxing Day are the two big Tests of the year. The first morning of the opening Test of the summer is always an exciting time, but this was something different, something I doubt I'll experience again. From the moment I woke up, everything seemed bigger than it usually is for a Gabba Test. The chatter in the hotel foyer seemed more animated, the traffic on the way to the ground was heavier, the mood among the players was tense. There was no point thinking, *this is just another game*. At the ground, people took their seats early, as if they wanted to make sure they didn't miss anything. Often was the time I looked at my watch or a clock to see how much longer before we got underway, and then, suddenly, it was time for the toss, then the national anthems. I'm not sure if an Australian cricket team has ever been more inspired by *Advance Australia Fair*, as the big crowd got right into it after Ian Healy and Ian Botham had brought the Aussie flag and Union Jack onto the Gabba. We had talked about not letting the pre-game ceremony distract us, yet this celebration was so heart-pumping. But as I stopped briefly to observe the lads in the dressing room, as Lang and Haydos got set to leave us, I realised that everyone was worrying only about what they had to do to play well *today*.

There was never any doubt that we'd bat first if I won the toss. The first hour at the Gabba can be awkward, but the pitch usually settles down into a nice batting track. This time, though, it seemed to be friendly from the opening wide, an outcome that came about, in my view, because of the skill and attitude of the batsmen, who bludgeoned the bowling into mediocrity. Harmison's first 'spell' lasted just two overs and 17 runs, including four fours to Langer. My little mate was on fire, dominating the first hour, and I couldn't help thinking that he'd taken all the pressure he'd been under about whether he should be in the side and turned it into the catalyst for this aggressive start. He had not been in the greatest of form, but he knew better than anyone how to respond positively to criticism, and that going into his shell to try to grind out a solid 40 (which might keep him in the team for another game) is never the way to go. Instead, he went at the bowling quite brilliantly, and at the first drinks break he was unbeaten on 38. We were 0–57. If I was writing the script, this is exactly how the first hour would have gone.

It wasn't until Andrew Flintoff came on that the bowling got anywhere near its 2005 standard. Suddenly, the pitch was more lively, the batsmen tested, the fieldsmen a little chirpier, and the England captain made the first breakthrough in his fourth over, when Hayden edged a catch to Paul Collingwood at second slip. This setback brought me out half an hour before lunch to get involved in one of the most enjoyable partnerships of my career. Lang was buzzing along, 50 not out, and I jumped on for the ride.

WHEN A NEW BATSMAN walks onto the ground at the fall of a wicket, there is a real responsibility on the shoulders of the man who has been batting for a while. *Partnerships are so important*, was a message I reminded myself as I walked out to the middle, *we don't want to lose two wickets in a row*. Inevitably, a fresh batsman is a little susceptible early on, so the more established guy has to do all he can not to throw his wicket away, so a new stand can be built. The need to consolidate the openers' fantastic start was about all that Lang and I talked about when we met near the pitch.

Saying the right thing during this mid-pitch 'introduction' is a skill in itself. It's all about knowing how your partner is going to react to any advice or opinion you might offer. But you never want to fill up your mate's mind with too much information, or say or imply that it's diabolically hard or too easy. On this occasion, Lang admitted he was feeling good, but he said it in a fairly underwhelming way. The impression I was left with was that he was in control and on a mission to bat for a very long time.

I've always loved playing and batting with Justin, going back to the West Indies tour in 1995, my first trip away with the Australian Test team, when he and I were on the bench throughout the Test series and for all but the last of the five one-day internationals. We were in the Caribbean for two months, young blokes sharing the same experience, training with each other, getting to know each other. We made a pact that when we got the chance to play for Australia we'd take it, and every time we bat together is in itself a reminder for each of us of that commitment. Lang is so determined to make the most of absolutely every ball he faces in Test cricket, it's almost inspirational to be out there with him. You don't want to let him down. He's a rare cricketer.

I was very disappointed for him when he was dismissed on the verge of what would have been a very satisfying hundred. It wasn't a great shot, a mistimed slash to point, but that was the way he'd played throughout the day and the out happened at a time when Flintoff was bowling extremely well. Lang's 82 had come from just 98 deliveries. Many is the time, during a great bowling spell, that an ordinary delivery gets the breakthrough, because the batsman gets too excited, and loses just too much concentration, at finally seeing a scoring opportunity.

MY INNINGS EVOLVED INTO one of my best centuries; I can't recall doing much wrong. It is true that, Flintoff apart, the England bowlers were not at their best, but when they did land the ball in the right areas, I had to be wary, as there was something in the wicket for them. As I approached three figures every corner in my brain emphasised the fact that if I did get to the landmark I had to go on and make a really big score. The hundred, in this sense, was just a number. The fact that it would be my 32nd Test century (equalling Steve Waugh's Australian record, an achievement I wasn't aware of until afterwards) was nice, but nothing more than that. Yet when I did get there my celebration was just about the most animated of my life — a release, I think, after all the stress and strain that surrounded the build-up to the series. It meant a lot to me, maybe even more than I'd realised — the self-analysis, all the sifting through the post-Ashes criticism, those early-morning training sessions, running up those bloody sand hills, the new balls at the nets, it was all worth it! In the same way, I was a little disappointed with myself after I got out on day two, because I walked off the ground in an apparent huff without acknowledging the crowd. I shouldn't have done that, but my mood reflected my regret, not so much that I got out for 196, so close to an Ashes double century, but that I got out at all. I was keen to continue to send messages to the Englishmen. We were going to be relentless, keep giving them nothing. We were in control of the game by then, 5–467 after lunch on the second day, but I wanted to really ram our advantage home.

Over the next couple of days, I became aware that some people were suggesting I was the best Australian batsman since Sir Donald Bradman. Steve Waugh wrote that in his column in the News Limited papers, and I think Bill Lawry said something similar. To be honest, it is how people compare me to other players from my era that is of more interest to me. The greatest batsmen in my time have been Sachin Tendulkar and Brian Lara, and if I can be rated somewhere near as good as them, then I'll be very satisfied.

The fact The Don could score hundreds just about all the time suggests he possessed an insatiable appetite for runs, which to me translates into him having an enormous desire to do his job as well as he could. If people want to say that about me, too, I'll definitely take it, because that is what I am trying to make a feature of my character and the way I play my sport. It's never about records for me, rather about being able to adapt my game to suit any scenario that might arise in a game. If I can come through in most situations the runs will come, and if I play long enough I'll move up the run-scoring lists. Just as surely, however, any records I might set will get broken in the future. That's the nature of cricket ... unless you're able to average 99.94. That's the one record that will live forever.

After this innings, a number of people wanted me to recall some of the best shots I'd played, but the truth is that when you contribute a big innings of this kind you often can't recall the specifics afterwards. I think this is because I get so much 'in the zone' when I'm batting at my best — I don't hear the crowd, I'm not conscious of getting tired, or of any other potential distractions. Afterwards, I can sit in front of a television and watch the highlights and think to myself, *did I really play that shot?* My mind is committed only to the next ball. That zone is a mysterious place, if you think about (which I try not to), and impossible to locate. It finds you. As has been said many times, if it was easy to discover, we'd all go there all the time. I just go with the flow, working on the theory that if I've done the work beforehand, more times than not I'll be okay.

THERE WERE THINGS I did during our innings to show England we were ready for them. After the last ball before the break was bowled at lunch (1–109), tea (3–217) and stumps (3–346) on day one, at lunch (4–427) on day two, I yelled to my batting partner to run off the field with me. I wanted the Poms to know we still had plenty of energy, at a time when they were dragging their butts, that we were a better team than we had been last time round.

During those tea and stumps breaks, my batting partner was Mike Hussey, with whom I added 209 for the fourth wicket. In many ways, Huss is the same as Lang to bat with, though more animated. He'll shout at you from the non-striker's end; you might cream a cover drive or hit a pull shot one bounce for four and he'll be screaming, 'Next ball, next ball, don't worry about anything else.' I'd never call Huss 'relaxed' out in the middle, but I love his intensity and the value he places on his scalp. We've had some good fun batting together. With him usually batting at No. 4 or No. 5, it means I've usually been in at least a little while when he comes out, and in such circumstances I find his competitiveness refreshing. Same as when I'm batting with Lang, there is this nagging motivation in my mind that I don't want to let him down.

At stumps after day one I made a point to the guys that while we had enjoyed a terrific start, it was just one day out of 25 as far as this series is concerned. The runs and psychological advantages we'd banked wouldn't really count for anything unless we followed up with more good performances on day two and beyond. The memory of the Test we lost to India in Adelaide in 2003-04 is always there for me — when we scored 556 batting first but lost pretty comfortably three days later. The loss of the 2005 series after winning the first Test at Lord's quite decisively is a similar spur. We knew that batting on this Gabba wicket would be easier on days two and three, so it was magnificent to see Michael Clarke make a polished half-century and then our late-order batsmen smash and swing our score towards 600. When I declared at 9–602, McGrath was 9 not out, another 50 nipped in the bud.

Throughout the 2005 series, we found Flintoff to be their most dangerous bowler, because he had that golden touch of being able to come on and take a wicket straight away, which often changed the mood, so we were mindful of guarding against him doing that in this series. Because of the way he likes to hit the seam, we thought the Gabba wicket would suit his bowling more than any other pitch in Australia, and we also felt that if we could blunt his impact that would have an effect on the rest of the attack. And I think it worked that way. He bowled really well on the opening day, but we were still three-for-plenty at stumps, and when we followed up by going all the way to 600, a psychological battle had been won. There's always a lot to be gained by mastering a team's best bowler, especially when he really stands out. The best example is Murali and Sri Lanka. Conquer him and you're usually in front.

Maybe the Englishmen wanted to do the same with McGrath. If they did set out to do this, it didn't work; instead, he strode out to put his critics very firmly in their place. Stuart Clark was outstanding, too, and we won ourselves a 445-run first-innings lead.

It started on the second afternoon, in Pidge's third over, after Alastair Cook and Andrew Strauss had begun okay. We'd spoken about Strauss liking the pull shot, but because he doesn't move his feet too much, he can be a chance to top-edge a short one behind square, and Pidge got it exactly right, the ball flew up in the air, and Mike Hussey (who had been placed slightly deeper than a conventional square-leg) and Brett Lee at deep fine leg both converged on the ball. Huss was closer, and going at top speed, and he took a terrific catch, but in the process spiked Bing's leg above the knee. We were lucky here; Huss' sprigs could have ripped Bing's leg wide open, but though our fastest bowler had to leave the field we soon learned that the prognosis was positive. A bit of tape over the wound and he was back bowling as fast as ever.

(We tried this tactic of testing Strauss on the pull shot again in the second innings and it worked again; this time he was caught by a substitute fieldsman, Ryan Broad. Falling for this trap twice in the same game is not a good feeling for an established Test player — you're supposed to be smarter than that — and we wondered if we might have done some damage on Strauss' psyche that might last for the rest of the series.)

The very next ball after Strauss was caught by Hussey, Cook couldn't handle a McGrath special, the trademark off-cutter that zipped off the pitch, and he edged a catch to Shane Warne at first slip. Soon after, Stuart Clark captured his first Ashes wicket — Collingwood caught behind down the leg-side for 5 — and we were in a remarkably powerful position, something we held on to tenaciously throughout the England first innings.

At the end of it, Glenn McGrath made a point of 'limping' off the field, holding his back like an old man — his response to the 'Dad's Army' jibes that had been aimed his way. The sell-out crowd (which in three days had broken the previous Gabba Test-match attendance record) had a nice old chuckle, but I must confess I held my breath when I saw him do it, and sure enough he slightly hurt his left heel during the Poms' second innings. But he had proved again the old adage I have always believed in: when champions *have* to deliver, they usually do. The pick of his six wickets was Kevin Pietersen, lbw without offering a shot, after a sequence of 22 McGrath deliveries to Pietersen that morning that included just two scoring shots, a single and a three. The great bowler didn't give him a thing.

And then, after four more balls for one single from Ian Bell, Brett Lee knocked over the England captain for a duck.

While we had waited for Flintoff to come to the crease, I had a chat with Binger about where he was going to bowl his first ball. My feeling with Flintoff is that early in his innings — because he doesn't move his feet too much (a product, I believe, of his wide batting stance) and at the same time he is committed to asserting himself by trying to hit the ball hard from the jump — he is susceptible to the delivery that seams away from him. It doesn't matter so much where the delivery pitches, it's the line and the away movement that counts. Brett's instinct was to bounce him first ball — not just to make a statement, but also because we felt Flintoff might try to pull a short ball before he was set (the memory of Jaipur during the Champions Trophy, when Shane Watson seemed to rattle him with a short one, is still strong). But the batsman in me was very keen on that good-length ball on that outside-off-stump line. Putting myself in Flintoff's boots, that's what I'd have least liked to receive. Brett delivered the perfect ball and Flintoff nicked it straight through to Gilly. England were 5–79. The Gabba was rocking.

THREE HOURS LATER, THE innings was over, and I surprised a lot of people by not enforcing the follow-on. I must confess to being very surprised that this decision was bagged as heavily as it has been, and also that a lot of this criticism came from former players who showed again how easy it is to become negative once you trade in your bat for a media pass.

In my view, the people doing the knocking failed to appreciate the way of 21st century cricket, with schedules so tight and demands on players sometimes being extremely hard. The old timers also seem to forget the way we play our cricket, scoring our runs so quickly that there is plenty of time left to bat again and still win. That wasn't true in days gone by, when teams might need two and a bit days to score 600, which meant that you had to send opponents back in if you could because otherwise you'd run out of time before could bowl them out twice. I have had a number of opportunities to make our opponents follow on since I became Test captain and have only done so once, when rain at Wellington in New Zealand made that decision mandatory, and I have memories of occasions before I became captain — against India in 2001, England in 2002-03 and in the West Indies in 2003 — when Steve Waugh did ask the opposition to bat again and we lost the Test after the one in which we enforced the follow-on. In each case, that Test we lost began almost immediately after the match in which we had to field through two consecutive innings. The second Test of this Ashes series, at the Adelaide Oval will start on December 1, just four days after the scheduled fifth day of this match.

Of course, the weather is an issue, but we had all the relevant forecasts and the odds were very much in our favour. As always, I had a chat with some of the senior blokes — in this case John Buchanan, Adam Gilchrist and Shane Warne — about what was the right thing to do. I certainly wanted to bat again, and the consensus supported me. Despite the manner in which the England first innings had disintegrated, the third-day wicket was still really good to bat on, but I felt it was going to crack up, making batting last potentially awkward. The idea of Warney bowling in the fourth innings appealed to me, especially with England having no hope of winning, when their only option would be to try to bat out a stack of time. The pitch had been taking turn from the first afternoon, when Pietersen got a few of his off-breaks to bite, and I don't know of too many batsmen around the planet who like the idea of facing the greatest spinner the world has ever seen on a wearing wicket.

The chief advantage of batting again, though, was that it would give our four frontline bowlers a rest. They were ready to go again, no doubt about it, and I would have been disappointed if they weren't, but I'm sure the rest was a good thing for them. McGrath, don't forget, had bowled 23 overs in what was for him a 'comeback' Test, and as things turned out he did have some problems with that left heel when the Poms finally batted again.

It didn't matter when we won, and not enforcing the follow-on didn't reduce our chances of victory one iota. I'd like to think it didn't hurt us here, might have helped us, and it definitely boosted our chances for Adelaide.

AS THINGS TURNED OUT, England batted very well in the fourth innings. I missed a fair bit of it, being off the field after I felt pain in my back when we batted again (an innings in which Justin Langer made up for missing out on a ton on the first day by scoring 100 not out). It was an old injury — caused this time quite innocently, as I backed up for a quick single, Lang sent me back and I had to pivot quickly — where tiny bone spurs on the joints in the middle of my spine cause my back to 'lock up' and I have to rely on massage and time to get it right again. It's stopped me maybe half a dozen times before, most notably in Sri Lanka in 2004, my second Test as captain, when Gilly had to move up to No. 3 and scored 144. Missing out on runs always hurts.

This time, Kevin Pietersen batted beautifully, and had a running battle with Shane Warne that generated most of the headlines, featuring as it did some fruity language and one moment when Shane threw the ball back to Gilly and it went a little closer to the batsman than might have been necessary. The big crowd loved the confrontation, I don't think there was any harm in it, and Pietersen was so theatrical in his response I'm guessing that deep down he really enjoyed it as well. Paul Collingwood also played really well, but Warney outsmarted him in the end, getting him stumped for 96 when Collingwood couldn't resist trying to go to his hundred with a big hit over mid-on. Shane realised the batsman wanted to come down the pitch and hit a boundary, so he dished up a delivery that was considerably slower and wider than most balls he bowled during the match. The dismissal wasn't an accident, it was classy bowling.

After the game, though, some English observers tried to argue that Shane hadn't bowled well and might be past his best, even though he had taken four top-order wickets on a good batting wicket and in different ways had seemed to rattle their two leading run-scorers. As Glenn McGrath had found in the lead-up to the Test, standards are always set higher for the really great players, especially if their age is on the other side of 35.

England were 5–293 at stumps on day four, still needing 357 to win. Pietersen was 92 not out, but the new ball was due and we knew that if we could get into the English tail we were a good bet to knock them all over pretty quickly. Straightaway, with Brett bowling, we put a short mid-wicket in, a fielding position that had been vacant for most of the previous day even though we'd spoken about putting someone there for the tourists' most dangerous batsman, because he does walk across his stumps and sometimes hit in the air through that region. Marto was duly positioned, and fourth ball of the day Pietersen chipped a catch straight to him. One metre either side of him and it's four; instead it looked like a clever piece of captaincy.

It took us another 20 overs and 77 runs to get the final four wickets, and then it was time for the post mortems. Inevitably, it wasn't long before people were reminding us that we'd also won the opening Test in 2005, as if we weren't aware of that fact. No doubt, England would be better for the run, and someone made reference to the 1954–55 Ashes series, when Len Hutton's England side was thrashed by an innings in the first Test, at Brisbane, but came back to win the series 3–1. Few people were suggesting that this series had anything other than a long, long way to run.

Still, a win by 277 runs is a huge one, and one I would have taken for sure at the start of the match. I know some people thought we'd allowed England back into the game by sending them straight back in, but they were wrong. Sure, England did regain some respectability in their second innings but whether that had anything to do with the fact we batted again is very debatable. A lot of teams that are dismissed cheaply in their first knock do better the second time around — playing for lost pride is part of that, as is the fact that they are more used to the conditions the second time around. In this instance, Pietersen and Collingwood both played beautifully, and Alastair Cook at the top of the order also went pretty well.

BECAUSE OF THE SHORT turnaround between Test matches, we were conscious not to go too hard with the celebrations. The fact we were only one game up in a five-Test series played a part in this attitude as well. Because the game was over around midday, there was plenty of time to savour the win and to sit back and think about what we might have been thinking going into the second Test in 2005. As I said at the post-match media conference: 'This time, we need to make sure we're better the second time around.' We had a terrific time in the rooms that for some of us went well into the evening, and today we were a tired but happy lot as we were bundled onto an afternoon flight to Adelaide.

One of the journos at that media conference yesterday had asked me about Steve Harmison's bowling, and how he'd improved as the game went on. This was true, as he seemed to find some pace and rhythm in our second innings, even though the pitch offered him less than it had on the opening day. 'Well, he had to get better,' I replied with a grin, which led to reports that my facetiousness was some sort of psychological mind game, a case of the winning captain cruelly putting the boot into the bloke while he's down. Harmison is a bowler who I reckon you can distract on the field — say something about his bowing action or where his front foot is landing and you might get him thinking too much — and from what I understand he isn't a big fan of touring life so he might not be a happy camper out here in Australia, but my crack wasn't an attempt to get into his head. When another writer had asked me if I was worried about rain washing out the day, I replied, 'It can rain as much as it likes for the rest of the day now.' These were just ordinary jokes made by a bloke who was relaxed and feeling pretty good about life, one-nil up in a five Test series and captain of a team that is going all right.

CHAPTER 6

SECOND TEST

Wednesday, December 6

Second Ashes Test, at Adelaide (December 1–5): England 6–551 dec
(PD Collingwood 206, KP Pietersen 158, IR Bell 60) and 129 (SK Warne 4–49)
lost to Australia 513 (RT Ponting 142, MJ Clarke 124, MEK Hussey 91,
AC Gilchrist 64; MJ Hoggard 7–109) and 4–168 (MEK Hussey 61*) by six wickets

BEFORE THE SERIES STARTED, we talked about the idea of playing two leggies in Sydney (definite chance), Adelaide (possibly) and Perth (not likely, but if the pitch is like the one they gave us for the Test against South Africa last season, then maybe). The continued injury problems besetting our No. 1 all-rounder, Shane Watson, makes the move much less appealing, and with the excellent form shown by Stuart Clark and Michael Clarke in Brisbane, Stuart MacGill not setting the world on fire in the Pura Cup, and the fact that the Adelaide Oval wicket has changed significantly in recent years, the selectors deemed it unnecessary for the second Test.

The Adelaide pitch used to crack up during the course of a game and turn considerably on the final day. In recent seasons, though, it stayed together and, if anything, became an even better batting wicket as the match proceeded. My feeling going into this Test was that, in such conditions, we might need a fifth bowling option of some sort before the game was through, and my thinking stayed that way for most of the game, even though Glenn McGrath's crook heel hardly bothered him. As it turned out, the pitch did turn on the last day, especially in the minds of our opponents.

The Test developed into one of the truly great ones, and I will have plenty of brilliant memories that will stay with me for a long time. But one of the least likely of these recollections, given the manner in which the Test played out, is the one that nagged me for much of the second day. England were cruising towards 450 in their first innings, and just three wickets down. According to most people, an Australian victory was already out of the question. Paul Collingwood was nearing his double century, Kevin Pietersen was past his hundred, Shane Warne and Glenn McGrath both had bowling figures of none-for-plenty. And I just kept thinking: *an extra bowler would be bloody handy*. At this time, the same reversal of fortune that occurred in 2005, when England came back from a heavy loss in the first Test at Lord's to square the ledger at Edgbaston, was obviously on the agenda.

BY STUMPS ON DAY two we were 1–28 chasing 6–551 declared. Before play began the next morning, I gathered the team together and told them I genuinely thought we could still win, not least because I remembered clearly what happened against India here in 2003–04, when we made 556 on the first day and a half and lost. The only difference I could see was that we had scored our runs quicker in that Test than England had in this one (India were 4–180 in their first innings at stumps on day two in 2003–04). This meant that for us to win here we had to score our runs reasonably quickly when we batted, and then — as things turned out — we had to make things happen on day five.

My point really was that everyone was saying we *couldn't* win, and I knew that wasn't true. It wasn't that I thought we were going to win, but that we could, and then I emphasised how beautiful it would be to prove everyone wrong. It always is. I will never forget talking to the guys and the feeling that *all* their eyes were locked on me; I think everyone was with me in the belief that if we played our best cricket from that moment to the final ball of the Test match we could come back and win.

BEFORE THE MATCH, AMID the Ashes buzz that we knew from Brisbane but which was now invigorating Adelaide, and the pre-match ticket sales that promised we'd be playing in front of the biggest Adelaide Oval Test cricket crowd since bodyline, there had been stories about that Michael Vaughan, England's captain in 2005 who had been battling injury for much of the time since, was preparing to make a comeback before the series was through. I wasn't sure how such a move might impact on the rest of the England squad, especially on Paul Collingwood, the bloke most likely to make way if Vaughan returned. At the same time, Rod Marsh — a man whose opinion I respect — had commented that he didn't think Collingwood had the technique to be a Test No. 4.

Of course, the much maligned batsman promptly came out and made a double hundred. I think we all underrated him, failed to appreciate what a tough and smart competitor he is, but after this innings, when we assessed how he'd batted both here and back at the Gabba, we concluded that we'd probably made a mistake in the way we bowled to him. Collingwood is a batsman who leans a little to the off-side when he tries to hit straight or forward of the wicket on the leg-side, and most guys who play that way can be susceptible to an lbw or a catch to the area around mid-wicket. So we attacked his stumps, but we've learned over the course of his two long innings that once he gets his eye in, that weakness becomes a strength. From England's second innings of this Test on, we resolved not to bowl anywhere near his stumps at all.

One bloke who'd been talking in the press before the game was England coach Duncan Fletcher, who was quoted as suggesting that Shane Warne was past his best and that Kevin Pietersen might have his measure. After Pietersen made his big hundred in the first innings here, playing Shane extremely well, many observers reckoned Fletcher might have been right on both counts, but I wasn't concerned. Bowling leg-breaks on a first-day Adelaide pitch against a couple of very good players is always a tough assignment, even for Warney, but we knew the wicket would start spinning a little bit more later in the game and that he would bounce back.

It wasn't too long ago that spinners weren't expected to extract big turn and take wickets in the first innings, but Shane changed all that. Everyone in our squad believed he was bowling well, despite what was being said and written elsewhere, and Shane himself — a bloke who's always honest about how he's performing — also thought he was going all right. Even the greatest have days when they take one-for-plenty. In this instance, because we didn't have that fifth bowler, I had to ask him to bowl more overs and more defensively than he or I would have liked. Even Pup bowled a lot (his previous longest spell in Test cricket had been 6.2 overs; this time he sent down 17), as we were reduced to waiting for Andrew Flintoff to declare.

On the second day, Shane was roundly criticised for consistently pitching outside the leg stump to Pietersen, but I thought some of this commentary was over-the-top, made by pundits who've been spoilt by all the attacking cricket we've played in recent years. Much of the criticism was directed at Shane, but it should all have been aimed at me, because it was my idea to bowl to Pietersen in this way. I wanted to slow down his rate of scoring and try to frustrate him a bit, not least because he can be so destructive if he's allowed to keep playing the way he wants. Within two overs of Shane changing his line, Pietersen was throwing his head around, kicking up a stink about our negativity, but when the score was three for 350, the pitch was dead and the batsman set, what did he expect us to do, keep serving up runs on a plate? *Deal with it, Kevin*, I thought to myself as he carried on. *Do something about it*. We mightn't have got him out, and the scoreboard kept ticking until they closed at 6–551, but if we got his brain out of whack for a period, then the tactic worked.

It was funny, the two things I was bagged for in the first two Tests were not enforcing the follow on in Brisbane and then slowing the game down in Adelaide. If I hadn't done the former, we might not have been in a position to force a victory here, because the act of bowling for so long at the Gabba might have flattened the bowlers and thus prevented their fifth-day heroics. And if we'd let Pietersen continue on his merry way when he and Collingwood were going so well, Flintoff might have been able to make his declaration when the Poms took their total beyond 600. If he'd done that, there'd have been no thrilling final afternoon. The other irony about the criticism of Shane's conservative style was that plenty of it came from the English media, who happily forgot that Ashley Giles has made a living out of this style of bowling.

I was delighted when Pietersen was just padding away and making a bit of a show, even though I knew that our best bowler didn't like it much. Warney wants to be attacking and aggressive all the time, wants to keep testing his wicket-taking skills against any player in any situation. But he didn't have much in his favour. He couldn't generate any worthwhile turn and he was bowling to an excellent player of spin, one of the better batsmen in the world. Normally, Shane will only pitch it outside leg stump when he has footmarks to aim at and he thinks he can bowl the batsmen around their legs. However, this time I judged that the situation of the game warranted the defensive tactic, so that's what we did.

I understand how powerful momentum is in sport, and liken what we did to what they call 'tempo football' in the AFL, a strategy designed to give a team that has been battling the chance to claw back into the contest. The Sydney Swans have been the masters of it, and it's one of the reasons they've been in the past two AFL Grand Finals. When teams get away from them, the Swans shut the game down by getting control of the ball or stifling the game at the breakdown until the pulse of the game stops throbbing; only then do they start playing their own aggressive footy again. The way scoring rates are in 21st-century cricket, it can only take half an hour of blazing by someone such as Pietersen and a Test match is gone. A captain has to be aware of that.

What do you do if you're batting five and in at 3–20? You don't try to smack it all over the place ... first thing you do is settle in, try to arrest the momentum the bowling team has. Only when you've done that can you think about a counter-attack. Was what we did negative, or smart? I think some of the stories written after the second day's play were looking pretty silly when we won the game in exciting circumstances three days later.

PIETERSEN'S INNINGS ENDED WHEN he was on 158, the same score he hit at The Oval in 2005, when I ran him out. I was fielding at mid-wicket at the time, working with Michael Clarke, who was patrolling the covers, the two of us trying to stop the single, when Pietersen jabbed one to my left and took off. I ran round, picked the ball as I was diving and hit the stumps with an underarm throw. I've always taken the attitude that every ball in a Test match is an opportunity for me to impose myself on the game, so I was feeling pretty satisfied in the huddle after this dismissal, given that it had only happened because I'd been able to maintain my concentration and enthusiasm. My view is that you have to keep up the intensity when you're in a contest, because you never know what might be the consequence of relaxing or giving up prematurely.

I find myself in the slips a lot these days, so I don't get to field in the circle as much I used to. I was always in the cover-point area when I was a younger player in the team, and loved it, and though I might be older now it's still good fun. This is especially true when a batsman such as Pietersen is at the crease, because he can be a somewhat feverish runner between the wickets, especially when he first comes in. When he comes out these days, I make sure there are athletic fieldsmen at mid-on and mid-off and bring them in a bit closer than normal, because he likes to just hit the ball and go to break his duck. Because he's also keen to play very straight at the start of his innings, he's liable to hit it too hard and find himself stranded halfway down the wicket. He's also a chance for a run out in similar style when he's 99, because he suddenly becomes a big fan of the short one. In fact, we could have got him this way, but he survived.

We followed up Pietersen's dismissal by getting Geraint Jones two runs later (Warney's one wicket of the innings, in the 155th over), but that was it until Flintoff declared after we'd been in the field for nearly 12 hours. It was England's highest total in a Test in Australia for 20 years. Lang then fended a catch to the gully in our second over, we went to stumps at 1–28, and by the first drinks break on day three we were 3–65. Then came 'the moment' that turned the Test. From when it happened to the end of the Test, I don't think we could have played much better cricket than what we did.

THE MOMENT OCCURRED WHEN Ashley Giles at deep square-leg dropped a fairly rudimentary above-your-head catch I'd offered him when I was 35 and the score was 3–78. The irony about Giles spilling that chance is that he's a really good fieldsman, whereas Monty Panesar, the bloke most people believed should be playing in his place, is not.

My thought, as the ball sailed towards him, was fairly straightforward, if somewhat incredulous: *how did I pick him out when there is so much empty space out there?* I'd hit the long hop from Matthew Hoggard right off the middle of the bat, and to see it go straight to him was a weird sensation, a type of mistake that I hadn't made in ages. Huss and I had just taken Harmison for 11 off one over, after the first 14 overs had gone for just 2–39, and maybe I got over-excited when I saw such a clear run-scoring opportunity and dropped my guard for a second. Fortunately, Giles put the catch down and immediately I reacted, *start again, make them pay.* That was my very first thought; that's what I always think when I get a 'lucky' break.

We'd already lost two wickets that morning: Matthew Hayden caught behind and Damien Martyn caught in the gully, and I'd had one awkward moment when Harmison bowled a knee-high full toss that I failed to pick up and forced me into a half angry, half 'stunned mullet' reaction as I tried to work out exactly what was going on. Marto actually looked pretty good while he was out in the middle, playing one nice hook off Harmison, but Hoggard bowled nice and tight to him and eventually got one to nip away a little a delivery after Marto had played one of his trademark caresses through the off-side field that almost reached the boundary.

You're not a 'lucky' batsman until you learn how to take advantage of your good fortune, and Huss and I managed to add 179 in 59 overs after Giles' made his blue. After the chance was missed and I resolved to take advantage, I took a moment to get my thoughts back in order, and then said to myself, 'Forget about it. Worry only about the ball in front of you.' In my view, what every batsman should be searching for, whatever the situation, is a means of preventing negative thoughts from entering his head; for me that's about keeping my thinking as uncluttered as possible. I'm big about having the same routine. I prepare for each innings in the same way. When I arrive in the middle to begin a knock, I take guard and then stride up the pitch, do some stretches and then walk back to take up my batting stance. By doing this every time, I'm not giving anything else a chance to infiltrate my concentration. As the bowler runs in, I'm reminding myself of the same simple mantra, *watch the ball, watch the ball* — I say this first when the bowler is midway in his run-up, and again when he reaches his delivery stride. Again, that routine keeps every other thought away. I do that for every ball. After I regained my composure following Giles' error, I knew that was what I had to get back to, pronto. Over the past two or three years, I've managed to do this just about every time I've been given a second chance.

WHEN I WAS DISMISSED, caught behind, I did the same thing I'd done in Brisbane, departing with my head down, hearing the ovation but not acknowledging it. This time, for good measure, I also kicked the ground after umpire Rudi Koertzen gave me out, walked off holding the blade of my bat, not the handle, and kicked a security guard's chair over when I stormed into the dressing room, all of which must have looked a bit petulant. Again, I was wrong to ignore the applause, but I was extremely disappointed to get out when the job was far from done.

We were getting ourselves back into the game and Hoggard, who was magnificent for England throughout this innings, was bowling the first over with the second new ball. This is a time in an innings that I've always rated as one of the best times to bat. I love being in when the second six-stitcher is called for, yet this time I got myself out with a fairly basic mistake. With the old ball, I'd been taking strike to Hoggard a fair way out of my crease, to take the lbw out of play, because he was reverse-swinging one away every now and then, and then would push one back into the stumps. That's how he dismissed me in Brisbane. I had decided that wasn't going to happen again, but when he took the new ball I should have moved my stance back nearer to the crease, as I had decided to do when I planned my innings the night before. I reckon if I had been back in my crease the split second of extra time would have allowed me to adjust, either to hit the ball in the middle of the bat or to let it go, rather than to nick it.

Adding to my annoyance, Huss and I had talked about the need to get through the second new ball and then to get to stumps, so I felt I'd let my mate down. It was an important time in the game. We were still 294 runs behind, and I'd missed an opportunity to ram home the fightback that Huss and I had began.

As it turned out, Huss also fell before stumps, but Michael Clarke played brilliantly that evening and well into the morrow. The state of the game rarely gets more important: 5–286 chasing 551. Pup was 17 when he was joined by Adam Gilchrist, who'd been struggling for runs. One more wicket and the Poms would definitely have been on top.

Pup didn't play an innings of this stature during the 2005 series, but he never looked like failing us now. He is a much better player, stronger mentally and more aware of what he needs to do. As I've said before, I saw a lot of me when I was a young player in Pup when he first came into the team — in the way he felt a lot of pressure to not just score runs but score runs quickly and with style. In his first stint on the Test XI, late 2004 and most of 2005, he was dismissed in the same manner a few times but still kept playing the same way, as if he wasn't learning, but the reality was that he didn't have faith in any method other than the one that had got him into Test cricket and had proved successful until opponents studied his way. Pup needed to work hard on his technique, and tighten up in a couple of areas, and the only way that could happen was if he was prepared to spend plenty of hours in the nets. Which is what he did during his time out of the team. Then he got lucky when Watto was ruled out of the first Test of this series because of injury, and it'll be hard for anyone to chisel him out of the team now. I think he knows how to prepare for a Test-match innings now, what he has to focus on and what isn't important; it's just a matter of him doing it over and over again for the rest of his career.

Gilly also played well, even if 64 from 79 deliveries is not overly quick for him. He was very disappointed when he got out, caught in the deep off Giles when he and Pup were in a position to push on and maybe even give us a first-innings lead, which psychologically would have been huge for us. Instead, we were still 167 behind and needed Warney to demonstrate once again what an excellent late-order batsman he can be. He and Pup added 118 and Shane only got 43 of them, as he thwarted the English bowlers for more than two and half hours. In the wash-up of our famous victory, among all the adulation for Warney's bowling on the final day and our clinical run-chase, the value of this partnership was largely forgotten.

WE'D STARTED THE FOURTH day 249 runs behind, but ended it in a position where we probably had more chance of winning than England. We were visualising getting a few early wickets to put the pressure on, whereas I imagine they would have been dreaming only about getting themselves in a position where they couldn't lose. Not till that was achieved would they consider an unlikely victory. Hope helps, fear doesn't, and when a couple of cards fell in our favour in the morning session, a momentum began that eventually became irresistible.

We'd been a little disappointed the previous evening when England got away from us before stumps. While wickets were what mattered, we knew we couldn't concede too many runs either, but Andrew Strauss and Ian Bell batted very well and they went into the fifth day with a lead of 97, and nine wickets in hand. I guess there might have been a temptation on our part to just think, *we've done really well, they won the toss, they batted, they got all those runs, let's take the draw and go to Perth one-up, one better than 2005.* But we sensed that they wouldn't risk losing the game, so for us the worst-case scenario was that they'd bat out most of the day and maybe make a token declaration late in the day. Best case was we'd put them under plenty of pressure and they might crack ...

If we can prevent the scoreboard from ticking over, I was thinking, *and the greatest leg-spinner who ever lived has one of his best days on a wearing wicket ...*

Those thoughts came to dominate our mindset, and we were bubbling in the dressing room before play. The fact that only 17 wickets had fallen in the previous four days on a pitch that had been roundly criticised as being too flat didn't slow us down at all. We'd convinced ourselves that what everyone else thought was impossible was actually a real chance. During our warm-up and then for half an hour in the rooms we talked about all the things we had to do if we were going to win. Warney was a real leader, adamant that this win was possible. He knew, we knew, that he was the man who'd win it for us, and he clearly felt he was up to that challenge. Once the boys heard it from him, they began thinking, *damn right, we can do this, let's get out there and give it a red-hot go.*

Any time there is a game on the line is Shane Warne's time. That's the perfect stage for him. For all that, such adrenalin can only fire for so long and we were fortunate early on when Strauss was given out when he probably wasn't. It was the last ball of the 11th over of the day, and though only 10 runs had been scored in that period a few more overs of wicketless stonewalling might have stifled our surge for victory before it even began. Instead, two overs later, Bell ran himself out and then Warney bowled an absolute pearler to Pietersen, one that pitched just outside leg and ripped across the batsman as he tried to swing away to leg. As the ball crashed into the top of off-stump our roars of delight must have been heard across the country. From that moment, an Aussie victory seemed as likely a result as anything.

I'll never forget that ball, that wicket. Warne to Pietersen. Through the day, I reckon Shane took leg-spin bowling to another level in terms of the way he was able to sustain pressure, turn the ball appreciably but not give any runs away, getting into the batsmen's heads. But the ball with which he knocked over their most dangerous batsman was the standout, one that will surely become an iconic moment in Ashes history.

We had to get Pietersen out quickly or we couldn't win. We'd spoken about the importance of this battle in the rooms before play, just as we'd talked about not letting them score and how we had to get some wickets in the first session. It was playing out like a dream. Once we had Pietersen, the pressure on the blokes who batted after him, from Flintoff down, was massive, and for us it was just so much fun to be out there, seeing them stressed, watching them react so negatively to what Shane was doing to them. Collingwood was taking his instructions to bat for time to the extreme, and though he survived for more than three hours I'm not sure if he helped them too much. They couldn't find a partnership, and though their tail held us up for a little while, it cost us time but not many runs, and I felt reasonably confident when we set off on the chase for 168 in 36 overs. In 54 overs since the start of play, England had lost nine wickets and scored just 70 runs, but that wasn't a true indication of the state of the pitch. We weren't over the line at the change of innings, but we were in front, which — given where we'd been early on day three — was a substantial victory in itself.

NEXT TO THE PIETERSEN wicket, the other thing that stands out for me as I write this is our celebration at the end of that game, the way we all charged out on the ground and mobbed Mike Hussey and Michael Clarke after Huss hit the winning run. The crowd, which had been relatively small at the start of the day's play but grew as word got around the city that something special was happening, was as vibrant and joyful as anything I've ever seen in Adelaide. It was the best Test-match win, at least in terms of coming back from nowhere, that I've ever been involved in, so I reckon we were entitled to carry on a bit.

The only victory that ranks near it is our win in the first Test against Bangladesh last April, but no one remembers that one, because it was 'only' (as others see it) Bangladesh and consequently the win wasn't really on the radar of a lot of Australian sports fans. But as good as that win was — fighting back from being 6–93 in reply to 427 to win by three wickets — this one was better, predominantly because we never lost the belief among ourselves that we could win, and also because we came up with a game plan to win from that difficult position at the end of day two and we followed that plan perfectly.

I'd become supremely confident we'd complete a successful run-chase as soon as the start of the ninth over. After Warney's exploits, it was no surprise that Ashley Giles was brought on early after Flintoff and Hoggard each bowled only three overs in our second dig. The score was 2–33. Huss scored a single off the third delivery, which got me back on strike. He was bowling left arm over the wicket into some big footmarks outside the line of my leg stump, and there was a slip, a backward point, a couple of blokes in front of square on the off-side, and the rest on the leg-side. With the spinning ball landing in those foot holes, it was hard for me, a right-hander, to attack without taking risks. Last ball of the over, Giles landed the ball where I least wanted it, and all I could do was fend it off and watch it spit off high on my bat and fly just wide of slip. It was a let-off, no doubt about it, and I felt pretty relieved as we hustled through for two. Flintoff bowled another over, and then as I prepared to face the first ball of Giles' second over I noticed that the slip had been dropped back to a short third man. I looked up at Huss right then and muttered, 'We've got 'em.'

I'd like to think that in the same situation I would have brought an extra slip in. With this new field, Giles changed his line, and I started getting runs through the off-side field. They weren't trying to get us out — to me, it felt a bit like the middle overs of a one-dayer when the bowling team seems happy to concede five or six an over. In this situation, Huss was perfect, deflecting ones and twos, charging between the wickets, full of energy, a complete contrast to our bewildered and beleaguered opponents.

I'd promoted Huss up the order purely because he bats left-handed. Again, I was worried about Giles and those footmarks and thought having a left-hander and a right-hander batting together would make it harder for him to consistently bowl the correct line. If I'd been the second wicket to fall, Marto would have batted four. I've promoted Huss a couple of times in one dayers against Daniel Vettori of New Zealand for the same reason, and also when we've lost a couple of early wickets because he's got plenty of experience as an opener and goes all right against a swinging ball. His adaptability is one his most valuable qualities. After I was dismissed for 49 and Marto fell for 7, Pup came out and looked strong and secure from his very first ball, and a famous victory was achieved with 19 balls to spare. As the Englishmen watched Huss hit Jimmy Anderson through the covers for the winning run, they must have been wondering — given how well they'd played for the first two days and an hour of this Test — if they'd ever beat us again. The mental scars inflicted by this stunning win could be deep.

THERE HAVE BEEN TIMES when it's been hours before we've sung the team song after a Test win, but we're making a conscious effort to do it sooner during this series. Traditionally, we'd sit around for a while, have a few beers, get the boys a bit charged and then sing the song. That's what I used to do when I was in control, but it reached the stage where it was almost the last thing we'd do before we packed up to go back to the team hotel. This could get silly if we won a Test around lunchtime, as we did in Brisbane, when we'd stay in the rooms until sunset, maybe even later, and the song became almost an afterthought. This time, quickly, Lang stood up and shouted, 'I have heard a bit of a rumour that Australia is two-up in the Ashes.' And then we were roaring. Most times, we'll sing *Under the Southern Cross* twice. This time, we belted it out three times, and each time, especially the third time, it was bloody fantastic.

I had to go and talk to the media, and by the time I returned most of the English team had entered our room for a post-match ale. They had come in after the first Test, too, but this time they stayed a lot longer. However, there were some exceptions. Kevin Pietersen was among a small group who had their shower and then walked across the ground, jumped on their bus and went home. Eventually, I found myself with Steve Harmison, and it was a bit weird — he seemed very keen to explain how much he hated touring, how he wished he could stay at home, how he had family out here with him to try to make the experience less aggravating, and how he'd had a blue out on the field with his South African-born team-mate.

At one point in our run-chase, so the story went, Harmison had been bowling indifferently and apparently Pietersen yelled something from the field along the lines of, 'Get him off!' Later, Pietersen, of all people, picked the ball up, had a random throw at the stumps — as he does every now and then — and it went for four overthrows. Harmison chipped him back. After that, the two apparently had a bit of a confrontation, but it couldn't have been much because we weren't aware of it on the field. Hearing stories like this confirmed what we had suspected: they aren't a happy team.

I had no problems at all with having a drink with our opponents midway through the series. Cricket has always been like that — tough, take-no-prisoners on the field, at fulltime have a beer together, and then, later, the battle is resumed. But this sort of thing is up to the individual, so I didn't feel any negativity towards the blokes who went straight back to their team hotel. Personally, I've never been a big one for going to opposition dressing rooms. If they come into our rooms I'm always happy to have beer, but the truth is I'm a bit of a shy bloke who has never been able to just plonk myself down next to someone I don't know that well and quickly start a conversation. I'm not being rude, snobbish, or precious; it's just the way I am. Simply because I've played a lot and I'm captain now, doesn't mean I can be someone I'm not. A bloke like Adam Gilchrist is really good at it, and I sometimes wish I had his openness. He'll come off the ground after a game, grab a couple of beers and head down to opponent's room. He'll say, 'C'mon Punter, we'll go down for a beer. It'll be good.' But it's not for me.

ON THIS OCCASION, IN our rooms where I always feel at home, we had a terrific time, a lot of fun, and it kept going back at the team hotel much later into the night than I'm used to. The next morning, I did an early phone interview with Alan Jones for his breakfast radio show back in Sydney, which I think went okay, and then I slept all the way on the flight home. Before Pup and I disembarked, the pilot came over the intercom and asked everyone to give us a round of applause, which showed me that the nature of our win had obviously touched a lot of people.

Damien Martyn had been one of the last to leave the party after our big win. In all that time, though, he never offered me even the slightest clue as to the negativity and doubt that must have been spinning like a Warney leg-break through his mind.

CHAPTER 7

MARTO

I LEARNED THAT DAMIEN Martyn had retired three days after the second Test. I was playing golf with Stuey Clark at The Australian in Sydney, and after nine holes decided to check my phone, which is when it all got a bit bizarre. I saw I had a 'missed call' from Michael Brown, Cricket Australia's General Manager, Cricket Operations, and immediately turned to Sarf and said, 'I reckon Marto's retired.'

I have no idea why I reacted to the message in that way, but sure enough that's what I was told when I returned Michael's call. Cricket Australia CEO James Sutherland had just received an email from Damien Martyn, in which Damien had retired from all forms of cricket. No formal farewell to the team, no press conference, no call to me, his mate, to explain why. I was more confused than gutted. The suggestions were that, having made his decision, Marto didn't want anyone to talk him out of it — which sort of made sense — and that with the team so close to regaining the Ashes he didn't want to be a distraction, didn't want any of the attention to be on him. One newspaper report suggested he'd quit because he'd been told that he was about to get dropped. But I knew the selectors were about to announce the team and that Marto was going to be in it. Another story claimed that, during the celebrations in the Adelaide Oval dressing room, Marto had quietly told an unnamed Cricket Australia employee that the best time to retire is when 'you're on top'. That could be true, but he never said it to me.

It's not for me to say whether Marto's decision to retire was right or wrong. I was disappointed because we had lost an excellent player, someone who'd bailed us out of difficult situations many times in the past. I was frustrated because I was left answering questions about something I knew nothing about, when one media appearance by him would have cleared the air. Any number of theories were circulating, and I knew some people just didn't believe me when I said I didn't have any idea what was going on.

I think Marto would have assumed I'd be feeling let down, because I had pushed hard for him to be brought back into the team after he was dropped following the 2005 Ashes series. But I honestly didn't feel let down, because I know what a big decision giving it all away is for a long-time player. Playing for Australia gets in your blood — not just the actual cricket, but also the multitude of experiences you share together, from the grind to the glory. We become absolute best mates, living with each other's shadows and seeing so much of each other and our families. We play golf in our spare time together, sing songs together, laugh and cringe together, argue with each other, forgive each other. We know the stress involved with always trying to be excellent, supremely fit, and clever enough to avoid the pitfalls from being a celebrity and dealing with the media.

It's probably only when one of us walks away that we stop to think about the unique nature of our lives. Over the past few years we have been amazingly successful, with just a few down times that have never lasted too long. This has been true, too, on an individual basis. Adam Gilchrist apart, we've all had periods of mediocre form and even Gilly has struggled a little with the bat in the past 18 months. Warney has never lost form, but he has had other worries, such as the suspension after he failed that drug test in 2003. I've been lucky, touch wood, I haven't felt that sort of pressure that comes from lack of form for a while — except, maybe, briefly, straight after the 2005 Ashes when a lot of people jumped all over my captaincy style. But I still remember the lean spells I had early in my career, so I know how debilitating stress and negativity can be and how it can take a lot of the joy out of the game, especially, I'd imagine, if you're getting close to retirement. If you can find ways to deal with it and get over it, the experience is character building; if you can't, it's as if the whole world is against you.

I'D FIRST COME INTO contact with Damien Martyn in December 1992, in my first season of first-class cricket with Tasmania, when we travelled to Perth for a Sheffield Shield match against Western Australia. It was my third Shield game, and the second day of the contest was my 18th birthday. Damien, who was already a Test cricketer by then, having made his debut three weeks earlier against the West Indies at the Gabba, scored a sensational 139 on the opening day, while I managed to scrap together 25 two days later, after Dene Hills, now the Australian team's assistant coach, had hit 138 in our reply. The match was drawn.

The first time I played with Damien, as best as I can remember, was for the 'ACB Chairman's XI' against the touring Englishmen at Lilac Hill in WA at the start of the Poms' 1994–95 Australian tour. Looking back over the scorecard of that game, I was one of only two blokes in our team who hadn't played Test cricket at the time; the other being Brad Hogg. The full team was Geoff Marsh, Tom Moody, me, Marto (captain), Greg Chappell, Hoggy, Tim Zoehrer (who bowled leg-breaks), Brendon Julian,

Rod Marsh, Dennis Lillee and Jeff Thomson — not a bad crew for a 19-year-old from Mowbray, Tasmania, to be part of! As that season went on, I played some more under Marto's captaincy, for an Australian XI against the Poms in Hobart, when we enjoyed our first significant partnership (133 for the fourth wicket), and for Australia A in the World Series Cup. The first time we were members of the same Australian team for a one-day international was in India in 1998, but we weren't part of the same Test XI until December 2000, when Marto replaced the injured Steve Waugh for the third Test against the West Indies in Adelaide (Marto had actually replaced me in the Test team for the tour to New Zealand earlier that year, after I damaged my ankle in the one-day finals, but the Windies match was our first together). From 2001 to 2006, we were Test and one-day team-mates, and grew so close that I was best man at his wedding to Annika in May '06.

From that first time I saw him bat I knew Marto was an unbelievably gifted cricketer. Back then, he was naturally flamboyant, the sort of player who could and would hit the first ball of the day over cover. He never lost that touch of genius, that extraordinary ability to time the ball better than the rest of us, which meant he could just lean into a shot and it would zip away to the boundary. As late as the 2006 Champions Trophy in India, in the game against England when he scored 78 and played a huge part in us winning the game, he was literally 'dead batting' forward defensive shots that raced through the covers for four, and in the dressing room, we were looking at each other and asking, 'How can he do that?'

To lock up a place in the Australian side he had to transform his whole life. He had become a Test batsman not long after his 21st birthday, but after the infamous loss to South Africa at the SCG in 1993–94, when he scored 6 from 59 balls in Australia's second innings (having hit 59 in the first) as the team crashed to a shock five-run loss, he was cast aside and wasn't picked again for six years. There were times during those 'lost years' when he might have been dropped from the WA team. But he was brave enough to re-assess his approach to his sport, went on a strict diet, disciplined himself, and when he earned his second chance he grabbed it. Indeed, he was so brilliant in England in 2001 — when he came into the side to bat six, with me moving up to No. 3 — that he made a few of us look at our own attitudes and the way we prepared. I think, through his actions, he had an impact on the whole team; I know I noticed, and I became a better, more confident cricketer as a result.

I know to some he appeared to be a fairly laid-back character, but that wasn't true about his cricket, certainly not from the day he returned to the Aussie squad. He was always trying to find ways of challenging himself, making small modifications to his technique, working even harder, that might give him an edge, even though he never dramatically changed the way he batted. It was important his rare talent was allowed to express itself. He was a bit like Sachin Tendulkar in that he never really moved his feet much, but he also kept his head still, which allowed his fantastic hand-eye co-ordination to take over. He was able to wait for the ball to come on to his bat, never reach out to it, just let his hands almost fall on the ball, always hit it when it was right under his eyes. I remember the way he played in Sydney against South Africa in 2001–02, when — with eight wickets down and still needing 12 for his hundred — he reverse swept his way to three figures, as if that was the perfectly natural way to do it. He liked to bag me about how far forward I'd go, as if that was extravagant and unnecessary, but the differences in our methods was why he didn't hit the ball down the ground like I do, or like Matty Hayden does; he was always more prolific square of the wicket, between point and cover and forward of square leg. Marto also got plenty of runs down to third man, and in one-day cricket he could deflect the ball into gaps as well as anyone.

My favourite on-field experience with Marto occurred on the biggest stage: the World Cup final of 2003 in Johannesburg. He was carrying a broken finger, and on the morning of the game I asked him, 'Mate, I need you to tell me if you are okay to play or not okay to play.' He looked straight at me and said confidently, 'I'm right to go.' We ended up adding an unbeaten 234 for the third wicket, and he scored 88 not out, as we enjoyed one of the best partnerships of our lives. Off the field, the memories of Marto I treasure most are simple things — when we'd sit down and have a coffee and talk 'rubbish'. Occasionally, we'd chat about cricket, but mostly it would be about things far removed from our sport. I got to know him better than most people, certainly better than the fans, because he rarely opened up to the media, and was never able to come to terms with the public scrutiny that comes with being a 'celebrity'.

Marto always tried to shy away from this attention, and hated it when anything he was involved in got blown up into a major issue. The incident at the 2006 Champions Trophy presentation is a good example; media speculation about his place in the side would always get to him, more than most people realised. He was wary of reporters and dismissive of 'hangers-on'. Consequently, the Damien Martyn the public think they know and the Marto we in the Aussie team do know are two different people. He's actually one of the funniest blokes around. The dressing room won't be the same without him.

When it came to Test cricket, I reckon his greatest knock was the hundred that won us the third Test against South Africa at Johannesburg last summer. That was the game in which Justin

Langer was clobbered first ball by Makhaya Ntini and didn't bat in either innings, and we had to score 292 in the fourth innings on a pitch that had not given up a hundred to any player until Marto produced his masterpiece. It was typical of the bloke, in that he always seemed to bat at his best when things were tough. Nine of his 13 Test hundreds were achieved away from home. His record in India is outstanding, while his effort in my first series as captain, in Sri Lanka when he scored two centuries, was magnificent. His performances in the recent Champions Trophy, most notably his back-to-back 70s against England and India, were similarly inspired. I reckon he enjoyed playing in these 'exotic' locations, when he felt he didn't have the eyes of all of Australia looking at him. Once while we were in a café in India I offered the opinion that it didn't get much harder than playing Test matches on the subcontinent, and he replied flatly, 'It's better than playing in Australia. I'll play here any day of the week.'

I guess this insecurity was his biggest weakness, because he never managed to totally overcome it. Most likely, it hastened his retirement. With Michael Clarke scoring runs in the first two Tests and Shane Watson due to come back from injury, suddenly Marto was on the edge again and perhaps he just didn't have the desire and energy to keep fighting. I just think it's a great shame he left the way he did, because the cricket community will probably never get the chance to celebrate his career, to say thanks for all he's done. More than anything, whenever I'm on tour now, I'll miss his friendship, his winning attitude and the fun that he brought to the team. We all loved playing with him. And I'll miss those coffees, when we rarely talked about anything too important but always made a lot of sense.

CHAPTER 8

THIRD TEST

Tuesday, December 19

Tour match, at Lilac Hill, Perth (December 8): England XI 8–259
(50 overs: AJ Stewart 69, RS Bopara 53; CD Matthews 3–38) lost to Cricket
Australia Chairman's XI 3–260 (40.1 overs: L Ronchi 89, AC Voges 71,
MJ North 58) by seven wickets

Tour match, at Perth (December 9–10): Western Australia 8–322 dec
(L Pomersbach 101*, CJL Rogers 66, SE Marsh 59) drew with England XI 5–356
(AN Cook 106, AJ Strauss 88, EC Joyce 73, CMW Read 59*)

Third Ashes Test, at Perth (December 14–18): Australia 244 (MEK Hussey
74*; SJ Harmison 4–48, MS Panesar 5–92) and 5–527 dec (MJ Clarke 135*,
MEK Hussey 103, AC Gilchrist 102*, ML Hayden 92, RT Ponting 75) defeated
England 215 (KP Pietersen 70) and 350 (AN Cook 116, IR Bell 87, KP Pietersen
60*, A Flintoff 51; SK Warne 4–115) by 206 runs

WITH MARTO OUT, THE selectors needed to make a change, and
they responded by recalling Andrew Symonds and coming up
with the name of West Australian batsman Adam Voges, after
Shane Watson and Brad Hodge were ruled out due to injury.

I knew very little about Adam, though what I had heard from the WA guys was all good. Justin Langer, Adam Gilchrist and Mike Hussey were all very keen on his ability, and also spoke highly about what a good fella and excellent team man he is. He's averaging 160 in the Pura Cup this season, having already scored two unbeaten centuries, and a couple of years back he smashed a century from 62 balls in an ING Cup game at North Sydney Oval. Lang told me I'd love having him around. But I had never played a match against him. I haven't played a four-day or one-day game against WA since December 2002, haven't scored a run against them since I made 94 in an ING Cup in November 2001.

I had come into contact with Adam at the Centre of Excellence. I can remember him from a couple of pre-season camps, doing a bit of slow left-arm bowling in the nets, so I may have spoken with him, but it wasn't until after the third Test squad was announced that I had my first real conversation with him. I rang him a few times in the lead-up, and then made a point of saying g'day as soon as I could after I landed in Perth. The media made a point of revealing he was a greyhound enthusiast, so it was natural I'd ask him about the dogs. It is true that he likes a wager and, like all the WA boys, he's a poker fiend, being right into 'Texas Hold 'Em'; more importantly, I quickly came to the conclusion that he's a keen and sensible young bloke who I sense we're going to see more of in the next few years. He was closer to making his debut here in Perth than most people realise.

IN THE END IT was the wicket that tipped it in Symonds' favour. The WACA had been ridiculously in the batsmen's favour in the first-class games played in Perth before the Test (WA had scored 3–608 declared in their match against Victoria), and the local boys thought the Test strip might be similarly gentle. Under these circumstances, we felt we'd needed the fifth bowler for sure, which tipped the scales Symmo's way. *Maybe that was why Marto pulled the pin*, I thought for a minute as I listened to reports about the square, because he knew his home pitch so well and he thought he knew how the selectors and I would be thinking.

The Queensland and WA boys had all told me that Symmo had been the pick of the bowlers in their Pura Cup game at the WACA last month. On the first day, he'd bowled upwind, medium pace, and nipped the ball about and finished with 3–18 from 10 overs. In the second innings, he bowled seamers and off-breaks, and took a couple more wickets as Queensland won by an innings. In my mind, Symmo's bowling could be useful in two ways during the Test — as a genuine attacking option if this wicket was doing something and, more defensively, by bowling up into the breeze if the pitch flattened out and I needed to give our frontline men a decent break.

My first reaction when I saw the Test pitch for myself was to think how weird it looked. It was quite motley, with patches of brown and green grass. It looked like it might turn. Back in the '90s, the WACA pitch was sometimes close to white, and incredibly quick and bouncy, but it's nothing like that any more. In the lead-up to this Test, the curator found himself under heaps of pressure. He would have known another flat deck like the ones he produced earlier in the season would have been unacceptable, and no one wanted another pitch like the one we had for the Test against South Africa last season, when only three wickets fell on the final day, yet he also couldn't go too far the other way, because the authorities desperately wanted the game to last the full five days. As it turned out, he put plenty of water in the pitch, so it did quite a bit on the first morning, but after that it dried out and played pretty well.

The curator wasn't the only person under the microscope in the days before the Test. It seemed to me that the papers were trying to build up conflict between Andrew Flintoff and Duncan Fletcher, because — as the reporters saw it — both were apparently trying to avoid blame for various selections. It looked like a bit of a beat-up to me, but I still wondered if it might eat away at what was left of morale in their squad. My understanding was that Fletcher had actually said words to the effect that he didn't have total responsibility for the selection of the side, in response to the criticism of Ashley Giles and Geraint Jones playing in the first two Tests. Fletcher made the point that there were other selectors on tour. The media twisted that to the coach saying, *it's the captain's fault*, which was not quite what he said.

For this match, Jones retained his place, but Monty Panesar came in for Giles. During the Test we would learn that Ashley was returning home to care for his wife, who had fallen ill. Again, like the sad situation with Marcus Trescothick earlier in the tour, this put everything in perspective. Cricket matters, it matters a lot, but there are more important things in life and we should never forget that.

My fear leading into the Test was that all the talk about us regaining the Ashes at the earliest opportunity might distract us from the task at hand. I didn't want us to get ahead of ourselves, so I decided to ban any talk of an Ashes win from our team talk. It was a bit of a gimmick, because it was impossible to forget that we were just one win away from claiming the series, but I knew we had to stick solid with the 'striving for excellence' formula that had been so productive for us. We had to have exactly the same attitude and ambition going into this Test, into every Test, as we had before the first day in Brisbane, when the series was level at nil-all, and nothing was being taken for granted.

The English media, meanwhile, were advising their team to try to get 'under my skin' out on the field. They based this theory on examples such as the incident at Trent Bridge in 2005, when I was upset after being run out by a substitute fielder, and the incidents in Bangladesh and Malaysia, when I was reported for talking inappropriately with the umpires. In each case, I'd put my hand up and said I made a mistake, but at the same time I didn't see how these episodes, or any other, demonstrated that an angry streak was impacting on my cricket. It wasn't as if my judgment has ever been blurred, that I made poor decisions or got myself out because I was in a rage. If I have lost my composure for a second, I've always rediscovered it before the next delivery has been bowled.

I PRIDE MYSELF ON being able to stay 'in the moment'. It's something I remind myself about all the time. A method I have adopted in recent years is to write notes, every night before a day's play, in which I list the things I have to do the next day to play well. One item that is always included on my checklist is to make sure I don't get locked in a one-on-one battle with the bowler, where things get 'personal'. If I become involved in such a confrontation and try to dominate the bowler as a result, I'll get out.

My list usually starts with the same key points. Then I'll go through the opposition bowlers and write a few pointers about how I believe they will try to get me out — what they do with the ball, what line they might bowl, how they might try to exploit the local conditions. I'll keep working on my list, studying it, pondering it, improving it until it covers every base.

Always, number one on my list is 'watch the ball'. Number two is 'play straight early on'. Three, I always emphasise my calling. I'm really conscious of calling loudly when I first go out to bat; I find it gets me going. Being 100 per cent positive with everything I do, whether it's leading the team or playing a shot, is on my list. Batting for long periods of time is another thing to write down, then in brackets I add, 'Make a hundred.' I visualise these things over and over in my head — I might picture Matthew Hoggard or Steve Harmison coming into bowl and me playing the right shot or letting the ball go or watching the ball — and then I underline each one as I feel it has been successfully programmed into my motor. Only when the final item is locked away can I get to sleep. That last thing I write down is this: 'I want to be man of the match in every game I play.' I write this not because I'm a glory hunter, or because trophies mean more to me than anything else, but on the basis that if I manage to achieve all the other things on my list, then I've got to be a chance to win the award.

The things I include in my checklist always relate to the next day's cricket. They never go beyond that. I'm not one to write long-term goals. I'd rather concentrate on breaking the next day down, to keep it simple. It's a process that works for me, gives me confidence, and underlines for me the profits that come not through just preparing, but through preparing thoroughly.

I can't actually recall exactly when I started doing this. It just evolved, from scratching out a few notes to doing the job properly, and I am not saying it would work for anyone else. Matty Hayden likes to sit on the wicket the day before a game for up to an hour, and visualise how he is going to play and the way the bowlers will bowl to him. That's how he prepares. When you think about it, my way isn't much different.

THE THIRD TEST WAS due to start on December 14. On the night of December 12, the WACA staged an 'Ashes Legends' Twenty20 match at the Test venue, using a pitch just two across from the Test wicket.

Well before that game got underway, as is our custom before every Test, we moved all our gear into our dressing room. It's our home for the week, something of a haven, and we like to reorganise it in the way we want. Each player will set up his locker, with his whites, gloves, pads, everything else, in places that suit him. This day, after we finished training at the WACA, we returned to the rooms and were stunned when we told that we had to pack up all our gear and move it out, because the legends were soon to move in. Every single one of us had the same thought: *what are you talking about? You can't stage a game on the Test-match ground two days before the Test starts. Can you?*

Yes, apparently, you can.

'We're not moving our gear,' I explained to team management. 'The old blokes will have to work around us.'

The Legends game began at twilight, and not long before the first ball was due to be bowled I heard the familiar beep of my mobile. It was a text message ... from Dean Jones, no less. 'I'm at the WACA mate,' it read, 'just want to know if I can borrow your gear?'

I figured he was joking, so I quickly replied: 'Yeah mate no worries there is a new bat in my bag that needs knocking in.'

Typical Deano, always confident, shot back with, 'It's about time someone uses one of your bats properly.'

Apparently the game was a big success, drawing 17,000 people. This Ashes hype is unbelievable. Next morning, we arrived in the dressing room, and it wasn't just my new bat that had been used, just about everyone's gear had been sampled. My new bat hardly had a mark on it, which suggested that if Deano did use it, he didn't use it very well. Matty Hayden had brought some new Nike footwear with him to Perth, which he was saving for the Test, but now he opened up his kit bag to find a note from

Terry Alderman saying, 'Thanks for letting me use your boots.' All we could hope was that the legends hadn't damaged the Test wicket, which we assumed had been covered while they were doing their thing.

A LOT OF PEOPLE were surprised when the Poms had their noses in front at stumps on the first day of the third Test. They were 2–51, pursuing 244. Many, I guess, expected them to fall apart after what happened on the final day in Adelaide, but maybe it was us who weren't as ready as we should have been. It's not that we were deliberately complacent, but maybe our preparation leading into this Test wasn't quite as sharp, because subconsciously we were thinking that nothing could beat Adelaide. In contrast, the Englishmen now had nothing to lose, and people can often achieve unlikely things when that is their mindset. If the team in front isn't quite 'on song', while their pursuers are fearless, things can go pear-shaped pretty quickly for the leaders.

Monty Panesar marked his Ashes debut by taking 5–92, while Steve Harmison, who'd taken 1–288 in the first two Tests, came back to take four wickets, including Ponting, lbw for 2. The big crowd revelled in another clever innings from local boy Mike Hussey, but they seemed stunned when our innings folded so quickly. But as the Test developed from this point, once England started thinking about winning, and we 'woke' from our temporary slumber, the two teams' fortunes reverted to how they'd been for much of the first two Tests. That we were able to do this so quickly was extremely satisfying.

The only blokes who batted for any significant length of time in the two first innings were Hussey and Kevin Pietersen, and while Pietersen batted very well, his approach with the tailenders was somewhat peculiar, as if he wasn't quite sure whether to bat as he normally would, try to defend and manipulate the strike, or just slog. After he was dismissed, Panesar and Harmison — who had both bowled nicely on the opening day, taking five and four wickets respectively — added 40 for the last wicket, which was comical (because they are both fair dinkum No. 11s), frustrating and a little comforting, because it suggested the pitch was flattening out. We were 1–119 at stumps on the second day, a lead of 148, and in control. Matty Hayden and I were both past fifty, and that night I went to sleep having visualised all the things I needed to do to go on and make a very big score.

I was thrilled by the way our bowlers responded to the task of getting us back into the game. We had talked about getting the length right, and each of our quicks did the job perfectly, and from the first ball of the day. This was important, because the pitch had something in it during the first session, when the ball was hard, but grew tamer the longer the day went on. Stuart Clark was superb, taking three wickets which gave him 14 scalps at the halfway point of the series, while McGrath bowled the perfect line to Collingwood, finally getting him caught in the gully after their top-scorer from Adelaide had laboured for 45 minutes.

One person who was having an interesting Test was Andrew Symonds, who'd smashed a rapid-fire 26 (including 17 runs, featuring two sixes, from one Panesar over) and then took 2–8 from four overs when I brought him on earlier than most people expected, just after drinks during the opening session on the second day. But I'd told him before the Test started that I thought he'd get Andrew Flintoff out, because I've always had a suspicion that at least a couple of the English bats, Flintoff among them, are susceptible to medium-pace bowling. This is due to a certain stiffness in their batting stances, and their initial movements when the ball is delivered. If a delivery hasn't got a lot of pace in it, they can be off-balance when it gets to them, and jab at the one that pitches just outside off stump and nips away a little. This flaw can reveal itself in the way these batsmen often struggle to time the ball when they're facing medium-pacers, or in Flintoff's case by the manner in which he tries to smash the ball or block it. I was so confident about Symmo's chances against the England captain that I told the boys before play started that I 'had a hunch' that he'd do the job, so no one in our camp was surprised when I brought him on when Flintoff was only seven, and the Poms were 4–94. Not only did he get the big wicket, caught by Warney at first slip, he then snared Geraint Jones as well.

People might say that the fact we got that wicket in part because I followed a hunch demonstrates what a clever captain I am. For me, all it proves is that a captain needs his players to do the job so they can make him look good. It's the same for the coach. You can be the shrewdest captain and the most perceptive coach in the game, but if the team you're in charge of isn't much good, then you're going to struggle. This, of course, sounds obvious, but it's amazing how few people seem to accept it as reality.

OUR AMBITION ON DAY three was to bat them right out of the game, and we sure managed that. The weather had been warm on day one, hot on day two and sweltering on day three, perfect conditions for a batting side to put the boot in. Sadly, though, I didn't contribute much at all. Matty and I were stunned when Pietersen bowled the first over of the day, but it suited us as we had resolved to push the accelerator from the jump, and we took 24 from his two overs, including 15 from a sequence of four balls. But one delivery after I hit Harmison through the covers for an all-run four, I went to push a good-length delivery into the off-side and nicked a catch behind. We'd scored 25 runs in 3.4

overs that morning, the beginnings of a surge that would build during the day, but I was still very dirty on myself that I not gone on with it. I didn't feel as if I'd got too excited, too aggressive, too soon, but maybe I did drop my guard just a fraction, and when I got a good ball in among the rubbish that had been served up previously, I pushed a little too hard. Fortunately, the rest of the boys batted beautifully — and, in Adam Gilchrist's case, unbelievably — and by stumps, barring rain, the Test and the Ashes were just about ours.

Having scored four fifties in his first four innings of this series, Mike Hussey finally reached his maiden Ashes hundred, on his home turf, which meant a lot to him, while Michael Clarke played as faultlessly here as he had in Adelaide, ending up 135 not out. However, these superb achievements were lost somewhat because of what Adam Gilchrist did. And what did Adam Gilchrist do? Just reeled off a hundred from 57 balls, a single delivery more than Viv Richards' record for the fastest century in Test history. The previous fastest hundred by an Australian in Test cricket, from 67 deliveries, was made by Jack Gregory at Johannesburg back in 1921. Here, Gilly took 22 deliveries to make his first 25 runs, 32 balls to get past 40, and 40 balls to reach 50. After that, he went berserk, though I found it a bit funny the way he talked afterwards — that he just teed off because the plan was to get some quick runs so we could have a bowl at them before stumps. As far as I knew, that had never been mentioned, mainly because we would have had to score at some ridiculous run rate to do so. Of course, Gilly promptly did score at a ridiculous rate and we were able to send down six overs (and take the wicket of Andrew Strauss) before the end of the day's play.

Later, he talked about how, back at the boot camp, we'd talked about communication skills, about how we could improve them. 'Obviously, we didn't pass,' he said with a laugh.

The dressing room, of course, was full of guys with plenty of experience, who've witnessed some amazing things during their cricket careers. But the talk in the viewing area was often along the lines of ... 'DID YOU SEE THAT?' ... as Gilly bludgeoned another colossal blow. A few times, I saw him swing and my instinct told me where the ball would land, but then I'd do a double take and realise that it was flying way further, like a long-iron approach to a green that looks good at first but then sails way over the flagstick. Fast and slow deliveries were the same to him. Twenty four, including three spectacular sixes, came from the last five balls of one Panesar over. An image that stays with me comes from the television coverage on the big screen, of Flintoff watching open-mouthed as one of those sixes sailed over his head and into the top deck of the grandstand. Panesar had bowled pretty well to that point, but Gilly just took him apart, showed him no respect. As it became apparent our master blaster was a chance to beat Richards' record, someone suggested we send a message out to him, but then we realised, what was the point? It was not like he could score any faster.

The funny thing was that Gilly could have been out before he scored a run, and he'd been out for a duck in the first innings, so he came perilously close to a pair. Imagine if that had happened; the scribes would have been writing gloomily about his batting slump, how he was just a shadow of the player who averaged 60 over his first 47 Tests. Flintoff brought in five guys in the catching cordon when he first came in, plus a cover and a mid-off, and was obviously going to bowl that nagging line just outside off stump that had often proved successful against the great keeper-batsman in the past. Second ball, Gilly prodded at one and it sliced at catchable height past gully and down to the fence for four. Two more dot balls and then he crashed a glorious back-foot drive through the covers for four. Within a few minutes he was in top form. A few minutes after that, he was 100 not out.

AT THE START OF day four, England were 1–19, needing another 538 to win. Not too long before stumps, when I brought back Glenn McGrath for one last spell for the day, they were 3–245, with Alastair Cook past his hundred and Pietersen going okay. As crazy as it sounded, an England victory was not totally out of the question, though it needed these two blokes to bat for a long while longer. Instead, in the third over of this spell, McGrath got the breakthrough, with a perfect-length delivery that Cook edged behind. Two balls later, the stumps of nightwatchman Matthew Hoggard were shattered; Flintoff had to come in before stumps and we were able to sleep a lot easier that night.

Cook, who became the fifth youngest Englishman to score an Ashes century, and Bell, who has now made a fifty in each of the first three Tests, were both very impressive, but in the end it was typical of McGrath to have the last word. So often during his career, he has found a way. Champions can get their teams out of awkward situations, and they love doing it, love the challenge. This might be the most important thing that separates them from the blokes who are just very good. The great ones want centre stage during the vital stages of a contest, because, deep down, they know that's where they belong. And their opponents know that, too.

Shane Warne had bowled for much of the day — 24 overs straight in one spell — which got me some criticism from those who thought I was over-bowling him. Maybe the critics had a point, but he wanted to keep going. Sometimes, as captain, I can recognise that Warney is not quite getting the amount of work on the ball that he does when he's at the absolute top of his game, but even then the quality of his bowling doesn't drop off much.

If you go down and ask him if he wants to have a break, he'll invariably reply, 'No, just one more over.' Often, he'll add that he has a plan that he's been working on, which is just about to come to fruition. On this occasion, he was having a running battle with Bell; not once, but maybe 6000 times here and in Adelaide, Warney called him 'The Sherminator', after the geeky character in the movie *American Pie*. Bell, who was now coping with the great spinner really well after struggling big time in 2005, just smiled, shrugged his shoulders and said he'd been called worse. The other thing about Warney bowling long spells is that he doesn't go for many runs, which is how it worked out this day, so the pressure never goes away. And, finally, he got his man, as Bell lifted a catch to Justin Langer at short cover.

WITH ENGLAND'S LONG TAIL, we realised at the start of the fifth day that we need to break just one more partnership and we were as good as home. Unlike in Brisbane, where we got Pietersen straight away and wrapped it up soon enough, this time we had to wait a while, largely because Flintoff played his first significant innings of the series. Pietersen was able to settle in, while his captain basically just teed off at the start and then hit the ball really sweetly, in a cameo that resembled some of his best moments from 2005. Finally, Warney slid one past him after about an hour and a half of play, and as the ball crashed into the stumps we knew the game — and the Ashes — were ours. Thus, it was no surprise that the celebrations at the fall of this wicket were pretty animated; only trouble was, I ran straight into Gilly's elbow, not the first time I've been tagged in this way. It's the price I have to pay for being a little bit shorter than everyone else.

Two balls later, I ran out Geraint Jones. A ball from Warney struck the batsman on the pads, everyone appealed for lbw, Jones stumbled down the wicket, and I picked the ball up and underarmed it into the stumps. Because everyone else — including Jones, who was on a pair and consequently very nervous — was concentrating on the umpire's decision (which was not out), I was later given a lot of credit for being the only person who was aware the run-out chance was on. But it's the nature of fielding close in on the off-side to a spinner, especially when Warney is bowling, that the run out is always on when the batsman plays forward and it is simply my job to look for any such opportunity. It was funny straight afterwards, as I got excited because I knew Jones was out, and a few of the blokes who'd been concentrating on the leg-before shout joined my celebration and asked, 'What happened?' all at the same time.

The final wicket — Panesar, bowled Warne, 1; his 699th Test wicket — fell second ball after lunch, and the events afterwards became something of a blur. We had some time out on the ground, completed lots of interviews for television and radio, and also went around the WACA, to thank the crowd for their support. In the confusion, I wasn't able to immediately shake Andrew Flintoff's hand, but I set that straight as soon as I could, seeking him out in their dressing room. Then it was a lot like the first two Tests, in that there were more media commitments to be kept, after which we spent a long time in our room. Again, most of the English guys came in, as did Mark Taylor and the Channel Nine cameras. The time for reflection came later, maybe not even until today, when I began thinking about not just the players' efforts but also the mighty contributions of the men who were brought into the set-up after the 2005 Ashes series: blokes such as Troy Cooley, Richard McInnes and Mike Young. Someone brought up, not for the first time, the controversy about whether the Ashes urn should now stay in Australia. 'Surely it's got to be too frail to fly back,' I quipped. 'It'd look quite good in Cricket Australia's offices, I think.' *Under the Southern Cross* was sung with much gusto out on the centre wicket. But what I remember most about the hours after the final wicket was taken was when Warney dragged me to one side and said, 'Punter, I've got something I want to talk to you about.'

Immediately, I replied, 'Mate, I don't want to hear this, do I?'

'It's my time,' he said quietly. 'I'm going to retire after Sydney.'

Even though we talked for a while, it never occurred to me to say, 'Are you sure?' It wasn't for me to try to talk him out of it, because — same as Marto — it's a big decision that he must have thought about a great deal. I'd always had a feeling that Shane would have retired from Test cricket in 2005 if we'd retained the Ashes in England, so maybe part of me wasn't all that surprised that he was doing this now, so soon after our great redemption. Of course, it wasn't my job to tell anyone what Shane had just told me, and I don't know if he mentioned it to anyone else, but I sensed that the mood among us changed as the evening went on. For me, it was almost bizarre to have a shred of sadness in my mind during such a joyous occasion. Gradually, the adrenalin rush that accompanied our victory subsided, and people began to sense that while regaining the Ashes was a dream come true, it was also the beginning of the end of something special. Shane Watson and Mitchell Johnson sent messages from Adelaide, where they were playing a Pura Cup game for Queensland, but we couldn't get Marto on the phone. The family was starting to break up. In my own mind, the need to win 5–0 was more imperative than ever.

Yesterday, the day we regained the Ashes, was a Monday. There isn't a lot happening in Perth on a Monday night, but there's enough and we ended up in a good pub that has a beer garden out the back, and that was where we had a very low-key but really excellent party. It was way better than going out to a busy nightclub, where we couldn't have heard ourselves talk and would have lost each other any way. Instead, we simply sat around a big long table, and enjoyed a few nibblies, pizzas and beers, chatted happily and celebrated well. At midnight, we toasted my 32nd birthday, and not too long after that I went to bed feeling unbelievably satisfied.

Yet still I have this nagging thought that the job isn't finished. The vibe among the team last night was that we want to continue to play excellent cricket until the very last ball of this series is bowled. And beyond that, too. Having set a new standard for ourselves, as individuals and as a team, as to the way we prepare and play, the last thing we want to do now is retreat from that, even a fraction. If rain prevents us from achieving a series clean sweep I'll be fine; in that sense, it really doesn't matter whether we win 3–zip, 4–zip or 5–zip. But if we miss an opportunity to make history because we take it easy, because we stop trying to get better, then I'll be very disappointed. We all will be.

CHAPTER 9

FOURTH TEST

Saturday, December 30

Fourth Ashes Test, at Melbourne (December 26–28): England 159
(AJ Strauss 50; SK Warne 5–39) and 161 (B Lee 4–47) lost to Australia 419
(A Symonds 156, ML Hayden 153; SI Mahmood 4–100) by an innings and 99 runs

FOR A WHILE IT looked as if the lead-up to the Boxing Day Test
would be all about Warney, after he revealed his retirement
decision in a newspaper column on December 20 and made it
official the next day at a media conference at the Melbourne
Cricket Ground. But then, over breakfast at our team hotel on
December 23, Glenn McGrath informed me that he was calling
it quits as well, via a media conference later that day, though his
intention is to keep playing until the end of next year's World
Cup. Immediately, speculation turned to the other senior
members of the team — Matthew Hayden, Justin Langer and
Adam Gilchrist — and I must confess that for a little while I felt
a streak of trepidation run through me whenever any of that trio
asked for a word.

I had enjoyed a short break in Sydney after the third Test,
spending most of my time with Rianna and the rest with some

cappuccinos and my golf clubs. But once we had all gathered in Melbourne, despite all the talk about the twin retirements, for the team it was — as best we could — business as usual. We had to concentrate on improving the quality of our play and not worry about 'doing it' for Shane and Glenn. This said, I did think of our two retiring warriors when I read a quote from David Collier, chief executive of the England and Wales Cricket Board. 'We were slightly short of experience,' Collier told *The Guardian*, as he sought reasons for his team's defeat. Does this mean those 'Dad's Army' jibes we'd heard before the first Test — the ones that led to Glenn 'limping' off the Gabba after he took six wickets in the first English innings of the series — aren't relevant anymore?

Following our third Test win, I'd come up with what I thought was a nice idea for Christmas. I have been working as a brand ambassador, Australasia wide, for Raymond Weil, the maker of luxury Swiss timepieces, and successfully pitched an idea to them — that we'd present a suitably engraved sports watch, as a memento of the Ashes win, and as a thank you for the effort and commitment shown over the last 15 months, to the members of the Aussie team. After the order was placed, I learned that Sir Donald Bradman had done something similar after the Invincibles tour, presenting each player at his testimonial game, which was played at the Melbourne Cricket Ground in early December 1948, with a set of gold cufflinks that featured a cricket bat and a cricket ball joined by a chain. For me, this was a nice, if unintended link between the two Ashes triumphs, 58 years apart. On a similar theme, after training on December 24, John Buchanan asked us all to go with him to the Long Room in the Melbourne Cricket Club's members' area, where he had tuxedos and bow ties waiting for us. Buck had seen an old photograph of the Invincibles in formal attire and wanted something similar featuring his Ashes team. A few of the boys really got into the spirit of the idea, by greasing their hair up in the manner of the Brylcreem boys of '48, with Mitchell Johnson, very much your modern man, looking a particular treat with his hair slicked back behind his ears.

That testimonial game was The Don's final match at the MCG, and it would have been a very different ground to today's modern stadium. We were all looking forward to playing in front of a capacity crowd at the 'G', now that the major renovations that took place for the 2006 Commonwealth Games were complete. The fact that Warney would be going for his 700th Test wicket in his farewell to home fans only added to the general Ashes buzz, and to the sense of history that surrounded the match, which was promoted as the 100th Test to be staged in Melbourne. Last year, there was a big crowd in for the first day of the Test against South Africa, but the construction of the new grandstand wasn't finished, so it wasn't quite a full house. However, I remember how after that game everyone kept saying how much they wanted to come back when it was finished, to experience something very special.

The media, inevitably, were all over the retirement stories. Every time I spoke to a reporter or commentator, from the time Shane and Glenn announced their retirement plans through to the on-field interview following the Boxing Day toss, I emphasised the point that I'd already put to the team — that the Australian squad was concentrating on the game, rather than the fact that two of our best players were saying goodbye. I said the same thing to the two guys. 'I'm not trying to be rude,' I explained, 'but I'm not going to mention your retirements at our team meetings.' Of course, they were sweet with that; it was the way they wanted it. I liked the idea of playing a winning brand of cricket in the last two Tests (and on to the World Cup for

Glenn) that would serve as an appropriate send off, and had no doubt that the best way to celebrate their careers was to clean sweep the series.

In other words, I didn't want any of us playing on emotion rather than skill. I've seen many examples of players underperforming when their concentration gets blurred. Ironically, McGrath is as good an example of this is any — when he starts yakking to the batsman, rather than letting his bowling do the talking, that's usually the time to take him off. Few players can be outwardly aggressive in that way and still play at their best. The memory of Steve Waugh's last season was also strong, when I believe there were times when the focus was more on getting Steve's farewell right than the team performing at its best.

CHRISTMAS DAY FOR US involves an optional training in the morning, which I always go to, followed by Christmas lunch with families at Crown Casino. That lunch was once an event that all the members of the squad went to, but in recent times a few of us, mostly the guys without kids, have chosen a quieter option, and this year I just had a nice lunch with Rianna. Afterwards, it was a typical night before a Test match, as I made sure my mind was locked into what I would be doing the following day.

I must confess I wasn't sure what to expect from the Englishmen now that the fate of the Ashes had been decided. Teams in their situation usually perform surprisingly well, because the pressure is off, or really poorly, because the gloom that comes with a devastating loss sucks away the last traces of enthusiasm. I kept thinking that because they're not a bad side, they'd come good at some stage, that their batsman would play again as they did in the first innings at Adelaide, that Steve

Harmison would start firing and Andrew Flintoff would return to form. One look at the Test pitch told me it would be much livelier than the road on which we'd played the Pura Cup last month, and I wondered if the promise of such a wicket might fire them into action. There was a lot of grass on it, and on Test-eve I was asked what I thought of it.

'We're actually considering playing the four quicks and leaving Warney out,' I said, trying to keep a straight face. Everyone laughed. Given the media hype that had been everywhere since Shane announced he was retiring, there was little doubt the capacity crowd would have burned the new grandstand down on the first morning if he'd been announced as 12th man.

GIVEN THAT THE PITCH had plenty of moisture in it, Flintoff made a big call by deciding to bat when he won the toss. It was a positive move, in my view, and a gutsy one, because not only was the wicket wet, there was a full house in that was sure to be pumped up as they got behind Shane Warne. The attendance for the day was later announced as 89,155, second biggest for a day's play in Australia and the largest ever for Boxing Day. I would have batted, but that was mainly because we had Warney in our line-up and in Australia I always like the idea of Shane bowling in the fourth innings of a match. That's what we'd done against South Africa in Melbourne last season, even though the pitch was so wet we started late and I knew it would be tricky for our top order for at least the first couple of hours.

I was impressed that they backed themselves to get through the morning, and they started pretty well. It did take a while for our bowlers to get their line right, maybe because of the occasion, more likely because it was cold and a little bleak, with thick clouds overheard and rain threatening. Glenn's first ball, to

Alastair Cook, went sideways like a quick off-break, which wouldn't have sent any joy through the away dressing room, and quickly we learned that there was even more in the wicket than we'd expected.

Brett Lee responded by bowling his best but unluckiest spell in the series. Bing had been struggling for rhythm — a disaster for a bowler who relies on the smoothness of his run-up and delivery stride to get his pace and late swing. We've seen in the past how when he's out of kilter he can struggle, bowl a lot of no-balls and lose his speed down into the high 130ks, when he should be touching 150. I had spoken to Troy Cooley a few times, expressing my concerns, and the two had worked on a few things, but mostly on Brett's run-up and especially on his stride pattern. Things started to work better in the days leading up to the Melbourne Test, and keen observers on this first day of the game would have noted the way Bing often paused at the top of his run, as if he was going through a checklist in his mind before he took off.

Again, how this played out demonstrated a difference to this Australian team and the set-up we had in 2005. In England, Brett would have had to work out his problem for himself. Here, at least in part because of Troy's input, he got his run-up right, then his pace came back, and then he started swinging the ball again. When all that happens, he is one of the most dangerous new-ball bowlers in the game.

Besides Troy's contribution, what I also liked about this outcome was that it came to fruition because Brett was mature enough to acknowledge he was struggling and then he did something about it. It wasn't as if he just shrugged his shoulders and hoped things would improve, or kept doing what he had been doing until he had a headache from belting his head against a brick wall. Instead he was proactive, went out to the nets with a coach whose opinion he trusted and worked it out, and I thought he bowled beautifully at different times in the Melbourne Test. On the first day, he had Cook caught behind after beating him for pace, and then he had Paul Collingwood caught at second slip by bowling precisely the right line. And in the England second innings, he made Strauss hurry a few times, and then cleaned up the tail by bowling quick and smart.

THE MELBOURNE CRICKET GROUND is my favourite venue in Australia. It was especially so this season. Right through this summer I'd kept thinking, I think we all did, *how good is Boxing Day going to be this year?* I love the Boxing Day Test itself, I love Christmas the day before, I love the guaranteed huge crowd on the first day, I love it that my family is always there. There's always a sense that something special or controversial might happen. In my first Boxing Day Test, back in 1995–96, Muttiah Muralitharan was no-balled for throwing; this time, Murali's great rival, Shane Warne, took his 700th Test wicket, and finished with 5–39 from 17.2 overs on the first day, even though I didn't introduce him into the attack until not long before three o'clock, when England were 2–82 after 40 overs.

I'd delayed his appearance until this point because it was a fast bowlers' pitch, and I will always believe that because the best friend a fast bowler has in Test cricket is a new ball, I've got to give them every opportunity to take advantage of it. I'm always on to everyone in the field to look after the ball 'like it's a baby', because it's so important to the quicks. In this instance, I was also guided by the answer to a question I kept posing in my head, *who would I least like to be facing?* For the first 40 overs, it was our quicks. Lee, McGrath and Clark all bowled excellently, and I imagine England would have been reasonably happy with the total they'd achieved by the time I brought Shane on to bowl. It was also genuinely cold, which meant Warney would need some time to get the fire into his spinning fingers. And, I figured, once he was on, he'd have the rest of the day to bowl as the ball grew older and softer.

Shane doesn't agree with me that the pacemen should get priority on a seaming deck. As he says all the time about cricket pitches, 'If it seams, it spins.' Which is true for him, but he's most likely the greatest spinner in Test cricket history. I'd bet he is definitely the best spin bowler *on the first day* there has ever been. Strauss, a world-class player, should have been full of confidence and looking like he was on his way to a very big score. Instead, when Warney came on, there was a negativity about his body language, not quite like he was on death row, but close. The crowd, which had been cheering his every move (and letting me know they thought he should be bowling), roared their approval at the sight of him handing his hat to the umpire. The MCG has never been more like the Colosseum. This is what we're going to miss most when Shane's gone — that sense of trepidation in the opposition camp that comes with the realisation that to win they have to overcome the legendary leg-spinner. The number no statistician provided as Shane's 700 wickets were discussed and dissected was how many wickets he'd earned for the bowlers at the other end. Trust me, it's been plenty.

I was fielding at mid-wicket when Strauss was dismissed, off the second ball of Shane's fourth over, bowled for 50. I found out later that just before it happened, Warney had actually told Glenn McGrath at deepish mid-on that he was going to knock Strauss over with a big-turning leg break. Apparently, Pidge called out to him, 'How are you going to get him out?'

'Through the gate, sweeping,' Warney replied confidently.

Which is nearly what happened, though Strauss was trying to drive when the ball drifted slightly away from him, dipped and then fizzed through the gap between bat and pad. As Shane started his celebration, he looked over at me for a second, as if to say, 'I told you so!' And then he kept running, a long circular extension of his follow-through, right arm pointing skywards, until Justin Langer got him in a bear hug behind the umpire at the bowler's end. Soon he was engulfed by the entire Australian team. The noise was unbelievable.

For the rest of the innings Shane took five wickets for 24 runs, as England lost their last eight for 58. Sure, some of the batting was ordinary (Kevin Pietersen batted a fair while, but he didn't seem sure what to do after a few of his team-mates got out and ended up holing out to Andrew Symonds at long-off), but the spin bowling was irresistible. It was only late in the day, when Andrew Flintoff took the wickets of Langer and nightwatchman Lee in consecutive balls, that the Barmy Army discovered its voice.

USING A NIGHTWATCHMAN IS not something we do that often; the decision can come down to the situation of the game or simply how the next bloke going in feels at the time. In this case, there was nothing to be gained at all by me going out that night: the ball still hard and shiny, wicket most likely doing more then than it would be the next morning. Sometimes it depends on who is available to be nightwatchman. I remember once against New Zealand in Christchurch, we used Jason Gillespie and he did a terrific job to get through the stumps. However, when he and I went back out the following day, I started scoring a single early in the over and then Dizzy would defend for the rest of it. Consequently, the game was going nowhere, and I got myself out after about half an hour. Dizzy went on to bat for two hours for 12 runs, but I'm not sure if he helped us too much, at least until he came out later and bowled beautifully in the Kiwis' second innings. We won by nine wickets, so I guess no real damage was done.

Because Brett didn't get through to stumps, our tactic of trying to protect the specialist batsman, in this case me, got a bit of attention. However, that mild criticism was nothing compared to the examination the English bowling tactics received on day two, after their bowling plans were 'leaked' to the media. My understanding is that the information was actually dropped by someone from the visitors' camp, picked up by a local fan, handed to someone in the pressbox, and thus caused a kerfuffle, especially when their strategy for bowling to Andrew Symonds was spectacularly unsuccessful. By the end of our innings, they seemed to be, tactically at least, in disarray.

I didn't pay a lot of attention to the document, on the basis that as an experienced player I should know how bowlers like Steve Harmison or Andrew Flintoff are trying to get me out. If they're trying something different during an innings, even during an over, I soon get a feel for it, and I'd like to think I have the nous to counter it. More generally, I've always felt that making bowling tactics too complicated or asking bowlers to do things they're not proficient at can be self-defeating. As Matty Hayden likes to say, if you consistently put the ball on a good line and length around the off stump, you're going to take wickets. Glenn McGrath has lived on that game plan, and Stuart Clark does much the same thing. It's one of our bowlers' biggest assets: we do the simple things better than anybody else.

THIS WAS A TEST with a wonderfully strange scorecard: essentially low-scoring except for one massive partnership, put together by two Queenslanders who off and on the field are the best of mates. For Symmo, it was a crucial contribution, as he finally found his feet as a Test batsman, and it was important for Haydos, too, as he scored his first hundred of the series.

All of us had been waiting for Symmo to flourish on the Test-match stage. Given the state of the game — Australia 5–84 in reply to 159 — and the way the wicket was playing, it was his ultimate challenge. The crowd, 75,000 strong, was not quite as big as day one, but still massive. In the first hour and a quarter of the second day's play, I had mistimed a pull shot off Flintoff to Cook at mid-wicket, Mike Hussey had failed to reach double figures in a Test for only the third time in his life (in his 15th Test) and Michael Clarke had nicked a good one from Harmison. The England quicks were bowling well, the crowd had gone quiet; there was plenty of juice in the pitch and pressure on the batsmen. A bit more than four hours later, you could see by the way the two Queenslanders celebrated Symmo's hundred how much their joint experience meant to both of them.

Both were using bats adorned with pink grips, to raise awareness for the National Breast Cancer Foundation. I can't imagine the people who thought up this promotion could have thought it would have received so much exposure, as the boys contributed mightily to two worthy causes: a fantastic charity and our big first-innings lead. The stand added up to 279 runs, the third-highest sixth-wicket partnership by an Australian pair in all Test matches, behind Don Bradman and Jack Fingleton's 346 against England in 1936–37 and Damien Martyn and Adam Gilchrist's 317 at Johannesburg in 2002.

More than anything else that has happened in the first four Tests, this effort was the best example of the difference in the Australian side between 2005 and now. In the same situation in '05, Symmo and Haydos might have added 30 or 40, given promise of a fightback, but then, as if that was enough, one of them would have got himself out. This time, they went right on with it, fighting hard until we had our noses in front, continuing to battle until the gusto went out of the English attack, and then they put the boot right in, not being separated until late in the day, when Matty was out for 153. On this pitch, it was an extraordinary effort, and that's forgetting the fact that one of the pair was playing for his Test-cricket life.

Symmo's a bloke who can think too much about his game, and he didn't look comfortable early on, but he kept fighting. England probably went on the defensive too quickly, and once he was 'in' he made up for all the frustrations and struggles of the past. After he came off the field at stumps, 154 not out, he turned on his phone and it was loaded with messages. One of them was a beauty from Queensland sport's poet laureate, Rupert McCall, who had come up with a few inspiring verses as he watched his mate carve up the England attack, and then recited them down the line. Symmo loved it, we all did, and he played it over and over. I can't remember much of it now, but it ended 'You ripper, Roy!' and it summed up the excitement we all felt.

Symmo's mistake in the past has been to try the big shot at the wrong time. Some people might have perceived that as over-confidence, but it was actually the reverse of that. He wouldn't feel comfortable out there, and go for the blazing drive or hoick over the top as a means of escape. His unconquered 143 off 125 balls against Pakistan in our first game of the 2003 World Cup — a sensible, brilliant innings — put his mind at ease as far as one-day cricket was concerned, and hopefully this knock will do the same for his Test career. He now knows he can do it ... his way ... but without having to slog or score at a run a ball to keep everyone, including himself, happy.

I know that in the past I've been watching him bat in Test cricket and he'd go for a low-percentage shot, and I'd sigh, 'Why is he doing that?' And Buck might reply, 'That's just Roy, that's the way he is.' *But with his talent*, I've thought to myself, *he should have 50 or 60 first-class hundreds by now!* There was no reason why his cavalier spirit couldn't assert itself in Test cricket, but only if he applied it wisely. And he is a smart cricketer, despite the knockabout image. This time, he waited until he was set before going for any big strokes — in fact, he only scored one three and one single in his first 32 balls — and it wasn't until he got all the way to 91 that he really opened up. At that point, he'd hit only seven fours, but then he smashed Panesar over mid-wicket for four, swung Collingwood over long-on to reach his hundred, and went at just about a run a ball until stumps. One interesting stat was that he hit Panesar for just one boundary from 32 balls; the other 14 fours he hit came from the quicks whenever they pitched too short (which was often) or too full. That he only took the spinner for one boundary reflected two things: one, the way he was happy to be patient; and two, the fact that for most of the partnership, Panesar bowled with four fieldsmen on the boundary.

Apparently the media conference at the end of the day was real good fun, in a typical understated Symmo way. When asked about the pressure as he took 21 deliveries to get off the mark, he answered, 'I was thinking to myself, "How hard's this?" Times were slightly tough!'

Slightly tough! I can imagine the anguish he was actually going through, but he fought it and won. Then, when probed as to his mindset as he approached his hundred, Symmo responded: 'When I was a handful away from it, I was thinking, should I do this in ones, or if he slips one up there, should I give it some Larry Dooley. And I decided that if he slips one up there, I'll give it some Larry Dooley.'

Which led to a posse of English journalists asking later, 'Who the hell is Larry Dooley?'

Lost in all the excitement of Symmo's big day out was the quality of Haydos' 27th Test century, made in his 88th Test. It was one his finest, for so many reasons: the state of the game and the wicket; the quality of his strokeplay; the way he supported Symmo; the way he worked so hard to get himself back to such magnificent form, because he had been under a bit of pressure, having not made a hundred in the series; the way he kept going, batting the opposition right out of the game. The Poms bowled too short to him, at least in part because he intimidated them into doing so. Even though there was still something in the wicket, Sajid Mahmood was conned into trying to outmuscle him, with dire results. Despite all Matty's runs and achievements over the years, I think there has been a tendency to underrate him in some quarters, though never in the Australian dressing room. He's now equal fourth on the list of Australian Test century-makers, level with Allan Border, who played in 156 Tests.

WARNEY'S FINAL TEST INNINGS at the MCG, made before 80,000 adoring fans, was a polished 40 not out, and a little bit of him was probably relieved to see McGrath fall for a duck, as it was the 35th Test zero of Pigeon's career, one more than Warney's 34. England began their second innings 50 minutes before lunch, 260 runs behind, and though Strauss and Cook survived through to the main break, after that it was only a matter of whether the Test would get into its fourth day. They went to tea four wickets down, the last drinks break at 7–122, and then Brett Lee ran through the tail, leaving Shane, who took 2–46 (including Mahmood, bowled by a well-pitched flipper — Shane's way of reminding the hapless England No. 8 that he'd bowled too short at Symmo and Haydos), with 999 international wickets: 706 in Tests, 293 in one-day internationals. At the end, it felt like everyone had stayed to watch the hero of the day get chaired from the ground on the broad shoulders of Haydos and Symmo, like an AFL champion after his 300th game. For me, there was something very appropriate about this trio leaving the playing field together. It had been quite a Test for each of them

I wasn't quite sure what to think when Kevin Pietersen came out batting at four in England's second innings. A number of people had been arguing that, as their best batsman (which he undoubtedly is), he should have been moved up the order, but their previous No. 4, Paul Collingwood, had made a double hundred just four innings ago. In one sense, for Pietersen to come out now at the fall of the second wicket was a positive thing, but at the same time, if the only reason for doing so was to keep the press happy, or to keep him happy, then it sent the wrong message to the rest of the team. More than anything, to me it said that they weren't really working to any plan, but making it up as they went along.

This gave me a cruel sense of satisfaction, because to me it said they were completely rattled, so different to the confident outfit that beat us last time. When Stuart Clark knocked Pietersen over straightaway it could only have made things worse for them, as if their last throw of the dice had spun off the table. When poor Collingwood came out to replace him, to labour for nearly an hour for 16, with no fours, we in the slip cordon couldn't help but point out how ineffective his demotion down the batting order had been.

I think the pitch was probably at its best for batting on day three, but our four frontline bowlers produced their best effort of the summer so far, getting their length perfect and giving nothing away. Stuart Clark was sensational, bowling Cook, a left-hander, and Pietersen, a right-hander, with balls that seamed back between bat and pad, and then trapping Flintoff leg before with a delivery that jagged back and beat the England captain as he tried to drive. Sarf's match figures of 5–57 from 33 overs gave a true indication of the way he operated. During one over, while I was at second slip, I turned to Gilly and Warney and commented about how it seemed like he was landing nine out of 10 balls in *exactly* the right spot. They had been thinking the same thing. Not many bowlers of any style can do that. Shane has done it at different times in his career, and Glenn would be just about the best in the world at it, but few other blokes in the game can land it so consistently. If a bowler does that, it means he's asking a question of the batsman every single ball, and I've never met a batsman yet who likes that. It's what I hate most.

Because so much had been made of the retirements of Warne and McGrath, Stuey had to do something for the highlight reel, like shatter Pietersen's stumps for 1, to get himself noticed. Sarf was so reliable throughout the series in South Africa and now here, and has started to build an imposing Test-match record. From his first eight Tests, he's taken 42 wickets at 17.76. Sure, there have been times when the conditions have suited him, in South Africa and here in Melbourne, but not always, yet every single time he's delivered. Back at the start of the series, there were a number of critics who were saying that he was too much like McGrath for the pair to gel in the same attack, but they've both put that theory to bed. It is still true, though, that next season, when Pidge is gone, we have in Sarf a ready-made replacement. Indeed, in my view the four quicks apart from Glenn who've been part of our squad this Test series — Clark, Lee, Mitchell Johnson and Shaun Tait — are potentially as good a quartet of quicks as Australian cricket has possessed in quite a while, and I'm not putting down bowlers such as Jason Gillespie and Michael Kasprowicz at all when I write that.

These young blokes are good. And you've got to like the balance: one in the style of McGrath, one left-handed, three who can bowl at 150k, all four who can swing it and seam it around. Throw Shane Watson into the mix, and I reckon Troy Cooley might be having some fun during the next couple of years.

AT THE POST-MATCH press conference I made a point of talking up the value of team unity. It was true that we're tight, and you could see it in the way we train, and the way we celebrate key wickets. The manner in which two great mates like Symmo and Haydos had looked out for each other and seemed happier with the other's success than their own highlighted our harmony, at a time when the Poms seemed less and less united. We didn't bother with cheap gestures such as gently punching each other's batting gloves every time one of us scored a single. When Warney said after the Test, 'It's a really good time to be playing cricket for Australia,' he could have been talking for any of us. But I'd like to think that this unity had been a characteristic of the Australian team for many years, since long before I was captain. We pride ourselves on being closer than any other team and looking out for each other. I think that's been pivotal to our success over the years and I've always had the feeling that other teams and other players are not that way. We need to never forget this.

It was also pointed out to me that at the press conference I used the adjective 'relentless' more than once to describe the Australian team. It's been an ambition of mine to have the team this way, and I think we've attained that right at the moment. It wasn't just the players ducking the bouncers who noticed how ruthless the West Indies teams of the 1980s were. I was just a kid, but I'll never forget how dominating they were, how they set the benchmark for other teams to dream about. When I first placed my kit in an Australian dressing room, I heard stories from blokes such as David Boon, Steve and Mark Waugh, Mark Taylor, Ian Healy and Craig McDermott, about the bruises and the way the Windies sought to not just pin their enemy down, but bludgeon them into submission. These were lessons that had been absorbed and need to be passed down to future generations. That was one of the reasons I kept stressing at team meetings that we had England under extreme pressure, and it would be a crime to produce a lazy session or even a lazy hour that let them wriggle free. This Australian team's relentlessness comes not from a barrage of bumpers but from a desire to be consistently excellent in *everything* we do. The little misgivings Flintoff's men had in their minds after the first couple of Tests must be huge doubts now.

Our celebration after this Melbourne Test was less reserved than it had been for the three earlier victories. Part of this was because we won so decisively, in doing so proving beyond doubt that we were the better side. There was also a feeling that we had to give Shane a proper send off, and he certainly seemed in the mood to party. I know that he remained right to the end because I stayed there with him — I just wanted to be part of everything that happened for him that night. Brian Lara, who's been in Melbourne, came into the room for a while, and there were a number of AFL footballers about, including Essendon captain Matthew Lloyd.

Everything is now in place for us to emulate Warwick Armstrong's Australian team of 1920–21, which swept that summer's Ashes series. I feel like nothing is going to stop us. Yet we must never take winning a Test match for granted. We were 4-up after the Boxing Day Test four years ago, and lost in Sydney, and that win by Nasser Hussain's team served as a bit of a springboard for the Poms going into the next Ashes series. We have to make sure history doesn't repeat itself.

CHAPTER 10

WARNEY

I FIRST MET SHANE Warne at the Australian Cricket Academy in Adelaide during the winter of 1992, when I was 'studying' there and Shane was preparing for the Australian Test cricket team's tour of Sri Lanka. He had made his Test debut at the start of that year, against India in Sydney, when he took 1–150, and he would have his first taste of success of the highest level a few weeks after we met — at Colombo, when Australian captain Allan Border risked him at the end of an exciting Test, and Shane responded by taking three late wickets without conceding a run. Four months later, he spun his country to victory in the Boxing Day Test against the West Indies, taking 7–52 on the final day, including the prized wicket of the Windies captain with a brilliant flipper. One of cricket's greatest international careers had been launched.

I was 17 years old and it was my first year at the academy. Shane was 22, nearly 23, but despite the age gap he headed in my direction and we shared some time together. He was the bloke responsible for my nickname, 'Punter', assigned to me because of my habit of sneaking down to the TAB on Monday and Thursday nights to have a bet on the greyhounds. I can't remember if he ever came with me, but I think he was impressed with my nerve, and the fact that I liked a bet. He tried to corrupt me a little, to get me into nightclubs even though I was under age, but I had one problem: I didn't own a pair of jeans and a good shirt. Finally, he dolled me up in decent gear and we did venture out, but I was like a rabbit in the headlights; I was more comfortable at the TAB.

The thing I recall about him most was that he was so far ahead in his cricket development than the rest of us were with ours. We were young kids waiting for buses; he zipped around in his own car. One day, his Australian Cricket Board contract turned up in a big yellow envelope, and we were agog at the numbers on it, thinking, with proverbial stars in our eyes, *how good is that?*

As a spin bowler, he was miles ahead of anything I'd faced before, but that was true of a number of bowlers I faced at the Academy. It was a new world to me and I lapped it all up. For me, it was like every net session was my first Test innings. Shane was working with the man who became known as his 'spin doctor', the former Test leg-spinner Terry Jenner, and I was always keen to get into the nets against him and they were happy for me to be there. Of course, the ball bounced and spun a lot on the indoor synthetic wickets; thinking back, his control was excellent even then, but it wasn't until I faced other first-class and Test spinners that I realised he was in a class of his own.

Years later, I heard Terry describe Shane as the 'natural unnatural'. Bowling out of the back of the hand is such an unnatural movement, yet his protégé is a natural at it. A lot of us have tried to bowl leggies, in the nets, the backyard, on the beach, so we know how hard it is, to just land them let alone land them and spin them like a top, and disguise the one that goes straight on, and change the pace and the loop and every so often, when its least expected, fire down a flipper which makes the batsman look like a goose.

There have been a few bowlers who have spun the ball as much as Warney, few if any slow bowlers who were as strong and explosive through their delivery stride, but what has really set him apart is that consistency and his ability to not leak runs, whatever the circumstances of the game. Until Warney, no one thought a leg-spinner had a role in one-day cricket, and batsmen had always known that while leggies could bowl unplayable deliveries, they were also prone to offer the occasional long hop or full toss. With Shane, batsmen were stressing out about how they were going to score off him. If he conceded a boundary, more often than not it was because he wanted to; it was part of the trap. Furthermore, from the moment he got the ball in his hand, he became the most competitive person I've ever seen on a cricket field. And he loved the big occasion, the bigger the better. When the game was on the line, he wanted to be there. The spin, the control, the competitiveness and the desire — it adds up to the greatest spin bowler of all time.

When a game is just rolling along and not much is happening, Warney is often just another bowler, but when a game is there to be won, or something ignites his competitive fire, a transformation takes place. In the Tasmania–Victoria Pura Cup game in 2006–07, I could sense that he was more energetic when I came out to bat. He took longer with his field placements, stood longer at the end of his run-up before each delivery, and resented every single.

Six months after he knocked over Richie Richardson, Warney bowled England's Mike Gatting with one of the most famous deliveries in Ashes history. Soon he had a reputation as a freakish bowler that he never lost, and with that came an aura that intimidated opponents as no spinner had ever done before. He's a winner. I was always astonished at the manner in which good players would be dismissed by him, and then, next time, they'd play him exactly the same way. He'd get them out again, and again, and still they'd play him the same way. They were too scared to change, unable to take risks because they thought he'd embarrass them. I can't think of anyone who thought, *right, today I'm going to take him on and see how we go*. It was as if it was better to get out than look stupid, and of course a spinner can make you look like a real goose if you charge down the pitch and get stumped, like Paul Collingwood did in the first Test of this series, at the Gabba. It seems almost strange to think of batsmen being frightened as they face up to a spinner, but it did happen. Shane was aware of it and preyed on it.

His feel for the game, its ebbs and flows, is second to none. No cricketer has read body language better, or been quicker to sense weakness. There have been 20 or 30 occasions when I have been standing at second slip, Warney next to me at first, and all's been quiet, when suddenly he'll say, 'This one is coming straight to me.' Sure enough, it did. At a lunch break during the '05 Ashes series, when we were bowling, he pulled me to one side to explain how he was going to attack Kevin Pietersen straight after the break. 'I'm going to start round the wicket,' he said, before telling me the field that he required, which included a short cover and with cover point and mid-off pushed back. 'First five balls, I'll bowl slow and outside leg stump. He'll pad them away. Then I'll go back over the wicket, and bowl a slower, loopy leggie that'll pitch outside off stump. Because he's seen that the off-side field is pushed back, but he hasn't scored a run off the over, he'll try to slog a six over mid-wicket.'

Which is exactly how it panned out. Warney's hope was that Pietersen would top edge a catch, but in fact he missed the ball completely.

The long lonely walk off the Adelaide Oval, after I was dismissed for 142 late on the third day of the second Test.

A famous moment. Shane Warne bowls Kevin Pietersen, and England are sliding towards a stunning defeat.

Adelaide was, without doubt, the greatest comeback win I have been involved in.

Above: Mike Hussey jumps for joy. while Kevin Pietersen can only look to where the winning run has just been hit.

Above: In front of the Adelaide Oval scoreboard.

Left: With Michael Clarke after the Australian team charged on to the field at the end of the Test.

The three century-makers from our second innings at the WACA: Mike Hussey (top left), Michael Clarke (top right) and Adam Gilchrist (below, hitting Monty Panesar into the crowd).

Above: Glenn McGrath dismisses Alastair Cook late on the fourth day of the third Test.

Left: Shane Warne bowls Monty Panesar second ball after lunch and Australia has regained the Ashes.

Below left: My reflex run out of Geraint Jones on the final day.

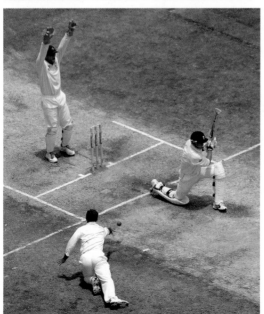

Above: Adam Gilchrist reflects the joy we felt after the last wicket fell.

With a replica of the Ashes urn in the WACA change room.

Shane Warne takes his 700th Test
wicket: Andrew Strauss bowled for 50.

Warney looks over in my direction at
midwicket, before beginning an exuberant
celebratory run.

Images from the fourth Test at Melbourne.

Above left: Andrew Symonds and Matthew Hayden celebrate the six that brought Symmo his first Test hundred.

Above right: Stuart Clark knocks over Kevin Pietersen on the final day.

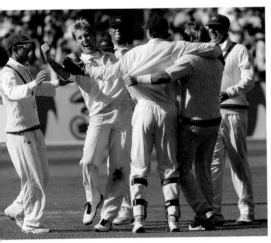

Below: Shane Warne is chaired from the field after his farewell appearance at the MCG.

Above: Brett Lee celebrates after bowling Matthew Hoggard to end the Test.

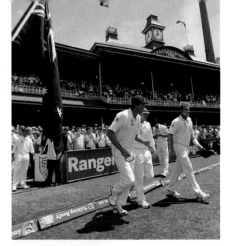

Right: Glenn McGrath, Justin Langer and Shane Warne lead us on to the SCG at the start of the fifth Test.

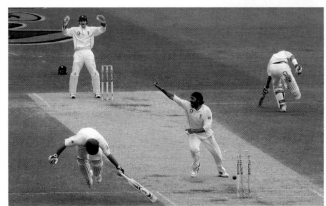

Left: I'm run out by a direct hit from Jimmy Anderson on day two in Sydney.

A team photo of a different kind. The 2006–07 Australians wait for the TV umpire's verdict on a possible stumping of Andrew Flintoff during the fifth Test. This would be Shane Warne's 706th and last Test wicket. From left: Mike Hussey, Matthew Hayden, Andrew Symonds, Mitchell Johnson, Brett Lee, Glenn McGrath, Adam Gilchrist, Stuart Clark, Shane Warne, Justin Langer (obscured), me, Michael Clarke.

Left: Justin Langer walks through his 'guard of honour' before our final Test innings of the summer.

Right: Langer with Matt Hayden after Hayden had hit Sajid Mahmood for six to move us to within a single of an Ashes clean sweep.

Glenn McGrath shows the Ashes Trophy to his legion of Sydney fans.

However, even though it didn't end in a dismissal, the over was still a terrific exhibition of Shane's all-round skill, because not only was he able to land each delivery in exactly the right spot, he was also able to predict exactly how the batsman would react to the pressure he created. It's a rare gift being able to stay ahead of the game; Warney was often further ahead than anyone else.

He was as unique off the field as he was on it. I'll never quite be able to come to terms with his diet. He could be quite worldly in many ways, but his menu was mostly cheese pizza and toasted cheese sandwiches. I've seen him walk into McDonald's, order a cheeseburger and eat it minus the beef pattie. The moment that best captured his food preferences came in India in 2001, when he revealed that he was going to spend most of the tour eating baked beans. Within days, a pallet of baked beans had been shipped to the subcontinent by an enterprising producer, and parked in a storeroom at our hotel. It all seemed a bit ridiculous, but Warney's reaction was, 'You beauty!'

He was a one-of-a-kind cricketer, very much his own man, yet also a sensational team player. When analysing his greatness, we must never forget his longevity. At training, he works hardest when he has a cricket ball in his hand or when a football comes out. He loves bowling and he loves footy. He might not have been the fittest guy in the squad, but I can't think of an instance when his fitness cost him or the team, and his ability to back up after a hard day in the field was remarkable. Niggling injuries were par for the course. Ian Chappell has written about how hard it was to get the ball out of Dennis Lillee's hand. Warney was exactly the same.

Many is the time that someone has met Shane, spent time with him, and then walked away thinking, *what a nice bloke, nothing like the arrogant so and so I thought he'd be*. Because Warney was always easily the biggest celebrity in the team — always in demand from the sponsors, the media, the fans and the gossip merchants — he's suffered more than the rest of us from those hangers-on who whinge loudly that he wouldn't give them an autograph, not caring that he'd signed 50 million of them before they stuck their particular scrap of paper in his face. There are not too many kids who can say they've been knocked back by Australian Test cricketers over the years, and this is especially true of Shane.

I loved playing with him, loved touring with him. He was always the guy whose door I'd knock on first when I was looking for a golf partner. He is as competitive on the course as he is on the cricket field. And he's a good winner. Yet the on-field experience that stands out for me involving Warney was not really a win, though it was as good as a win — the tie against South Africa at the 1999 World Cup that got us through to the final.

That morning, Warney was not his usual self. I've never forgotten that. He'd been going through a difficult time, having missed most of the 1998–99 Ashes series because of a major shoulder injury, been dropped from the Test XI in the West Indies, and then been struggling for his best form in the early games at the Cup. It's just a gut feeling, and I've never asked him about it, but I think he might have retired from one-day international cricket if we'd lost that game. He was so intense, so pumped up, as if the game was death or glory. When Steve Waugh brought him on early in the South Africans' innings, with the score at 0–45 after nine overs, he struck immediately, bowling Herschelle Gibbs with an unbelievable leg break, and reacted in as animated a fashion as I ever saw him celebrate a wicket. He quickly knocked over Gary Kirsten and Hansie Cronje as well, came back to get Jacques Kallis later in the innings, and was named man of the match in this game and in the final. It was a joy to be on the same field as him, to see the maestro at his absolute best.

Of course, there have been so many brilliant performances. In England in '05, he was the best bowler from either side, taking 40 wickets and always threatening even though he often lacked support. If we'd won that series, and we nearly did, his effort would be remembered as one of the greatest of all time. Even this summer at Melbourne, he must have been so anxious to bowl well, to give all the fans who were cheering him a decent show, if he'd been slightly below his best everyone would have understood. Having to wait for ages before his captain gave him a bowl couldn't have helped his composure, but the bloke is nerveless, and he bowled as well as I've seen him. A lot of excellent athletes across many sports dread those moments; Warney lives for them.

Of all the things I learned from watching Warney, the thing I'd put top of my list would probably surprise most people. Patience is an unlikely thing to learn from such an aggressive cricketer, but many was the time that I'd be fielding at bat-pad on the off-side, and he'd bowl three or four overs where I thought nothing was happening. So up I'd trot to say, 'Why don't we change things up a little? We'll put a "45" in and you can straighten your line and we can try and get him leg before. Or maybe he'll go for a sweep and get a top edge?'

'No, no,' Shane would reply. 'Just leave it, everything is fine, everything is going great.'

To me, he didn't look like he was going to get a wicket, but he could read his victims better than I could, and he knew that if he persisted, his plans would come true. He is undoubtedly one of the greatest wicket-taking bowlers of all time, yet it wasn't as if he was constantly sending down unplayable deliveries. Instead, he would often chisel players out, and because his control was so immaculate he could stick to what he knew was going to work for long periods of time. This said, if you needed a wicket immediately, he was usually the man I turned to. He could do it on first-day wickets or fifth-day wickets, defending small totals or with plenty of runs to play with. Always, he had that innate self-belief that allowed him to be patient, confident and deadly, all at the same time.

I was happy for him when he announced his impending retirement, because he was happy and very comfortable with the fact that he was going out on top. Like one of those big back foot drives that came to characterise his batting, I sense he's got the timing right. He is, though, perhaps more than any other cricketer in the game, irreplaceable. It is a funny thing about the truly great bowlers — you would expect that they would inspire a generation of clones, as boys try so hard to imitate their heroes, but it usually doesn't work that way. The West Indies have never produced another Malcolm Marshall, Pakistan have not found another Wasim Akram, New Zealand are still looking for the next Richard Hadlee, there'll never be another Shane Warne. If we who are left in the Australian team can maintain our winning record of recent years without him ... well, that might just be our greatest achievement.

CHAPTER 11

FIFTH TEST

Saturday, January 6

Fifth Ashes Test, at Sydney (January 2–5): England 291 (A Flintoff 89, IR Bell 71) and 147 lost to Australia 393 (SK Warne 71, AC Gilchrist 62) and 0–46 by 10 wickets

IN THE DAYS BEFORE the fifth Test, John Buchanan was critical of Kevin Pietersen, suggesting the England No. 4 or No. 5 is a cricketer who played for himself. 'Pietersen certainly talks about himself as a team player,' our coach said. 'Personally, I don't see any evidence of that.' I wouldn't have been astonished if it had been Shane Warne or Glenn McGrath coming out with such a comment, but I was surprised that it was Buck giving the media such an opinion. I think he did so for a reason, to remind us that there was a Test match coming up, to make sure we were thinking of our opponents and what we had to do to beat them again, rather than us worrying more about sending our retiring champions off in style. Perhaps, he was worried that the contest was losing its edge, and wanted a sense of confrontation to re-emerge.

Not long after Buck made his comments, the number of retiring champions in our side grew to three, when, on New Year's Day, Justin Langer arranged a media conference to reveal this fifth Test would be his last. With Buck also handing in his Australian coaching badge after the World Cup, the feeling that this game would mark the end of an era in Australian cricket history was becoming more and more powerful. For the first time in my cricket life, I was feeling a little old — of the guys in the squad who are not retiring, only Matty Hayden made his Test debut before I did.

This time, unlike before Melbourne, I didn't place a strict embargo on talk of the retirements, but I still stressed the need for us to concentrate on the game. I searched for signs that we might be switching off, that somehow we wouldn't be as committed to this Test as we'd been for the previous four, but there was none of that. The desire to win 5–0 was strong; we all saw it as a once-in-a-lifetime opportunity to make some history and to devastate the ghosts of '05 for good.

We had decided during the series that if a Test ended early, we would have the option of going home to our families for a day or two, if that's what we preferred. So the morning after the fourth Test, I flew to Sydney while Justin stayed with his family in Melbourne, to mull over his future. Apparently, it was during a coffee with his father that his mind was finally made up, and after that he went through it one last time with his wife Sue and then gave me a call. I must confess I wasn't completely surprised, mainly because after what had already occurred with Marto, Warney and Pigeon, I knew ending up or not ending up had to be on the minds of all the senior players. With Lang, I knew he found the constant conjecture about his place in the side a little wearing, and there was also the memory of him being pinged by Makhaya Ntini in Johannesburg last April. That concussion, if you'll pardon the pun, really shook him up, made him think about his future with Sue and their four girls. In a way, after this Ashes series, 105 Tests, 23 Test centuries, he had nothing left to prove, yet at the same time no man alive has ever loved the baggy green more. Walking away from the Australian Test set-up would cut him deep. Whereas with Warney and Pidge, I knew they were 100 per cent comfortable with their decisions, with Lang I sensed that while he knew in his gut that he was doing the right thing, that didn't mean he had to like it. Not even a little.

I watched Lang's media conference, and was struck by one particular part of it, when he recalled the anguish he went through in Jo'Burg, as he tried to decide whether he'd try to bat in our second innings:

> *'The thing that struck me most about that was that everyone — my family, friends, I'd say 98 per cent of people — said, "You can't bat, it's just a game."*
>
> *'But it's not just a game to me. The baggy green cap, I have had the same one for 13 years. Yeah, it's just a game of cricket, I love it. But it is not just a game for me.*
>
> *'It has been the vehicle for me to learn how to handle success, failure, criticism, how to fight back from adversity. I have learned about mateship, about leadership. So many things. I have hopefully forged a strong character, and it is all because of the baggy green cap ...'*

When Pigeon and I had fronted the media together earlier in the day, the mood was often jovial. At one point, I was asked to nominate my favourite memory of the bloke sitting next to me, which made me stop and think for a moment. I was just about to begin my response, when McGrath started coughing and mumbling: 'Sixty-one ... 61 ...'

The journos thought it was quite funny, but I'd heard it all before, many, many times. Here is a great pace bowler, who has taken more Test wickets than any other quick, who has starred at Lord's, Cape Town, Melbourne, Port-of-Spain, dismissed Tendulkar, Lara, Dravid and Pietersen, and he'd rather talk about his one Test-match fifty.

'That's one of my worst, actually,' I muttered, while Pidge just grinned, happy that his one batting triumph would now be mentioned in a number of newspaper reports (and to think he's got it in this book, too!) For the record, when I was pressed for my best McGrath memory, I went for two from Lord's — in 1997, when he took 8–38, and in 2005, when he bowled us back into the game on the first day, taking his 500th Test wicket in the process.

It was a very strange feeling, going into this Test knowing that three key players were doing so for the last time. Add in Damien Martyn, and it meant that a third of the XII, four of my best mates, were saying goodbye. Little wonder that at the end of the game, I cried my eyes out …

THERE WERE NO SURPRISES in my pre-match talk to the boys. Last thing before we ran onto the field, I said again what I had underlined many times in the previous week: make sure we play on skill and not emotion. Justin was very nervous, extremely keen to make his last Test a big one, but I think his anxiety fired up the rest of the team. The three of them went out together, McGrath first of all (Shane had led the team out in Melbourne), and as had been the case throughout the series there was genuine passion about when the two flags were brought on to the field and when the national anthems were belted out, and an extra buzz as the full house waited for the first ball to be delivered. To all the guys' credit, we went out to play the cricket we had to play, and it really wasn't until right near the end, when our openers went out to get the small total we needed to complete the clean sweep, that we started talking about ideal farewells.

The game was actually quite even for the first two days, but it all fell apart for the Poms on day three. Critically, it was a tale of two lower orders: England were 4–245, all out 291, in their first innings, despite Andrew Flintoff playing his best innings of the series. In reply, we found ourselves in a little bit of difficulty at 5–190, and made 393. McGrath got two key wickets on the first afternoon — Pietersen caught at mid-wicket by Hussey for 41 after he tried to charge the bowler but got the ball up near the splice and, a run later, Ian Bell bowled by a beauty for 71 — and then all our bowlers pitched in as we ran through their tail. Then Andrew Symonds, Adam Gilchrist and Shane Warne came together to rescue our first innings, after which we took five cheap second-innings wickets before stumps. As I went to sleep that night, as hard as I told myself not to believe that the series was as good as over, I couldn't help thinking that it was.

OFF THE FIELD, THERE was a minor controversy on the first day when the boss of Virgin, Sir Richard Branson, announced he was mounting a campaign to have the Ashes remain in Australia. This led to an interesting scene when Sir Richard stood up at a media conference to explain his position, but was made to look a bit silly when his lack of knowledge of cricket history was exposed. I was on the periphery of this, as I'd signed a petition supporting the idea.

Ian Botham had approached me during the fourth Test, to explain that he believed that the Ashes urn should stay in the country that 'held' it. Did I agree with him? When I said that I did, he asked me if I'd sign a document backing the notion, which would eventually be handed to the Marylebone Cricket

Club, who are responsible for the caring of the urn and keep it under lock and key in their museum at Lord's. I saw no reason not to, and I was hardly the first prominent cricketer, past and present, or cricket identity, to think that way. I read that the editor of *Wisden* is also of this view, as is the Australian Prime Minister. Cricket Australia looked at the petition, and said they had no problem with me autographing it.

When Sir Richard raised the matter in Sydney, he had Botham and Allan Border with him, but I'm not sure he got as much public support as he expected. To me, that was a pity — I appreciate that the urn is frail and was never intended to be a trophy, that the 'Ashes' are more mythical than something akin to a premiership cup, but that urn is still real, in itself a symbol of Ashes glory. It's hard to believe that in the 21st century we can't find a way to protect it and care for it whether it's in a glass case at Lord's, the MCG, or flying first-class in between.

WHEN, ON THE SECOND day, I ran myself out for 45, it was as far as I can remember the only mistake I made during my innings. I'm not sure I've ever batted better ... and then I took on the wrong fieldsman and it was all over, because Jimmy Anderson was too good for me, after I pushed a ball to mid-on and tried to pinch a single. I knew I was in trouble from the split second after it was too late to change my mind. I saw Anderson, who moves best of all the Englishmen in the field, attack the ball, pick it up in one motion and shape to throw. I put my head down, closed my eyes, slid my bat and hoped, but then I heard the clunk of the ball hitting the stumps and knew I was dead.

All I could do was walk off, sit down in my corner of the dressing room and wonder grimly, *how many runs have I left out there?* These sort of days, when *everything* hits the middle of your bat and you feel a million dollars, don't come round very often. But it's crazy how often on such days, when it's almost too easy, you do something stupid and get yourself out, whereas on the days when you have to battle and work hard, and you make a lot of mistakes, you survive. There's a lesson there somewhere.

IT WAS NO ACCIDENT our lower-order guys batted well. It's something we've talked about a lot, the profit that comes from everyone in the XI respecting their batting role. A highlight as the boys built a substantial lead was a verbal stoush between Shane Warne and Paul Collingwood, which continued throughout Warney's innings and was actually the culmination of a running battle the two had enjoyed for much of the series. I remember during the second Test, when Collingwood made his double hundred, Warney was in to him, telling him flatly, 'You're no good.' It got better here, after Collingwood said something from slip not long after our No. 8 had arrived at the crease with the score at 6–260 and the game still fairly evenly poised, and Shane backed away, basically refusing to take strike until the fieldsman shut up. Umpire Bowden felt obliged to walk in from square-leg to find out what was going on.

Warney's next move, which came over loud and clear via the stump microphone, was to ask his English sparring partner: 'You got an MBE, right? For scoring seven at the Oval? It's an embarrassment.'

Cruel but fair. Collingwood had only played in one Test in 2005, the last one at The Oval, when he scored 7 and 10 and took 0–17 from four overs, but as every one who played for England in that series was awarded a gong he is now Paul Collingwood MBE. Good luck to him, I guess. The two kept going, with Shane at another time, turning around and saying something like, 'You're not putting me off, you know. You're making me concentrate even more.' Then he clubbed Monty

Panesar into the crowd at deep mid-wicket and spun around and thanked Collingwood for his help. The crowd loved it, I'm sure it made great viewing, and I saw no harm in it. Just when it looked like Warney might be a chance to finally get that elusive Test century, with McGrath there to guide him through, he swung one too many times and was stumped.

The Warne-Collingwood chat was just one of a number of sledges that happened during the Test, but because it was picked up by the on-field mikes, and also because Shane won the exchange so convincingly, it received all the publicity. Earlier in the game, when I was batting with Matty Hayden, the Pommie slip cordon decided to have some fun by doing their best Warney impersonations every time a ball missed the outside edge or hit the pad, basically whenever they could. This went on for ages, long past the time when it might have been funny, and later I think Haydos told Warney about it, which might have been one of the reasons he was so fired up when he went out there to bat. To me, it looked pretty juvenile, hardly the actions of a side trying to win back some pride after being thrashed so comprehensively in the first four Tests. So when the England openers, Andrew Strauss and Alastair Cook, went out for the second dig, I made a point of walking up to Strauss, one of the offenders, to let him know what I thought, and we had our own little battle until Brett Lee sconed him on the helmet with a very quick ball in his second over. I was glad he was okay, and admired the way he refused to go off, but that lack of respect still annoyed me.

THE LAST WICKET TO fall on the third day, Andrew Flintoff stumped for 7 to make then 5–113, a lead of nine, turned out to be Shane Warne's last Test wicket. It was the exclamation mark on an excellent day's work, a highlight of which for me was

McGrath's afternoon spell, when he sent down 13 overs into the breeze for 22 runs, a build-up of pressure that led to wickets falling at the other end. Everyone bowled and fielded well, and it set up one of the most enjoyable on-field experiences of my life: the fourth morning, when we took the last five English wickets for 31. It was brilliant because it was perfect.

It started with the dismissal of Kevin Pietersen in the first over of the day, the same scenario as had occurred back on the final day at the Gabba. This time, he was dismissed exactly how we'd planned. The idea was for Glenn McGrath to aim at a good length, just outside off stump, in the expectation that the batsman would be keen to get his first run of the morning. He jabbed at the third ball and nicked to the keeper. Then Monty Panesar, the nightwatchman, was run out by a sensational piece of fielding by Andrew Symonds: a pick up, throw, and the stumps exploded.

If ever a team could have been distracted by the excitement of an impending victory, it was us that morning, but instead we were at the absolute top of our game. Quickly, they were nine wickets down, and I got sentimental — one last time, it was Warne and McGrath working in tandem, until Anderson hit a slower ball straight up in the air, for Mike Hussey at mid-on to take the catch.

FORTY SIX TO WIN, and it was no longer necessary to play the charade that this was just another day. Many of us — having lived through Shane in Melbourne, and having now seen Glenn being cheered off the ground by the Sydney faithful after taking a wicket with his last ball — were already starting to choke up. We all dearly wanted Justin to bat out our second innings, but there was one guy in our room who wouldn't have been too upset if Haydos had been dismissed. I know I'm not supposed to think like that, whatever the circumstances, and Matty and I are really close, but I really wanted to be out there with Lang at the end of the series. However, I knew that it was exactly what the other guys *didn't* want. Hayden and Langer had become like a good luck charm for us, the flag bearers who led us into many a battle. In was only fitting they were the two out there when the series sweep was completed.

When the two of them strode out to start the innings, the Poms did something I thought was superb: forming a 'guard of honour' for Justin to walk through on his way to the wicket. In our room, we were all struck by what a magnificent tribute it was, a real credit to the person or people in the English camp who inspired it, as it underlined the respect Lang has earned across the cricket world. We did, though, think it was a bit rich for Haydos to walk through it as well! A bit ridiculously, Steve Harmison then stepped up and bowled just about his most dangerous spell of the series, touching up Lang a couple of times. The bruises must have hurt, but deep down, Lang would have loved it, wouldn't have wanted it any other way. It was the way he always played his Test cricket, wear a couple on the ribs, the arm, the fingers, tough it out, get on with it, get through.

Which is what the two of them did, quickly moving us close to victory, at which point I turned to Glenn and said, 'Okay mate, put the pads on.' I could picture the roar of the big crowd (and it was a big crowd, packed for the fourth day straight, despite the fact there would be much less than a complete day's play) as they looked down to see me walk out at the fall of the first wicket ... and instead it would be ... for the very last time ... Glenn McGrath!

Pidge just looked at me and deadpanned, 'Punter, I either bat first or last.'

That cracked everyone up. But ironically there was a fraction of truth in his remark. Whenever Glenn batted at No. 10 in his Test career, he couldn't handle the pressure. He never once reached double figures going in second last, and averaged just 3.25. As last man in, he averaged 7.78.

Meanwhile, out in the middle, the target was down to seven and Lang was growing increasingly nervous, as the stress of not getting out in his final Test innings began to kill him. So he walked down the pitch and said to Haydos with a very serious look on his face, 'Mate, how about a six and a one to finish it?'

What could Matty do? He walked back down the pitch, and said to Andrew Flintoff as the England captain went past, 'The little fella doesn't want much. Just a six and a one to finish it!' And then he promptly slammed Sajid Mahmood over the boundary rope at mid-wicket and pushed him into the covers for the last run of the rubber. Immediately, we were all rushing out on the ground. I reckon I ran so fast to be with Lang, I met him on the edge of the square. As soon as someone managed to separate him and Haydos, I wrapped my arms around them. Soon, there were TV cameras and commentators in among us, and tears everywhere, many of them mine. I just couldn't get the idea out of my head that I would never play another Test match with Langer, McGrath and Warne; it's crazy to think that the fact we'd just won an Ashes series 5–0 was running second among my thought processes. All up, that sadness, plus the joy, the excitement, the pride that came with the knowledge that we'd worked so hard, the satisfaction I felt because our plans had come true, plus just a little sheer relief that it was all over added up to an emotional overload. Gilly, ever the pragmatist, had brought his sunnies out with him, but I wasn't that smart, so until I settled down, I stayed as far from the media as I could.

No one was more emotional than Matty, and he and John Buchanan had a long and heartfelt bear hug out there on the field. Part of that I think, was simply a case of the coach looking after his man, to hide a few of the tears, but mostly it reflected the length of time the two have worked together, the things they've be through. Their relationship is not as close as father and son, but it's more than just coach and cricketer. With Queensland during the '90s, and then with Australian from 2000 to now, Buck has constantly pushed and challenged Haydos. There have been moments when they've clashed, haven't agreed with the other's methods, but the respect has constantly been there, and always they've known they wanted the absolute best for each other, and for the team.

THE HOURS WE SPENT in the rooms went like a blur. All the English boys joined us and most of them stayed for a long time, as did Damien Martyn, which is something I wasn't expecting. It was the first time I'd seen him since Adelaide. Other high-profile visitors included the champion fighter Kostya Tszyu, George Gregan and Phil Waugh from the Wallabies, and the Prime Minister. At one stage, I shared a beer with Andrew Strauss and Paul Collingwood and they quizzed me about how we handled difficult egos within the Aussie team set-up. *Even if I did know*, I thought to myself, *I'm not sure I'd tell you.* The thing about this Australian team is that — while it is made up of a variety of characters with an assortment of interests on the park — on game day every single fellow turns up ready to play.

Shane Watson also came in (once he'd sorted out a problem with one of the gatekeepers at the members' entrance, who didn't like the shirt he was wearing because it didn't have a collar), but Mitchell Johnson couldn't make it, because officials had insisted he stay in Brisbane to play for Queensland in a Twenty20 game. Of course, we could understand the Bulls wanting him, because he is such a good bowler and if a game's worth staging it's worth trying to win, but we felt he'd miss more by not being here feeling part of our triumph than he'd lose by not bowling four overs in the 20-over game.

The mood at the post-game media conference was mostly light-hearted, as the journos had a chance to interview both captains and also all three of the guys playing their final Test. When I was asked to describe the series, I replied simply that it was 'the best little period of my cricketing life'. I then surprised a few people when I nominated the first hour of the Brisbane Test as the key moment of the campaign, but I don't think we should ever underrate the impact of that opening delivery from Harmison, or the manner in which Langer and Hayden then exploded out of the blocks. 'In Adelaide, they batted well on the first day, but otherwise we've been in front in every other Test match as far as I'm concerned,' I continued. 'Brisbane was a magnificent win and the series was set up because of the pressure we put them under immediately in the series.'

Of course, I was asked about the retiring players, and also John Buchanan. I made a point of praising the level of planning that went into our performances, and obviously much of the credit for that has to go to the coach. I then started to describe how he had called the team together before the final day, to offer some advice. 'Buck's never really got a lot to say,' I said. 'He'll have his input but try and keep it pretty short and precise. He just mentioned three things to the group this morning: about controlling the controllables, which is something he's said to us a thousand times, I think; staying in the moment and playing the moment; and ... um ... ah, I mustn't have been listening too close to the third one.'

Once the laughter died down, I attempted to set things straight. 'Whatever Buck has to say is usually spot-on. And those messages he gave us this morning ... or at least two of them ... were spot-on.'

Some time after six o'clock, someone shouted it was time. Not that the party was over, just moving. Initially, we were a bit hesitant when someone proposed the idea of celebrating the end of the series aboard James Packer's 32-metre luxury yacht on Sydney Harbour, not because it wasn't a brilliant concept, but the worry was if the Test concluded not long before sunset, then with all the celebrations, the media commitments and getting back to the hotel, we might not be getting to the wharf until very late. Everything would have been rushed, which is the last thing we wanted, but then we were informed that the boat could be put on standby, there if we wanted it. When the game ended at the time it did, not long after midday, we quickly thought, *gee, that harbour cruise is looking good.*

The night was terrific. There was probably about 40 to 50 people — cricketers, family and friends — on board. Steve Waugh joined us and Glenn McGrath wore his baggy green, which was a little bit ironic only because after the game he'd been chiding Justin Langer for wearing his cap to bed. One pace bowler, who will remain nameless but who did win the man of the match award here in Sydney, didn't handle the experience too well, though, not because he drank too much but because his sea legs are not in the same class as his seamers. One of the highlights of the cruise was to be when Lang would reveal to whom he was handing the privilege of leading the team in the singing of *Under the Southern Cross*, and we hadn't been on the water long when our landlocked quick came up to Lang and me and said, 'Can you get on with it. I'm not sure I'm going to last too long out here.' Eventually, the honour was given to Mike

Hussey, who immediately did the job for the first time, sharing the stage with his predecessor, and doing it brilliantly, while everyone — cricketers, support staff, wives and partners — joined in.

A FEW HOURS EARLIER, IMMEDIATELY after the official on-field presentations had been completed, we'd gone on a 'lap of honour', another terrific experience. We've never stopped appreciating the crowd support throughout the summer, and as we slowly moved around the SCG we took enormous pleasure from all the smiles, handshakes and cheers that came from beyond the boundary rope. I hope all our fans feel they were part of the victory. At one stage, I grabbed Michael Clarke and said quietly, 'How good is this? This is the way we're going to finish every series against England, right?'

I've always been big on passing lessons on, to make sure future generations are aware of the past and can learn from it, because that is what the senior players did when I first came into the team. Guys like me and Pup know how low it feels to lose the Ashes, and now we also know how glorious it is to win them back. One thing I'll do from time to time in future years, as long as I'm part of the Australian team set-up, is tell young blokes coming into the team about 2005 and 2006–07, about the mistakes we made, the hard work, the commitment to excellence. A lot of lessons were learned from the first over at Lord's to the last at Sydney, and we must never forget them.

CHAPTER 12

LANG

I FIRST RAN INTO Justin Langer at the Australian Cricket Academy in 1992–93, when I was there to learn and he was training and also doing a bit of coaching. I first played against him in a first-class match during that same season, in the same game that I first saw Damien Martyn, on the weekend of my 18th birthday. Later that summer, Justin made his Test debut, against the West Indies in Adelaide. Two and a bit years after that, we were on a plane together, flying to the West Indies, the two reserve batsmen on what would evolve into one of the most important cricket tours ever undertaken by the Australian Test team. Neither of us played a Test on that tour, but we did forge a strong friendship and, importantly for our educations, we were on the inside as the team captained by Mark Taylor became the first side to win a series in the West Indies since 1973.

Back then, Lang was a scrappy sort of batsman, an excellent defensive player with a reputation as a fighter. He was in and mostly out of the Test team for six years until 1998–99, when he scored hundreds against Pakistan, England and the West Indies, and I'm not sure he was ever seriously considered for the Australian one-day team, even when he turned his game around from 2001, after he started opening the innings. This was true even though for the next five years, he was as good at putting the bad delivery away as anyone, and scored his Test-match runs at a faster rate than just about every other opening batsman in the game. No instance captured his revamped aggressive style better than the Test against New Zealand at Hobart in late 2001, when Lang was 58 not out before drinks on the first morning. His partner, Matthew Hayden, was still there with him, on 1.

Even with freakish days like that, he could never make the media happy. I can't think of any other Test batsman with his record for runs, hundreds, partnerships and clutch innings who was cut so little slack by the people responsible for writing stories about players whose position in the side is in jeopardy. No matter what he achieved or how much we talked him up, he just never managed to become fashionable. Yet he always kept everyone in and around the team delighted by the way he was training, preparing and playing.

His greatest strength is his character; that was the ingredient that kept him on the championship path. Throughout his Test career, he had an overwhelming desire to be the best that he could be for every single ball he saw. Because of the scrutiny he was always under, and also because he just loved playing cricket for Australia, for Justin it was like every delivery was his last, a great and infectious attitude that rubbed off on a lot of people around the team, including me. I know, after Phil Jaques scored a couple of centuries against the Englishmen before the first Test this summer, that there was talk of Lang being dropped, but I had told him months before that I wanted him to be the guy in Brisbane facing the first ball of the series. I remember clearly at Marto's wedding last May, when Lang whispered to me that he had been thinking about his future. I felt like a teacher who had just been told by the usually dedicated student that the dog had dined out on the homework. 'Mate, don't you ever say that to me again,' I snapped back. 'We're going to beat England, then we'll see what happens after that.'

I knew what the selectors thought, and that such a show of faith would bring something special out of him, and he duly scored 82 and 100 not out in the first Test. As I've already explained, that first knock was crucial, because it set the mood for the entire series.

When I became captain and had to hand on the honour of leading the squad in the singing of the team song, I nominated Justin, because in my view playing cricket for Australia means more to him than anyone else I know. I'll never forget how I informed him about his elevation. We were in Sri Lanka, sitting in a circle in the room after winning the first Test, at Galle. Lang and I were perched on the same esky, it was about time for the song to be sung, but I hadn't told anyone they were going to be in charge. Now I had to do it quietly, so I grabbed my phone and wrote a text message which read: 'Mate, I want you to sing the team song.' Then, instead of hitting 'send', I handed Lang the phone, and watched his face as he read it. The reaction was priceless. He was so emotional he had to duck out to the showers for a moment, to compose himself, after which he took us up to the grand old fort situated on the hill overlooking the Galle ground. There, looking down on the field where Australia had just won a Test against Sri Lanka in Sri Lanka for the first time in 11 and a half years, we sang *Under the Southern Cross* with our shirts off, like professional boxers, and the baggy greens on.

When asked about the greatest accomplishment from his career, Lang didn't go for one of his own innings, or a match in which he played the pivotal role, but for a team achievement — when we won 16 Tests in a row between 1999 and 2001. After we beat the West Indies in 1995, even though he didn't play in the series, the victory fired him up so much he went out and got a small tattoo of a boxing kangaroo splitting a palm tree. Everyone thinks the line about him sleeping with his baggy green is a joke. It might be. I can never remember him fielding in anything else, unless he was at short leg with the Australian helmet on his head and the cap placed carefully in his pocket.

MY FAVOURITE ON-FIELD MOMENT with Lang is a little 'left field', and it might sound a bit callous, but then you've got to know the bloke. He is a ridiculously tough cricketer, one of those batsmen who gets hit quite a bit on the hands, arms and upper body, but never flinches. In the New Year's Test in Sydney in 2005, he was batting against Rana Naved, the Pakistani swing bowler whose top speed would be no more than 135k, probably less. The delivery was a short one, and Lang went back to pull it through it mid-wicket, but it came through a bit quicker than he expected and hit him in the gut. For a moment all was quiet, he took a step ... and then it floored him. The poor bloke was prostrate on the deck, all curled up, and all I could do as I ran down from the non-striker's end was try not to laugh. 'You weak little bastard,' I said when I reached him, as he gasped for breath. 'Get up. I've seen you wear bouncers from bowlers twice as quick as this bloke.'

He was trying to say something to me, but nothing was coming out of his mouth. In his mind, I'm sure he was hating the embarrassment, but laughing at himself, too. He can do that. It's something Haydos and I constantly remind him about — the day he was decked by Rana Naved.

Off the field, we've had plenty of good times. He loves his football, claims to be a West Coast Eagles fan, but I think he's a Kangaroos man at heart. He says they're his 'second team', but I think he might have followed North Melbourne before the Eagles entered the VFL and you really never forget your first relationship. Throughout his Test career, he was intense on the field and at training, but afterwards, if we'd won an important game or especially a series, he'd enjoy a few beers and a cigar, usually with his shirt off but always with the baggy green glued on. One thing he and I always did, after a big win and a couple of quiet ones, was to have a wrestle, no holds barred, sometimes up to half an hour, which might leave us with a few scratches on the nose the following day. After we played Zimbabwe in 2003, the game in Perth in which Matty Hayden scored a then Test record 380, John Buchanan had a go at the team because he thought we didn't celebrate appropriately, that we seemed keener to get out of the dressing room and on our way home than stay to dwell on what we'd achieved. So after the next Test, in Sydney, Lang and I thought we'd set things straight by putting on a classic, and we grappled for ages, to the point that the rest of the team got physical, too, and there were friendly skirmishes everywhere, scrums in the room, and eventually a big wooden bench was busted. Our wrestles became a tradition, and the one after the fifth Test this season took on extra significance, because it was our last. I almost nailed him this time.

I learned a lot from Lang. More than anything, he taught me that you must never take anything for granted. It's no good being ready for the opening delivery some of the time; it has to be *every time*. That doesn't mean we have to all prepare the same way, but to not be ready is a crime. Lang is a guy who can stay in the nets and bat and bat and bat for hours at a time, until he feels like he's hitting the ball all right. Only then does he feel prepared for battle. Haydos works the same way, and Steve Waugh was like that, too. I'm different; usually, if I'm not having a great net, I'm better off getting out of there, going away, and returning later, maybe tomorrow, and starting again. If I've been having a good run, one bad net session is never going to damage my confidence.

But on game day, whatever our methods, we were all right to go, and we knew it. The strength that gave us could be awesome.

I'M NOT USUALLY BIG on statistics, but in Lang's case I reckon they're important, because they emphasise the extent of his contribution to the Australian cause. His Test career aggregate of 7696 runs puts him sixth all-time among Australian batsmen, behind Allan Border, Steve Waugh, Mark Waugh, Matthew Hayden and me. His 23 Test hundreds is seventh most scored by Australians, behind Steve Waugh, Sir Donald Bradman, Border, Hayden, Greg Chappell and me. His three Test double centuries ties him with Bob Simpson for fourth on the Australian all-time list. Twenty-four Australians have played 30 Test innings and averaged more over their careers than Lang's 45.27, and of these men, seven were openers: Hayden (53.01), Bill Ponsford (48.23), Bill Lawry (47.15, Bill Brown (46.82), Simpson (46.82), Arthur Morris (46.49) and Bill Woodfull (46.00).

The record of Langer and Hayden as an opening partnership is truly magnificent. The excellent cricket stats website *howstat.com.au* tells me that they went out first together in 64 Tests and totalled 5655 runs at an average of 51.41. Only the West Indies pair, Gordon Greenidge and Desmond Haynes, scored more: 6482 at 46.63. The closest Australian pair to Langer and Hayden, in terms of total runs, is Mark Taylor and Michael Slater, who put together 3887 runs as a partnership, at 51.14.

Langer and Hayden opened the batting for us 113 times, and they went past 50 together on 38 occasions. One out of three times they opened up, Australia made it to 50 before the first wicket fell. They shared 14 century partnerships, and six double-century stands. For the bloke batting three, these numbers represented a very comforting reality.

The three of us came to think of ourselves as the 'engine room' of the Australian batting order, even though we had contrasting styles and various ways of getting the job done. A winning attitude was the thing we had in common, a pride in our country and a great love for the game. But something as simple as the way Lang and I treated our bats showed how we could be different. Once I've found a good bat and I'm getting some runs with it, I'll keep it until it can't be used any more, whereas Lang is never happy, the handle feels strange, or he's forever sticking tape over the blade, hoping to get it right.

Against England in 2002–03, he made a brilliant 250 at the MCG, which I think might have been his best innings (Lang goes for the 127 he scored against Pakistan in Hobart in 1999–2000, when he and Adam Gilchrist took us from 5–126 to 6–364, chasing 367, to win us a Test most thought lost, as his best knock). I reckon he changed his bat at least once every session during that epic double hundred. Just before a resumption in play, the little bloke would decide he needed a heavier bat, so he'd pick one out of his kit, rehearse a few shots in front of a mirror, and out he'd go. But after an hour, he'd signal to the rooms that he needed to make another swap. With Lang, everything had to be perfect. When he was in the Australian team, it often was.

CHAPTER 13

COMMONWEALTH BANK SERIES

Tuesday, January 9

Twenty20 International, at Sydney (January 9): Australia 5–221
(20 overs: AC Gilchrist 48, RT Ponting 47, CL White 40*; MS Panesar 2–40)
defeated England 9–144 (BW Hilfenhaus 2–16, A Symonds 2–24) by 77 runs

TONIGHT'S TWENTY20 GAME WAS remarkably popular, drawing a vibrant capacity crowd to the SCG and colossal TV ratings. The game itself was full of big hits and plenty of laughs, and though I don't yet find Twenty20 as enjoyable as other forms of cricket, it was impossible not to notice that the crowd was having a really good time.

The Australian team had a couple of new faces in Victoria's Shane Harwood and Tasmania's Ben Hilfenhaus, while Cameron White enjoyed his return to Australian colours by smashing 40 from 20 balls, including four enormous sixes. As was the case last season, we had our nicknames on our back, and a couple of them generated some discussion. Adam Gilchrist decided to have

'Church' sown across his shoulders, which goes back to a tour some years back when a fan asked for his autograph by saying, 'Aren't you Eric Gilchurch?' I actually think Gilly would be very happy if we called him 'Churchy' all the time! Andrew Symonds went for 'Roy', which I know the majority of people and especially his mates from Queenslanders use when they're talking to or about him, but I've always called him Symmo. Same with Brad Hogg — many people refer to him as George (after his first name, as in George Bradley Hogg), but he'll always be 'Hoggy' to me.

Cameron White is 'Bear', because he resembles the polar bear from the Bundy Rum commercials, and Nathan Bracken went with 'Andy G', after the co-host of *Australian Idol*, who has a similarly dud haircut. Shane Harwood is 'Stickers', because of his predilection for tattoos, while Michael Clarke went with 'Clarkey', because, I think, he feels he's outgrown 'Pup'. The other nicknames — Haydos, Huss and Hilfy — speak for themselves, and I liked the line from one slightly cynical individual who, as he pondered nicknames of ex-players such as Warney, Lang and Heals, pointed out that if Mike Hussey's surname was Huss his nickname would be Hussey.

The game itself, which we won comfortably, reinforced my view that Twenty20 cricket is a total power game. It doesn't really pay to be subtle, to try, for example, to play a delicate leg glance instead of trying to club another six over mid-wicket. We hit 14 sixes in 20 overs. The nature of the game also means that luck is as important as tactics, which I think means the fans might tire of the game quickly if administrators fail to get the balance right. In my opinion, too much of this style of cricket could hurt rather than help the sport in the long run. But we definitely had a good time tonight as we ran away with the contest, and as I looked around the happy faces at the ground I couldn't help but think that this annual Twenty20 international is now locked into the cricket calendar. And looking forward to the one-dayers, I also pondered the thought that if we can smash 5–221 from 20 overs on an Australian ground, there's no reason why a team can't make 400 from 50, too.

From a cricket perspective, perhaps the most interesting time of the game was when Andrew Flintoff came on to bowl. It was always hard during the Test series to get a gauge on how much Flintoff's surgically-repaired ankle was bothering him, but there was no doubt that while he bowled well at various times, his pace was down on what he delivered in 2005. But then, suddenly, in this game, he started bowling like the wind, at one point hitting Cameron White flush on the helmet. Maybe it was because he only had to bowl four overs, so he could afford to let himself go, or perhaps it was because Michael Vaughan is back as captain, which freed him of the shackles of the leadership. Whatever the reason, it seemed almost incongruous that he'd bowl his fastest spell of the tour in what was, in many respects, an exhibition game.

Saturday, January 13

Commonwealth Bank Series Game 1, at Melbourne (January 12):
England 8–242 (50 overs: KP Pietersen 82, A Flintoff 47*, PD Collingwood 43; NW Bracken 3–46) lost to Australia 2–246 (45.2 overs: RT Ponting 82*, AC Gilchrist 60, MJ Clarke 57) by eight wickets

THE UNIFORMS WE'VE BEEN given for this summer's Commonwealth Bank Series (the successor to last year's VB Series) are unlike anything we've been decked out in before. The dark-green colour matches that of the baggy green cap, while the shirts come complete with a 'sun protection neckline' and a zip neck at the front. They are lighter than the old shirts, and apparently the fabric represents the very latest in garment technology. They look classy, and the fact that the zip at the front enables us to keep the collar 'up' — and thus protect the backs of our necks from the summer sun — provides an added bonus.

Outside this tournament, we'll keep the predominantly gold uniforms in one-day internationals, because that is accepted across the cricket world as our national colour, but for home series — especially when there is no colour clash with the opposing teams — I'd be more than happy to keep the sharp green look.

WHAT I AM SEEKING from the members of the Australian one-day team over the next four months is a small but critical improvement in each of our games that when combined will make us an even better team than we've been in the past. It's important we keep trying to stretch ourselves. Before the first game in the competition, against England in Melbourne — a game in which Kevin Pietersen broke a rib after he was struck on the body while trying to charge Glenn McGrath — we scheduled a team meeting at which we tried to compare where we are now compared to the same time in 2003, when we were preparing for the World Cup in South Africa. The view that came out of that meeting is that we have to be at least a five per cent better team than what we were four years ago if we want to win the World Cup this time round. Based on what we did in the Champions Trophy, I think it's fair to say that the team, as a unit, is working well, so the onus is on each of us as individuals to ask, *What little things can I do to be a better player?*

In my case, I've pondered the wickets we will be likely to see in the Caribbean, and then tried to imagine how opposition teams will try to exploit these conditions when they are bowling to me. Most likely, quite a few of the middle overs during games at the Cup will be bowled by spin bowlers, and I feel I need to expand the range of shots I have available to me in these circumstances. In the past, if a good right-arm off-spinner has bowled a leg-stump line to me, I have often found it difficult to get him away, so I've resolved that whenever I come across an offie, maybe England's James Dalrymple, I'll try to stay on leg-side of the right delivery and hit it 'inside out' over cover. Most offies in one-day cricket work with three men on the fence on the leg-side, leaving a big gap on the boundary between point and long-off, but I haven't always been able to exploit that. Hopefully, this can change.

Monday, January 22

Commonwealth Bank Series Game 2, at Hobart (January 14): Australia 8–289 (50 overs: A Symonds 69, AC Gilchrist 61, CL White 45; SE Bond 4–61) defeated New Zealand 184 (38.3 overs: RL Taylor 84) by 105 runs

Commonwealth Bank Series Game 3, at Hobart (January 16): New Zealand 9–205 (50 overs: NJ Astle 45; JM Anderson 4–42) lost to England 7–206 (49.5 overs: A Flintoff 72*, IR Bell 45) by seven wickets

Commonwealth Bank Series Game 4, at Brisbane (January 19): England 155 (42 overs: NW Bracken 3–24, GD McGrath 3–24) lost to Australia 6–156 (38.4 overs: MEK Hussey 46*; J Lewis 4–36) by four wickets

Commonwealth Bank Series Game 5, at Sydney (January 21): New Zealand 218 (47.4 overs: CD McMillan 89; SR Clark 4–54, GD McGrath 3–24) lost to Australia 8–224 (48.4 overs: MJ Clarke 75, MEK Hussey 65*) by two wickets

IT WASN'T TOO LONG ago that the Australian team used to start the home one-day series slowly, as if they were suffering from some sort of hangover after the Test matches. However, this is now a thing of the past, and we began the 2006–07 competition in some style, thrashing England at Melbourne and New Zealand at Hobart. I sensed after these two games that some observers were fearful the whole summer might turn into one giant whitewash, but experience has taught me that it is almost impossible to maintain such dominance throughout an entire season, and within the Australian camp the fact that we've reshaped our training this year, in response to the extended program we're facing, leaves us wondering what these changes might do to us in the short-term.

The coaching staff has decided to really pump the fitness work into us through most of January, with an eye to the World Cup, and this is being done with little consideration for our immediate playing schedule. During the past week and a half, we have trained much harder on the day before a game than we've done in the past, and at other times we've completed substantially more 'physical' work than usual, rather than focusing on our post-game recovery or skills work in preparation for the next game. I'm sure this workload isn't ideal at a time when we are playing so regularly, but in a way I see it as a good test for us. We should always be ready to play, whatever is put in front of us.

The reality that this fitness work might be impinging on our cricket became apparent in Brisbane, when we beat England by four wickets in a low-scoring game. All the players who were up there went through a full-scale fitness test the day before the game, and a few blokes mentioned to me afterwards that they needed time on game day to run the stiffness and soreness out of their system. I had that game off, instead staying in Sydney for my annual short break (which received little attention this year, I guess because we're winning), so I must confess I was a little sceptical. But then I went through my fitness test on the following afternoon, 24 hours before we edged out New Zealand by two wickets at the SCG. This examination involved a beep test, sprint work, just everything they could think of, and it did knock me about a bit.

Saturday, February 3

Commonwealth Bank Series Game 6, at Adelaide (January 23): New Zealand 210 (50 overs: JDP Oram 86; A Flintoff 4–21) defeated England 120 (37.5 overs: EC Joyce 47; DL Vettori 4–24, JEC Franklin 3–17) by 90 runs

Commonwealth Bank Series Game 7, at Adelaide (January 26): England 110 (34.3 overs: MG Johnson 4–45) lost to Australia 1–111 (24.3 overs: RT Ponting 51*) by nine wickets

Commonwealth Bank Series Game 8, at Perth (January 28): Australia 5–343 (50 overs: ML Hayden 117, RT Ponting 111) defeated New Zealand 5–335 (50 overs: JDP Oram 101*, L Vincent 66, BB McCullum 46*) by eight runs

Commonwealth Bank Series Game 9, at Perth (January 30): New Zealand 7–318 (50 overs: L Vincent 76, RL Taylor 71, JDP Oram 54*; LE Plunkett 3–54) defeated England 8–260 (50 overs: EC Joyce 66, PA Nixon 49) by 58 runs

Commonwealth Bank Series Game 10, at Sydney (February 2): England 7–292 (50 overs: EC Joyce 107, IR Bell 51) defeated Australia 200 (38.5 overs: ML Hayden 51; LE Plunkett 3–24) by 92 runs

AFTER OUR FOURTH GAME of the competition, our halfway point of the qualifying games, I made a public plea to our batsmen, me included, to pick up our games. Yes, we were unbeaten, but my feeling was there were a few areas we needed to improve. 'The last couple of games we've played we haven't been chasing big totals,' I said, 'and we've managed just to scrape across the line both times.' In both instances, it was only one or two batsmen (Hussey in Brisbane; Hussey and Clarke in Sydney) who batted well, after the rest of the top-order fell cheaply. At around the same time, John Buchanan went in a different direction, complaining about the mediocre form of our opponents.

'Unless there is an unbelievable turn around in the playing performances of all sides,' he wrote in a regular column that is posted on the Cricket Australia website, 'New Zealand and England should be fighting it out for second place and a place in the finals.' I was surprised Buck had gone public in this fashion, but I also knew he had been concerned after the first two games that he hadn't been able to gauge how we were going, because we'd won those matches easily. 'Our ability to deliver yorkers, length balls, bouncers, variety balls (such as slower balls, cutters, etc) has not been placed under constant scrutiny by an opposition batting lineup,' he continued. 'This testing of our bowlers' response to situations when we have lost control (temporarily hopefully) is not happening. In essence, the batting efforts of our opposition are not assisting the development of our bowlers' one-day skills and the decision making that accompanies being placed under the microscope of competition. And while this is not occurring, we cannot have our fielding tested also for its ability to create and make opportunities.'

I'm not sure if Buck was actually trying to cause some trouble, to add some spice to the contests, but his comments started to look out of place when our form fell away and England — despite missing Pietersen, Harmison and Vaughan — came back to beat us in our seventh one-dayer of the summer, played at Sydney yesterday, on the back of an Ed Joyce century. This setback came five days after the New Zealanders — most notably Jacob Oram, who smashed a hundred off 72 deliveries — showed in Perth that we do still have a problem conceding runs in the late overs of a one-day innings.

'Our bowlers, in the last 30 overs of that game, were put under some pretty intense pressure and we didn't cope as well as I would have liked,' I commented after Oram and Brendon McCullum had belted us to distant parts of the WACA, to get the Black Caps within nine runs of a very unlikely victory. 'Our lengths towards the end were all wrong. I am disappointed with the way we responded and reacted, and hopefully we will improve on that when the finals come around.'

OPENING THE BATTING FOR the Black Caps in that Perth game was Lou Vincent, who was making his first appearance in the competition as a replacement for Nathan Astle. He scored 66, had a bit to say on the field, but made a bigger impact with his comments after the game, when he tagged us as egotistical and complained that we thought we were bigger than the game. 'They're very close-knit,' Vincent was quoted as saying. 'They hunt like a pack of dogs. There's not just one guy going at you, there's a little bit here, a little bit there. I mean, I love that part of the game, I think it's brilliant but as soon as they start calling you all sorts of stuff it gets a bit tiring. I personally think that they think they're bigger than the game ...'

Frankly, I don't care what Lou Vincent thinks, and I take some pride in his statement that we 'hunt like a pack of dogs'. I know it wasn't meant as a compliment but it captures precisely the sort of environment we want to create out on the field. There were some 'edgy' moments during the game at the WACA, which started as some words between Vincent and Andrew Symonds, and then Michael Clarke jumped in to support his mate.

Eventually, a few of us were into him. It was good, tough but fair cricket, and he should have enjoyed it.

DROPPING A GAME TO England was very disappointing, but losing Andrew Symonds to a serious injury was much worse. Symmo hurt his upper arm while batting in that game at the SCG, as our pursuit of the Poms' 7–292 went badly wrong, and it is one of those injuries we knew was a bad one from pretty much the moment it happened. Symmo is not a bloke to show pain easily. Our physio, Alex Kountouris, went out and realised straightaway just by looking at his arm and hearing the pain in Symmo's voice that he had done some serious damage to his right bicep, but rather than bringing the injured man back with him, he was talked into taping it up.

'He wants to keep going,' Alex explained when he returned to the dressing room. 'He promised me he'll just work the ball around … unless he sees something that's got to go. Then it's got to go.'

A couple of people chuckled. 'Typical Roy,' someone said. But I wasn't amused. After he continued to feel for the arm during the next couple of overs, I said to Alex, 'Mate, we've got a World Cup just round the corner, you've got to go and get him.'

When Symmo came in, the bicep was basically sitting in a clump just about his elbow. The muscle was ruptured, and we all had the same despondent thought about the World Cup: *He's gone.* I was told that he'd need at least three months, time we did not have, though Symmo was quick to tell us that he's a quick healer. I dug out my World Cup itinerary, did some mental arithmetic, and worked out it that the Super Eights stage of the World Cup is due to begin in eight weeks. However, my understanding is that if we pick Symmo injured and he doesn't recover in time then we'll have to cop it sweet — we won't be able to seek a replacement because the injury was suffered before the team was chosen. Thus, we could be putting ourselves at a significant disadvantage if we pick him and he doesn't come up, but I know how important and influential a player he is for our team. He'd make anyone's World XI one-day side. What he gives our team with his batting, fielding and bowling is prodigious, and for that reason I reckon taking him with us is worth the risk. I hope the selectors agree with me.

Monday, February 5

Commonwealth Bank Series Game 11, at Melbourne (February 4):
New Zealand 7–290 (50 overs: L Vincent 90, PG Fulton 60) lost to Australia 5–291 (48.2 overs: RT Ponting 104, BJ Hodge 99*) by five wickets

WITH SYMMO OUT, BRAD Hodge kept his place in the side for the game against New Zealand at the MCG. I reckon he was just about playing for his international cricket life, because after being dropped from the test team last season (a little unluckily, after scoring a double hundred in just his third Test) he had scored 0 and 1 in his two innings in this season's Commonwealth Bank series. One more failure might have been the end of him, but instead he played beautifully, sharing a 154-run third-wicket partnership with his captain and finishing 99 not out.

I've known Hodgey since we were teenagers and have never had any doubts about his batting ability. I saw this innings in front of his home crowd as terrific reward for him in itself, because rather than moping after being dropped he had gone back to domestic cricket and worked hard and smart to be the best player he can be. He made this point clear to me when he compiled a big hundred in the Pura Cup game against me earlier in the season, when I had Ben Hilfenhaus test him out with some short stuff and he came through more than unscathed.

MOMENTUM IS EVERYTHING IN modern cricket, especially modern one-day cricket, and when a batting team gets going it can be hard to stop. A fielding team under pressure will drop two or three catches in a row as the pressure builds, while bowlers often seem to get in a rut where they keep bowling the wrong line or length. Batsmen have learned to attack from the jump, so one wicket might not change anything; you need two, three or four. Further adding to the pressure on the fielders, the way many of the top batsmen run between wickets these days is exceptional.

Twenty years ago, a brilliant runner such as Dean Jones stood out, because he was a pioneer, but today every team has half a dozen blokes who work between the wickets that way. Back in Deano's day, people thought he was a champion runner because he was quick, but that was only part of it. He had a great technique which allowed him to grab every run. At training these days, we do sprint work and practise pushing the ball into gaps and running, but more importantly we work on getting our turns right, to save every scrap of ground we can. Video replays demonstrate that many run outs are a matter of centimetres, one way or the other.

A target of eight or nine runs an over in the last 10 is rarely intimidating, especially if you have wickets in hand and the opposition scored at that rate during the latter part of their innings. That's what I kept saying to Hodgey when we were hunting the target down against New Zealand in Melbourne. I'd made a point of checking exactly how quickly the Kiwis had rattled along at the end of their innings: 86 from their last 10; 54 from their final five. After 32 overs, we needed more than eight an over, and Hodgey, who'd scored only 19 from 37, was concerned. But I told him not to worry. 'Mate, if they can score eight-and-a-half from their last 10 overs, so can we.' With eight overs to go, the required rate was exactly eight; with five to go it was closer to seven-and-a-half. We finished up winning with 10 balls to spare, and Hodgey had faced only 86 deliveries.

Wednesday, February 7

Commonwealth Bank Series Game 12, at Brisbane (February 6):
England 7–270 (50 overs: PD Collingwood 106, AJ Strauss 55; SE Bond 4–46) defeated New Zealand 8–256 (50 overs: SP Fleming 106; LE Plunkett 3–60) by 14 runs

SYMMO WENT UNDER THE surgeon's knife two days back, and 24 hours later he was with us at the Allan Border Medal night. 'When I woke up from the operation I felt like my arm had been shot off,' he said, 'but now I feel pretty good.' As early as yesterday morning, down at the hotel reception, he had tried (with a cheeky grin) to convince me about all the movement he already has in the joint! I'm not sure whether finishing second in the one-day player of the year voting would have made his arm feel better or worse, given that he could easily have won if he hadn't missed the high-scoring game against New Zealand in which his replacement, Brad Hodge, scored 99 not out.

I had a real good night as far as the awards went, but just about my most priceless memory of the evening was the look on Brett Lee's face when they showed, up on the big screen in all its glory, the video of the pop song he has just recorded in India. We thought it was sensational, but Bing didn't seem quite so keen. Another moment, not nearly as amusing, came when a senior journalist came up to me to say how much he enjoyed the yarn he'd heard about the game in Sydney against New Zealand, when Michael Clarke had to bat at No. 3 because I was listening to a greyhound race. 'What are you talking about?' I said. 'That never happened.'

'Gee, that's no good,' the scribe replied. 'I put it in my column.'

All I could do was shake my head. I don't know where he got the story from, but it was completely false. What happened was no more complicated or sinister than a wicket fell when I was having a toilet break. If it had happened a ball or two later, I'd have been fine. As it turned out, Pup scored 75 and won us the game, on a pitch that wasn't easy to bat on because it had a crack running right along the middle of it, and the Kiwi bowlers aimed at it all night. I batted four and was out for 5.

IN MY VIEW, THE Australian cricketer of last year was Mike Hussey, who I just think has been fantastic from the day he first wore the baggy green, and has been remarkably consistent in both forms of the game. So I was surprised to win the Border Medal, and genuinely stunned to be named both Test and one-day cricketer of the year — especially the former, because I thought Shane Warne was a certainty. Chris Rogers was the player of the year from Australian domestic cricket, my Tassie team-mate Ben Hilfenhaus won the Bradman young cricketer-of-the-year award, Lisa Sthalekar was the women's player of the year, and Richie Benaud and Charlie Macartney were inducted into the Australian Cricket Hall of Fame.

It was a good night this year, with fitting tributes paid to our retiring warriors. But for me the best thing about the entire show was that 12 months earlier I had stood up there and almost guaranteed that a year on I would be captain of a better Australian team which had achieved more impressive results. At the start of 2006, we had played well in Tests against the World XI, the West Indies and South Africa, but the memory of the Ashes loss cut deep. It was good to be able to stand up there last night, knowing that we had delivered on my promise.

EARLIER TODAY, I WAS at Trinity Grammar School in Melbourne to have a yarn with the members of the Kangaroos AFL team. In one way, it was just a catch-up, and I always enjoy mixing with the lads from my favourite team, but I was also invited to speak to them as a group about how I go about my cricket business and how the Australian team has gone about improving in the last 18 months. This struck a chord with the footballers, who are seeking to rebound from an unsuccessful 2006 season. The session started with a Q&A between me and Channel Nine's James Brayshaw, who is on the board at the Kangaroos, and then I answered a few questions from the lads.

I loved footy as a kid, and had a little bit of ability, enough to get invited to an under-16 state training camp in Hobart. The idea was that they'd choose the rep team after the camp, and I'll never forget my dad's last words to me as I was getting ready to go. 'Don't you dare get yourself picked in that team,' he said firmly. Like me, his preference was that I set out on a cricket career. Last year in my diary I told the story of the time in India when I bought a DVD player to watch some Kangaroos DVDs that had been sent over to me, because the hotel we were staying at didn't have players in the rooms. But that is not the only slightly crazy example of my devotion to the men in blue and white.

The Australian cricket team was in Galle on Grand Final day 1999: Kangaroos v Carlton. The fourth day was the Saturday, and it dawned wet and miserable, with little chance of any cricket for the day. As soon as play was called off, I raced back to the team hotel and called a mate of mine in Tassie, a Carlton fan, and asked him if he could put his phone up next to his television. And that's how I heard the final quarter, as the Kangaroos ran away to a 35-point victory. It was magic. The mobile charges were around $10 per minute, and it cost me a fortune. But it was worth every penny.

Monday, February 12

Commonwealth Bank Series First Final, at Melbourne (February 9):
Australia 252 (48.3 overs: ML Hayden 82, RT Ponting 75; A Flintoff 3–41) lost to England 6–253 (49.3 overs: PD Collingwood 120*, IR Bell 65; B Lee 3–41) by four wickets

Commonwealth Bank Series Second Final, at Sydney (February 11):
England 8–246 (50 overs: PD Collingwood 70, MB Loye 45, A Flintoff 42) defeated Australia 8–152 (33 overs: BJ Hodge 49; LE Plunkett 3–43) by 34 runs (D/L method)

I FEEL SOMEWHAT GUTTED over the way our home summer ended, with us losing the finals to England in two straight games. I'm very confident we'll bounce back at the World Cup, but disappointed our winning run has ended in such a miserable fashion. I kept saying to the guys that — because we'd worked so hard for so long — I didn't think England deserved to win a game against us. However, I have to give the Poms credit, because it takes some character to find some form when things have been going badly for so long, especially when some of your best players are unavailable.

The two players most responsible for their revival were Paul Collingwood, who climbed out of a prolonged slump to top-score for England in three games straight, and the unheralded

Liam Plunkett, who had a real night out in yesterday's second final, taking three top wickets in his first four overs. We had talked about the fact Plunkett could be dangerous in the right conditions, because he has the ability to swing the new ball at reasonable pace, so we didn't underestimate him. He was just too good for us.

Inevitably, questions were asked about our training program. All I hope is that no one within the team is using it as an excuse. We're professionals, and we have to be able to carry little niggles and be tired but still be able to win, and if the process we've been through has shown that we're not up to that yet, then we've got some more work to do. I reckon we'll benefit big-time from what we've been through in the past month. And it's funny, the hardest training session we did over the past month occurred in the lead-up to the game against England in Adelaide on Australia Day, when we bowled them out for 110 and got the runs in 25 overs.

I am disappointed we couldn't raise our games when we needed to in the finals. About the only highlight for us was that Glenn McGrath managed to dismiss England keeper Paul Nixon with his last ball in one-day international cricket in Australia. Though we'd conceded too many runs in a few of our qualifying games, we'd still played some reasonable cricket, but in the finals we went backwards, instead of returning to our best form. This was highly disappointing, but I did wonder about some of the media comments, which suggested we were 'embarrassing', 'humiliated' and that our World Cup campaign was 'unravelling'. I'm glad we're not as negative as they are.

'As far as our World Cup preparations are going at the moment, I don't think this really changes too much,' I said at the media conference after we'd lost the second final. 'Though I'm sure the selectors will now be asking a few more questions of me at their meeting in regard to selection for the World Cup squad.'

That meeting will be happening today, because the ICC had ruled that all World Cup line-ups must be lodged by tomorrow night.

Wednesday, February 14

THERE WERE A COUPLE of surprises when our World Cup squad was announced yesterday, most notably that Brad Haddin has been chosen to provide cover for Adam Gilchrist (who will be allowed to leave for the Caribbean after the rest of the squad, so he can spend some time with his new baby). Hadds will also come in handy in the group games, because it is extremely unlikely that Andrew Symonds will be available at that stage, as he continues his recovery from his bicep injury. The decision to select Symmo was made a lot easier when we were informed that our earlier understanding was wrong, that he can be replaced if he does not recover in time. As long as a player is genuinely injured, and can demonstrate that to the tournament's medical committee, then a substitute can be brought in. What we can't do is leave Symmo out because he's not fit, but then bring him into the squad during the tournament to replace a healthy player because he has made a sudden recovery.

The more I'd thought about the dilemma as to whether we should pick him, even before I knew he could be replaced, the more I'd come to the view that we had to take the risk. If he is away with us, he will obviously get the best possible treatment from our support staff, which will hasten his recuperation and make it more likely he'll be able to contribute. He'll also be able to do all the fitness work that doesn't involve his right arm, so his body will be ready to go from the day he's okay to play.

I also thought about Symmo's off-field influence, that unique, bubbly personality he brings to the group. Put simply, he's a terrific bloke to have around. He works very hard on his game, but he also possesses that light-hearted touch around the dressing-room and that ability to tell the right joke at the right time that keeps things in perspective. That boost to team spirit he provides was one of the reasons I pushed for him to be included in the 2003 World Cup side, and nothing has changed in the four years since. Even if he's not playing in the West Indies, he'll still be an excellent and experienced team-mate, who'll add plenty to the squad set-up.

In other major selection news, Shaun Tait was preferred to Stuart Clark, while Brad Hogg and Shane Watson won the all-rounder spots, meaning Cameron White unluckily missed out. The full squad is: Ricky Ponting (captain), Adam Gilchrist (vice-captain), Nathan Bracken, Michael Clarke, Brad Haddin, Matthew Hayden, Brad Hodge, Brad Hogg, Michael Hussey, Mitchell Johnson, Brett Lee, Glenn McGrath, Andrew Symonds, Shaun Tait, Shane Watson.

The decision to choose Tait over Clark was a tough one, but I like the 'X factor' Taity offers us — he can bowl quick, and contain and even threaten batsmen in the powerplays. I thought he did well against New Zealand in our last Commonwealth Bank game before the finals, when he bowled two overs during a powerplay and conceded a single, and then he came back later and bowled three overs for five runs between overs 32 and 36. Whenever Taity gets his yorker right, he'll be handy in the latter overs of an innings, and with the old ball a chance to reverse swing in the West Indies, he can take advantage of that swing if it happens as well. Picking him over the player of the series from the Ashes Tests is a gamble, and I do feel very sorry for Stuey, but I see this selection as an attacking move, and I'll always welcome that.

I also don't believe that Sarf's omission is a sign his one-day career is over, that from now he is considered a Test-match cricketer. For me, he's a natural to replace Glenn McGrath in our one-day line-up from the start of next season.

CHAPTER 14

CHAPPELL–HADLEE TROPHY

Friday, February 16

Chappell–Hadlee Trophy Series Game 1, at Wellington (February 16):
Australia 148 (49.3 overs: MEK Hussey 42; SE Bond 5–23) lost to New Zealand
0–149 (27 overs: L Vincent 73, SP Fleming 70) by 10 wickets

WE MADE A MISTAKE last year when I scheduled my mid-season
break to coincide with the Australia Day game in Adelaide. It
didn't look good for the Aussie cricket captain to miss that
particular day.

With hindsight it shouldn't have happened, and it was the
main reason I had my time off this year earlier in the
tournament, which seemed to keep everyone happy. However,
there was some quite strident criticism in the papers when it
was announced that Adam Gilchrist and I would miss the
Chappell–Hadlee Trophy series, on the basis that sending a
team without its usual captain and vice-captain meant we
weren't treating the games seriously.

I can't help noticing that the knockers had come out after we've lost a couple of games. The reality is that Gilly desperately needs a break — he's played in every game, Tests, one-dayers and Twenty20, since the start of the Champions Trophy — and furthermore, his wife Mel is very pregnant with their third child, and everyone agrees it can't be a bad thing for him to spend a little time with his family. But I was a different matter. I sensed people just didn't believe my reason for withdrawing from the short tour, to the point that one newspaper positioned a photographer at each end of my street, like private detectives behind a tree, trying to prove I'd made a fake worker's compensation claim.

Maybe the wrong perception was created by the fact that my unavailability for New Zealand was announced on the same day I scored a run-a-ball 75 in the first Commonwealth Bank final in Melbourne. But my back has been causing me problems throughout the summer, most notably during the Gabba Test when I didn't field on the fourth day, and it made a lot of sense for me to listen to our medical staff's advice and give my spine a break before the World Cup. The day after the second final, I received three cortisone injections, which will reduce the inflammation around the bone spurs on my vertebrae and should get me through the next couple of months.

I HAD ALSO MISSED our second-last qualifying game for the Commonwealth Bank Series, against England in Sydney, because of a hip injury. I hurt it in the nets the day before that game, 24 hours after I'd been put through another full-on fitness test. Brett Lee also missed the game, and in a roundabout way it might have cost him a trip to the World Cup. Bing had been a mainstay through all the cricket we'd played to that point of our long season, and because he was suffering a couple of little 'niggles', I was keen for him to do as I was doing, and miss the short trip to New Zealand.

However, after he was rested for the game at the SCG, his manager publicly criticised the decision and that led to a change of heart.

I was annoyed at this intervention, because we had spoken to the bowling group at the start of the competition, and explained that everyone was going to miss out at some stage. Brett did go to New Zealand and almost immediately did serious damage to his ankle at training at the Basin Reserve at Wellington. My understanding is that X-rays have cleared Brett of a broken bone, but we won't know the extent of the ligament damage until tomorrow at the earliest. It doesn't seem good, though, and it won't surprise me if he is ruled out of the World Cup.

The irony is twofold: one, if he'd stayed at home he probably wouldn't have been hurt; and two, because of the rotation policy that Bing's manager was complaining about, we are better placed to cover for him, as his replacement will have had some experience playing with the one-day team in recent weeks. However, there is no doubt that losing the best one-day bowler in the game would be a major setback.

Then, 24 hours later, it was announced that Michael Clarke has a hip problem and is coming home to get his body right for the West Indies. With Symmo also in grave doubt, the squad is looking a little frayed and I'm beginning to feel the same way I did in 2003, when Michael Bevan, Shane Watson and Jason Gillespie all had injury concerns, Darren Lehmann was suspended for the first game, and Shane Warne tested positive for a diuretic.

Monday, February 19

Chappell–Hadlee Trophy Series Game 2, at Auckland (February 18):
Australia 4–336 (50 overs: MEK Hussey 105, BJ Hodge 97*, BJ Haddin 49,
CL White 42*) lost to New Zealand 5–340 (48.4 overs: RL Taylor 117,
PG Fulton 76*, CD McMillan 52) by five wickets

TROY COOLEY IS NOT in New Zealand with the team. Instead, he is currently working at Cricket Australia's Centre of Excellence in Brisbane, where he'll be until we depart for the World Cup. So Troy has been like me, watching the games on television, and I'm sure he would have similarly been dismayed by the way the Kiwis chased down a huge total in yesterday's game at Eden Park in Auckland.

When some reporters cornered our bowling coach after the game, he conceded his troops had 'some work to do', but then he reminded everyone that 'this group of bowlers did a great job of hitting the right lines and building pressure in the first half of the one-day series. You don't just lose that skill.' Troy continued:

> 'We have to get back to what we do right, and find that right balance. [But] I think there's a danger sometimes that you can go in search of things that aren't there, and I think we have to be mindful of that. You don't go from being a good side one day to a bad side the next. It's a matter of getting their minds right before the games.
>
> 'We've lost a couple of games. You never like losing, but there is a bigger picture. There have been a lot of things happening around the team, with World Cup selections and injuries, and I think they have all played a role. It's also the end of a pretty long season, and there is always that thought of the World Cup.

'There was so much talk about the six fast bowlers battling for five spots to go to the World Cup. These kind of issues can play on a player's mind. I think the sudden injury to Brett hasn't helped things, and there's also been the re-entry of Shane Watson and trying to get him some match practice before the World Cup. There are a lot of factors. It's a combination of things we need to look at.'

Tuesday, February 20

Chappell–Hadlee Trophy Series Game 3, at Hamilton (February 20):
Australia 5–346 (50 overs: ML Hayden 181*, SR Watson 68) lost to New Zealand 9–350 (49.3 overs: CD McMillan 117, BB McCullum 86*, PG Fulton 51; MG Johnson 3–81) by one wicket

THE NEW ZEALANDERS PLAYED excellent cricket throughout the Chappell–Hadlee Trophy series. They're a good batting side, and when players of that quality get on a run with the bat on small grounds there's not much you can do about it. It was the same with the South Africans in Johannesburg last year, when they smashed us for more than 400. Very good batsmen on a roll can be unstoppable when the boundary rope isn't too far away, because they never have to play outside their strengths to keep the score rocking along at eight, nine or 10 an over. I often wonder if, over the last decade, batsmen's skills have increased more rapidly than bowler's skills; that the game is going through an evolution that will only correct itself over time. When you look at the list of highest innings totals in one-day international cricket, and see that seven of the eight highest scores in history have been made in the past two years, you've got to think this is the case.

Further evidence of this had come in the game last Sunday at Eden Park, when Mike Hussey scored 105 from 84 balls and Brad Hodge hit 97 not out from 86, but our bowlers gave away more than nine runs an over in the final 10 overs. Today, at Hamilton, Matthew Hayden broke the Australia record for the highest individual score in a ODI, but we conceded nearly eight runs per over in the last 10, to lose for the second time in a row a game in which we'd scored a very big total. The Kiwis' two successful run-chases, of 337 and then 347, have only been surpassed once in ODI cricket (not including games involving ICC 'composite' teams such as an 'Asian XI'), by South Africa in that fateful match at Jo'burg I'm constantly trying to forget.

AS THE AUSTRALIAN LOSSES piled up, the papers continued to talk down our World Cup chances. I must confess to being astonished by this. The sweep in the Chappell-Hadlee Trophy series does mean we've lost five in a row, but except for the first game in New Zealand, when we batted first on a seaming deck, we could have won the other four without too much changing. The challenge for all of us since the DLF Cup had been to keep ourselves physically and mentally up for each game, which is a tough gig, so maybe it was natural that at this stage of the season some guys were looking ahead rather than playing for today. An irony was that the one bloke who was up for it in New Zealand was, naturally, Mike Hussey, the stand-in skipper. Unfortunately, his record as Australia's one-day captain is now four games, four losses, even though he's scored centuries in two of those matches.

I've spoken to Huss a couple of times in recent days and the last time we talked he said, with what might have been a laugh, 'You can have your job back! I don't want it ever again.' I also received some interesting text messages from him after the first two games. 'How are you? Are you on the next flight over' is one I can remember.

In a sense, as far as one-day cricket is concerned, Huss has become a victim of his success. He has been so productive batting at or around No. 6, there have been plenty of people arguing that he should be pushed up the order, especially now that Marto has departed. He scored his hundred in Auckland batting four. But I think he is best suited staying at six, to play the 'Michael Bevan role', which he has done superbly at times. There is almost an obligation on batsmen at the top of the order to be 'power' players, and I'm not convinced Huss is equipped to do that role as brilliantly as he can manage a run-chase if we're batting second, or help make the most of the final 15 overs if we've gone in first.

He is a dynamic and relentless runner between wickets, and like Andrew Symonds he has that priceless knack of being able to find the boundary even when there are five blokes back on the fence. What is undoubtedly true is that there are few men in world cricket better able to get an innings back on track, if there has been a sudden fall of wickets either at the start of an innings or in the middle overs.

MATTHEW HAYDEN WENT ALL the way to the Australian record score in the game at Hamilton despite hurting his toe during the innings. It was a stunning knock, and as he played it my mind went back to the Commonwealth Bank Series game in Perth, when he'd scratched and scraped his way to three figures in a knock that might have saved his one-day career. In his first five one-day innings in Australia he had never made it past 30. At the WACA, he was dropped first ball, on four and on 79, top-edged a couple of shots into gaps, and could have been out half a dozen other times. But he survived, made it through the finals and managed to lock up his World Cup place.

Even with the promise Shane Watson showed in the Champions Trophy, and as keen as I am to get Shane into our one-day team, I've never really been able to shake my belief that Matty is best person around to partner Adam Gilchrist in our one-day side. The appeal of Watto opening is that it adds to our bowling options, and as I've said I feel he has the skill to be an opener in Tests, but it's still always comforting to have big Haydos striding out there to take on the opposition.

Friday, February 23

AS OUR FORM FELL away over the past month, conjecture grew as to whether the training we'd been doing has been too arduous, or just plain wrong. As planned, we had continued the endurance and strength work for three solid weeks in January, but then eased off around the time of the Commonwealth Bank finals. The boys got back into it in New Zealand, and there will be more tough times at the start of the World Cup before we lighten off again when the group games in the West Indies begin.

There was plenty of logic to the concept of working our butts off now, so that we'll be right for the World Cup. People have compared our strategy to that of an Olympic swimmer 'tapering' before a big meet, but though that might sound trendy I'm not sure it's quite as scientific as that. For me, it's more us being proactive, so that we won't be arriving in the Caribbean with some catching up to do, or suffering from a post-Ashes hangover. If we needed to do this work — and I think we did — then it had to happen through January.

Quite frankly, our loss of form doesn't worry me. After the experiences we've been through in the past two years, I feel really confident about what we have to do to get things back on track.

We've just got to get our preparations back on track, unclutter our brains so we can concentrate on the job at hand, and take comfort in the fact that our fitness will look after itself. But then I spoke to John Buchanan after the Chappell–Hadlee matches, after the team had lost those five games in a row, and found him a little downcast, worried that he's overcooked it. I thought it was the coach's job to rev up his players, but here I was telling Buck everything is going to be sweet. If the coaches do their job, I said emphatically, we'll do ours.

TWO DAYS AFTER THE Chappell–Hadlee series concluded, I fronted the media to talk about my back complaint, the way the team was going and the World Cup. First, my fitness:

> *'My back's fine. [The doctors] said on the day that I had the injections it would be three to four days of not doing much before the injection settles down. It's been about a week and the last few nights I've slept a lot better and felt a lot better in the morning. Hopefully, when I get to the West Indies I'll be pain-free and ready to go.'*

I'd even managed a round of golf late last week — on doctor's orders. My medico really said that swinging a club would help maintain movement in my back while not aggravating the inflamed area.

Of the team's form in New Zealand, and what we might expect at the World Cup, I made comments that weren't too dissimilar to what I'd said when I returned to Australia after the 2005 Ashes loss, only this time there was no sense of deep concern in my voice, more a quiet confidence that we'd be okay. As I said, I truly believe that, once the Cup gets underway, we'll prove that our recent form is an aberration:

'We've got to look at what we haven't done in the last few games and find ways to improve.

'It was only a month ago that everyone was saying we were odds-on favourites to win the World Cup, and now, all of a sudden, we can't win it ...

'I don't think the team's in any dire straits at the moment. We've had a few injuries and lost a few guys, but I'm pretty confident that we'll be ultra-competitive in every game we play as we have been in the five games we've lost.

'We've just got to tighten up a few little areas and I think things will change.'

CHAPTER 15

PIGEON

I'M ALWAYS A LITTLE surprised when people recall their earliest memory of Glenn McGrath and they only talk about the cricket trousers he wore, which finished halfway down his shin. This look was particularly fetching because he had seriously raw-boned legs, which were the cause of his nickname of 'Pigeon' (on the basis that his legs resembled those of a pigeon). However, what I remember just as much, maybe more, are his bowling boots — huge leather-soled clodhoppers that were laced, like boxer's boots, all the up to his shin, where they met the bottom of those pants. And there is another thing I vividly remember. He bowled fast back then. Real fast.

In 1992, when he was fresh out of the bush, we toured South Africa together with a Cricket Academy team captained by another cricketer from the NSW country, a young wicketkeeper/batsman named Adam Gilchrist. I remember Glenn and another quick, Mark Atkinson, who later played Shield cricket for Western Australia, taking wickets for fun in some of the tour matches. Glenn had been living on his own in a caravan in Sydney's south, having moved to the big smoke from Narromine in western NSW after impressing the great Dougie Walters in a Toohey's Cup exhibition game. He landed in Sydney with no cricket gear, so he'd headed down to the local sports store to buy himself a pair of pads, a pair of gloves and a bat, which he then brought to Adelaide after he received an Academy scholarship.

I scored 125 and 69 in Glenn's first Sheffield Shield game, at the Sydney Cricket Ground in January 1993 (he took 5–79 and 0–29 for NSW), learning very quickly that patience was a key virtue when batting against him. An irony of that first game is that he was injured the second innings, and couldn't complete an over — in the seasons that followed, more than any other of his many positive attributes, it was his persistence and durability that I came to admire the most.

A lot of that came from his easy, economical bowling action. When he was operating, it all seemed natural, as if he'd been born to bowl, and though he did cop his fair share of injuries, he had the healing powers, dedication and toughness to fight back every time. There was nothing complicated about his bowling at the highest level — he rarely swung the ball, was not quite express pace, but he knew that if he put the batsmen under enough pressure for long enough periods of time then the dismissals would follow. It helped that he was quick enough, could seam it, and could get bounce out of most pitches, but he was still a boring line-and-length bowler. I mean that as the greatest compliment. He landed the ball precisely where he wanted it to go 99 times out of 100. If that was easy, everyone would do it.

Pidge might never have been Australian skipper, but for just about my entire Test career he was the 'captain' of the bowling group. If someone asked the question, 'How are we going to bowl to Jacques Kallis?' or to any other key opponent, his opinion would always be the first one sought. This is something I have always encouraged as captain — to have plenty of 'leaders' within the team. I may be the one with the 'c' next to my name, but in my time there has always been at least four or five other guys in the Australian dressing room who could just as easily be captain, so it would be foolish of me not to seek alternative views as to how we should be playing our cricket.

Pidge understands the game, no doubt about it; you could see it in the help he gave to the young bowlers who came into the team. His advice was like his bowling: never complicated, always spot on. Of course, fast bowlers aren't supposed to be smart. That's what we batsmen say, anyway. But I did always find it funny when parents would come up to Pidge and ask for a couple of tips they could pass on to their sons and daughters. 'Just bowl the ball in the right spot all the time and you will be successful,' he would reply. Unfortunately, this wasn't the pearl of wisdom people were after, so they'd walk away disappointed. But that was his 'secret'.

At the media conference before this summer's fifth Ashes Test, I nominated Lord's in 1997 and 2005 as Glenn's greatest performances. They probably were his best *bowling* efforts, but what he did in the West Indies in 1995 was about more than just overs and wickets. He went to the Caribbean as probably our third quick, but then Craig McDermott and Damien Fleming were injured and Pidge had to step up, which he did in a remarkable way.

For 20 years, a succession of West Indies quicks — Andy Roberts, Michael Holding, Joel Garner, Colin Croft, Malcolm Marshall, Courtney Walsh, Patrick Patterson, Curtly Ambrose and Ian Bishop — had been pitching short at all batsmen, from openers to last-men-in. Here, it was as if Glenn said to himself, *Right, I know I'm going to get some bouncers, I know the rest of our bowlers are going to get some bouncers. But I don't care. I'm going to give it back to them.* From the opening day of the series, when he, Brendon Julian, Paul Reiffel and Shane Warne bowled the West Indies out for 195, he forced the Windies players onto the back foot in a way they hadn't experienced for 20 years, a shift in mood and momentum that Australia retained for most of the series and beyond.

Glenn was no cagey veteran when he stood up to Ambrose and Walsh in this way. He'd played nine Tests since his debut at the start of the 1993–94 Australian season, but never more than three in a row, and he had absolutely no idea with the bat. So he needed plenty of courage as well as bowling talent and a fierce competitive streak to do what he did during that series, and through his actions he became the standard bearer for a new generation of Australian Test cricketers. I never lost my respect for him. Never will.

He has a reputation as a nuisance and a funnyman in the dressing room, but when people ask me what comes to mind first in regards to his off-field persona, I always go for the way he has been able to separate his personal life and his sport. The reality of his wife Jane's battle with illness is well known. The fact that he has been able to play such a consistently high standard of cricket in such circumstances is unbelievable. There have been times on long tours when he has been just about the only bloke in the side without his family there with him, but it has not affected his performance or, outwardly at least, his character.

As a contributor to team morale, he has always been fantastic. As a pest, he really is second to none. I would be sitting, having my lunch, when I would feel a tap on my right shoulder and instinctively look to my right. Pidge, meanwhile, would be standing to my left. He would 'get' you 10 times a day, 'get' everyone 10 times a day, and each time he would walk away laughing as if he had just perpetrated one of the all-time great practical jokes.

He is a man who doesn't take himself too seriously, though you might not think so after another poor umpiring decision has cut short a potentially long innings. One of the highlights of his career was the outfield catch he took at the Adelaide Oval to dismiss Michael Vaughan in 2002–03, a spectacular diving effort he likes to remind us about from time to time. Few people know that he was 30 metres out of position when Vaughan played his fateful shot. If Pidge had been fielding where he should have been, the ball would have gone straight down his throat. I was fielding at bat-pad on the off-side and Steve Waugh was behind me at short cover, and when the ball was hit up in the air out towards deep square-leg, we both reacted exactly the same way: *where the hell is he?* Then he came into view, running hard to his left, and he dived full-length, held the catch, and they were advertising memorabilia the following day. Of course, Glenn tells it differently. 'If I had been standing where you wanted me,' he said flatly, 'he would not have played the shot in the first place.'

Glenn's hand–eye skills are uncanny. If he could have transferred them to his batting, he would have been Bradman. During a drinks break, he might grab an empty drink bottle and, with a flick of the wrist, send it spinning through the air to land perfectly, maybe eight times out of 10, in one of the small square spaces in the 12th man's drinks tray. At other times, he could pick up a grape and flick it across the room at someone 20 metres away and, sure enough, clip the victim behind the ear. Of course, he would then look the other way, innocent as ever. Our days at the Academy coincided with the Australian Institute of Sport's release of their own breakfast cereal, Kellogg's 'Sustain', so there was never any shortage of cereal boxes around the place. Glenn would set some of them up, side by side, in his room. Then, he would take the dinner knives out of the cutlery drawer, and like an army commando throw the 'weapons' across his bed at the boxes. *How do you come up with this stuff?* I'd think to myself as he gave me a demonstration of his new game. *And how is it that you hit the centre of the boxes every single time?*

At Lord's in 2005, he took his 500th Test wicket during one of his greatest spells. We had been dismissed for 190 in less than two sessions on the opening day of the series and England were 0–10 at tea, after six overs. The home attack, led by a fired-up Steve Harmison, had bowled quick and hostile and hit a few bodies. 'I think we have bowled a little bit too full and a little bit short,' I said to the team during the interval, as I reviewed the start of the home team's innings. 'Straight away when we get back out there, we need to get the length perfect.'

Pidge did that magnificently. First ball after the break, Marcus Trescothick became dismissal No. 500, caught in the slip cordon. Four deliveries later, Andrew Strauss was held at first slip. Every ball pitched in exactly the right area, and suddenly, without warning, some deliveries were scooting through low, after four hours where many balls had been flying through at rib-cage height. Michael Vaughan couldn't cope with a delivery that seamed back, kept low, and bowled him. Ian Bell was knocked over by one that cut back miles through the gate. Andrew Flintoff's stumps were shattered by a devilish ball that almost ran along the ground.

Glenn had made a living proving that while pace is important for a quick bowler, it is not as vital as line, length and that extra bounce that surprises batsmen, reduces their confidence. When I had batted, Harmison had cut my cheek with a nasty riser, and while his final bowling figures looked impressive, he and his colleagues had not relentlessly attacked the length batsmen hate most, especially on an unreliable pitch like this, where you don't know whether to play back or forward. McGrath did, and it made him unplayable. His bowling figures after Flintoff's dismissal were 5–7 from 8.1 overs, and England were 5–21. They recovered to 155 all out, but we had taken control of the Test, and three days later we were celebrating a 239-run victory. We only lost two Tests in England in 2005 — the two Pidge didn't play.

That Lord's Test was just one of many examples between 1995 and 2007 when the Australian team needed a bowler to make a statement and Glenn McGrath came through. Shane Warne did this often, too, which made the two of them irresistible as a combination, easily the best quick-slow bowling tandem of my experience. They were the 'go-to' guys for Mark Taylor when he was captain, for Steve Waugh and for me. This will be the test for their successors: do they have the ability to consistently rise to the occasion?

Glenn had his knockers in the latter stages of the 2006–07 Commonwealth Bank Series and during the Chappell–Hadlee Trophy games, when his form did dip below its usual standard. A couple of writers even wondered if he'd gone on too long, and suggested it might have been better if he'd finished up at the same time as Justin Langer and Shane Warne. When I read this, I just shook my head at the short memories. I still have that image in my head of Pidge 'limping' off the Gabba after taking six-for in England's first innings of the recent Ashes series. The great players make a habit of proving the critics wrong. In recent times, Matt Hayden has done it, Lang has done it, Gilly has done it, Warney has done it.

Now, once again, it was Pidge's turn ...

CHAPTER 16

ICC WORLD CUP

Saturday, March 10

World Cup warm-up match, at St Vincent (March 6): Australians 7–290
(50 overs: MJ Clarke 82, SR Watson 81, BJ Haddin 47) defeated Zimbabwe XI
7–144 (50 overs: SC Williams 44) by 146 runs

World Cup warm-up match, at St Vincent (March 9): England XI 197
(48.3 overs: MP Vaughan 62, IR Bell 56; SW Tait 4–33, SR Clark 3–16) lost to
Australians 5–200 (40.5 overs: AC Gilchrist 72, SR Watson 55) by five wickets

WE LEFT FOR THE Caribbean on February 28, without Brett Lee,
who'd been ruled out because of his damaged ankle, and Adam
Gilchrist, who stayed behind with his wife, two older children
and new son Archie. Stuart Clark received the late call-up to
replace Bing. Two days later, after 22 hours in the air and the rest
in airport terminals, we finally landed in St Vincent, having
flown via Los Angeles, Miami and Barbados. For most of the
journey, our gear travelled with us, but for the last 40-minute leg,
some of the luggage went missing and didn't arrive until a day
after us. But we didn't lose anything, so all things considered the
long trip went reasonably well.

One of the first things I did after we'd settled in to our new surroundings was organise, first with the coach and then with each of the players, one-on-one meetings to find out how each member of the squad is feeling and to outline the role I see each of them playing over here. I was imagining that some of the younger guys might have had the stuffing knocked out of them over the past month, when we started losing matches, but quickly I discovered that to a man they are positive and confident. I still think the heavy training we undertook during January played a part in our slump, but I think the key factor was that during the last part of the summer and in New Zealand, everyone had one eye on the World Cup rather than being in the moment. Obviously, neither factor is an issue here; at the moment, I can't see any outside influence that should hold us back during the tournament.

Mike Young had left Brisbane for St Vincent a couple of days before the rest of us, to make sure our training facilities in this important first week were in place. Unfortunately, he didn't have a lot of luck, and quickly we sensed, from what we've seen and stories we've heard, that it is going to be a tight race to see if the facilities and infrastructure for the World Cup are going to be in place before the tournament begins. I can picture the last coat of paint being applied as the first ball is being bowled. Mike tried his best, but it seemed we were going to be disappointed, until overnight before our first session, nets, wickets, everything suddenly appeared and we were able to practise on schedule, and well.

The entire support staff has been working hard. Not long after we arrived, I'd had breakfast with Buck one morning and I could sense that he was still concerned about our chances. The team had suffered five losses in a row, conceding 340 and 350 in two games, and he was worried, probably the least optimistic person in the squad. That is not usually his style. 'I'm not sure if we are ready,' he said. 'And the coach has to take the blame for that.'

'Mate, we've had a couple of years to get prepared,' I replied. 'Where we are at, is where we are at. All we have to do now is create an environment that is going to make all the guys happy, where we can work hard and prepare as well as we possibly can. It's not up to you to worry about what might not have been done. We can't change the past, not that I'd want to. But if we create the right environment, get the guys all on the same page, then I'm sure we'll be competitive.'

From that morning on, Buck has made a point of ensuring that each training session is as well-run, efficient and effective as they could possibly be. Each day, the coaching staff leaves for training at least half an hour before the players, so when we get down to the ground everything is set up for us. Our bags are all lined up, nets are all ready to go, bowling machines are cranked up and in position, the fielding stations were laid out. For us, it's just a matter of putting our boots on, having a jog and a stretch, and then we're in to it. This attention to detail makes us feel important, suggests that every aspect of our training is planned and thought through, and shows that our support staff really cares. We have no excuse but to be committed to practice; to give anything other than our best would be an insult to the work our coaches are putting in.

ADAM GILCHRIST ARRIVED LAST Tuesday evening, the same day we played our first warm-up game, against Zimbabwe, and we were all waiting for him at the bar, to share a beer and (for some, but not me) a cigar. He was weary after the long flight, but also very proud of himself, and I had to ponder just how hard it must have been for him to drag himself away from his family. There is no option for international cricketing dads, but that doesn't mean it's easy to do. The next morning, Gilly got stuck into his work as professionally and diligently as ever, as if he'd never been away. It was good for all of us to have him back among the group.

I CONSIDER THE DEFINING of players' roles to be one of the most important pre-game things I do as captain. I remember back when I first came into the Australian one-day team, I batted at No. 6, which was hard for me because I had never done that before. Even in Test cricket, batting down there was hard for me as well and I'm not sure I ever really worked it out. I have never been as comfortable at five or six as I am at No. 3.

I think the importance of knowing your role has been downplayed in cricket. It's not as simple as everyone bats, everyone bowls and everyone fields, so you have to be adaptable. Nor should it be a case that if you can't work it out for yourself, you drown. I don't think Andrew Symonds was given enough direction as the way he should play when he first came into the Australian team. He now knows his role, and what he has to do to play well, and he keeps doing it over and over.

During these one-on-one meetings, I sensed that some of the bowlers had been a little confused as to their roles. Mitchell Johnson and Shaun Tait provide good examples of this. Mitch had played in all four of the one-day competitions we'd been involved in before the World Cup — DLF Cup, Champions Trophy, Commonwealth Bank Series and Chappell–Hadlee Trophy — and done well, at times exceptionally well. But in every series he also received the dreaded 'tap on the shoulder' that meant he wouldn't be playing in the next game. Naturally, whenever he received his next chance, he was worried about conceding too many runs because he wants to cement his spot, so his natural instinct would have been to try to bowl 'dot balls'. But that might not necessarily be what I want him to do. I might want him to be aggressive, a wicket-taker. He needs to be clear in what we want him to do, and we need to show faith in him, to give him every chance to succeed in the role we want him to do.

Taity was as nervous as all hell for his ODI debut in Sydney last month, and he conceded a lot of runs. But most of those were shots that went really fine. Because of his pace, little flicks to fine leg flash past the wicketkeeper down to the fence, while slashes can race down to the boundary before the third-man fieldsman even moves. He actually bowled a little better in that game than his figures suggested. I used him differently in the game against New Zealand in Melbourne two days later, and he responded superbly, tightening things up in the power plays beautifully, and achieving some reverse swing. After that, we put a lot of thought into how we were going to handle the conditions in the West Indies, and I keep coming back to the idea that Shaun is perfect for a very specific role that would see him opening the bowling for just a couple of overs, and then coming back to play an attacking, wicket-taking role in the middle of the innings. By taking him off after two overs, we'll get Glenn McGrath into the attack sooner rather later, which will be better for him as well, because he'll also have a newish, harder ball to bowl with. One day, someone is going to prove my theory that powerplays can be an attacking option, as long as you possess the right weapon, and Shaun Tait could be my man.

Like just about every captain I have ever met, I love to have genuinely fast bowlers at my disposal. For one thing, it's very exciting. In my time, Tasmania have never had any genuinely fast bowlers. Whenever I played against sides that had quick bowlers in their line-up, I could only imagine how much more fun it would be to be out in the field if you knew your team featured bowlers who could intimidate the opposition batsmen. It was only when I started playing for Australia in 1995, and we had Craig McDermott and Glenn McGrath (who was quick back then), that I got to enjoy this experience, and then Brett Lee came along in 1999. Fielding, all of a sudden, became a lot more exciting, as I saw close-up the ball whizzing past the batsman and through to the keeper. When we played at the WACA, I was standing on the 30-metre circle when we were in the slips. I don't call blokes like Brett Lee and Shaun Tait 'fast' bowlers, they are *express* bowlers. If they get it right, they take wickets. Only a skipper who has never faced men of this pace would underrate their value. There is nothing like them.

NATHAN BRACKEN HAS A key role in our plan to bowl Taity first, because Taity — given his reputation for inaccuracy — could go for some runs, so we need Bracks to be frugal, which is something he has consistently done at the start of the innings for the last couple of years.

I spoke to Bracks before our second warm-up match, against England, to ask him to try a different style of bowling that could prove useful during the World Cup. The wicket in St Vincent was very slow, and the ball was really grabbing the pitch surface, so I put to him the idea of him bowling slow, heavy, left-arm off-cutters to the right-hand batsmen. After his first spell, that's what he bowled exclusively, with only three guys on the leg-side, and they struggled to score a run off him.

Of the two games, the one against Zimbabwe was more of a practice hit out, a chance to get used to the conditions. But to be honest I never like to use the term 'practice game' — as far as I'm concerned, they were both contests we wanted to win. Because of those five losses in a row, I wanted to send a clear message right from the start, especially against England, and we smacked them. I think this victory, and the fact we won comfortably, has given all the guys a kick along.

Michael Vaughan and Ian Bell batted really well at the start of the game, adding 116 for the second wicket. They were going along beautifully, but then we brought Brad Hogg on and he dismissed both of them, which was good for him because he hadn't taken a wicket in his five previous ODIs and had also gone wicketless against Zimbabwe. As with Nathan Bracken, we got Hoggy to bowl slightly differently in this match. But where we'd slowed Bracks down, with our No. 1 spinner we asked him to bowl significantly faster through the air. I brought mid-on up for the right-handers and asked Hoggy to bowl his wrong 'un more, to try to tempt them to hit across the spin towards long-on, and it worked, especially when Bell was stumped after he tried to hit a googly over the top.

ONE OF THE SUCCESS stories of the first week was that our two 'casualties' — Andrew Symonds with his arm and Matthew Hayden with his toe — both 'survived'. We had to keep a close eye on them. I know myself that when you are touring and you see the team training, the hardest thing to do is to stay away. You always feel you can help out, by hitting catches or under arming some balls or catching some balls or just doing something to make yourself useful. But Symmo especially just couldn't afford to receive any sort of bump or knock on his arm, because that would have knocked him completely out of the World Cup. I needed to have a word to both of them a couple of times to tell them to go and do what they had to do somewhere else, to get away from the nets, where balls were flying about and the risk of a setback was real.

I broke my thumb before the India tour in 2004, and when I finally went over there, mid-tour, I did all the training leading into the third Test. I shouldn't have, but the series was on the line and I wanted to play. I had plastic guards made up on my thumb, which basically would have prevented the joint from moving, and I intended to wear them at practice and in the field, even though I knew I shouldn't be doing any of that. It was just impossible to keep myself out of it.

Haydos didn't play in either of the warm-up games, but he will be right for the opening game against Scotland in St Kitts. At this stage, it looks like Symmo will definitely be right for the first Super Eights game, and might even be okay for the last group game, against South Africa. In both cases, they have worked amazingly hard to get their bodies right, and in doing so have boosted everyone. So many different things are happening within the squad that show just how much we want to win this competition.

ONE DAY WHILE WE were in St Vincent we went up to the 200-year-old Fort Charlotte, where you can look out over the sea and the southern half of the island. This was John Buchanan's idea. He had made the 200-metre climb to check it out, and then decided to take us all up there. We sat around as a group, out of the wind, and Buck asked us to cast our minds back to the boot camp. We spoke about some of the values we had learnt during that experience, and about the reality that in any major sporting competition there are lots of distractions. You have to be able to keep these out if you want to give yourself the best chance to win. We started talking about the fort itself — what's its purpose? A fort is built to preserve the safety of those inside and to keep everybody else out. We want to build a similar 'fort mentality' within our group.

Buck persevered with this theme, asking each of us to nominate one thing that we wanted let into our fort and kept inside, and one thing we wanted kicked out of our fort and then left outside. When it came to my turn, I suggested we should strive to keep negative influences outside the fort throughout the World Cup campaign. I know we have a strong group and I believe that the only thing that can get in our way is other people's negative thoughts. I want to snuff that negativity out.

What I want to create and retain is a real fun environment for the squad. I've seen it over the years — whenever we are having fun and enjoying what we do we usually play well. I want this to be true for not just the players, but for the support staff, too. I also want an untiring work ethic to be a constant, in every way — not just at training, but with our punctuality, recovery work, treating injuries, massage, sleep, diet, everything.

AS PART OF THE fun element, our team kit had one extra item in it: a box of yo-yos. During the Sydney Test, a cardboard box had been placed next to my locker, with a letter stuck to it. I opened the envelope, and learned that enclosed in the box were 30 of the world's finest yo-yos. Also in the note was a line that said something like, 'We hear you are not very good, or that your current yo-yo doesn't work well for you.' I had no idea what this was all about — I'm actually a yo-yo superstar — and forgot about it, after I put the box in the kit.

Weeks later, I learned that the following short article had appeared in the papers during the Boxing Day Test ...

'We keep hearing that Ricky Ponting could have been anything if he hadn't chosen to pursue a cricket career — a golfer, a footballer or a master of many other sporting pursuits. He could not, however, have been a champion yo-

yoer. We know this because the toy in Ponting's Christmas cracker was a yo-yo, which he simply could not get to spring back to him. Finally, the Australian captain has found something he is not good at.'

I don't know where this came from, as I didn't even attend the team Christmas party this summer, but from the time we landed in St Vincent we've all been stuffing around with these yo-yos in our spare time. The only possibility I can think of was that before the Melbourne Test the English journos presented me with a Christmas bonbon that had something in it that didn't work. I didn't even realise it was a yo-yo, in fact I'm pretty sure it wasn't. This is how some newspaper stories can start.

THE ENGLAND GAME FINISHED late yesterday afternoon, and this morning we flew back to Barbados, and then on to Jamaica for the World Cup opening ceremony.

The flight from St Vincent to Barbados was a chartered flight, two teams and both teams' support staff piling onto one plane. It was a 48-seat plane and there were 55 of us, so seven people missed out. What to do? We took off, landed in Barbados, and then the same plane flew back to get the other seven. The rest of us waited and waited. Finally, the plane returned and we all flew to Jamaica together. Once more, there were numerous signs that the organisers have left it very late to get things finished for the tournament. I must confess I can't quite get a handle on how the event will go. The one thing I'm sure of is that our cricket will be excellent, because the vibe within our playing group is as positive as I've known it. I can't guarantee that we'll win the World Cup, but I do know that our opponents will have to be at the very top of their games if they want to get past us.

Monday, March 12

THE OPENING CEREMONY WAS staged at the brand new Trelawny Stadium in Montego Bay. It started at around five o'clock in the afternoon, at a time when all the seats that had been set aside for the 16 participating teams were looking directly into a setting sun. It was hot, maybe 40 degrees, so the start of the three-hour event wasn't that pleasant for us.

Still, there were 12,000 people inside, and an estimated 2.6 billion people from various parts of the planet watching on television. The legendary Sir Garfield Sobers officially declared the tournament open after which West Indies captain Brian Lara gave a pledge that we would all play the game the right way:

> *We the cricketers promise that we shall play to the best of our ability, respect the laws and spirit of cricket, observe all the rules which govern this tournament and commit ourselves to the highest standards of fair play, ethical conduct and good sportsmanship. This we pledge on behalf of our teams for the good of the tournament and in honour of this glorious game.*

The ceremony featured a host of Caribbean entertainers, including reggae stars Jimmy Cliff and Shaggy, and at least a thousand singers, dancers and performers. For me, though, it was a rare chance to be in the company of so many of the game's elite players all at the same time. I think that was why I came away from the evening sensing that this might be the beginning of something special.

OF COURSE, AT THE start of any contest, many of the competitors retain an optimistic attitude. I was constantly being told that the

World Cup was 'open', as in anyone could win it. Journalists have looked me in the eye and offered the opinion that, based on recent form and our injury worries, that Australia might struggle. My reply is simply, 'We will see.'

One English television reporter stood out. Throughout our time in St Vincent, he must have asked me the same thing 100 times. 'Ricky, this must be the most open World Cup we can ever remember?' he'd gasp. Or, 'Ricky, no one can recall a more open World Cup!' Or, 'Ricky, everyone is saying this is the most open World Cup.' Eventually, I said to him, 'Mate, if you don't think we can win it, why don't you just say so.' He replied, 'Oh no, I think you're the favourites.'

'Okay,' I said, 'what's your next question?'

'Well Ricky,' he said, 'You've got to admit this is the most open World Cup we've seen ...'

At the end of the interview, I muttered to myself, 'We'll see how open this World Cup is!'

Wednesday, March 14

Group A match, at St Kitts (March 14): Australia 6–334 (50 overs: RT Ponting 113, ML Hayden 60, AC Gilchrist 46, GB Hogg 40*) defeated Scotland 131 (40.1 overs: CJO Smith 51; GD McGrath 3–14) by 203 runs

THE CRICKET SIDE OF the World Cup kicked off yesterday with a win for the hosts over Pakistan at Sabina Park in Kingston, Jamaica, and then today our campaign began with a big win over Scotland at Warner Park in Basseterre, St Kitts. For me, the Cup started in the best possible way, as I made a hundred, which was handy given that I'd scored 2 and 7 in our two warm-up games. By the end of our innings, I felt like my game was in pretty good shape.

An innings I really enjoyed came when Brad Hogg clubbed 40 from 15 deliveries at the end of our 50 overs. While we all enjoyed seeing Hoggy in full cry, I don't think it did much for our morale, which was already excellent, but it must have made an impact on the other sides watching us, to see one of our 'fringe' players looking so good. It is true that the ground is tiny, maybe 20 metres too small from point to square leg, so our total of 6–334 was only good, not great, but it was too many for the Scots, who couldn't withstand the pace of Shaun Tait or the guile and seam of Glenn McGrath. As a first-up performance, this was excellent.

Sunday, March 18

Group A match, at St Kitts (March 18): Australia 5–358 (50 overs: BJ Hodge 123, MJ Clarke 93*, AC Gilchrist 57) defeated Netherlands 129 (26.5 overs: GB Hogg 4–27) by 229 runs

THE WORLD CUP IS reeling tonight, following the news that Bob Woolmer has passed away. We learned about the Pakistan coach's death during our game today against the Netherlands, when Brad Haddin ran drinks out after we had taken a wicket and informed us of the appalling news.

Nothing prepares you for a situation like this. We issued a statement in which I, on behalf of the team, passed on 'our condolences to the Woolmer family and everyone he has known over the years'. I also responded to questions at the media conference after our game against Holland today, but I must confess I felt almost numb as I answered.

'Everyone just stood back in shock for quite a while,' I explained, as I recalled our reaction after Brad told us the news.

'When I was out in the field I was thinking about lots of different things for probably the last 10 or 12 overs of the game.

'Everybody was immediately saddened by what we heard. We have played a game of cricket, but there are a lot of bigger things happening around the world and there always is. We sometimes get a bit carried away with what we do in sport. But when something like this happens it certainly rams home that there are other things happening around you all the time.'

THE PREVIOUS DAY, WE'D ALL been stunned when Pakistan had been beaten by Ireland. On the same day, India lost to Bangladesh, but that wasn't quite as big a shock. In fact, Dav Whatmore, the Bangladesh coach, had told our strength and conditioning coach, Justin Cordy, and our performance analyst, Richard McInnes, who have worked with Dav in the past, that he thought that his men could beat India. They had done so once before, in a game at Dhaka on Boxing Day 2004, and they genuinely believed they could do it again. But never in my wildest dreams did I think Ireland could beat Pakistan.

Friday, March 23

Pura Cup Final, at Hobart (March 19–23): Tasmania 340 (DG Wright 67, LR Butterworth 66; DE Bollinger 5–73) and 460 (SG Clingeleffer 107, LR Butterworth 106, MJ Di Venuto 64, GJ Bailey 50) defeated New South Wales 230 (PA Jaques 82, GM Lambert 61; LR Butterworth 4–33) and 149 (DG Wright 5–13, BW Hilfenhaus 4–22) by 421 runs

THE NIGHT AFTER OUR game against the Netherlands, we had the first big team dinner of the trip. We were being looked after magnificently by a couple of local businessmen who were on the

St Kitts World Cup Organising Committee, and they invited us out to their restaurant and laid everything on: beer, champagne, wine, fish, crayfish, it was magnificent. During the night, a group that included Haydos, Gilly, Hodgey (who'd scored a superb century against the Dutchmen), Taity and a few others made plans for a deep-sea fishing trip the next day. Of course, our new friends knew who to talk to, a couple of calls were made, and soon the boat was booked and plans for an early start had been locked in place.

Because we'd been working so hard since we arrived in the Caribbean, and there were six days between our second and third group games, this was a chance to relax and have a good time. No practice was scheduled for the Monday or Tuesday, but there were still a few scratchings for the fishing expedition, with only the previously mentioned Aussie quartet up to the task. They clambered on board, the boat's engines sparked into life, and off it went out into Basseterre Harbour, on its way out to the beautiful blue waters of the Caribbean Sea. Just a few hundred metres from the wharf, Taity started to feel crook. Seasickness had got him. He looked back longingly at the wharf, and asked if he could be dropped back on dry land, but it was too late, there was no turning back. They made him stay out there for hours, and the poor bloke never improved.

FOR EVERY DAY FROM March 19 to March 23, I would leave my computer on the Cricket Australia website, to get regular updates from the Tasmania–New South Wales Pura Cup final from Bellerive Oval in Hobart, and I also received a variety of text messages, making sure I was aware of the latest developments. I had spoken to Tim Coyle, the Tassie coach, once or twice leading into the game, and to a few of the players, and the one piece of advice I gave them all was to play to win. To think about the draw was a mistake, even though such a result would be enough for them to win the title, because they topped the points table after the home and away season. As soon as you start thinking that way, everything can go wrong.

As things turned out, I had nothing to worry about. I also sent the guys a fax before the game, which Tim was going to read out during their last team meeting. The ultimate victory was a special moment not only for Tasmanian cricket, but Tasmanian sport.

I guess, technically, I'm the captain of the team that won the Pura Cup this season, but as I only played in one game, that draw in Melbourne last November, I'm probably not entitled to shout this fact out too loudly. Whether I should be captain of the team, given that with international schedules being so crowded nowadays I'm hardly ever there, is something I've tossed around in my mind for the past couple of years. In my view, it would probably be easier for everyone if there is one captain for the whole summer, but my attitude is that it depends on what Tasmanian Cricket wants. If they want me to remain 'in charge' and come back and captain the side whenever I'm available, then I'll keep doing it.

I've also been asked why I'm still playing for Tasmania now that I'm a resident of Sydney. The history of the Sheffield Shield/Pura Cup is littered with examples of players who changed teams when they moved interstate — including legends such as Don Bradman, Keith Miller and Allan Border — but it's never occurred to me to 'transfer', and I have never sensed that anyone in Tassie, NSW or Cricket Australia thinks I should be playing for the Blues. The irony is that even when I was living in Launceston and playing cricket full-time in Tasmania, I never trained with the state team. In the 1990s, most of the players in the Shield squad were based in Hobart, but Shaun Young (who played one Test for Australian in 1997) and I used to train with the Northern Tasmanian Cricket Association squad in Launceston, and only see the rest of the state XI on match days. So, in a sense, little has changed. Maybe it would be easier for me if I did play for NSW, but I feel a strong loyalty to Tasmanian cricket, and would be very disappointed if anyone ever told me things had to change.

Two days ago, I went to sleep with Luke Butterworth and Sean Clingeleffer involved in a fourth-day partnership that looked like it might bat NSW right out of the game. When I woke the next morning, I learned that they'd exceeded even my most optimistic expectations, by both scoring hundreds, and the visitors required an impossible 568 runs on the last day. Yesterday, the first person I sought out was Brad Haddin, the regular NSW captain, to make sure he had heard the latest scores. For some reason, I missed him at breakfast, and he was hard to collar at training, but when I finally caught up with him he told me he had been speaking to a couple of the Blues players and they were going to just block out the last day, to prevent Tassie from gaining the satisfaction of a Pura Cup final victory.

I just laughed and then asked straight-faced, 'What's the use of doing that? A draw is a loss for you blokes. The game is over, finished, you've lost.' As it turned out, NSW were bowled out for nothing, and I will spend the next few days, maybe the whole tour, making sure everyone, especially Hadds, is aware of the final result.

The man-of-the-match performance by Butterworth, who scored 66 and 106 and took 4–33 and 0–19, didn't surprise me at all, because I remember him from the one Ford Ranger Cup game I played this season. He wasn't in the Pura Cup team at that point, and only took 1–36 and scored 20 batting eight in the game we played together, but I said to Tim Coyle, based purely on what I'd seen from him that day, that he should be in the Pura Cup team for the remainder of the season. As it turned out, he didn't come into the four-day side until late January, but he then took 18 wickets in the three games before the final, and looks a real prospect.

THE STORY OF BOB Woolmer's passing has turned sinister. Last Tuesday, the police announced that they are treating the death as suspicious, and Jamaican police have finger-printed every member of the Pakistan touring party. Both Pakistan and India have been eliminated from the World Cup, and a feeling of gloom hangs over the tournament.

Because we are in St Kitts, and Woolmer died in Kingston, we do feel a little bit removed from the story, and we are reading the same reports and hearing the same rumours as everyone else. Inevitably, I am often being sought for comment, but there is really nothing I can say, so every time I point the inquirer in the direction of our media manager. Some people are arguing that the entire World Cup should be called off, but until we know the facts to me that would be premature.

Inevitably we have been talking about the affair. It is such a tragic, terrible situation. With all sorts of stories flying around, including the allegation Bob had been murdered, it is natural that we've stopped to think about our own safety. But while it is truly horrible to even consider the thought that someone connected with our sport has been assassinated, it is also a concept far removed from my experience as an international cricketer. There is nothing in our lives to suggest we were under threat, and in such circumstances my view is that we should keep playing.

Sunday, March 25

Group A match, at St Kitts (March 24): Australia 6–377 (50 overs: ML Hayden 101, RT Ponting 91, MJ Clarke 92, AC Gilchrist 42) defeated South Africa 294 (48 overs: AB de Villiers 92, GC Smith 74, JH Kallis 48; GB Hogg 3–61) by 83 runs

IN THE LEAD-UP TO yesterday's game against South Africa, Jonty Rhodes, arguably the finest fieldsman of the 1990s and currently working with Graeme Smith's team, publicly claimed that his team was a better fielding outfit than Australia. Frankly, I doubted this, and while I have no idea what Rhodes brings to the South African set-up I do know how influential Mike Young has been with the Aussie squad ever since John Buchanan introduced him to us a few years ago.

Mike's background is in baseball, coaching in the minor leagues in America and at the top level in Australia. While he offers us no cricket knowledge whatsoever, there is plenty he can teach us in regard to fielding technique, especially throwing but also catching. This is all good, but in my view the best thing Youngy gives us is his attitude, a positive persona that is highly contagious.

For me, the key to being an excellent fieldsman, even a capable fieldsman, is to enjoy it. If you don't enjoy fielding practice and fielding on game day, you'll never get much out of it and you won't be much good at it. Even when I was a kid, this was the one thing I always tried to bring to my team — to make sure I was the first one out there for fielding practice, to really enjoy it, and to do lots of work. Youngy is cut from the same cloth, and he has created an atmosphere within the current Australian squad where guys actually go looking for him, so they can do some more work, rather than him having to go and drag blokes out of the change rooms to get their drills done.

Youngy has introduced a real aggression into our fielding. He wants us to throw it at the stumps, and his view is that if it goes for overthrows, it's never the fault of the thrower, it's the fault of the two or three guys who didn't back up. Consequently, there is a lot more movement in the field when the Australians are out there these days, because on any play (as he calls them), almost every fielder should be running to a position where the ball might go.

Mike loves being with the team, and fancies himself as a motivator. Often, he will write a note for a player and slip it under that man's door, or in his locker. It might be something he's noticed about the opposition, or reinforcement for some praise he offered the day before. I think one of his biggest plusses has been the work he has done with the bowlers on their fielding. It's rare in 21st century cricket to see an Australian bowler who can't also field well, but this wasn't always the case. In today's one-day cricket, I believe a player has to be better than average in two of the three components of the game: batting, bowling and fielding. If you can only do one of these, then you have to do it unbelievably well to stay in the side. If you are batsmen you have to bat and field; if you are a bowler you have to be able to bowl and field. If you are the wicketkeeper, you must be able to keep and bat. Because of this, the fielding coach is now regarded as a key member of the support staff. In Mike Young, we have one of the best.

Fielding drills are much more specific now. In days gone by, everyone in the team would run around the outfield at practice, catching plenty of high balls, or get in close and take a lot of sharp ones. But in my case, a slips specialist who usually fields inside the circle in limited-over cricket, I don't need to be catching 1000 high balls a day. I need to be rehearsing for when I'll be throwing from different angles, hitting the stumps side on, doing short catching. We are also aware that we shouldn't be throwing too many balls in any one day, and we should use the right technique when we are throwing, because no one wants to 'blow' an arm up. Youngy also realises that one cricketer might not be as athletic as the next, so that while some blokes can throw from different angles in different ways, others can't and shouldn't try. If they do, they'll hurt themselves. Same if they slide the wrong way as they try to prevent a boundary.

Youngy hates players getting injured doing dumb things in the field, and genuinely cares about their welfare. He worked hard with Andrew Symonds to help get him back on the park as quickly as possible, and must have taken great satisfaction when his mate was passed fit to play against South Africa in our last group game. I'm not sure if anyone else really believed Symmo would be right to go before the Super Eights.

THE PREVIOUS TIME WE played South Africa in a one-day international we scored 4–434. Only trouble was, they replied with 9–438. We might have beaten them in five of six Tests last season, but that one-day loss in Johannesburg still rankles with us, and they are currently ranked the No. 1 team in limited-over international cricket. We desperately wanted to win.

The thing that struck me before the game was the way everyone in our team was training. Our batsmen were going into the nets and not worrying about simply hitting a few balls in the middle; they were going in there preparing themselves to play a certain way. I'll never forget Matt Hayden and Adam Gilchrist going in there to face bowling machines that had been set up to mimic Shaun Pollock's delivery, and belting the balls all over the place.

We have talked about getting through the first three or four overs of the games over here, just seeing if the new ball is going to do anything, and then, once we're through that period, opening up and playing with freedom. But the two of them hardly waited at all, and then in the fifth over, Haydos took Pollock for 17 in five balls — 4, 0, 6, 6, 1. After five stunning overs, we were 0–50. At the team meeting, Haydos had argued that Pollock's strength, his consistency, could also be his weakness, because he tends to be fairly predictable. He was 'taking him down'. In doing this so brutally, he made one of the greatest one-day bowlers look mediocre. And the carnage wasn't over until he reached his century from just 66 deliveries. It was the fastest hundred in World Cup history, and the local St Kitts government was so impressed they awarded Matty honorary citizenship.

In contrast, I felt as if I hardly hit a ball in the middle all day. When I was out there with Haydos, I felt like a flyweight batting with George Foreman. The fact I managed 91 from 91 balls was purely a reflection on the short distance from the middle to the boundary rope. Even when I got out, caught on the long-on boundary, the ball hit the toe of the bat and I was surprised it flew that far. On paper, the fact that every one of the Australian batsmen scored at a run a ball or better looks imposing, but it wasn't that amazing a feat.

Michael Clarke played really well with me. He was constantly trying to pick me up, tell me that I was 'going all right', because he knew I wasn't hitting them well at all. A total of 377 was excellent but not unbeatable, and Smith and AB de Villiers took 160 from the first 21 overs, to get them right back in the game. Fortunately, though, Shane Watson produced a freakish piece of fielding, a direct hit from deep backward square to end that opening partnership, and from there we were always going to win.

Afterwards, I was asked if I was thinking abut Johannesburg as Smith and de Villiers were smashing the ball to all parts, and

I replied, 'No, what made me think about Jo'burg was the run out.' What I meant by that comment was that right through the historic game where we couldn't defend 434, I had always expected something to happen to stop the flow of South African runs. One good catch, a couple of excellent overs in a row, a poor shot, a run out, even an umpiring mistake — that's all we needed to slow the momentum for long enough to make such a colossal run-chase impossible. Over the course of 50 overs, that shouldn't have been too much to expect. This time, Watto got his run out to end de Villiers' outstanding knock, and Smith started cramping up, and our score proved more then enough.

The other thing that worked in our favour was the manner in which Jacques Kallis batted. Kallis came at No. 3, in a situation where he had to get going immediately, but instead he only scored six runs from his first 16 balls. From 1–160 after 21, they slowed to 1–213 after 31, and never recovered. Watson, Shaun Tait and Brad Hogg all bowled extremely well during this period, and Bracken came back at the end to concede only 17 runs from his final six overs, and take the last two wickets. Hoggy's wrong 'un that led to Herschelle Gibbs being stumped was a beautiful delivery.

Taity's effort during the powerplay we took as soon as Kallis arrived in the middle, conceding only nine runs in three overs, convinced me for good that my theory that he is the right man to bowl during these critical spells is spot on. The fact his first four overs had cost 33 runs was all but forgotten.

At the post-game media conference I made some news by being openly critical of Kallis' display. I didn't go into that gathering intending to have a shot at him, but when I was asked if I was surprised by the way he batted in that situation, I just replied, 'No, that's the way he plays.' To me, it's a flaw in his make-up, the reason why I don't rate him a great batsman, just a very good one. There have been at least a few occasions I can think of when he's needed to step up if his team was going to win, but he hasn't been able to do so. As I said, there was no premeditated plan on my part to try to put him under pressure in future games, but when the reporters persisted with their inquisition, I thought to myself, *It can't hurt to add a little bit of fuel to the debate.* We'll probably see the South Africans again before this tournament is over, and if Kallis is thinking too much about his game when that rematch happens, it will work to our advantage.

I don't usually think this way. Most times, I think the concept of off-field 'mind games' is vastly overrated. Team-mates such as Shane Warne and Glenn McGrath might get into it, but I'm usually happy to worry about my own game. Why did I have a gentle shot at Kallis now? Maybe because I'm sick of hearing from the South Africans about how they don't fear us. They say it so often, they obviously do.

Wednesday, March 28

Super Eights match, at Antigua (March 27–28): Australia 6–322
(50 overs: ML Hayden 158, MJ Clarke 41) defeated West Indies 219
(45.3 overs: BC Lara 77; GD McGrath 3–31, GB Hogg 3–56) by 103 runs

WHEN WE ARRIVED IN Antigua, as soon as he could, John Buchanan took us to the new Sir Vivian Richards Stadium. Our game against the Windies was the first match of the Super Eights, so we landed, went to our hotel, which is about 40 minutes out of St John's, ditched out bags, and then made the 20-minute journey to the ground. It is an impressive venue, except it's not finished yet. Neither are the roads that lead to the stadium. The outfield is ridiculously sandy, to the point that the first thing I thought about when I walked on it was a torn leg muscle. We gathered in the centre of the field for a short period, talked about different challenges this venue throws at us, and then we headed back to the hotel. I guess this meant we were accustomed to our new surroundings.

In the same way the totals we achieved in St Kitts weren't that fantastic because the ground there is so small, here the score we managed was remarkable, because neither the field nor the dead wicket leant themselves to fast run-getting. These conditions made Matt Hayden's innings one of his greatest — 158 from 143 balls on a slow pitch, and on a field where the outfield was slow and the ball basically plugged if you hit it in the air. There were 51 fours or sixes hit in the game and Matty hit 18 of them.

As I have already explained, our batting group has identified the opening few overs of an innings here in the Caribbean as being perhaps the most important segment of the entire 50 overs. The new ball loses its shine very rapidly on these grounds, but there is some swing at the start, so it is important that the top-order batsmen stay wary during this time. To make the big scores that are needed to win one-dayers during this competition, we need to survive those overs, and if that means adopting a defensive mindset for a short period that is what we expect our top-order batsmen to do. The run-fest from ball one against South Africa was something of an aberration. Here, Matty didn't score a run off any of the first 17 deliveries he faced, but he recovered to reach his century from 110 balls.

The value of Haydos' early caution really came through the next morning, when the game resumed with the start of the West Indies innings. Rain the previous day had caused an adjournment at the halfway stage of the match, and under the tournament conditions a game could go over to a second day in such circumstances. There was some moisture in the track on the second morning, and Bracken, Tait and McGrath reduced the home team to 3–20 after 10 overs. I actually think the Windies total of 219 was reasonably adequate for the conditions, but of course they were roundly criticised for being beaten by such a wide margin. All our bowlers performed admirably — especially Glenn McGrath, who has worked himself into outstanding form, and Brad Hogg, who got the key wicket of Brian Lara — but more than anything, the Windies were beaten by one great innings.

THE SAME COMMENTATORS WHO were writing us off a month ago are now starting to suggest we're invincible, but I've been seeing signs of our relentless form since even before the tournament started. Mainly, it's been little things, such as what time the guys have been getting down for breakfast. This might sound a bit weird for some, but I've always thought that a way of telling if a team is switched on is if they are ready to go in the morning; if they are only giving themselves five minutes for breakfast before they jump on the bus for training I often wonder if their minds are elsewhere.

There is a kind of controlled freedom about our cricket at the moment, and also about the way we were going about our preparation, as if we know exactly how far we can push things without getting reckless. Because we've fought back from the slump we suffered at the end of the Australian summer so completely, there is an enhanced spirit and strength about our cricket that is bigger than anything we've enjoyed during the past 18 months. It's not arrogance, because the Ashes loss in 2005 (and to a lesser extent the down spell right before this tour) taught us humility, more a sense of supreme confidence that is heightened because we all have total faith in our games, each other and our support staff.

If one bloke is more responsible for this mindset than anyone else it is Matt Hayden, who has gone from being a guy who was just hanging on to his spot in the side to a legend who is consistently producing a brand of cricket no one has seen him deliver before. *If he can do it*, we all think, *I can do it*. Because Matty has been so diligent and dedicated in his preparation, and that has so obviously helped get him into the dynamic form he is in, he has inspired the rest of us.

The other bloke who has given us a real kick along is Brad Hogg, who has taken 11 wickets in our first four games, making him our leading wicket-taker to this point in the World Cup, two ahead of Glenn McGrath and four clear of Shaun Tait. Hoggy's spirit is invigorating. He has been in and out of the side all season, mainly out to be honest, but we'd always thought he'd be handy during the World Cup. He's one of the most popular blokes in the squad, yet he's also one of those cricketers who is always unlucky when his name is brought up at selection meetings. When a change needs to be made, he's the guy who usually gets squeezed out. It could even have happened here, too, with Matt Hayden entrenched in the opening batting spot and Shane Watson and Andrew Symonds coming back into the team, but Hoggy bowled nicely in the warm-up games and then started taking wickets in big numbers in the group games. Against the West Indies, he took three wickets, including the key scalp of Brian Lara. Suddenly, there is no way we can leave him out.

IT WAS IMPOSSIBLE NOT to notice during the West Indies game that the new stadium was a long way from full. Especially after the constant buzz of the Ashes series, it felt almost bizarre to be playing such a big game — favourites versus the hosts — in front of so many empty seats.

There are a number of reasons behind this situation, but a couple stand out. One, it is almost universally agreed that the ticket prices are too high for the locals. And two, the rules that ban musical instruments and the like from being brought into the grounds have taken a bit of the 'Caribbean' out of the World Cup experience, and upset a number of potential spectators.

In my years travelling the world, I've always thought that one good way to get a feel for the vibe of a place is to talk to the taxi drivers. Here in Antigua, most of the cabbies I've talked to don't want anything to do with the cricket. With a lot of West Indian people, if you lose them, you lose them forever, and it appears the World Cup organisers have a lot of work to do in the next few days if they want to get them back.

Wednesday, April 4

Super Eights match, at Antigua (March 31): Bangladesh 6–104 (22 overs: GD McGrath 3–16) lost to Australia 0–106 (13.5 overs: AC Gilchrist 59*, ML Hayden 47*) by 10 wickets

UNFORTUNATELY, OUR GAME AGAINST Bangladesh degenerated into something akin to the Twenty20 game, after the new playing field at the Sir Vivian Richards Stadium failed to handle the rain that fell before the game. The water didn't drain away and the field became very sticky in parts, especially in the outfield. The eight or 10 metres from the edge of the spectator area out onto the 'turf' was just a sandy bog, and we realised soon enough that if the game was going to be played that day it was going to be something like 25 or 30 overs a side.

To get the game started, the authorities proposed bringing the boundary ropes in so the worst of the mud would be outside the actual field of play. I didn't like that idea, because the purist in me thought that was downgrading an important World Cup game and the pragmatist in me realised such a move would suit the less powerful Bangladeshis more than us. So I stood my ground. 'If the only way we can play is to bring the boundaries in,' I said, 'I think we should wait until tomorrow.'

The reason the officials were so keen to get the game over and done with lay in the playing schedule, which seems to have gone a bit skewiff. Our next clash, against England, isn't scheduled until April 8. Bangladesh, in contrast, were due to play New Zealand here in two days time. If our game was held over, they'd be playing on successive days.

Following this stand-off, the situation deteriorated. The one 'super sopper' on location broke down, after which the ground staff seemed happy enough to let the ground dry at its own pace. I felt as if my bluff was being called, but the umpires, Aleem Dar and Billy Bowden, refused to be pressured into starting the game prematurely. Like me, they were concerned about the integrity of the contest, and also wanted the surface to be safe to play on. It would have been a disgrace if we had started early and someone had been hurt. In the end, we won a 22-over game by 10 wickets with nearly nine overs to spare, after Glenn McGrath bowled another superb spell, but we came away feeling as if we'd escaped. It was one of those days when you almost expected something to go wrong.

AFTER THE BANGLADESH GAME, because we had that long break before our next game, we were given three days off. Rianna, who is following the team, and I took off to the island of St Barths (Isle de St. Barthélemy), a tiny island, no more than 15 square kilometres, situated north-west of Antigua, in what is known as the 'French West Indies'. It was a total escape, where I could move about totally unnoticed and savour some magnificent (and expensive) restaurants and cafes.

It is a bit of a contradiction with me, in that I love cricket dearly but I often try to get right away from it. In this instance — even though there has been plenty of time between matches — it has been relentless, partly because of the natural stress that comes with being captain of the tournament favourites, partly because the tragedy and mystery of Bob Woolmer's death has brought a whole new element to the media scrutiny, and also because of the time difference with back home which has meant that sometimes you feel like you're on call 24 hours a day.

So for three days, the members of the Australian team went their separate ways. Some stayed in Antigua, many returned to St Kitts, where we'd been treated so royally. If we had just kept training, I think we might have started to go 'stir crazy', and the constant jibes from outsiders that the tournament is too long might have overwhelmed us. I'm not saying we've returned feeling refreshed and as if we're about to start a new season, but in football terms for us it feels now more like the start of the third quarter of a grand final, halfway in an event we really want to win, rather than as if we are running a marathon and the finish line is nowhere in sight.

Sunday, April 8

Super Eights match at Antigua (April 8): England 247 (49.5 overs: KP Pietersen 104, IR Bell 77; NW Bracken 3–33, SW Tait 3–41, GD McGrath 3–62) lost to Australia 3–248 (47.2 overs: RT Ponting 86, MJ Clarke 55*, ML Hayden 41) by seven wickets

THE MEDIA HAD SOME fun in the days leading up to the England game, mostly by asking provocative questions and then going to town with the responses to them. For example, John Buchanan was asked about Michael Vaughan's one-day record, how Vaughan only averages 27 in ODIs without a hundred, and Buck agreed that record wasn't that impressive. The resulting story focused on our coach's criticism of the England captain's record in one-day cricket. I was quoted as saying we would target Kevin Pietersen's ribs, but I don't think I said that. I was asked what would happen if Pietersen charged the bowlers as he'd done to ill-effect back in Melbourne in January, and I replied light-heartedly it would be lovely if was hit in the ribs again, but that doesn't mean we'll be going out to try to hurt the bloke. People started interpreting these comments of ours as being part of the psychological ploys we reputedly scheme in the lead-up to big games, but as I've said before I hardly ever try to plan my responses. I just answer whatever questions come as best I can. If I devoted a few hours to planning my press interviews, I'm sure I'd do my own head in before I made any impact on an opponent.

This is not to say we don't think about our opponents' psyche, and where we might be able to win an advantage, big or small. In the team meeting before this game against the Poms we resolved not to talk to Pietersen at all on the field, because we thought the silent treatment might have an impact on his extroverted I-want-to-be-noticed character. I think he is a bit like Steve Waugh or Brian Lara, who used to like getting in a slanging match with his opponents out on the field. Quite often, these blokes would go looking for a blue to fire them up. Unfortunately, on this occasion the plan didn't work too well, because first Pidge spoke to him, then I got in an argument with him, and he went on to make a hundred. But I still think there were signs that he could be distracted in the future.

It started not long after Shaun Tait had claimed two early wickets, when McGrath bowled a bouncer and Pietersen hit it to deep square leg for a single. As the batsman strolled to the non-striker's end, he said something like, 'You won't get me bowling that sort of pace.'

Pidge responded with, 'It was good enough to break your ribs a couple of weeks ago.'

I said something similar — so much for the no-chat strategy — to which Pietersen came back with: 'I read what you said in the papers this morning. I thought you were one of the good guys.'

'Don't worry about me being a good bloke, mate,' I shot back. 'I've heard plenty of stories about you from your dressing room. I'd be looking after my own backyard if I were you.'

This was in the 11th over, by which time I'd already brought Michael Clarke on to bowl ... during a powerplay. Clarke and Pietersen played together at Hampshire, and I have a theory that Pietersen doesn't like facing him, because he'd be embarrassed if he lost his wicket to him. In Pup's second over, straight after we'd had a go at him, Pietersen blocked five balls straight, but I should have taken Pup off then. Instead, Pietersen had time to regain his composure, and he and Ian Bell took 22 runs from two overs. Still, the episode suggested we'd got inside his head a little bit, if only for a short period of time.

England really tested us in this game. I think we were lucky in that Pietersen might have got a little obsessed with his hundred during our innings, because they didn't score as many from the late overs as they needed. He was dismissed for 104 in the 49th over. It was certainly strange to see the manner in which he celebrated getting to three figures, as if he'd just completed the innings of his life. After 40 overs, England were 5–196, but they finished up with only 247. In reply, we were only a wicket or two away from some trouble at 2–89 in the 20th over, but Pup and I added 112 for the third wicket, and we ended up getting home with seven wickets and 16 balls to spare.

An important moment in this match came when I delayed our third powerplay until the 27th over, when I brought Tait and then McGrath back on. England were 2–146 at the time, with Pietersen and Bell going well, and I'd been waiting for a wicket to fall, in the hope that I could bring Shaun back for the powerplay with a new batsman at the crease. They took eight runs from Shaun's first over of this new spell, but then we conceded only 18 runs during the next four overs and took the wickets of Bell and Paul Collingwood. We could have got Pietersen, too, but Brad Hogg and Matthew Hayden mucked up a skied catch at mid-off. Still, the mood had changed, because our two quicks were able to use the powerplay as an attacking option, and England never regained the momentum.

Friday, April 13

Super Eights match, at Barbados (April 13): Ireland 91 (30 overs: GD McGrath 3–17, SW Tait 3–39) lost to Australia 1–92 (12.2 overs) by nine wickets

THE KENSINGTON OVAL AT Bridgetown has been completely renovated, to the point that I hardly recognised the ground when we first went down there. It used to be old and run down, dominated by dreary concrete stands, but it looks terrific now. They've done a really good job; it's a pity that the infrastructure problems, disappointing crowds and criticism over the length of this World Cup have masked a number of things that have worked well. It must have been a logistical nightmare trying to organise a tournament that has been in so many different nations, and overall I reckon they have done it more than adequately.

We had been told to expect that the Barbados wicket would be a lot quicker and bouncier than any other pitch we had seen so far.

Right: The four retirees — Damien Martyn, Justin Langer, Glenn McGrath and Shane Warne — in the SCG change room after the final Ashes Test.

Left: Cameron White and Shane Harwood celebrate the dismissal of Andrew Flintoff for a duck in the Twenty20 International in Sydney.

Right: England's Jon Lewis is caught by me at backward point during the opening Commonwealth Bank Series match at the MCG.

Above: Matthew Hayden during his important hundred against New Zealand at Perth.

Above: Brad Hodge after finishing 99 not out at the MCG.

Above: With the Allan Border Medal.

Above: England's Liam Plunkett celebrates my wicket in the second final in Sydney.

The former great South African batsman Barry Richards, on commentary duty, Scotland captain Craig Wright, me and the former Indian paceman Javagal Srinath, the match referee, at the toss before our opening match of the 2007 World Cup, in St Kitts.

Australia's bowling coach and his World Cup pacemen among the ruins of the fort on Brimstone Hill at Basseterre, St Kitts. From left: Troy Cooley, Glenn McGrath, Stuart Clark, Shaun Tait, Shane Watson, Nathan Bracken and Mitchell Johnson.

Left: Shaun Tait and Matthew Hayden at centre-wicket practice in St Kitts.

Below left: Andrew Symonds with fielding coach Mike Young in Antigua.

Below right: The Australian team trains in Grenada before our final Super Eights game against New Zealand.

Left: Matthew Hayden glides a single through the raindrops during his epic 158 against the West Indies in Antigua.

Left: Shane Watson is all smiles after his 65 from 32 balls against New Zealand.

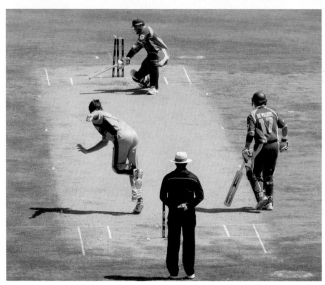

The first two wickets to fall in the second semi-final, in St Lucia. Above: Nathan Bracken bowls South African captain Graeme Smith. Left: Glenn McGrath gets through a retreating Jacques Kallis.

Adam Gilchrist during his extraordinary, dynamic hundred in the 2007 World Cup final.

It was a great privilege for me to bat in a fourth straight World Cup final.

Kumar Sangakkara (left) and Sanath Jayasuriya are caught in the Barbados sunshine during their stirring partnership that threatened to get Sri Lanka back into the final.

Below left: Brad Hogg after claiming the key wicket of Sangakkara.

Below right: Premature Aussie celebrations, after the Sri Lankans agreed to go off for bad light.

Left: Michael Clarke bowls to Chaminda Vaas as the final descends into gloom.

Above: Our celebrations after the final took place under a blaze of fireworks and camera flashes.

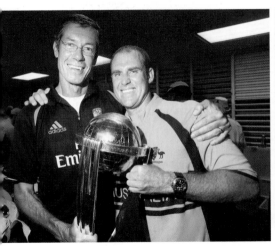

Above left: John Buchanan, on his last day of duty as Australian coach, with Matt Hayden.

Above right: Glenn McGrath receives his player of the tournament award from Sir Garfield Sobers.

Left: On the beach the morning after the final, showing the Cup to the world ... and to some of the boys up on our hotel balcony.

I'm not sure the track for the Ireland game was that good, but I do know that the first ball Shaun Tait bowled in this match was one of the fastest balls I've ever seen in my life.

From our experience here and previously in Australia, we had come to expect that Shaun would commence a bowling spell with a wide, often a big wide, as he sought to pitch his first ball up near the blockhole. After he bowled that wide, his pace would drop for a few deliveries as he tried to land the ball in something like the right area, but we wanted him to be electric in the first over. After the game against Bangladesh, Troy Cooley and I sat down with him and said, 'Look, first ball, why don't you just run in and bowl a bouncer? Just to loosen yourself up and get the first one on target, bowl a bouncer. You won't have to worry about the ball swinging or spearing down the leg-side. This way, you won't put yourself under pressure right from the start.'

I'm sure we said 'loosen yourself up'. Against England, first ball, he bowled Michael Vaughan a fast bouncer and then here against Ireland I was at second slip when he sent down a rocket to William Porterfield. Gilly managed to intercept it, and Haydos and I just looked at each other and mimed, 'Wow!' It was seriously fast, and Porterfield did well to get out of the way. I couldn't help thinking, *If Taity gets a couple on line here they're gonna need the luck of the Irish.*

MORE OFTEN THAN NOT, I bat first when we win the toss in all forms of cricket. But this time I sent the Irishmen in, purely because I wanted to get the game over and done with as soon as possible. We also changed our line-up and batting order, using the game to give Stuart Clark a run in conditions that suited him and to get Mike Hussey some time in the middle.

Huss has been having one of those runs where he wasn't getting much of an opportunity, and on the rare occasions he wasn't having any luck. After the West Indies game, when he unluckily chopped a wide one back onto his stumps, I began to think that we needed to get him up the batting order, to give him a chance to feel bat on ball in match conditions. He was telling us that he was batting well in the nets, but as we all know net practice doesn't necessarily do you much good if you are getting starved of opportunity on match day.

Part of me wanted to push him up the batting order as soon as the match against Bangladesh, regardless of the situation of the game, on the basis that an in-form Mike Hussey is so important to us that the disruption to normal transmission would be worth it. But another part of my brain kept insisting that we didn't want to be making such changes when overall things were going so well. Sometimes, trying to help one bloke out can impact unfairly on a team-mate, and you just have to let the normal run of things look after itself. And, of course, there is the happy reality that if the No. 6 isn't getting many chances, it means the top order is going all right. Huss made that point himself. One of the negatives of batting five or six in a one-day side is that the only time you get a chance to build an innings is when the blokes in front of you have failed.

Thursday, April 19

Super Eights match, at St George's, Grenada (April 16): Sri Lanka 226 (49.4 overs: DPMD Jayawardene 72, LPC Silva 64; NW Bracken 4–19) lost to Australia 3–232 (42.4 overs: RT Ponting 66*, Symonds 63*, ML Hayden 41) by seven wickets

WE'D RECEIVED SOME MIXED messages about the wicket in Grenada. South Africa and the West Indies had played a high-scoring game there a week ago, but since then the totals have been getting smaller and I'd seen one report where the pitch was described as a 'compost heap'. When we had a chance to look at the square, it was patchy, but it actually played okay. I probably wouldn't have wanted to chase too many more than the 227 Sri Lanka set us three days back, but a wicket doesn't have to give up 350 runs a side to be a fair one-day pitch. By the end of the match, the pitch was beginning to break up, and it was spinning, and if Muttiah Muralitharan had been playing, I doubt we would have won by seven wickets.

However, the great off-spinner was 'resting', one of a small group of the Sri Lankans' best bowlers who didn't front for this encounter, which lost a fraction of its edge because both teams have already qualified for the final four. There was much conjecture and some criticism about their decision to play an under-strength side, but I preferred to look for the positives out of our display. Number one for me was that Sri Lanka didn't leave any of their excellent batsmen out, and we knocked them over for a relatively small total.

TWO DAYS AFTER THE Sri Lanka game, while they were beating Ireland 2–81 to 77 in a game that lasted less than 40 overs, we spent five long hours out on the water looking for a marlin. We might have seen one after an hour, but that was it, until when it was finally just about time to come back in, one of the six rods exploded into life and a deck hand started yelling, 'Marlin! Marlin! Marlin!' Matty Hayden, a mad keen fisherman, had organised this day out, but at the time he was below deck having a sleep, which meant that someone else was going to enjoy the experience of reeling the big fish in. But before any of us could even think about to whom that role would fall, Haydos suddenly came to life, like Superman bursting out of a phone booth, knocked everyone else out of the way and strapped himself in behind the fiercely vibrating rod. After 25 minutes, and some spectacular action as the marlin leapt out of the ocean, the catch was completed.

When we returned to shore, I saw Tom Moody, the Sri Lankan coach, and told him to go and have a look at Haydos' catch. 'It's as big as you!' I told him. This was not the first time Haydos had enjoyed some luck with a fishing line on this trip. Back in St Vincent, he and Symmo had ventured out with some locals and caught a stack of tuna, which they brought back and barbecued for us. I remember that clearly because of the text message I received that day: *We've got the fish, organise the bbq and make up the salads.*

BECAUSE THE WEST INDIES is a collection of different countries, whenever we 'island hop' we have to fill out various immigration and customs forms. On one occasion, I was next to Brad Hodge when he filled out his documentation and when he came to 'Occupation', he turned to me and said with a half-smile, 'Should I write "Professional fieldsman"?'

This wasn't a disgruntled bench player having a dig at the captain. Hodgey has been having a good trip and when he has had the chance to play in the early games, before Andrew Symonds came back into the side, he looked sensational. He had made an explosive 123 from 89 balls against the Netherlands, and then came back into the side for three Super Eight games after Shane Watson was hurt in Antigua. Unfortunately, Hodgey never got a hit in those three games, which we won by seven wickets, nine wickets and seven wickets. Hence, the 'professional fieldsman' crack.

When it comes to picking squads for big tours and tournaments, the character and commitment of the blokes who might not play is an important ingredient. Just a little bit of public dissension from a bloke or blokes out of the top XI can quickly choke team morale, not least because it can cause others in the touring party to 'pick sides'. I have read of past teams being divided on state lines, as small groups from the same part of Australia stick together in response to real or perceived injustices. Something as simple as a reserve dragging his butt at practice because he's not getting a game can have a negative impact.

I remember back to the 1995 West Indies tour, when I knew I wasn't going to play a game unless something bad happened to one of the Test batsmen, that I had to keep revving myself up and enjoy the experience, rather than let my lack of playing time get me down. I think the memory of that tour helps me now, because I know what the guys who aren't playing are going through, and appreciate the effort they are putting in for little personal reward. There have been times — and Andrew Symonds at the 2003 World Cup is probably the best example — when what a player brings to the group in terms of positive attitude and team spirit was an important consideration in deciding who would be the last bloke selected in a squad. On this trip, the guys on the bench — Brad Hodge, Brad Haddin, Mitchell Johnson and Stuart Clark — have been superb.

Saturday, April 21

Super Eights match, at St George's, Grenada (April 20): Australia 6–348 (50 overs: ML Hayden 103, RT Ponting 66, SR Watson 65*, MJ Clarke 49) defeated New Zealand 133 (25.5 overs: PG Fulton 62; GB Hogg 4–29, SW Tait 3–32) by 215 runs

IT WAS GOOD TO go into the semi-finals on the back of a big win, especially as it came against the same New Zealand side that had beaten us 3–zip in the Chappell–Hadlee Trophy series. Even more encouragingly, this was one of those games where everything went just about perfectly, especially when we bowled and fielded. Maybe our opponents weren't at full throttle, because they have already qualified for the semi-finals, but we were certainly at the top of our games.

There was never any suggestion that we'd ease off. On the contrary, we saw this as a chance to inflict some psychological damage on a team that we might be seeing again in the final. Even the fact that the Black Caps were without Shane Bond, who was back at the team hotel suffering from food poisoning, and Jacob Oram, who has a heel injury, couldn't take anything away from our victory. 'I'd rather be in our room than theirs right at the moment,' I said straight afterwards. 'I'm sure they'll be having all sorts of meetings over the next few days to talk about today's game. We'll be having a beer tonight.'

ONE OF THE MEMORIES I'm going to savour from this World Cup experience, regardless of how the next week pans out, is the look on Shane Watson's face as he came off the field after scoring 65 from 32 balls against New Zealand. He's had such a bad run with injuries over the last few months — missing the Ashes series and most of the one-dayers back home, and then straining a calf muscle in the sandpit at Antigua — he was entitled to think the cricket gods are against him. Watto's body language has never been one of his strengths, yet here he looked so positive, as if he knew he'd turned a very important corner.

And he was entitled to be happy, as he had just produced some of the cleanest hitting of a cricket ball I have ever seen. The slaps to fine leg off the Kiwi pacemen, as they tried to stay away from his booming off-side shots, were a particular highlight.

Wednesday, April 25

Second Semi-final, at Gros Islet, St Lucia (April 25): South Africa 149 (43.5 overs: JM Kemp 49*; SW Tait 4–39, GD McGrath 3–18) lost to Australia 3–153 (31.3 overs: MJ Clarke 60*, ML Hayden 41) by seven wickets

MORE OFTEN THAN NOT, when the big games come around, this Australian team stands up. In the lead-up to this semi-final against our old adversary, South Africa, there were suggestions about that we might have 'peaked too early', but I wasn't concerned about that. Call me a raging optimist if you like, but I actually took the view that the way we'd kept improving from game to game was a sign that even bigger things were in store in the semi and the final.

We have never set upper limits on our achievements. If you score a hundred from 60 deliveries, there is no reason why next time you can't get that century from 55 balls. You can always take enormous satisfaction and pride from a great performance, but that should never mean that it's the best you can do. In cricket, a team game, even on the best of days, one or two blokes miss out. What if next time, those two guys don't miss out — how good will the side's performance be then?

The fact that this game was a knockout added something new, but we have known this stage of the tournament was coming and really relished the challenge. South Africa had lost to New Zealand and Bangladesh in the Super Eights, but then came back to thrash England to confirm their semi-final spot. I guess it might have seemed a little unfair if, having played so well for so long, we'd suddenly been eliminated by a team that had dropped a couple of games, but that is the nature of this competition. It's not like we didn't know the rules when we signed up to participate. I've stressed to the guys that we are not owed anything just because we've played well in every game since we've arrived in the Caribbean. All the teams in the final four were starting with a clean slate; our only advantage was the confidence our unbeaten run had brought us.

I THINK THAT COUNTED for plenty. While we went about our business as usual, South Africa obviously spent the time before the game trying to come up with something new strategy-wise to try to beat us. I was extremely surprised when they won the toss and batted, and not just because the pitch seemed to have something in it. They have usually fielded first against us, with some success, too. This time, it was as if they were trying to say, 'We'll take you on, on your terms. We're not scared of you!' But when Graeme Smith said, 'We'll have a bat,' I immediately thought, *Gee, they must be desperate.*

In the papers leading into the game, the members of the South African team hierarchy had talked about the need for their players to 'back themselves' whenever they played us. For me, 'backing yourself' is about having the courage to execute your game plans as well as you can for a long period of time. But it's also about being realistic, about 'swimming between your flags'. If you understand your game and don't try to do what you can't do, and work your hardest within those parameters, then you are giving yourself the best chance of playing your best cricket. That's brave and smart.

South Africa, on the other hand, just played dumb. Glenn McGrath had caused a stir earlier in the tournament by claiming that Smith's team lacks flair and is too structured for its own good, and that might have struck a nerve, judging by the way they played here. The best I could read into their strategy was that they'd decided to make a statement by batting first and scoring 400 in a World Cup semi-final, as if nothing less would guarantee them the victory they wanted. They were all trying to play the innings of their life in the same game, but they were cut down, one after the other. Instead of swimming between the flags, they drowned down the wrong end of the beach. Smith and Jacques Kallis were too aggressive, much too quickly, while Glenn McGrath, Nathan Bracken and Shaun Tait were magnificent, and by the 10th over the scoreboard read 5–27. If Herschelle Gibbs had been given out when we thought he got an inside edge off a very quick ball from Taity, they would have been 6–27, after winning the toss and batting.

McGrath was brilliant. In most of our earlier games he had bowled first change, coming on after Tait's opening burst, and there was no pre-conceived plan for him to take the new ball here. However, when we arrived at the Beausejour Cricket Ground here in Gros Islet, St Lucia, there was a strong wind blowing up and across the wicket at a particular angle that meant that whoever bowled from the pavilion end would be working up into a gale. But if Bracken bowled from that end, the wind would stifle his natural away swing, so we decided to start with Bracks, then Pigeon up into the wind, then Taity to bowl first change at high speed. McGrath responded by taking 3–14 from his first six overs, Tait was as dangerous as ever despite the slight change to his role, and in the end, considering their disastrous start, South Africa probably did well to get to 149.

In reply, we lost Adam Gilchrist straight away, and when I was dismissed we were 2–44, but Michael Clarke was outstanding and we got home with 18-and-a-half overs to spare. I had always rated South Africa the second best team at this World Cup, and believed a big game from them was just around the corner. So for us to win this game so decisively was almost unbelievable. This victory has to rank right up there with anything we have achieved over the past six months.

So now it's on to the final in Barbados, where our opponents will be Sri Lanka, who overcame the New Zealanders in Jamaica yesterday on the back of a century from skipper Mahela Jayawardene and four wickets from Muttiah Muralitharan.

Monday, April 30

World Cup Final, at Barbados (April 28): Australia 4–281 (38 overs: AC Gilchrist 149) defeated Sri Lanka 8–215 (36 overs: ST Jayasuriya 63, KC Sangakkara 54) by 53 runs (D/L method)

I ONLY STOPPED FOR a moment to think about how fortunate I am to be preparing for my *fourth* World Cup final. I am not sure anyone is entitled to be that lucky, and it proves that during my career I have been a member of some fantastic teams and played with some truly great cricketers. As quickly as I could, I stopped worrying about past finals, or wondering what the future might hold for me, and tried to think totally about what we needed to do to win this game.

We had played our first match of this World Cup more than six weeks ago, and at different times there had been gaps of eight days, six days and twice five days between our games. Now, before the final, we had our shortest break — just three days — which seemed a little weird, a strange time to be rushing things.

Overall, our record against Sri Lanka is very good, but they have beaten us in a couple of big games — the World Cup final in 1996 and the Champions Trophy semi-final in 2002. Alex Kountouris reckons they used to fancy their chances when they faced us, but in recent years that confidence has diminished. We have certainly long believed that Murali would rather bowl at anyone but us, because we tend to be more aggressive against him than other teams, while Nathan Bracken in particular has built a good record against them, especially against their left-handers. The memory of the Super Eights game, when they played a weakened bowling attack and we bowled them out, was strong. There were plenty of reasons for us to be confident.

The biggest mystery for us was their 23-year-old opening bowler Lasith Malinga, whom we have faced before, but who is a much better organised, more controlled express bowler now. His effort in taking four wickets in four balls against South Africa, almost pulling off an incredible victory, was a tournament highlight, and his explosive, round-arm, slinging action had generated plenty of positive comment and made a number of batsman jump and jive. On the eve of the final, we set up a bowling machine at the nets to try to mimic his delivery, taking part of the machine's legs off and moving it in front of the stumps at the bowler's end, because that is where the ball is coming from when he bowls. I must confess to not being that convinced about the merits of this kind of rehearsal, but Matt Hayden and Adam Gilchrist used it, and it worked for them.

DID IT EVER! BECAUSE Adam's hundred came in such a big game, I have to rate it up there with the greatest knocks I've ever seen. I was in the viewing area, sitting next to Michael Clarke, when the first ball of the final was bowled by Chaminda Vaas, and Gilly played a forward defensive push and hit the ball right in the middle of the bat and it flew to mid-off. That was enough. I whacked Pup on the leg and said quietly, 'This could be Gilly's day.'

Afterwards, there was considerable debate about Gilly batting with a squash ball in his left (bottom) batting glove, to help him with his grip. I've seen him use it before, but not often in games and was a little surprised when he used it this time. I think it might have been a last-minute decision. The start of the game was delayed by morning rain, the first ball wasn't bowled until a little after midday, and as we waited for the start, Gilly was out on the balcony, seemingly ready to go. Then, when it was time to walk out, he suddenly raced back into the room and grabbed the squash ball out of his kit. And then he went out to smash a century from 72 balls, with eight fours and six sixes. One blast over very deep mid-wicket off Murali almost cleared the Greenidge and Haynes Stand, while another off Tillakaratne Dilshan landed high up in the new Worrell, Weekes and Walcott Stand. He finished with 149, a record score for a World Cup final, from 104 deliveries, having gone past 50 for the third straight World Cup final.

The logic behind using the squash ball is that it stops you gripping the handle too tightly with your bottom hand, but part of me says it would be more of a hindrance, as it doesn't feel natural. But we all have little idiosyncrasies that work for us, but no one else. I went through a stage when I taped two fingers of my bottom hand together, to weaken my bottom-hand grip. One of the big things you are always guarding against is your bottom hand taking over, when it is your top hand and your front elbow that leads you through a stroke.

IT WAS A GREY, RAINY morning, hardly perfect weather for such a cricket showpiece. We tossed just before 10am. It had been raining, and as we walked out for that toss we could all see that it was going to pour with rain any minute. I said to Mahela Jayawardene, 'Mate, there's no point doing this now.' But the officials insisted, and as it turned out it didn't worry me, because I was always keen to bat first, to get out there and put some runs on the board. The rain did come not long after the specially minted coin had landed, and for the next two hours we were idle, wondering if the tournament would go yet another day. Finally, at around 11.45am, we were told play would begin in half an hour, the start of a 38 overs-a-side contest.

We'd stressed the need to keep wickets in hand for the middle overs, to counter Murali and his fellow spinners, but this didn't mean we were going away from our usual strategy of seeing off the early overs when the ball is new and shiny, and then getting aggressive from there. Vaas is a very cagey one-day bowler, always seaming the new ball and changing his pace up all the time, while Malinga, of course, is usually lightning quick, so we had to be wary. We were surprised their first change, Dilhara Fernando, was playing, and saw his overs as a chance to attack, and that was pretty much how it worked out. Gilchrist and Hayden were 0–46 after 10 overs, and then we went crazy. For the rest of the innings, we scored at nearly eight-and-a-half runs per over.

For a while when Sri Lanka batted, it looked like Kumar Sangakkara and Sanath Jayasuriya might bat them back into the game. They are two class cricketers, capable of producing remarkable innings, and I opted to take the powerplays as soon as I could, for two totally conflicting reasons. Because we were defending such a big score, part of me wanted to just get them out of the way. But because Sangakkara and Jayasuriya are arguably their two most dangerous batsmen, I wanted to attack them, to get them out. If we broke that partnership quickly, I theorised, we could not be beaten.

I must confess going away from the game plan we'd used throughout the tournament worried me, but it was clear that these two batsmen held the key to their innings. If we could make them go for big shots against our best bowlers, that was our best chance of getting them out. But they played brilliantly, and at the 19-over mark they were 1–117, requiring an imposing eight-and-a-half an over to claim a shock victory, but still definitely a chance. But the weather was closing in again, and then Brad Hogg stepped up and nailed the vital breakthrough: Sangakkara caught at mid-wicket for 54. When Jayasuriya was bowled by Michael Clarke three overs later, the match was almost won.

Quickly the required run rate moved into double figures, as the light deteriorated. With 10 overs to go, they needed nearly 11-and-a-half runs per over to win; five overs later, the ask was up to 21 an over; that is, three-and-a-half runs per ball. By this stage it was closer to night than day, and Sri Lanka couldn't win. I had the ball in my hand at the end of the 33rd over, and when I saw the two umpires in a huddle, I immediately thought, *They're going to offer them the light.* That was precisely what they did, and when the batsmen accepted the offer I threw the ball miles into the air and took off running. Soon we were jumping over each other and hollering with delight. The World Cup was over.

As usual, this moment went in a blur, but I reckon we must have celebrated for a couple of minutes. But then one of the umpires, Aleem Dar, tapped me on the shoulder and said, 'I'm sorry, we have to come back tomorrow. There are still three overs to bowl.'

'You've got to be kidding, don't you?' I replied. I was as incredulous as I have ever been on a cricket field. I honestly thought he was having a lend of me.

'No, we have to come back tomorrow.'

'Mate, 20 overs constitutes a game,' I argued. It's hard to describe my mood. I wasn't angry, more stunned, bewildered and bemused. 'Once the team batting second faces 20 overs, it's game over,' I pleaded. 'Twenty overs constitutes a game.'

I sensed that the two umpires were getting conflicting messages through their earpieces. Aleem Dar, who is a very good umpire, said, 'No, those rules are written for rain. It is different for bad light.'

This can't be happening, I thought. *We've won*. Even if we did have to come back tomorrow, we'd still win, because we were so far in front. But this was taking some of the gloss off our triumph. It was as if someone had come up with a scheme to prevent us from enjoying this huge moment in our lives. Meanwhile, there were conferences between umpires and officials, and who knows how it would have ended if Mahela Jayawardene hadn't stepped forward and said, 'We'll bat out the overs tonight. Let's finish it.'

I thought that was a sensational piece of sportsmanship, a gesture that should never be forgotten. Enough lights were available to allow us to see each other ... just. We bowled our spinners, and there was even the parody of a decision going to the TV umpire, just to slow the process down a fraction more. During the last over, I was fielding at mid-wicket and couldn't see a thing. And finally we won our third World Cup in a row. Later, the match officials admitted they had misinterpreted the rules, and the game should have been over when the light offer was accepted. For us, the fiasco of this last half hour didn't really matter. The only downer was that I couldn't engineer it so Glenn McGrath bowled the final over. It would have been nice if he could have ended his ODI career the same way he finished up in Test cricket, with a wicket from his final ball.

LATER THAT NIGHT, IT was Glenn who led us in the singing of the team song, though this didn't work out quite the way we planned it. It was late in the night when we decided to go out onto the field, onto the pitch, to sing *Under the Southern Cross*. After we'd gathered in a tight circle, arm in arm, Adam Gilchrist (who has led the one-day team in song since I became captain in 2002) put the question: 'What is your lasting memory of this World Cup?' And so it began, each of us recalling a personal highlight from the previous two months. For a while, we were oblivious to the outside world, but then I noticed a group of policemen had come up behind our scrum.

Soon, one of them approached us and said, 'Righto boys, time to go, you've got to get off the ground.'

'Oh, come on mate,' someone responded. 'We won't be long.'

'No, you've got to go now.'

'Hang on,' I said. 'We've just won the World Cup. Can't you give us one minute?'

Unfortunately, I added a swear word into that request, which the police officer did not appreciate at all. 'You cannot cuss like that in Barbados,' he said firmly, as his mood blackened. He stepped towards me, and my team-mates moved in behind me, as if a real stink was about to take place. I think they threatened to lock us up for the night, and we soon realised that we weren't going to be permitted to finish our ceremony. As a diplomat, I'd failed miserably, and I'm fully aware I shouldn't have sworn like I did, though I do wonder why they couldn't have given us a little more time. We went back to the dressing room, packed up our things, and returned back to the hotel, where we sang the anthem long and loudly by the pool, with Pidge at the forefront.

THE PARTY WAS ONE of the best and longest I've been involved in as an Australian cricketer. Some of the boys went through the night, and well into the following day. For the second time in four months, we found ourselves on James Packer's boat, though this was a vessel he'd hired, not the luxury yacht we saw in Sydney after the Ashes Test. Everything was laid on for us, and we really felt like the champions of the world. A couple of the lads had some fun with the jet skis that were stored in the boat, and we were all clowning around, throwing each other's sunnies and thongs overboard.

Earlier, Pidge (the retiring champion and player of the series), Gilly (the player of the final) and I (the captain) had been roused to go down to the beach for some TV interviews and a photo shoot with the World Cup, which we managed with a lot of laughs. At one point, we looked up to one of the balconies of the hotel to see Andrew Symonds and Mitchell Johnson not nude, but close. A season that had started in the Queensland scrub last August, with us all wearing white T-shirts and camouflage trousers, had ended on the beach in Bridgetown, with some of my mates in nothing more than their jockstraps. Our dress sense might not have always been impeccable, but our cricket had been. It had been some journey, and I am so grateful for the fact that I was part of it.

Later, as I thought about all our success, one thing kept coming back to me. We had earned all this. Everyone in the Australian team agreed, straight after the 2005 Ashes series, that we needed and wanted to play better cricket. We identified what had to change, and we put the infrastructure in place to allow that to happen. There has been a lot of skill involved in all the success we've achieved in the past 18 months, a lot of planning and a lot of character. But more than anything, our success has come about because we have worked harder than we have ever worked before. We could have talked about doing this or changing that as much as we liked, but we had to get out there and do it. It didn't matter if we were behind, had our noses in front, or were leading by a long way, we had to keep working. I'd like to think that throughout 2006–07 we demonstrated that this simple commitment can help turn any team around, in sport, in business, in life.

When I was just a boy, everyone in my family kept telling me that 'all I was going to get out of life was what I was willing to put in'. The philosophy at the Mowbray Cricket Club was the same. I think I forgot that a little during the 2005 Ashes series. I think we all did. Now, as I admired the World Cup trophy we've just won, and my mind wandered back to the Ashes series and the Champions Trophy, I kept thinking about all the good times we've had, and resolved to never again forget the value and importance of hard work. If we can do that — even without Marto and Warney and Lang and Pidge and Buck — I'm sure there are plenty more good times ahead for the Australian cricket team.

CHAPTER 17

BUCK

FOR ME, THERE IS a strong link between the Australian team's historic Test series victory in India in 2004 and the World Cup triumph in 2007, one that goes further than the two being among the Australian team's most important wins of recent times.

I broke my thumb at the Champions Trophy in England in 2004, which preceded the tour to India, so while the rest of the team went straight to India for the Test series, with Adam Gilchrist as captain, I returned home for a month. I rejoined the team in Nagpur, before the third Test, in the hope I'd be able to play in that game, but the thumb wasn't right and I was on the sidelines as the boys won that Test to take a 3–nil lead in the four-Test series.

Though I had kept hoping for a miracle recovery, there was never any real chance of me playing in that game, so on the first morning I was genuinely excited to be among the team, rather than suffering any anguish because I'd failed a last-minute fitness test. When the Test began, as Justin Langer and Matthew Hayden went out to bat, I was in my whites, wearing the baggy green, ready to do any 12th-man duties that might come my way. In fact, I wanted something, anything, to do, and after about half an hour I spotted coach John Buchanan sitting by himself in the viewing area, with his laptop in front of him, tapping on the keyboard. *What is he looking at?* I thought to myself. *What is he doing now?* It was someone else's job to capture all the statistics from the day's play, so it wasn't as if he was sitting there, recording where the last ball had pitched, or how often Lang had let the ball go. *What is Buck doing on his computer?*

I snuck up behind him, looked over his shoulder, and was somewhat stunned by what I saw. Our coach was planning the contents for a handbook he was compiling for the 2007 World Cup, a document he intended to hand to all the players who might be part of that campaign. Two things immediately struck me: one, *he must be very comfortable about our preparation for this Test, if he can be working on future projects*; and two, *the next World Cup is two and a half years away!*

I always knew Buck was a forward thinker and I had already been inspired by how well-organised he was. But it was only at this moment that I realised just how far ahead he planned. If something was going to be a factor in Australia winning the World Cup, even this far from the final, he wanted to know about it.

JUSTIN LANGER CALLS JOHN Buchanan 'the great visionary'. I had an inclination to use that description here, but to add the adjective 'cricket', as in 'the great cricket visionary'. But then I thought back to when Buck became Australian coach.

That was at the start of the 1999–2000 Australian season. Geoff Marsh had been in charge from after the 1996 World Cup to our Sri Lanka tour in August–October 1999, then, after Geoff resigned, Allan Border filled the role temporarily for our short trip to Zimbabwe, and then Buck took over, starting with the Brisbane Test against Pakistan. At our first team meeting, he wrote a few things up on a whiteboard — mainly about what we could expect from him and what he expected from us. He explained that he was going to be as honest and as loyal as he could be, and that he was going to do things slightly differently to how other coaches went about their business. He wanted to bring a family environment to the team, by getting the wives and partners more involved. More than anything, he wanted us to be open to all the ideas he had, to give him a fair go.

What I remember most clearly is that he spoke of his desire to make us *better people* as well as better cricketers. Seven-and-a-half years later, I reckon he'd be pleased with the results. To call him simply a *cricket* visionary is to underrate him. Buck is much more than that.

BACK IN '99, I was happy to give him a go. He had been the coach of Queensland for a number of seasons, helping them to their first Sheffield Shield title, and the blokes who'd played under him thought he was excellent, in his own way. I quickly learned that he did indeed do some things differently to how Geoff Marsh and Bob Simpson (the Australian coach from 1986 to 1996) had gone about the job. 'Swampy' and 'Simmo' weren't into whiteboards, computers and time management the way the new coach was; nor would they have talked about the value of being ambidextrous, of scoring 400 in a 50-over match, or becoming the 'new Invincibles', as Buck did.

For day one, no matter how well or how badly we were going, Buck would make us look at things in different ways, and work with us to identify the brakes — physical and mental — that were impinging or might impinge on our performance. That is where he was different to the other coaches. Other coaches only knew one way: if you weren't making runs, go to the nets and hit 1000 balls; if you dropped a catch, make sure you caught 1000 catches the next day. Buck didn't denigrate that approach, but to him it was based on the premise that such repetition would fix the flaw, which might be the case, but not always. Working hard was one thing; working hard and smart was his solution.

Importantly, he never forced his theories on players. With major training exercises, such as the boot camp, it was 'one in, all in', but in one-on-one dealings with players he was shrewdly flexible. He won over some blokes very quickly, while others took longer. As he readily admits, he never really gelled with Shane Warne or Stuart MacGill, yet both guys had great success while he was coach. This, I believe, reflects highly on all three of them, as it shows they were able to put the team and their performances ahead of any personal differences.

There was a lot of pressure on Buck when he joined the Australian set-up, because he didn't have what Swampy and Simmo had — international experience — so he had to rely on his expertise and personality to challenge us. In his first home season, Australia won every Test and all but one ODI, but he couldn't stand still. Buck had to keep reinventing himself as a coach, which he did brilliantly, except, maybe, in England in 2005, when the team needed something new and Buck and I were slow to respond. When we got home, we all had to re-evaluate the way we went about things, and the manner in which he, with the support of Cricket Australia, revamped the coaching structure was farsighted. This meant that instead of the Ashes loss bringing him down, it inspired his greatest achievement. The way the Australian team played from the start of the 2005–06 season to the 2007 World Cup was as much a credit to the head coach and his staff as it was to the players who received most of the acclaim.

His record in international cricket is imposing — 90 Tests as coach, for 69 wins, 11 draws and only 10 losses; 216 ODIs, for 160 wins, 46 losses, three ties and seven no- results — yet more than the victories, in my view, what makes Buck special is his extraordinary thoroughness. I noted from the start his penchant for getting things exactly right and, without he or I knowing it, I think he inspired me to work harder on my preparation. No idea or strategy was dismissed, in case it might be the one that made the team one per cent better, yet he wasn't a bloke who did things on a whim. He was big on us getting the most out of our time at training, while he could spend hours in front of a television or his laptop screen, studying videos of his players and our opponents, or poring over statistics that might give a clue to how batsmen scored their runs and were most likely to be dismissed, or what style of bowling is likely to be most and least effective. Some old-style pundits lampooned his use of the computer when he first became Australian coach. Every team uses such technology now.

The players who presented the biggest challenge to Buck were the ones who were set in their ways. He didn't want blokes continuing to be good if he believed they could be great. A batsman might want to go to the nets, to feel bat on ball, but the coach had assigned that same half an hour for the players to work on 'wrong-handed' throwing. Such ideas were a waste of time for some, but a sign of where the game was heading for Buck. One day, he'd argue, all the best fieldsmen will throw powerfully with each arm, just as the best footballers can kick with both feet. He wanted us to be so dominant that we changed the rules in the game, like Phar Lap did in the early 1930s, when the authorities changed the rules of racing, to make it more competitive. We didn't get there, but we did win his first 15 Tests as coach, and his last 12, and his record in World Cups was two for two.

AS CAPTAIN, I LOVED having access to Buck's tactical know-how. The best example of how his 'thinking outside the square' approach worked to our advantage came in that series in India in 2004.

The way we bowled and the field placements we employed were very different to anything we'd tried in the past. We had talked for months about getting our strategies right, and a lot of the pre-tour planning came from Buck. He identified the Indian batsmen as 'boundary hitters' and had seen how, once they got on a roll, the crowd would get behind them and they'd be hard to stop. 'Let's try to take that away from them,' he argued.

Instead of bowling to their weaknesses, we bowled to their strengths, supported by field placements that many incorrectly interpreted as being defensive. We often only had one or two slips in at the start of the innings, instead of the customary three slips and a gully, and the 'spare' fieldsmen were used to plug the areas, in the ring and on the boundary, where the Indian batsmen liked to hit. Essentially, we said to them, 'You can keep hitting your favourite shots, but if you want to hit fours you are going to have to hit the ball harder and harder to get it through.' We made them play a different way, took the crowd out of the game and the momentum from their psyche, and it worked for us.

A dynamic batsman such as Virender Sehwag, whose method is all-out attack and who is hero worshipped in India because of his reputation for scoring heavily and quickly, didn't enjoy our method at all. A fieldsman was stationed on the boundary at deep point, and we could see Sehwag's frustration grow whenever he played one of his characteristic slashes through the off-side field, but only scored a single and lost the strike. The scorecards show that we out-batted India in the first three Tests of that series. We out-thought them, too.

Buck always tried to deflect attention from his contribution. His public comments were always well calculated, designed to help the way we were going and stifle any optimism our opponents might have been feeling. He is a public figure who has always tried to stay away from media as much as he can. In this regard, he modelled himself on another Queenslander, the great rugby league coach, Wayne Bennett.

It is true that some of his initiatives were a little bizarre. Once in New Zealand, he had us chasing albatross — I'm still not sure why — while at other times we've done triathlons in the West Indies, rowing on the Yarra River in Melbourne and mountain-bike riding in New Zealand. We've read books such as *The Art of War* and *Who Moved My Cheese?*. Not everyone enjoyed these exercises, but Buck's mantra is always: 'If you don't give things a chance, you'll never improve.' He was criticised at times for not having the technical expertise to, for example, help bowlers with their actions. I think people said that almost as a reflex, on the rare occasions when something went wrong, simply because he hadn't played cricket for Australia, as if they'd found a weakness. While it is true that his knowledge in this area is not as farsighted as his tactical nous or man-management skills, it is also a fact, surely, that players who reach the international stage should understand their techniques well enough to solve most of their problems themselves. It was interesting that the blokes he helped most in the technical area were the men he'd worked with for the longest time, fellow Queenslanders such as Matthew Hayden and Michael Kasprowicz. In doing so, I think he just confirmed something I've known for a long time. The guy who is best suited to analyse my technique is the current Australian assistant coach Dene Hills, who has been watching me bat since the days we were in the Tasmanian Shield squad together. It is impossible for a head coach to be across the individual needs of every one of his players, which is why Buck campaigned for so long for specialist batting, bowling and fielding coaches to be appointed. He finally got them after the 2005 Ashes series and the results speak for themselves.

This is one reason why Buck's successor as Australian coach, Tim Nielsen, whose promotion was announced in February 2007, during the latter stages of the Commonwealth Bank Series, has so much to offer. Tim knows the current group of players really well, because he has worked with them as Buck's assistant coach, and he knows the 'next generation' who will soon enter the Australian set-up because he has worked with them at the Centre of Excellence (where he has been head coach) in recent years. Tim is smart and intuitive, and his own man, so he will bring plenty of freshness to the job as well.

I KNOW I'M A better person for having known John Buchanan, and I reckon most people would say that about their experience working with him. He was usually able to find the most effective way to get the best out of people. One thing I learned from Buck is how important it is to understand and appreciate the players' diverse personalities, so I can communicate with each of them in the most effective way. I'm sure this has helped my captaincy.

Most of the time, Buck was even-tempered, though occasionally he did give us some almighty sprays, if we played a brand of cricket he thought was unsatisfactory. And there were rare instances when he made his dissatisfaction public, such as in 2003–04, when he slid some notes under our doors in Adelaide after the second Test against India, a game we couldn't lose but we did. He tore strips of us that night, wrote his criticism down on paper, and then that criticism ended up not just in our hands but also in the papers. He made the judgment that we needed this private and public censure, and didn't care who he upset in the process, which showed he could be hard-nosed, but at the same time, he was a measured coach who usually knew the right way to respond to a predicament.

There were times when we would come off the field at the end of the day and I would drag him aside and say, 'Mate, I've got to give it to these blokes.'

'No, just sit back and take a couple of minutes,' he would advise quietly. 'Have a think about it. Is it worth doing? You are better off just letting them think about it. Take those two minutes. Don't do anything now.'

After that, I would stop, cool down a fraction ... and realise that while shouting might make me feel a little better, it wouldn't do anything for the team. Buck had read me and the situation well.

I've never seen him like he was leading into the 2007 World Cup. For most of the first week, I had to calm him down, tell him that he hadn't let us down, that he hadn't misjudged our preparation, that there was no reason to panic. His nervousness has spread among all the coaches, which with hindsight shows how much the Cup meant to them. Buck, I think, was fearful that if we flopped it would tarnish his legacy, that he'd be remembered as 'the coach who lost the World Cup'. It was a bit silly, really, because he had actually done everything possible to create the environment that allowed us to train and play well in the West Indies. There was a lot of John Buchanan in our ultimate victory; in fact, there was a lot of John Buchanan in all our victories between November 1999 and April 2007.

SO NOW WE HAVE to battle on without him, and without our other retired champions. The five of them were different in many ways, but in one crucial respect they were the same. No matter how good they were, what they achieved, players they improved, wickets they took, runs they scored, they would always find some way the next day to make themselves even better. At any time they were prepared to look at themselves and their games, to find one aspect of their cricket they could work on, so they would be a better player for the next game.

When you have achieved as much as John Buchanan, Justin Langer, Damien Martyn, Glenn McGrath and Shane Warne have, become so good at what they do, you'd think that at some stage of their careers they might have relaxed a bit, become satisfied, even if it was only for a moment, before they resumed their quest for greatness. But they never did.

SCORES AND AVERAGES

DLF CUP

In Malaysia, September 12–26, 2006

TOURNAMENT SUMMARY

Date	Match	Venue	Result
September 12	Australia v West Indies	Kuala Lumpur	Australia won by 78 runs
September 14	India v West Indies	Kuala Lumpur	West Indies won by 29 runs
September 16	Australia v India	Kuala Lumpur	No Result
September 18	Australia v West Indies	Kuala Lumpur	West Indies won by three wickets
September 20	India v West Indies	Kuala Lumpur	India won by 16 runs
September 22	Australia v India	Kuala Lumpur	Australia won by 18 runs

POINTS TABLE

Team	P	W	L	NR	T	BP	Pts	NRR
Australia	4	2	1	1	–	1	11	+0.553
West Indies	4	2	2	–	–	1	9	–0.305
India	4	1	2	1	–	–	6	–0.258

FINAL

Date	Match	Venue	Result
September 24	Australia v West Indies	Kuala Lumpur	Australia won by 127 runs

Notes

1. All matches were played at Kinrara Academy Oval, Kuala Lumpur
2. A team received a bonus point if, in winning a match, they achieved a run-rate of 1.25 times that of their opponents. A team's run-rate is calculated by dividing the runs scored in an innings by the number of overs faced.

GAME ONE
AUSTRALIA V WEST INDIES
Kinrara Academy Oval, Kuala Lumpur
12 September, 2006 (50-over match)

Result: Australia won by 78 runs • Toss: Australia
Umpires: Asad Rauf (Pak) and AL Hill (NZ) • TV umpire: MR Benson (Eng)
Match referee: BC Broad (Eng) • Player of the match: SR Watson (Aus)

Australia innings		R	M	B	4	6
PA Jaques	b Edwards	2	15	11	0	0
SM Katich	c Bravo b Bradshaw	36	107	69	4	0
RT Ponting	lbw b Bradshaw	54	74	53	9	0
MJ Clarke	b Bravo	81	110	79	9	0
MJ Cosgrove	c Lara b Smith	34	51	38	5	0
SR Watson	c Sarwan b Smith	2	17	15	0	0
BJ Haddin	b Taylor	23	26	19	3	0
MG Johnson	b Taylor	15	12	8	1	1
NW Bracken	b Taylor	1	2	3	0	0
DJ Cullen	not out	2	11	3	0	0
GD McGrath	not out	1	2	3	0	0
Extras	(lb 10, w 18)	28				
Total	(9 wkts; 50 ov)	279				

FALL OF WICKETS: 1–8 (Jaques, 3.2 ov), 2–107 (Ponting, 20.6 ov), 3–122 (Katich, 24.1 ov), 4–191 (Cosgrove, 36.2 ov), 5–205 (Watson, 40.5 ov), 6–258 (Clarke, 46.6 ov), 7–258 (Haddin, 47.1 ov), 8–260 (Bracken, 47.5 ov), 9–276 (Johnson, 49.2 ov)

BOWLING: Bradshaw 10–1–37–2; Edwards 6–0–38–1; Gayle 8–1–37–0; Smith 9–1–39–2; Taylor 10–0–59–3; Bravo 7–0–59–1

West Indies innings		R	M	B	4	6
CH Gayle	c Ponting b Watson	58	88	46	7	2
S Chanderpaul	c Haddin b Johnson	92	116	83	10	4
RR Sarwan	c Ponting b Watson	22	70	48	3	0
BC Lara	lbw b Johnson	1	6	3	0	0
DJ Bravo	c Jaques b McGrath	8	11	10	1	0
WW Hinds	c Haddin b Cosgrove	2	9	3	0	0
DR Smith	c Haddin b Bracken	2	24	9	0	0
CS Baugh	c Haddin b Bracken	0	2	5	0	0
IDR Bradshaw	lbw b Watson	0	2	1	0	0
JE Taylor	b Watson	0	1	1	0	0
FH Edwards	not out	2	3	3	0	0
Extras	(lb 2, w 7, nb 5)	14				
Total	(all out; 34.3 ov)	201				

FALL OF WICKETS: 1–136 (Gayle, 17.6 ov), 2–172 (Chanderpaul, 23.3 ov), 3–176 (Lara, 25.1 ov), 4–185 (Bravo, 28.1 ov), 5–196 (Hinds, 30.2 ov), 6–197 (Sarwan, 31.6 ov), 7–198 (Baugh, 32.6 ov), 8–199 (Bradshaw, 33.3 ov), 9–199 (Taylor, 33.4 ov), 10–201 (Smith, 34.3 ov)

BOWLING: McGrath 9–0–30–1; Bracken 6.3–2–45–2; Johnson 8–0–65–2; Watson 8–0–43–4; Cullen 2–0–15–0; Cosgrove 1–0–1–1

GAME THREE
AUSTRALIA V INDIA
Kinrara Academy Oval, Kuala Lumpur
16 September 2006 (50-over match)

Result: No result • Toss: Australia
Umpires: MR Benson (Eng) and AL Hill (NZ) • TV umpire: Asad Rauf (Pak)
Match referee: BC Broad (Eng)

Australia innings		R	M	B	4	6
PA Jaques	c Sehwag b Patel	25	39	25	2	1
SR Watson	c Raina b Harbhajan Singh	79	118	74	10	2
RT Ponting	c Tendulkar b Pathan	19	22	21	4	0
DR Martyn	c Dhoni b Singh	4	14	10	1	0
MJ Clarke	c Raina b Patel	64	101	94	5	1
MJ Cosgrove	c Dravid b Harbhajan Singh	4	9	9	0	0
BJ Haddin	run out	18	29	31	1	0
GB Hogg	c Dhoni b Agarkar	12	57	24	0	0
MG Johnson	c Dhoni b Agarkar	1	2	2	0	0
SR Clark	c Singh b Patel	7	7	5	1	0
GD McGrath	not out	1	2	1	0	0
Extras	(b 1, lb 4, w 5)	10				
Total	(all out; 49.2 ov)	244				

FALL OF WICKETS: 1–64 (Jaques, 9.6 ov), 2–92 (Ponting, 15.2 ov), 3–113 (Martyn, 18.1 ov), 4–157 (Watson, 27.6 ov), 5–167 (Cosgrove, 31.3 ov), 6–200 (Haddin, 40.5 ov), 7–230 (Clarke, 46.1 ov), 8–232 (Johnson, 47.1 ov), 9–243 (Clark, 48.5 ov), 10–244 (Hogg, 49.2 ov)

BOWLING: Agarkar 8.2–0–50–2; Patel 10–1–53–3; Singh 7–1–35–1; Pathan 4–0–32–1; Harbhajan Singh 10–0–26–2; Sehwag 10–0–43–0

India innings		R	M	B	4	6
R Dravid	c Martyn b Johnson	6	24	22	1	0
SR Tendulkar	c Haddin b Johnson	12	30	17	2	0
IK Pathan	b Johnson	0	1	1	0	0
V Sehwag	run out	8	6	5	0	1
Yuvraj Singh	c Jaques b Johnson	0	6	3	0	0
SK Raina	not out	1	3	1	0	0
Extras	(w 7, nb 1)	8				
Total	(5 wkts; 8 ov)	35				

DID NOT BAT: MS Dhoni, AB Agarkar, Harbhajan Singh, MM Patel, RP Singh

FALL OF WICKETS: 1–20 (Dravid, 5.5 ov), 2–20 (Pathan, 5.6 ov), 3–34 (Sehwag, 6.6 ov), 4–34 (Tendulkar, 7.2 ov), 5–35 (Yuvraj Singh, 7.6 ov)

BOWLING: McGrath 3–1–10–0; Johnson 4–0–11–4; Clark 1–0–14–0

GAME FOUR
AUSTRALIA V WEST INDIES
Kinrara Academy Oval, Kuala Lumpur
18 September 2006 (50-over match)

Result: West Indies won by three wickets • Toss: Australia
Umpires: Asad Rauf (Pak) and AL Hill (NZ) • TV umpire: MR Benson (Eng)
Match referee: BC Broad (Eng) • Player of the match: MEK Hussey (Aus)

Australia innings		R	M	B	4	6
ML Hayden	c Taylor b Bravo	49	111	77	5	0
SM Katich	run out	22	40	21	4	0
SR Watson	c Lara b Taylor	0	3	7	0	0
A Symonds	c Smith b Bradshaw	8	22	19	1	0
MJ Clarke	c Gayle b Bradshaw	1	7	8	0	0
MEK Hussey	not out	109	130	90	10	3
BJ Haddin	c Taylor b Bravo	70	92	77	3	4
B Lee	not out	1	1	1	0	0
Extras	(b 1, lb 5, w 6)	12				
Total	(6 wkts; 50 ov)	272				

DID NOT BAT: SR Clark, NW Bracken, DJ Cullen

FALL OF WICKETS: 1–41 (Katich, 9.3 ov), 2–42 (Watson, 10.5 ov), 3–57 (Symonds, 15.4 ov), 4–64 (Clarke, 17.4 ov), 5–104 (Hayden, 25.5 ov), 6–269 (Haddin, 49.3 ov)

BOWLING: Taylor 10–0–53–1; Bradshaw 10–0–35–2; Gayle 7–0–46–0; Smith 7–0–38–0; Samuels 7–0–42–0; Bravo 9–1–52–2

West Indies innings		R	M	B	4	6
CH Gayle	c Hussey b Watson	79	151	93	7	3
S Chanderpaul	c Haddin b Lee	0	19	10	0	0
RR Sarwan	c Haddin b Bracken	25	29	31	5	0
BC Lara	c Hussey b Lee	87	136	80	11	1
DJ Bravo	not out	37	73	53	2	1
WW Hinds	c Haddin b Lee	1	7	9	0	0
MN Samuels	run out	0	1	2	0	0
DR Smith	b Symonds	4	3	3	1	0
CS Baugh	not out	7	12	14	1	0
Extras	(lb 6, w 16, nb 11)	33				
Total	(7 wkts; 47.2 ov)	273				

DID NOT BAT: IDR Bradshaw, JE Taylor

FALL OF WICKETS: 1–12 (Chanderpaul, 4.2 ov), 2–44 (Sarwan, 11.4 ov), 3–195 (Gayle, 31.1 ov), 4–242 (Lara, 40.2 ov), 5–249 (Hinds, 42.3 ov), 6–249 (Samuels, 42.5 ov), 7–255 (Smith, 43.4 ov)

BOWLING: Lee 10–0–46–3; Bracken 9–0–31–1; Clark 7–0–87–0; Watson 10–0–42–1; Symonds 5.2–0–27–1; Cullen 6–1–34–0

GAME SIX
AUSTRALIA V INDIA
Kinrara Academy Oval, Kuala Lumpur
22 September 2006 (50-over match)

Result: Australia won by 18 runs • Toss: Australia
Umpires: Asad Rauf (Pak) and MR Benson (Eng) • TV umpire: AL Hill (NZ)
Match referee: BC Broad (Eng) • Player of the match: B Lee (Aus)

Australia innings		R	M	B	4	6
ML Hayden	run out	54	100	66	9	0
SM Katich	c Raina b Agarkar	9	35	23	1	0
RT Ponting	c Agarkar b Patel	4	13	9	0	0
DR Martyn	run out	19	60	38	1	1
A Symonds	lbw b Mongia	2	12	13	0	0
MEK Hussey	c Dravid b Harbhajan Singh	13	25	20	1	0
BJ Haddin	c Dhoni b Singh	46	74	63	1	4
GB Hogg	run out	38	59	49	2	1
B Lee	c Sehwag b Singh	7	18	8	0	0
SR Clark	b Agarkar	2	2	3	0	0
GD McGrath	not out	0	1	1	0	0
Extras	(lb 6, w 9, nb 4)	19				
Total	(all out; 48.1 ov)	213				

FALL OF WICKETS: 1–36 (Katich, 8.2 ov), 2–49 (Ponting, 11.1 ov), 3–87 (Hayden, 21.2 ov), 4–97 (Martyn, 24.2 ov), 5–97 (Symonds, 24.3 ov), 6–117 (Hussey, 31.3 ov), 7–194 (Haddin, 44.4 ov), 8–208 (Hogg, 46.6 ov), 9–213 (Clark, 47.5 ov), 10–213 (Lee, 48.1 ov)

Bowling : Agarkar 8-0-44-2; Patel 9-1-32-1; Singh 9.1-1-43-2; Harbhajan Singh 10-2-24-1; D Mongia 9-0-43-1; Sehwag 3-0-21-0;

India innings		R	M	B	4	6
V Sehwag	b Lee	10	24	11	0	0
SR Tendulkar	c Hussey b Lee	4	11	10	1	0
M Kaif	c & b Clark	21	45	37	2	0
R Dravid	lbw b Clark	7	36	21	1	0
D Mongia	not out	63	140	90	5	0
SK Raina	b Hogg	26	48	36	2	1
MS Dhoni	c Martyn b Lee	23	34	34	0	1
AB Agarkar	lbw b Hogg	9	17	12	0	0
Harbhajan Singh	c Haddin b Symonds	0	2	2	0	0
RP Singh	c Hussey b Lee	4	10	12	0	0
MM Patel	c Symonds b Lee	1	2	2	0	0
Extras	(lb 7, w 16, nb 4)	27				
Total	(all out; 43.5 ov)	195				

FALL OF WICKETS: 1–7 (Tendulkar, 2.2 ov), 2–20 (Sehwag, 4.4 ov), 3–47 (Kaif, 12.5 ov), 4–50 (Dravid, 12.6 ov), 5–96 (Raina, 24.5 ov), 6–158 (Dhoni, 36.2 ov), 7–185 (Agarkar, 39.5 ov), 8–186 (Harbhajan Singh, 40.2 ov), 9–193 (Singh, 43.1 ov), 10–195 (Patel, 43.5 ov)
BOWLING: Lee 8.5-0-38-5; McGrath 8-1-25-0; Clark 8-0-36-2; Symonds 9-0-41-1; GB Hogg 10-0-48-2

FINAL

AUSTRALIA V WEST INDIES

Kinrara Academy Oval, Kuala Lumpur
24 September 2006 (50-over match)

Result: Australia won by 127 runs • Toss: Australia
Umpires: Asad Rauf (Pak) and MR Benson (Eng) • TV umpire: AL Hill (NZ)
Match referee: BC Broad (Eng) • Player of the match: B Lee (Aus)
Player of the series: B Lee (Aus)

Australia innings		R	M	B	4	6
SR Watson	c Gayle b Bradshaw	1	9	27	3	0
SM Katich	c sub (MN Samuels) b Gayle	25	101	66	1	1
RT Ponting	lbw b Taylor	6	27	12	0	0
DR Martyn	c Morton b Bradshaw	52	92	77	5	0
A Symonds	c Morton b Sarwan	52	78	59	2	2
MJ Clarke	c Gayle b Sarwan	23	32	24	0	0
MEK Hussey	not out	30	36	24	2	1
BJ Haddin	not out	17	18	12	0	1
Extras	(lb 7, w 9, nb 1)	17				
Total	(6 wkts; 50 ov)	240				

DID NOT BAT: B Lee, NW Bracken, GD McGrath

FALL OF WICKETS: 1–24 (Watson, 6.6 ov), 2–37 (Ponting, 13.2 ov), 3–80 (Katich, 23.4 ov), 4–153 (Martyn, 38.2 ov), 5–173 (Symonds, 41.3 ov), 6–200 (Clarke, 46.1 ov)

BOWLING: Bradshaw 10–2–30–2; Smith 8–1–35–0; Taylor 10–1–36–1; Bravo 9–1–65–0; Gayle 9–0–46–1; Sarwan 4–0–21–2

West Indies innings		R	M	B	4	6
CH Gayle	lbw b Lee	0	1	1	0	0
S Chanderpaul	c Katich b Bracken	12	38	23	2	0
RS Morton	lbw b Bracken	0	56	31	0	0
RR Sarwan	run out	36	103	64	5	0
BC Lara	c Haddin b Bracken	5	13	18	1	0
DJ Bravo	c Ponting b Watson	8	27	23	0	0
WW Hinds	b Watson	0	2	5	0	0
DR Smith	c Ponting b Lee	30	40	30	2	2
CS Baugh	c Haddin b Lee	3	15	12	0	0
IDR Bradshaw	c Haddin b Lee	0	2	3	0	0
JE Taylor	not out	0	4	2	0	0
Extras	(b 2, lb 7, w 3, nb 7)	19				
Total	(all out; 34.2 ov)	113				

FALL OF WICKETS: 1–0 (Gayle, 0.1 ov), 2–16 (Chanderpaul, 7.2 ov), 3–20 (Morton, 9.6 ov), 4–32 (Lara, 15.3 ov), 5–55 (Bravo, 22.1 ov), 6–56 (Hinds, 22.5 ov), 7–106 (Sarwan, 30.3 ov), 8–112 (Smith, 32.1 ov), 9–112 (Bradshaw, 32.4 ov), 10–113 (Baugh, 34.2 ov)

BOWLING: Lee 8.2–1–24–4; McGrath 6–2–6–0; Bracken 7–0–16–3; Watson 6–0–30–2; Symonds 3–0–15–0; Clarke 4–0–13–0

DLF CUP — AUSTRALIAN AVERAGES

BATTING AND FIELDING

Batsman	ODI	Inn	NO	Runs	HS	Ave	100	50	Ct	St
MEK Hussey	3	3	2	152	109*	152.00	1	–	4	–
ML Hayden	2	2	0	103	54	51.50	–	1	–	–
BJ Haddin	5	5	1	174	70	43.50	–	1	12	–
MJ Clarke	4	4	0	169	81	42.25	–	2	–	–
GB Hogg	2	2	0	50	38	25.00	–	–	–	–
DR Martyn	3	3	0	75	52	25.00	–	1	2	–
SR Watson	4	4	0	99	79	24.75	–	1	–	–
SM Katich	4	4	0	92	36	23.00	–	–	1	–
RT Ponting	4	4	0	83	54	20.75	–	1	4	–
A Symonds	3	3	0	62	52	20.67	–	1	1	–
MJ Cosgrove	2	2	0	38	34	19.00	–	–	–	–
PA Jaques	2	2	0	27	25	13.50	–	–	2	–
MG Johnson	2	2	0	16	15	8.00	–	–	–	–
B Lee	3	2	1	8	7	8.00	–	–	–	–
SR Clark	3	2	0	9	7	4.50	–	–	1	–
NW Bracken	3	1	0	1	1	1.00	–	–	–	–
DJ Cullen	2	1	1	2	2*	–	–	–	–	–
GD McGrath	4	3	3	2	1*	–	–	–	–	–

BOWLING

Bowler	O	M	R	W	Ave	Best	4w
MJ Cosgrove	1	0	1	1	1.00	1–1	–
B Lee	27.1	1	108	12	9.00	5–38	2
MG Johnson	12	0	76	6	12.67	4–11	1
NW Bracken	22.3	2	92	6	15.33	3–16	–
SR Watson	24	0	115	7	16.43	4–43	1
GB Hogg	10	0	48	2	24.00	2–48	–
A Symonds	17.2	0	83	2	41.50	1–27	–
SR Clark	16	0	137	2	68.50	2–36	–
GD McGrath	26	4	71	1	71.00	1–30	–
MJ Clarke	4	0	13	0	–	–	–
DJ Cullen	8	1	49	0	–	–	–

AUSTRALIAN CENTURIES AND FIVE WICKETS IN AN INNINGS

Mike Hussey's 109 not out in game four was his first century in one-day international cricket, in his 41st ODI.

Brett Lee's 5–38 in game six was the sixth time he had taken five or more wickets in a one-day international innings, in his 137th ODI.

NOTABLE AUSTRALIAN LANDMARKS

In game four, against the West Indies, Mike Hussey became the 17th man to captain Australia in a one-day international. He also became the sixth Australian captain to score a ODI hundred while leading the side (after Allan Border, Mark Taylor, Steve Waugh, Ricky Ponting and Adam Gilchrist), and the first to do so on his ODI captaincy debut.

The 166 runs added by Hussey and Brad Haddin in the same match established a new record sixth-wicket partnership for Australia in ODI cricket.

ICC CHAMPIONS TROPHY

In India, October 7–November 5, 2006

GROUP A

Date	Match	Venue	Result
October 15	England v India	Jaipur	India won by four wickets
October 18	Australia v West Indies	Mumbai	West Indies won by 10 runs
October 21	Australia v England	Jaipur	Australia won by six wickets
October 26	India v West Indies	Ahmedabad	West Indies won by three wickets
October 28	England v West Indies	Ahmedabad	England won by three wickets
October 29	Australia v India	Mohali	Australia won by six wickets

GROUP A POINTS TABLE

Team	P	W	L	NR	T	Pts	NRR
Australia	3	2	1	–	–	4	+0.529
West Indies	3	2	1	–	–	4	+0.009
India	3	1	2	–	–	2	+0.482
England	3	1	2	–	–	2	1.044

GROUP B

Date	Match	Venue	Result
October 16	New Zealand v South Africa	Mumbai	New Zealand won by 87 runs
October 17	Pakistan v Sri Lanka	Jaipur	Pakistan won by four wickets
October 20	New Zealand v Sri Lanka	Mumbai	Sri Lanka won by seven wickets
October 24	South Africa v Sri Lanka	Ahmedabad	South Africa won by 78 runs
October 25	New Zealand v Pakistan	Mohali	New Zealand won by 51 runs
October 27	Pakistan v South Africa	Mohali	South Africa won by 124 runs

GROUP B POINTS TABLE

Team	P	W	L	NR	T	Pts	NRR
South Africa	3	2	1	–	–	4	+0.767
New Zealand	3	2	1	–	–	4	+0.572
Sri Lanka	3	1	2	–	–	2	-0.195
Pakistan	3	1	2	–	–	2	-1.107

SEMI-FINALS

Date	Match	Venue	Result
November 1	Australia v New Zealand	Mohali	Australia won by 34 runs
November 2	South Africa v West Indies	Jaipur	West Indies won by six wickets

FINAL

Date	Match	Venue	Result
November 5	Australia v West Indies	Mumbai	Australia won by eight wickets

Notes

1. Sri Lanka and the West Indies reached the group stage after a series of qualifying matches, also involving Bangladesh and Zimbabwe, played between October 7 and October 14.
2. Matches in Mumbai were played at Brabourne Stadium

GROUP A
AUSTRALIA V WEST INDIES
Brabourne Stadium, Mumbai
18 October 2006 (50-over match)

Result: West Indies won by 10 runs • Toss: West Indies
Umpires: MR Benson (Eng) and RE Koertzen (SA) • TV umpire: Aleem Dar (Pak)
Match referee: MJ Procter (SA) • Player of the match: RS Morton (West Indies)

West Indies innings		R	M	B	4	6
WW Hinds	c Ponting b Bracken	1	17	15	0	0
CH Gayle	c Gilchrist b Watson	24	57	26	4	0
DR Smith	c Hogg b Lee	8	14	13	2	0
RR Sarwan	lbw b Clarke	21	40	32	4	0
RS Morton	not out	90	161	103	7	1
BC Lara	c Symonds b McGrath	71	122	94	7	2
CS Baugh	c Ponting b Bracken	13	20	17	1	0
MN Samuels	not out	1	1	1	0	0
Extras	(lb 1, w 3, nb 1)	5				
Total	(6 wkts; 50 ov)	234				

Did not bat DJ Bravo, IDR Bradshaw, JE Taylor

FALL OF WICKETS: 1–10 (Hinds, 3.4 ov), 2–25 (Smith, 6.4 ov), 3–47 (Gayle, 11.5 ov), 4–63 (Sarwan, 14.6 ov), 5–200 (Lara, 44.2 ov), 6–233 (Baugh, 49.5 ov)

BOWLING: Lee 8–0–45–1; Bracken 10–1–42–2; McGrath 8–0–42–1; Watson 8–0–34–1; Clarke 5–0–18–1; Symonds 8–0–35–0; Hogg 3–0–17–0

Australia innings		R	M	B	4	6
AC Gilchrist	run out	92	189	120	11	0
SR Watson	c Sarwan b Bradshaw	0	11	3	0	0
RT Ponting	b Taylor	1	8	5	0	0
DR Martyn	c Bravo b Bradshaw	17	35	24	3	0
A Symonds	b Gayle	18	38	30	3	0
MJ Clarke	c & b Bravo	47	114	85	3	0
MEK Hussey	b Taylor	13	30	16	1	0
GB Hogg	b Taylor	10	20	11	1	0
B Lee	lbw b Taylor	0	1	1	0	0
NW Bracken	not out	3	12	5	0	0
GD McGrath	not out	3	4	3	0	0
Extras	(lb 8, w 9, nb 3)	20				
Total	(9 wkts; 50 ov)	224				

FALL OF WICKETS: 1–12 (Watson, 2.2 ov), 2–17 (Ponting, 3.4 ov), 3–44 (Martyn, 10.5 ov), 4–81 (Symonds, 19.6 ov), 5–182 (Gilchrist, 41.4 ov), 6–206 (Clarke, 46.1 ov), 7–214 (Hussey, 47.5 ov), 8–214 (Lee, 47.6 ov), 9–219 (Hogg, 49.1 ov)

BOWLING: Bradshaw 10–0–38–2; Taylor 10–0–49–4; Smith 3–0–16–0; Samuels 10–1–36–0; Gayle 10–0–39–1; Bravo 6–0–33–1; Sarwan 1–0–5–0

GROUP A
AUSTRALIA V ENGLAND
Sawai Mansingh Stadium, Jaipur
21 October 2006 (50-over match)

Result: Australia won by six wickets • Toss: Australia
Umpires: BF Bowden (NZ) and SA Bucknor (West Indies) • TV umpire: DJ Harper (Aus)
Match referee: JJ Crowe (NZ) • Player of the match: DR Martyn (Aus)

England innings		R	M	B	4	6
AJ Strauss	c Gilchrist b Symonds	56	138	90	6	0
IR Bell	c Hussey b Watson	43	86	60	7	0
KP Pietersen	c Gilchrist b Johnson	1	5	6	0	0
A Flintoff	c Hussey b Watson	4	31	15	0	0
MH Yardy	c Gilchrist b Watson	4	24	15	0	0
PD Collingwood	not out	22	73	38	1	0
JWM Dalrymple	c Ponting b Johnson	3	18	15	0	0
CMW Read	c Gilchrist b McGrath	0	5	2	0	0
SI Mahmood	c & b Bracken	8	14	13	0	0
SJ Harmison	c Gilchrist b Johnson	1	3	3	0	0
JM Anderson	b McGrath	15	18	19	2	0
Extras	(lb 3, w 3, nb 6)	12				
Total	(all out; 45 ov)	169				

FALL OF WICKETS: 1–83 (Bell, 18.2 ov), 2–84 (Pietersen, 19.2 ov), 3–110 (Flintoff, 25.5 ov), 4–115 (Strauss, 28.6 ov), 5–125 (Yardy, 31.1 ov), 6–135 (Dalrymple, 35.5 ov), 7–136 (Read, 36.6 ov), 8–150 (Mahmood, 40.2 ov), 9–151 (Harmison, 41.1 ov), 10–169 (Anderson, 44.6 ov)

BOWLING: Lee 9–3–25–0; Bracken 8–0–38–1; McGrath 9–1–36–2; Johnson 10–0–40–3; Watson 7–0–16–3; Symonds 2–0–11–1

Australia innings		R	M	B	4	6
AC Gilchrist	b Mahmood	10	27	10	2	0
SR Watson	b Anderson	21	40	26	3	0
RT Ponting	c Strauss b Mahmood	1	8	4	0	0
DR Martyn	c Read b Harmison	78	118	91	12	0
MEK Hussey	not out	32	126	85	2	0
A Symonds	not out	8	11	10	1	0
Extras	(b 4, lb 5, w 6, nb 5)	20				
Total	(4 wkts; 36.5 ov)	170				

DID NOT BAT: MJ Clarke, MG Johnson, B Lee, NW Bracken, GD McGrath

FALL OF WICKETS: 1–30 (Gilchrist, 3.6 ov), 2–34 (Ponting, 5.6 ov), 3–34 (Watson, 6.4 ov), 4–152 (Martyn, 34.1 ov)

BOWLING: Anderson 9–2–31–1; Mahmood 10–0–57–2; Harmison 4.5–0–45–1; Yardy 10–1–18–0; Dalrymple 3–0–10–0

GROUP A
AUSTRALIA V INDIA
Punjab CA Stadium, Mohali
29 October 2006 (50-over match)

Result: Australia won by six wickets • Toss: India
Umpires: BF Bowden (NZ) and SA Bucknor (West Indies) • TV umpire: MR Benson (Eng)
Match referee: RS Madugalle (SL) • Player of the match: DR Martyn (Aus)

India innings		R	M	B	4	6
V Sehwag	lbw b Johnson	65	136	90	9	0
SR Tendulkar	c Gilchrist b McGrath	10	46	26	2	0
D Mongia	c Hussey b Watson	18	45	30	3	0
R Dravid	c Clarke b Lee	52	91	63	6	0
M Kaif	b Lee	30	57	43	2	0
MS Dhoni	lbw b Bracken	28	44	23	2	0
SK Raina	c Watson b Bracken	13	23	19	2	0
IK Pathan	c Martyn b McGrath	10	5	7	1	0
Harbhajan Singh	not out	5	3	3	0	0
Extras	(lb 5, w 9, nb 4)	18				
Total	(8 wkts; 50 ov)	249				

DID NOT BAT: MM Patel, S Sreesanth

FALL OF WICKETS: 1–46 (Tendulkar, 9.5 ov), 2–89 (Mongia, 19.4 ov), 3–126 (Sehwag, 28.2 ov), 4–186 (Dravid, 40.2 ov), 5–197 (Kaif, 42.1 ov), 6–224 (Raina, 47.1 ov), 7–239 (Pathan, 48.6 ov), 8–249 (Dhoni, 49.6 ov)

BOWLING: Lee 10–1–54–2; McGrath 10–1–34–2; Bracken 10–2–56–2; Johnson 8–0–33–1; Watson 9–0–48–1; Symonds 3–0–19–0

Australia innings		R	M	B	4	6
AC Gilchrist	c Raina b Sreesanth	23	40	24	4	0
SR Watson	lbw b Mongia	50	83	46	8	0
RT Ponting	c Tendulkar b Sreesanth	58	109	69	8	0
DR Martyn	not out	73	116	104	8	0
A Symonds	b Pathan	20	36	24	3	0
MJ Clarke	not out	2	10	7	0	0
Extras	(lb 8, w 18)	26				
Total	(4 wkts; 45.4 ov)	252				

DID NOT BAT: MEK Hussey, B Lee, MG Johnson, NW Bracken, GD McGrath

FALL OF WICKETS: 1–61 (Gilchrist, 8.5 ov), 2–111 (Watson, 15.5 ov), 3–185 (Ponting, 33.5 ov), 4–230 (Symonds, 42.6 ov)

BOWLING: Pathan 7–0–42–1; Patel 8.4–0–61–0; Sreesanth 8–1–43–2; Harbhajan Singh 10–0–49–0; Mongia 9–0–36–1; Sehwag 3–0–13–0

FIRST SEMI-FINAL
AUSTRALIA V NEW ZEALAND
Punjab CA Stadium, Mohali
1 November 2006 (50-over match)

Result: Australia won by 34 runs • Toss: New Zealand
Umpires: SA Bucknor (West Indies) and RE Koertzen (SA) • TV umpire: MR Benson (Eng)
Match referee: MJ Procter (SA) • Player of the match: GD McGrath (Aus)

Australia innings		R	M	B	4	6
AC Gilchrist	c Oram b Mills	3	13	.11	0	0
SR Watson	c Fulton b Mills	0	10	4	0	0
RT Ponting	c Vettori b Mills	58	118	80	9	0
DR Martyn	lbw b Vettori	26	72	54	4	0
MEK Hussey	c Marshall b Franklin	35	93	52	2	0
A Symonds	b Bond	58	73	58	3	1
MJ Clarke	c Vettori b Mills	14	29	22	1	0
B Lee	b Bond	5	8	5	0	0
MG Johnson	run out	3	12	9	0	0
NW Bracken	not out	15	9	8	1	1
GD McGrath	not out	0	1	0	0	0
Extras	(lb 6, w 14, nb 3)	23				
Total	(9 wkts; 50 ov)	240				

FALL OF WICKETS: 1–3 (Watson, 2.2 ov), 2–4 (Gilchrist, 2.5 ov), 3–70 (Martyn, 19.3 ov), 4–123 (Ponting, 28.6 ov), 5–188 (Hussey, 40.1 ov), 6–211 (Symonds, 45.4 ov), 7–220 (Clarke, 46.5 ov), 8–223 (Lee, 47.2 ov), 9–236 (Johnson, 49.5 ov)

BOWLING: Mills 10–1–38–4; Bond 10–0–55–2; Franklin 8–1–48–1; Oram 10–1–43–0; Vettori 10–0–41–1; Astle 2–0–9–0

New Zealand innings		R	M	B	4	6
L Vincent	c Ponting b McGrath	1	23	15	0	0
SP Fleming	c Ponting b Bracken	15	51	28	2	0
NJ Astle	b Lee	0	3	4	0	0
HJH Marshall	c Gilchrist b McGrath	5	13	13	0	0
PG Fulton	b McGrath	2	18	13	0	0
JDP Oram	st Gilchrist b Symonds	43	111	59	5	0
BB McCullum	c Martyn b Bracken	1	2	4	0	0
DL Vettori	b Johnson	79	125	103	7	0
JEC Franklin	c Gilchrist b Watson	8	14	11	1	0
KD Mills	c Gilchrist b Lee	21	28	17	2	1
SE Bond	not out	9	12	11	1	0
Extras	(lb 7, w 13, nb 2)	22				
Total	(all out; 46 ov)	206				

FALL OF WICKETS: 1–16 (Vincent, 5.3 ov), 2–20 (Astle, 6.2 ov), 3–30 (Marshall, 9.2 ov), 4–30 (Fleming, 10.4 ov), 5–34 (Fulton, 13.4 ov), 6–35 (McCullum, 14.2 ov), 7–138 (Oram, 35.1 ov), 8–159 (Franklin, 38.6 ov), 9–180 (Vettori, 42.4 ov), 10–206 (Mills, 45.6 ov)

BOWLING: Lee 8–0–31–2; McGrath 10–2–22–3; Bracken 7–1–36–2; Johnson 7–0–38–1; Watson 7–0–27–1; Symonds 7–0–45–1

FINAL
AUSTRALIA V WEST INDIES
Brabourne Stadium, Mumbai
5 November 2006 (50-over match)

Result: Australia won by eight wickets (D/L method) • Toss: West Indies
Umpires: Aleem Dar (Pak) and RE Koertzen (SA) • TV umpire: BF Bowden (NZ)
Match referee: RS Madugalle (SL) • Player of the match: SR Watson (Aus)
Player of the series: CH Gayle (West Indies)

West Indies innings		R	M	B	4	6
S Chanderpaul	b Bracken	27	53	18	4	1
CH Gayle	b Bracken	37	27	27	6	2
RR Sarwan	c Hogg b Bracken	7	13	9	1	0
DJ Bravo	lbw b Hogg	21	86	47	3	0
BC Lara	c Gilchrist b McGrath	2	26	18	0	0
RS Morton	c Gilchrist b McGrath	2	16	9	0	0
MN Samuels	c Ponting b Watson	7	17	12	1	0
CS Baugh	lbw b Watson	9	9	13	1	0
IDR Bradshaw	b Lee	7	18	15	1	0
JE Taylor	not out	5	23	13	0	0
CD Collymore	run out	0	7	5	0	0
Extras	(lb 5, w 7, nb 2)	14				
Total	(all out; 30.4 ov)	138				

FALL OF WICKETS: 1–49 (Chanderpaul, 5.1 ov), 2–65 (Sarwan, 7.3 ov), 3–80 (Gayle, 9.4 ov), 4–88 (Lara, 14.5 ov), 5–94 (Morton, 18.2 ov), 6–113 (Samuels, 22.4 ov), 7–125 (Baugh, 24.6 ov), 8–125 (Bravo, 25.1 ov), 9–136 (Bradshaw, 28.6 ov), 10–138 (Collymore, 30.4 ov)

BOWLING: Lee 7.4–0–49–1; Bracken 6–0–22–3; McGrath 7–3–24–2; Symonds 3–0–16–0; Watson 3–0–11–2; Hogg 4–1–11–1

Australia innings		R	M	B	4	6
AC Gilchrist	c Gayle b Bradshaw	2	13	9	0	0
SR Watson	not out	57	121	88	4	0
RT Ponting	lbw b Taylor	0	5	2	0	0
DR Martyn	not out	47	100	71	6	0
Extras	(lb 4, w 5, nb 1)	10				
Total	(2 wkts; 28.1 ov)	116				

Did not bat MEK Hussey, A Symonds, MJ Clarke, B Lee, GB Hogg, NW Bracken, GD McGrath

FALL OF WICKETS: 1–12 (Gilchrist, 2.6 ov), 2–13 (Ponting, 3.6 ov)

BOWLING: Gayle 1–0–5–0; Taylor 7–0–42–1; Bradshaw 6–0–21–1; Collymore 6–1–19–0; Samuels 5–0–9–0; Sarwan 3.1–0–16–0

ICC CHAMPIONS TROPHY — AUSTRALIAN AVERAGES

BATTING AND FIELDING

Batsman	ODI	Inn	NO	Runs	HS	Ave	100	50	Ct	St
DR Martyn	5	5	2	241	78	80.33	–	2	2	–
MEK Hussey	5	3	1	80	35	40.00	–	–	3	–
A Symonds	5	4	1	104	58	34.67	–	1	1	–
SR Watson	5	5	1	128	57*	32.00	–	2	1	–
MJ Clarke	5	3	1	63	47	31.50	–	–	1	–
AC Gilchrist	5	5	0	130	92	26.00	–	1	12	1
RT Ponting	5	5	0	118	58	23.60	–	2	6	–
GB Hogg	2	1	0	10	10	10.00	–	–	2	–
MG Johnson	3	1	0	3	3	3.00	–	–	–	–
B Lee	5	2	0	5	5	2.50	–	–	–	–
NW Bracken	5	2	2	18	15*	–	–	–	1	–
GD McGrath	5	2	2	3	3*	–	–	–	–	–

BOWLING

Bowler	O	M	R	W	Ave	Best	4w
GD McGrath	44	7	158	10	15.80	3–22	–
SR Watson	34	0	136	8	17.00	3–16	–
MJ Clarke	5	0	18	1	18.00	1–18	–
NW Bracken	41	4	194	10	19.40	3–22	–
MG Johnson	25	0	111	5	22.20	3–40	–
GB Hogg	7	1	28	1	28.00	1–11	–
B Lee	42.4	4	204	6	34.00	2–31	–
A Symonds	23	0	126	2	63.00	1–11	–

NOTABLE AUSTRALIAN LANDMARKS

Brett Lee took his 250th wicket in one-day international cricket during the Group A match against the West Indies in Mumbai.

Adam Gilchrist became the first wicketkeeper to complete 400 dismissals in one-day international cricket when he caught Sachin Tendulkar during the game against India in Mohali.

Tendulkar was one of five catches Gilchrist completed in this game, an Australian record seventh time he has taken five or more catches in a ODI.

Damien Martyn is the only Australian to have scored more than 400 runs in ICC Knockout/Champions Trophy matches. At the end of this tournament, he had scored 492 runs in 12 matches between 1998 and 2006, at 61.50.

Glenn McGrath is one of only two men to have taken more than 20 wickets in ICC Knockout/Champions Trophy matches. McGrath took 21 wickets in 12 matches between 2000 and 2006, at 19.62. Sri Lanka's Muttiah Muralitharan has taken 23 wickets in 15 matches, at 16.43.

Australia has now played 13 ICC Knockout/Champions Trophy matches, for eight wins and five losses. The team was eliminated at the earliest opportunity in 1998 and 2000, and reached the semi-finals in 2002 and 2004.

THE ASHES

FIRST TEST

The Gabba, Brisbane
23–27 November 2006 (five-day match)

Result: Australia won by 277 runs • Toss: Australia
Umpires: BF Bowden (NZ) and SA Bucknor (West Indies) • TV umpire: PD Parker
Match referee: JJ Crowe (NZ) • Player of the match: RT Ponting (Aus)

Australia first innings		R	M	B	4	6
JL Langer	c Pietersen b Flintoff	82	136	98	13	0
ML Hayden	c Collingwood b Flintoff	21	88	47	2	0
RT Ponting	lbw b Hoggard	196	464	319	24	0
DR Martyn	c Collingwood b Giles	29	79	62	2	0
MEK Hussey	b Flintoff	86	257	187	8	0
MJ Clarke	c Strauss b Anderson	56	153	94	5	1
AC Gilchrist	lbw b Hoggard	0	3	3	0	0
SK Warne	c Jones b Harmison	17	42	26	1	0
B Lee	not out	43	90	61	6	0
SR Clark	b Flintoff	39	34	23	3	2
GD McGrath	not out	8	26	17	0	0
Extras	(b 2, lb 8, w 8, nb 7)	25				
Total	(9 wkts dec; 155 ov; 690 mins)	602				

FALL OF WICKETS: 1–79 (Hayden, 18.3 ov), 2–141 (Langer, 28.5 ov), 3–198 (Martyn, 47.2 ov), 4–407 (Hussey, 108.4 ov), 5–467 (Ponting, 126.3 ov), 6–467 (Gilchrist, 126.6 ov), 7–500 (Warne, 135.3 ov), 8–528 (Clarke, 141.3 ov), 9–578 (Clark, 149.1 ov)

BOWLING: Harmison 30–4–123–1; Hoggard 31–5–98–2; Anderson 29–6–141–1; Flintoff 30–4–99–4; Giles 25–2–91–1; Bell 1–0–12–0; Pietersen 9–1–28–0

England first innings		R	M	B	4	6
AJ Strauss	c Hussey b McGrath	12	25	21	2	0
AN Cook	c Warne b McGrath	11	27	15	1	0
IR Bell	c Ponting b Clark	50	228	162	5	0
PD Collingwood	c Gilchrist b Clark	5	24	13	1	0
KP Pietersen	lbw b McGrath	16	72	44	1	0
A Flintoff	c Gilchrist b Lee	0	4	3	0	0
GO Jones	lbw b McGrath	19	90	57	2	0
AF Giles	c Hayden b McGrath	24	61	39	4	0
MJ Hoggard	c Gilchrist b Clark	0	12	6	0	0
SJ Harmison	c Gilchrist b McGrath	0	5	5	0	0
JM Anderson	not out	2	9	8	0	0
Extras	(b 2, lb 8, w 2, nb 6)	18				
Total	(all out; 61.1 ov; 283 mins)	157				

FALL OF WICKETS: 1–28 (Strauss, 5.4 ov), 2–28 (Cook, 5.5 ov), 3–42 (Collingwood, 10.6 ov), 4–78 (Pietersen, 27.4 ov), 5–79 (Flintoff, 28.3 ov), 6–126 (Jones, 49.2 ov), 7–149 (Bell, 56.2 ov), 8–153 (Hoggard, 58.2 ov), 9–154 (Harmison, 59.2 ov), 10–157 (Giles, 61.1 ov)

BOWLING: Lee 15–3–51–1; McGrath 23.1–8–50–6; Clark 14–5–21–3; Warne 9–0–25–0

Australia second innings		R	M	B	4	6
JL Langer	not out	100	199	146	9	0
ML Hayden	run out	37	67	41	6	0
RT Ponting	not out	60	131	85	4	0
Extras	(lb 4, nb 1)	5			
Total	(1 wkt dec; 45.1 ov; 199 mins)	202			

FALL OF WICKET: 1–68 (Hayden, 15.3 ov)

BOWLING: Hoggard 11–2–43–0; Anderson 9–1–54–0; Flintoff 5–2–11–0; Harmison 12.1–1–54–0; Giles 5–0–22–0; Pietersen 3–0–14–0

England second innings		R	M	B	4	6
AJ Strauss	c sub (RA Broad) b Clark	11	51	31	1	0
AN Cook	c Hussey b Warne	43	128	94	4	0
IR Bell	lbw b Warne	0	11	4	0	0
PD Collingwood	st Gilchrist b Warne	96	216	155	13	2
KP Pietersen	c Martyn b Lee	92	227	155	14	0
A Flintoff	c Langer b Warne	16	37	26	4	0
GO Jones	b McGrath	33	68	48	5	0
AF Giles	c Warne b Clark	23	55	38	3	0
MJ Hoggard	c Warne b Clark	8	49	35	1	0
SJ Harmison	c McGrath b Clark	13	31	18	2	0
JM Anderson	not out	4	7	8	1	0
Extras	(b 8, lb 10, w 2, nb 11)	31			
Total	(all out; 100.1 ov; 445 mins)	370			

FALL OF WICKETS: 1–29 (Strauss, 10.4 ov), 2–36 (Bell, 13.2 ov), 3–91 (Cook, 29.2 ov), 4–244 (Collingwood, 63.3 ov), 5–271 (Flintoff, 71.4 ov), 6–293 (Pietersen, 80.4 ov), 7–326 (Jones, 87.1 ov), 8–346 (Giles, 92.5 ov), 9–361 (Hoggard, 98.2 ov), 10–370 (Harmison, 100.1 ov)

BOWLING: Lee 22–1–98–1; McGrath 19–3–53–1; Clark 24.1–6–72–4; Warne 34–7–124–4; Hussey 1–0–5–0

STUMPS SCORES
Day 1: Australia first innings 3–346 (Ponting 137, Hussey 63; 90 overs)
Day 2: England first innings 3–53 (Bell 13, Pietersen 6; 17 overs)
Day 3: Australia second innings 1–181 (Langer 88, Ponting 51; 40 overs)
Day 4: England second innings 5–293 (Pietersen 92, Jones 12; 80 overs)

THE FOLLOW-ON

Since Ricky Ponting assumed the Test leadership in 2004, the Australian captain has had seven opportunities to enforce the follow on, but has done so only once, in a rain-interrupted Test at Wellington in 2005. The six Tests where Australia did not make their opponents bat again resulted as follows:

Year	Match	Australia	Opponent	Result
2004*	1st Test v India	474 & 228	246 & 239	Aust by 217 runs
2004*	3rd Test v India	398 & 5–329d	185 & 200	Aust by 342 runs
2004–05	2nd Test v NZ	8–575d & 2–139d	251 & 250	Aust by 213 runs
2004–05	1st Test v Pakistan	381 & 5–361d	179 & 72	Aust by 491 runs
2005–06	1st Test v WI	435 & 2–283	210 & 129	Aust by 379 runs
2006–07	1st Test v England	9–602d & 1–202	157 & 370	Aust by 277 runs

* Adam Gilchrist was captain.

SECOND TEST
Adelaide Oval
1–5 December 2006 (five-day match)

Result: Australia won by six wickets • Toss: England
Umpires: SA Bucknor (West Indies) and RE Koertzen (SA) • TV umpire: SJ Davis
Match referee: JJ Crowe (NZ) • Player of the match: RT Ponting (Aus)

England first innings		R	M	B	4	6
AJ Strauss	c Martyn b Clark	14	63	44	0	0
AN Cook	c Gilchrist b Clark	27	90	57	2	0
IR Bell	c & b Lee	60	189	148	6	0
PD Collingwood	c Gilchrist b Clark	206	515	392	16	0
KP Pietersen	run out	158	377	257	15	1
A Flintoff	not out	38	101	67	2	1
GO Jones	c Martyn b Warne	1	10	7	0	0
AF Giles	not out	27	63	44	4	0
Extras	(lb 10, w 2, nb 8)	20				
Total	(6 wkts dec; 168 ov; 707 mins)	551				

DID NOT BAT: MJ Hoggard, SJ Harmison, JM Anderson

FALL OF WICKETS: 1–32 (Strauss, 14.3 ov), 2–45 (Cook, 20.5 ov), 3–158 (Bell, 61.4 ov), 4–468 (Collingwood, 145.5 ov), 5–489 (Pietersen, 151.6 ov), 6–491 (Jones, 154.2 ov)

BOWLING: Lee 34–1–139–1; McGrath 30–5–107–0; Clark 34–6–75–3; Warne 53–9–167–1; Clarke 17–2–53–0

Australia first innings		R	M	B	4	6
JL Langer	c Pietersen b Flintoff	4	9	8	1	0
ML Hayden	c Jones b Hoggard	12	57	30	1	0
RT Ponting	c Jones b Hoggard	142	353	245	12	0
DR Martyn	c Bell b Hoggard	11	42	33	1	0
MEK Hussey	b Hoggard	91	298	212	7	1
MJ Clarke	c Giles b Hoggard	124	318	224	10	0
AC Gilchrist	c Bell b Giles	64	111	79	8	0
SK Warne	lbw b Hoggard	43	157	108	4	0
B Lee	not out	7	47	33	0	0
SR Clark	b Hoggard	0	9	7	0	0
GD McGrath	c Jones b Anderson	1	25	21	0	0
Extras	(b 4, lb 2, w 1, nb 7)	14				
Total	(all out; 165.3 ov; 718 mins)	513				

FALL OF WICKETS: 1–8 (Langer, 1.6 ov), 2–35 (Hayden, 12.6 ov), 3–65 (Martyn, 22.2 ov), 4–257 (Ponting, 82.6 ov), 5–286 (Hussey, 90.4 ov), 6–384 (Gilchrist, 114.4 ov), 7–502 (Warne, 153.5 ov), 8–505 (Clarke, 157.1 ov), 9–507 (Clark, 159.2 ov), 10–513 (McGrath, 165.3 ov)

BOWLING: Hoggard 42–6–109–7; Flintoff 26–5–82–1; Harmison 25–5–96–0; Anderson 21.3–3–85–1; Giles 42–7–103–1; Pietersen 9–0–32–0

England second innings		R	M	B	4	6
AJ Strauss	c Hussey b Warne	34	125	79	3	0
AN Cook	c Gilchrist b Clark	9	48	35	1	0
IR Bell	run out	26	85	73	2	0
PD Collingwood	not out	22	198	119	2	0
KP Pietersen	b Warne	2	8	5	0	0
A Flintoff	c Gilchrist b Lee	2	25	24	0	0
GO Jones	c Hayden b Lee	10	41	24	1	0
AF Giles	c Hayden b Warne	0	14	8	0	0
MJ Hoggard	b Warne	4	27	24	0	0
SJ Harmison	lbw b McGrath	8	25	21	0	0
JM Anderson	lbw b McGrath	1	41	28	0	0
Extras	(b 3, lb 5, w 1, nb 2)	11				
Total	(all out; 73 ov; 324 mins)	129				

FALL OF WICKETS: 1–31 (Cook, 10.6 ov), 2–69 (Strauss, 29.6 ov), 3–70 (Bell, 31.6 ov), 4–73 (Pietersen, 33.1 ov), 5–77 (Flintoff, 38.6 ov), 6–94 (Jones, 48.4 ov), 7–97 (Giles, 51.6 ov), 8–105 (Hoggard, 57.5 ov), 9–119 (Harmison, 62.6 ov), 10–129 (Anderson, 72.6 ov)

BOWLING: Lee 8–3–35–2; McGrath 10–6–15–2; Warne 32–12–49–4; Clark 13–4–22–1

Australia second innings	R	M	B	4	6
JL Langer	c Bell b Hoggard	7	12	8	1	0
ML Hayden	c Collingwood b Flintoff	18	31	17	2	0
RT Ponting	c Strauss b Giles	49	95	65	5	0
MEK Hussey	not out	61	129	66	5	0
DR Martyn	c Strauss b Flintoff	5	4	4	1	0
MJ Clarke	not out	21	47	39	0	0
Extras	(b 2, lb 2, w 1, nb 2)	7				
Total	(4 wkts; 32.5 ov; 161 mins)	168				

FALL OF WICKETS: 1–14 (Langer, 2.2 ov), 2–33 (Hayden, 5.4 ov), 3–116 (Ponting, 21.4 ov), 4–121 (Martyn, 22.2 ov)

BOWLING: Hoggard 4–0–29–1; Flintoff 9–0–44–2; Giles 10–0–46–1; Harmison 4–0–15–0; Anderson 3.5–0–23–0; Pietersen 2–0–7–0

STUMPS SCORES
Day 1: England first innings 3–266 (Collingwood 98, Pietersen 60; 90 overs)
Day 2: Australia first innings 1–28 (Hayden 12, Ponting 11; 9 overs)
Day 3: Australia first innings 5–312 (Clarke 30, Gilchrist 13; 97 overs)
Day 4: England second innings 1–59 (Strauss 31, Bell 18; 19 overs)

FAMOUS COMEBACKS

Australia's victory was the sixth instance of a team conceding 500 runs in the first innings of a Test and still winning:

Year	Match	Batting 1st	Batting 2nd	Result
1894–95	Aust v Eng, at Sydney	586 & 166	325 & 437	Eng by 10 runs
2003–04	Aust v Ind, at Adelaide	556 & 196	523 & 6–233	Ind by 4 wkts
2006–07	Eng v Aust, at Adelaide	6–551d & 129	513 & 4–168	Aust by 6 wkts
1968	WI v Eng, at Port-of-Spain	7–526d & 2–92d	404 & 3–215	Eng by 7 wkts
1952–53	Aust v SA, at Melbourne	520 & 209	435 & 4–297	SA by 7 wkts
1928–29	Eng v Aust, at Melbourne	519 & 257	491 & 5–287	Aust by 5 wkts

THIRD TEST
WACA Ground, Perth
14–18 December 2006 (five-day match)

Result: Australia won by 206 runs • Toss: Australia
Umpires: Aleem Dar (Pak) and RE Koertzen (SA) • TV umpire: SJ Davis
Match referee: JJ Crowe (NZ) • Player of the match: MEK Hussey (Aus)

Australia first innings		R	M	B	4	6
JL Langer	b Panesar	37	116	68	6	0
ML Hayden	c Jones b Hoggard	24	48	33	3	0
RT Ponting	lbw b Harmison	2	19	11	0	0
MEK Hussey	not out	74	244	162	10	0
MJ Clarke	c & b Harmison	37	62	67	4	0
A Symonds	c Jones b Panesar	26	39	30	2	2
AC Gilchrist	c Bell b Panesar	0	7	4	0	0
SK Warne	c Jones b Panesar	25	32	22	3	0
B Lee	lbw b Panesar	10	32	25	2	0
SR Clark	b Harmison	3	13	5	0	0
GD McGrath	c Cook b Harmison	1	4	2	0	0
Extras	(w 1, nb 4)	5				
Total	(all out; 71 ov; 313 mins)	244				

FALL OF WICKETS: 1–47 (Hayden, 10.3 ov), 2–54 (Ponting, 13.3 ov), 3–69 (Langer, 24.1 ov), 4–121 (Clarke, 40.4 ov), 5–172 (Symonds, 49.6 ov), 6–172 (Gilchrist, 51.4 ov), 7–214 (Warne, 59.1 ov), 8–234 (Lee, 67.6 ov), 9–242 (Clark, 70.3 ov), 10–244 (McGrath, 70.6 ov)

BOWLING: Hoggard 12–2–40–1; Flintoff 9–2–36–0; Harmison 19–4–48–4; Panesar 24–4–92–5; Mahmood 7–2–28–0

England first innings		R	M	B	4	6
AJ Strauss	c Gilchrist b Clark	42	101	71	6	0
AN Cook	c Langer b McGrath	15	26	15	2	0
IR Bell	c Gilchrist b Lee	0	5	2	0	0
PD Collingwood	c Hayden b McGrath	11	45	33	1	0
KP Pietersen	c Symonds b Lee	70	180	123	8	1
A Flintoff	c Warne b Symonds	13	46	31	2	0
GO Jones	c Langer b Symonds	0	11	4	0	0
SI Mahmood	c Gilchrist b Clark	10	24	18	1	0
MJ Hoggard	c Hayden b Warne	4	47	39	0	0
SJ Harmison	c Lee b Clark	23	56	33	3	0
MS Panesar	not out	16	41	26	3	0
Extras	(w 1, nb 10)	11				
Total	(all out; 64.1 ov; 301 mins)	215				

FALL OF WICKETS: 1–36 (Cook, 5.6 ov), 2–37 (Bell, 6.6 ov), 3–55 (Collingwood, 17.2 ov), 4–82 (Strauss, 24.2 ov), 5–107 (Flintoff, 33.4 ov), 6–114 (Jones, 35.6 ov), 7–128 (Mahmood, 40.6 ov), 8–155 (Hoggard, 51.6 ov), 9–175 (Pietersen, 54.5 ov), 10–215 (Harmison, 64.1 ov)

BOWLING: Lee 18–1–69–2; McGrath 18–5–48–2; Clark 15.1–3–49–3; Warne 9–0–41–1; Symonds 4–1–8–2

Australia second innings		R	M	B	4	6
JL Langer	b Hoggard	0	1	1	0	0
ML Hayden	c Collingwood b Panesar	92	252	159	12	0
RT Ponting	c Jones b Harmison	75	194	128	9	0
MEK Hussey	c Jones b Panesar	103	224	156	12	0
MJ Clarke	not out	135	251	164	17	1
A Symonds	c Collingwood b Panesar	2	9	6	0	0
AC Gilchrist	not out	102	103	59	12	4
Extras	(lb 15, w 2, nb 1)	18				
Total	(5 wkts dec; 112 ov; 514 mins) 527					

FALL OF WICKETS: 1–0 (Langer, 0.1 ov), 2–144 (Ponting, 39.4 ov), 3–206 (Hayden, 58.4 ov), 4–357 (Hussey, 89.3 ov), 5–365 (Symonds, 91.6 ov)

BOWLING: Hoggard 20–4–85–1; Flintoff 19–2–76–0; Harmison 24–3–116–1; Panesar 34–3–145–3; Mahmood 10–0–59–0; Pietersen 5–1–31–0

England second innings		R	M	B	4	6
AJ Strauss	lbw b Lee	0	2	4	0	0
AN Cook	c Gilchrist b McGrath	116	389	290	9	0
IR Bell	c Langer b Warne	87	234	163	8	2
PD Collingwood	c Gilchrist b Clark	5	45	36	0	0
KP Pietersen	not out	60	243	150	6	0
MJ Hoggard	b McGrath	0	2	2	0	0
A Flintoff	b Warne	51	96	67	8	1
GO Jones	run out	0	11	7	0	0
SI Mahmood	lbw b Clark	4	14	10	0	0
SJ Harmison	lbw b Warne	0	3	1	0	0
MS Panesar	b Warne	1	8	9	0	0
Extras	(b 7, lb 8, w 6, nb 5)	26				
Total	(all out; 122.2 ov; 529 mins)	350				

FALL OF WICKETS: 1–0 (Strauss, 0.4 ov), 2–170 (Bell, 56.6 ov), 3–185 (Collingwood, 69.3 ov), 4–261 (Cook, 93.2 ov), 5–261 (Hoggard, 93.4 ov), 6–336 (Flintoff, 114.5 ov), 7–336 (Jones, 116.6 ov), 8–345 (Mahmood, 119.6 ov), 9–346 (Harmison, 120.2 ov), 10–350 (Panesar, 122.2 ov)

BOWLING: Lee 22–3–75–1; McGrath 27–9–61–2; Clark 25–7–56–2; Warne 39.2–6–115–4; Symonds 9–1–28–0

STUMPS SCORES
Day 1: England first innings 2–51 (Strauss 24, Collingwood 10; 14 overs)
Day 2: Australia second innings 1–119 (Hayden 57, Ponting 57; 36 overs)
Day 3: England second innings 1–19 (Cook 7, Bell 9; 6 overs)
Day 4: England second innings 5–265 (Pietersen 37, Flintoff 2; 96 overs)

ASHES REGAINED

This was the second instance of either England or Australia regaining the Ashes by winning the third Test of a five-Test series, after Warwick Armstrong's Australians in 1920–21. This was the seventh time Australia won the opening three Tests of an Ashes series, after 1920–21, 1921, 1924–25, 1950–51, 2001 and 2002–03. England won all three Tests in 1886 and the first four Tests of 1928–29. Australia won all three Tests v England in 1979–80, when the Ashes were not at stake.

FOURTH TEST
Melbourne Cricket Ground
26–28 December 2006 (five-day match)

Result: Australia won by an innings and 99 runs • Toss: England
Umpires: Aleem Dar (Pak) and RE Koertzen (SA) • TV umpire: RL Parry
Match referee: RS Madugalle (SL) • Player of the match: SK Warne (Aus)

England first innings		R	M	B	4	6
AJ Strauss	b Warne	50	206	132	1	0
AN Cook	c Gilchrist b Lee	11	49	37	1	0
IR Bell	lbw b Clark	7	46	30	0	0
PD Collingwood	c Ponting b Lee	28	115	82	4	0
KP Pietersen	c Symonds b Warne	21	104	70	0	0
A Flintoff	c Warne b Clark	13	36	31	1	0
CMW Read	c Ponting b Warne	3	28	17	0	0
SI Mahmood	c Gilchrist b McGrath	0	11	9	0	0
SJ Harmison	c Clarke b Warne	7	11	12	1	0
MS Panesar	c Symonds b Warne	4	27	19	0	0
MJ Hoggard	not out	9	15	10	1	0
Extras	(b 2, lb 1, nb 3)	6				
Total	(all out; 74.2 ov; 324 mins)	159				

FALL OF WICKETS: 1–23 (Cook, 10.5 ov), 2–44 (Bell, 20.5 ov), 3–101 (Collingwood, 45.6 ov), 4–101 (Strauss, 46.2 ov), 5–122 (Flintoff, 55.5 ov), 6–135 (Read, 62.6 ov), 7–136 (Mahmood, 65.4 ov), 8–145 (Harmison, 68.2 ov), 9–146 (Pietersen, 70.2 ov), 10–159 (Panesar, 74.2 ov)

BOWLING: Lee 13–4–36–2; McGrath 20–8–37–1; Clark 17–6–27–2; Symonds 7–2–17–0; Warne 17.2–4–39–5

Australia first innings		R	M	B	4	6
JL Langer	c Read b Flintoff	27	45	29	3	0
ML Hayden	c Read b Mahmood	153	418	265	13	2
B Lee	c Read b Flintoff	0	2	1	0	0
RT Ponting	c Cook b Flintoff	7	37	28	0	0
MEK Hussey	b Hoggard	6	37	20	0	0
MJ Clarke	c Read b Harmison	5	6	5	0	0
A Symonds	c Read b Harmison	156	327	220	15	1
AC Gilchrist	c Collingwood b Mahmood	1	10	8	0	0
SK Warne	not out	40	75	54	6	0
SR Clark	c Read b Mahmood	8	34	24	0	0
GD McGrath	c Bell b Mahmood	0	9	6	0	0
Extras	(lb 6, w 1, nb 9)	1				
Total	(all out; 108.3 ov; 505 mins)	419				

FALL OF WICKETS: 1–44 (Langer, 9.2 ov), 2–44 (Lee, 9.3 ov), 3–62 (Ponting, 17.3 ov), 4–79 (Hussey, 24.1 ov), 5–84 (Clarke, 25.2 ov), 6–363 (Hayden, 90.4 ov), 7–365 (Gilchrist, 92.3 ov), 8–383 (Symonds, 99.2 ov), 9–417 (Clark, 106.5 ov), 10–419 (McGrath, 108.3 ov)

BOWLING: Hoggard 21–6–82–1; Flintoff 22–1–77–3; Harmison 28–6–69–2; Mahmood 21.3–1–100–4; Panesar 12–1–52–0; Collingwood 3–0–20–0; Pietersen 1–0–13–0

England second innings		R	M	B	4	6
AJ Strauss	c Gilchrist b Lee	31	173	107	2	0
AN Cook	b Clark	20	64	46	1	0
IR Bell	lbw b McGrath	2	21	11	0	0
KP Pietersen	b Clark	1	7	8	0	0
PD Collingwood	c Langer b Lee	16	52	38	0	0
A Flintoff	lbw b Clark	25	60	45	2	0
CMW Read	not out	26	127	77	1	0
SI Mahmood	lbw b Warne	0	3	2	0	0
SJ Harmison	lbw b Warne	4	44	26	0	0
MS Panesar	c Clarke b Lee	14	20	19	2	0
MJ Hoggard	b Lee	5	21	20	0	0
Extras	(lb 12, w 1, nb 4)	17				
Total	(all out; 65.5 ov; 301 mins)	161				

FALL OF WICKETS: 1–41 (Cook, 14.5 ov), 2–48 (Bell, 19.2 ov), 3–49 (Pietersen, 20.5 ov), 4–75 (Collingwood, 31.4 ov), 5–90 (Strauss, 37.5 ov), 6–108 (Flintoff, 45.5 ov), 7–109 (Mahmood, 46.3 ov), 8–127 (Harmison, 56.5 ov), 9–146 (Panesar, 61.2 ov), 10–161 (Hoggard, 65.5 ov)

BOWLING: Lee 18.5–6–47–4; McGrath 12–2–26–1; Clark 16–6–30–3; Warne 19–3–46–2

STUMPS SCORES
Day 1: Australia first innings 2–48 (Hayden 17, Ponting 0; 11 overs)
Day 2: Australia first innings 7–372 (Symonds 154, Warne 4; 96 overs)

END OF AN ERA

Damien Martyn, Shane Warne, Glenn McGrath and Justin Langer all retired from Test cricket during 2006–07. Where they (and other prominent current players) rank in the lists of Australia's leading run-scorers and wicket-takers is as follows:

MOST TEST RUNS (AS AT SEPTEMBER 1, 2007)

Rank	Player	Tests	Inn	NO	Runs	HS	Ave	100	50
1.	AR Border	156	265	44	11174	205	50.56	27	63
2.	SR Waugh	168	260	46	10927	200	51.06	32	50
3.	RT Ponting	110	183	25	9368	257	59.29	33	36
4.	ME Waugh	128	209	17	8029	153*	41.82	20	47
5.	ML Hayden	89	159	13	7739	380	53.01	27	27
6.	JL Langer	105	182	12	7696	250	45.27	23	30
13.	AC Gilchrist	90	129	19	5353	204*	48.66	17	24
20.	DR Martyn	67	109	14	4406	165	46.38	13	23
28.	SK Warne	145	199	17	3154	99	17.33	–	12
114	GD McGrath	124	138	51	641	61	7.37	–	1

MOST TEST WICKETS (AS AT SEPTEMBER 1, 2007)

Rank	Player	Tests	Balls	Mdns	Runs	Wkts	Avg	Best	5w	10w
1.	SK Warne	145	40705	1762	17995	708	25.42	8–71	37	10
2.	GD McGrath	124	29248	1470	12186	563	21.64	8–24	29	3
3.	DK Lillee	70	18467	652	8493	355	23.92	7–83	23	7
4.	CJ McDermott	71	16586	583	8332	291	28.63	8–97	14	2
5.	JN Gillespie	71	14234	630	6770	259	26.14	7–37	8	0
8.	B Lee	59	12279	410	7301	231	31.61	5–30	7	0
13.	SCG MacGill	40	10211	344	5386	198	27.20	8–108	12	2

FIFTH TEST
Sydney Cricket Ground
2–5 January 2007 (five-day match)
Result: Australia won by 10 wickets • Toss: England
Umpires: Aleem Dar (Pak) and BF Bowden (NZ) • TV umpire: PD Parker
Match referee: RS Madugalle (SL) • Player of the match: SR Clark (Aus)
Player of the series RT Ponting (Aus)

England first innings		R	M	B	4	6
AJ Strauss	c Gilchrist b Lee	29	64	52	3	0
AN Cook	c Gilchrist b Clark	20	88	47	2	0
IR Bell	b McGrath	71	194	153	8	0
KP Pietersen	c Hussey b McGrath	41	162	104	1	0
PD Collingwood	c Gilchrist b McGrath	27	119	73	4	0
A Flintoff	c Gilchrist b Clark	89	195	142	11	1
CMW Read	c Gilchrist b Lee	2	13	9	0	0
SI Mahmood	c Hayden b Lee	0	2	1	0	0
SJ Harmison	lbw b Clark	2	51	24	0	0
MS Panesar	lbw b Warne	0	20	14	0	0
JM Anderson	not out	0	6	5	0	0
Extras	(lb 5, w 3, nb 2)	10				
Total	(all out; 103.4 ov; 462 mins)	291				

FALL OF WICKETS: 1–45 (Strauss, 14.2 ov), 2–58 (Cook, 19.1 ov), 3–166 (Pietersen, 58.3 ov), 4–167 (Bell, 60.1 ov), 5–245 (Collingwood, 85.6 ov), 6–258 (Read, 88.5 ov), 7–258 (Mahmood, 88.6 ov), 8–282 (Harmison, 98.6 ov), 9–291 (Flintoff, 102.1 ov), 10–291 (Panesar, 103.4 ov)

BOWLING: GD McGrath 29–8–67–3; Lee 22–5–75–3; Clark 24–6–62–3; Warne 22.4–1–69–1; Symonds 6–2–13–0

Australia first innings		R	M	B	4	6
JL Langer	c Read b Anderson	26	41	27	4	0
ML Hayden	c Collingwood b Harmison	33	113	77	5	0
RT Ponting	run out	45	96	72	6	0
MEK Hussey	c Read b Anderson	37	120	100	3	1
MJ Clarke	c Read b Harmison	11	39	24	1	0
A Symonds	b Panesar	48	138	95	6	0
AC Gilchrist	c Read b Anderson	62	118	72	8	0
SK Warne	st Read b Panesar	71	114	65	9	2
B Lee	c Read b Flintoff	5	14	10	1	0
SR Clark	c Pietersen b Mahmood	35	55	41	1	0
GD McGrath	not out	0	6	3	0	0
Extras	(lb 10, w 4, nb 6)	20				
Total	(all out; 96.3 ov; 432 mins)	393				

FALL OF WICKETS: 1–34 (Langer, 9.3 ov), 2–100 (Hayden, 25.3 ov), 3–118 (Ponting, 32.3 ov), 4–155 (Clarke, 43.1 ov), 5–190 (Hussey, 56.2 ov), 6–260 (Symonds, 73.1 ov), 7–318 (Gilchrist, 80.3 ov), 8–325 (Lee, 83.3 ov), 9–393 (Clark, 95.3 ov), 10–393 (Warne, 96.3 ov)

BOWLING: Flintoff 17–2–56–1; Anderson 26–8–98–3; Harmison 23–5–80–2; Mahmood 11–1–59–1; Panesar 19.3–0–90–2

England second innings		R	M	B	4	6
AJ Strauss	lbw b Clark	24	68	45	3	0
AN Cook	c Gilchrist b Lee	4	11	8	1	0
IR Bell	c Gilchrist b Lee	28	85	51	5	0
KP Pietersen	c Gilchrist b McGrath	29	139	95	3	0
PD Collingwood	c Hayden b Clark	17	67	36	3	0
A Flintoff	st Gilchrist b Warne	7	31	21	1	0
MS Panesar	run out	0	27	19	0	0
CMW Read	c Ponting b Lee	4	26	17	1	0
SI Mahmood	b McGrath	4	13	11	1	0
SJ Harmison	not out	16	42	26	2	0
JM Anderson	c Hussey b McGrath	5	37	22	1	0
Extras	(b 2, lb 3, w 1, nb 3)	9				
Total	(all out; 58 ov; 278 mins)	147				

FALL OF WICKETS: 1–5 (Cook, 2.3 ov), 2–55 (Strauss, 14.3 ov), 3–64 (Bell, 20.5 ov), 4–98 (Collingwood, 34.6 ov), 5–113 (Flintoff, 41.3 ov), 6–114 (Pietersen, 43.3 ov), 7–114 (Panesar, 47.2 ov), 8–122 (Read, 48.6 ov), 9–123 (Mahmood, 49.6 ov), 10–147 (Anderson, 57.6 ov)

BOWLING: Lee 14–5–39–3; McGrath 21–11–38–3; Clark 12–4–29–2; Warne 6–1–23–1; Symonds 5–2–13–0

Australia second innings		R	M	B	4	6
JL Langer	not out	20	44	43	2	0
ML Hayden	not out	23	44	22	2	1
Extras	(lb 3)	3				
Total	(0 wkts; 10.5 ov; 44 mins)	46				

DID NOT BAT: RT Ponting, MEK Hussey, MJ Clarke, A Symonds, AC Gilchrist, SK Warne, B Lee, SR Clark, GD McGrath

BOWLING: Anderson 4–0–12–0; Harmison 5–1–13–0; Mahmood 1.5–0–18–0

STUMPS SCORES
Day 1: England first innings 4–234 (Collingwood 25, Flintoff 42; 80 overs)
Day 2: Australia first innings 4–188 (Hussey 37, Symonds 22; 55 overs)
Day 3: England first innings 5–114 (Pietersen 29, Panesar 0; 43 overs)

CLEAN SWEEPS

The 2006–07 Ashes series was the ninth instance of a five-Test rubber being 'swept' by one team:

Series	Teams	Venue	Winner
1920–21	Australia v England	Australia	Australia
1931–32	Australia v South Africa	Australia	Australia
1959	England v India	England	England
1962	West Indies v India	West Indies	West Indies
1984	West Indies v England	England	West Indies
1986	West Indies v England	West Indies	West Indies
1998–99	South Africa v West Indies	South Africa	South Africa
2000–01	Australia v West Indies	Australia	Australia
2006–07	Australia v England	Australia	Australia

ASHES SERIES AVERAGES

AUSTRALIA BATTING AND FIELDING

Batsman	Tests	Inn	NO	Runs	HS	Ave	100	50	Ct	St
MEK Hussey	5	7	2	458	103	91.60	1	4	5	–
RT Ponting	5	8	1	576	196	82.29	2	2	4	–
MJ Clarke	5	7	2	389	135*	77.80	2	1	2	–
A Symonds	3	4	0	232	156	58.00	1	–	3	–
ML Hayden	5	9	1	413	153	51.63	1	1	7	–
SK Warne	5	5	1	196	71	49.00	–	1	5	–
AC Gilchrist	5	6	1	229	102*	45.80	1	2	24	2
JL Langer	5	9	2	303	100*	43.29	1	1	5	–
B Lee	5	5	2	65	43*	21.67	–	–	2	–
SR Clark	5	5	0	85	39	17.00	–	–	–	–
DR Martyn	2	3	0	45	29	15.00	–	–	3	–
GD McGrath	5	5	2	10	8*	3.33	–	–	1	–

AUSTRALIA BOWLING

Bowler	O	M	R	W	Ave	Best	5w	10w
SR Clark	194.2	53	443	26	17.04	4–72	–	–
GD McGrath	209.1	65	502	21	23.90	6–50	1	–
SK Warne	241.2	43	698	23	30.35	5–39	1	–
B Lee	196.5	32	664	20	33.20	4–47	–	–
A Symonds	31	8	79	2	39.50	2–8	–	–
MEK Hussey	1	0	5	0	–	–	–	–
MJ Clarke	17	2	53	0	–	–	–	–

ENGLAND BATTING AND FIELDING

Batsman	Tests	Inn	NO	Runs	HS	Ave	100	50	Ct	St
KP Pietersen	5	10	1	490	158	54.44	1	3	3	–
PD Collingwood	5	10	1	433	206	48.11	1	1	7	–
IR Bell	5	10	0	331	87	33.10	–	4	5	–
A Flintoff	5	10	1	254	89	28.22	–	2	–	–
AN Cook	5	10	0	276	116	27.60	1	–	2	–
AJ Strauss	5	10	0	247	50	24.70	–	1	3	–
AF Giles	2	4	1	74	27*	24.67	–	–	1	–
CMW Read	2	4	1	35	26*	11.67	–	–	11	1
GO Jones	3	6	0	63	33	10.50	–	–	9	–
SJ Harmison	5	9	1	73	23	9.13	–	–	1	–
MS Panesar	3	6	1	35	16*	7.00	–	–	–	–
JM Anderson	3	5	3	12	5	6.00	–	–	–	–
MJ Hoggard	4	7	1	30	9*	5.00	–	–	–	–
SI Mahmood	3	6	0	18	10	3.00	–	–	–	–

ENGLAND BOWLING

Bowler	O	M	R	W	Ave	Best	5w	10w
MJ Hoggard	141	25	486	13	37.38	7–109	1	–
MS Panesar	89.3	8	379	10	37.90	5–92	1	–
A Flintoff	137	18	481	11	43.73	4–99	–	–
SI Mahmood	51.2	4	264	5	52.80	4–100	–	–
SJ Harmison	170.1	29	614	10	61.40	4–48	–	–
JM Anderson	93.2	18	413	5	82.60	3–98	–	–
AF Giles	82	9	262	3	87.33	1–46	–	–
IR Bell	1	0	12	0	–	–	–	–
PD Collingwood	3	0	20	0	–	–	–	–
KP Pietersen	29	2	125	0	–	–	–	–

AUSTRALIAN CENTURIES AND FIVE WICKETS IN AN INNINGS

Ricky Ponting's 196 in the first Test was his 32nd Test century, in his 106th Test.

Justin Langer's 100 not out in the first Test was his 23rd Test century, in his 101st Test.

Ricky Ponting's 142 in the second Test was his 33rd Test century, in his 107th Test.

Michael Clarke's 124 in the second Test was his third Test century, in his 24th Test.

Mike Hussey's 103 in the third Test was his fifth Test century, in his 14th Test.

Michael Clarke's 135 not out in the third Test was his fourth Test century, in his 25th Test.

Adam Gilchrist's 102 not out in the third Test was his 17th Test century, in his 88th Test.

Matthew Hayden's 153 in the fourth Test was his 27th Test century, in his 88th Test.

Andrew Symonds's 156 in the fourth Test was his first Test century, in his 12th Test.

Glenn McGrath's 6–50 in the first Test was the 29th time he had taken five or more wickets in a Test innings, in his 120th Test

Shane Warne's 5–39 in the fourth Test was the 37th time he had taken five or more wickets in a Test innings, in his 144th Test.

NOTABLE AUSTRALIAN LANDMARKS

Ricky Ponting became the seventh man (after Brian Lara, Allan Border, Steve Waugh, Sachin Tendulkar, Sunil Gavaskar and Rahul Dravid) and third Australian to score 9000 runs in Test cricket during the second innings of the first Test.

Shane Warne scored his 3000th run in Test cricket in the first innings of the second Test. He became the first man to score 3000 Test runs without making a Test century, and the eighth man and first Australian to achieve the 3000 runs/100 wickets Test double.

Glenn McGrath became the third man (after Warne and Muttiah Muralitharan) and the first pace bowler to take 550 Test wickets during the second innings of the second Test.

Shane Warne became the first bowler to take 700 Test wickets when he dismissed Andrew Strauss on the opening day of the fourth Test.

Shane Warne's first wicket of the fifth Test was his 1000th in international cricket: 707 in Tests, 293 in ODIs.

Australia's win in the fifth Test was their 12th straight Test victory, a run that began with the Boxing Day Test against South Africa in 2005–06. The Test record is 16 consecutive wins, achieved by Australia between October 1999 and March 2001.

TWENTY20 INTERNATIONAL

AUSTRALIA V ENGLAND

Sydney Cricket Ground
9 January 2007 (20-over match)

Result: Australia won by 77 runs • Toss: Australia
Umpires: PD Parker and RL Parry • TV umpire: RJ Tucker
Match referee: RS Madugalle (SL) • Player of the match: CL White (Aus)

Australia innings		R	M	B	4	6
AC Gilchrist	b Panesar	48	36	29	2	5
ML Hayden	c Dalrymple b Anderson	20	15	8	3	1
RT Ponting	c Lewis b Collingwood	47	41	26	3	2
MEK Hussey	st Nixon b Panesar	18	7	9	2	1
A Symonds	not out	39	38	22	3	1
MJ Clarke	run out	5	5	6	0	0
CL White	not out	40	21	20	1	4
Extras	(lb 2, w 2)	4				
Total	(5 wkts; 20 ov)	221				

DID NOT BAT: GB Hogg, NW Bracken, BW Hilfenhaus, SM Harwood

FALL OF WICKETS: 1–28 (Hayden, 3.2 ov), 2–97 (Gilchrist, 8.1 ov), 3–123 (Hussey, 10.2 ov), 4–149 (Ponting, 13.1 ov), 5–155 (Clarke, 14.2 ov)

BOWLING: Flintoff 4-0-36-0; Anderson 4-0-64-1; Panesar 4-0-40-2; Lewis 3-0-31-0; Dalrymple 1-0-12-0; Collingwood 4-0-36-1

England innings		R	M	B	4	6
EC Joyce	c Hussey b Bracken	1	2	3	0	0
MP Vaughan	lbw b Symonds	27	28	21	4	0
A Flintoff	c White b Harwood	0	2	2	0	0
KP Pietersen	run out	11	12	6	2	0
IR Bell	b Hilfenhaus	22	26	22	1	0
PD Collingwood	c White b Hilfenhaus	5	8	11	0	0
PA Nixon	not out	31	38	22	2	1
JWM Dalrymple	lbw b Symonds	32	19	27	4	0
J Lewis	c Gilchrist b White	1	2	4	0	0
MS Panesar	run out	1	3	2	0	0
JM Anderson	not out	1	2	1	0	0
Extras	(b 4, lb 1, w 6, nb 1)	12				
Total	(9 wkts; 20 ov)	144				

FALL OF WICKETS: 1–3 (Joyce, 0.4 ov), 2–5 (Flintoff, 1.2 ov), 3–32 (Pietersen, 4.1 ov), 4–54 (Vaughan, 6.2 ov), 5–68 (Collingwood, 9.3 ov), 6–78 (Bell, 11.4 ov), 7–127 (Dalrymple, 17.5 ov), 8–129 (Lewis, 18.3 ov), 9–138 (Panesar, 19.3 ov)

BOWLING: NW Bracken 3-0-20-1; Harwood 4-0-44-1; Hilfenhaus 4-0-16-2; Symonds 4-0-24-2; Hogg 3-0-24-0; White 2-0-11-1

COMMONWEALTH BANK SERIES

In Australia, January 12–February 11, 2007

Date	Match	Venue	Result
January 12	Australia v England	Melbourne	Australia won by eight wickets
January 14	Australia v New Zealand	Hobart	Australia won by 105 runs
January 16	England v New Zealand	Hobart	England won by three wickets
January 19	Australia v England	Brisbane	Australia won by four wickets
January 21	Australia v New Zealand	Sydney	Australia won by two wickets
January 23	England v New Zealand	Adelaide	New Zealand won by 90 runs
January 26	Australia v England	Adelaide	Australia won by nine wickets
January 28	Australia v New Zealand	Perth	Australia won by eight runs
January 30	England v New Zealand	Perth	New Zealand won by 58 runs
February 2	Australia v England	Sydney	England won by 92 runs
February 4	Australia v New Zealand	Melbourne	Australia won by five wickets
February 6	England v New Zealand	Brisbane	England won by 14 runs
February 9	Australia v England	Melbourne	England won by 4 wickets
February 11	Australia v England	Sydney	England won by 34 runs

POINTS TABLE

Team	P	W	L	NR	T	BP	Pts	NRR
Australia	8	7	1	–	–	3	31	+0.667
England	8	3	5	–	–	1	13	–0.608
New Zealand	8	2	6	–	–	1	9	–0.007

THE ANNUAL ONE-DAY SERIES IN AUSTRALIA, 1979–2007

The first version of this tournament, the Benson & Hedges World Series Cup, was played in 1979–80. The competition was renamed the Benson & Hedges World Series in 1988–89, the Carlton & United Series in 1996–97, the Carlton Series in 2000–01, the VB Series in 2001–02, and the Commonwealth Bank Series in 2006–07. The performance records of all teams that have competed in the various guises of the tournament are as follows:

Team	First	Second	Missed Finals
Australia	18	7	3
Australia A	–	1	–
England	2	3	3
India	–	3	2
New Zealand	–	5	4
Pakistan	1	3	4
South Africa	1	2	1
Sri Lanka	–	2	5
West Indies	6	2	4
Zimbabwe	–	–	3
Totals	*28*	*28*	*29*

Notes

1. Four teams were involved in the World Series in 1994–95, with Australia beating Australia A in the finals and England and Zimbabwe failing to qualify.
2. Australia missed the finals in 1979–80 (the first year of the tournament), 1996–97 (first year of the Carlton & United sponsorship) and 2001–02 (first year of the VB sponsorship).

GAME ONE
AUSTRALIA V ENGLAND
Melbourne Cricket Ground
12 January 2007 (50-over match)

Result Australia won by eight wickets • Toss: England
Umpires: IL Howell (SA) and SJ Taufel • TV umpire: RL Parry
Match referee: RS Madugalle (SL) • Player of the match: AC Gilchrist (Aus)

England innings		R	M	B	4	6
AJ Strauss	c Hayden b Bracken	12	22	20	1	0
MP Vaughan	c Hayden b Bracken	26	40	32	4	0
IR Bell	c Hussey b Johnson	15	54	29	2	0
KP Pietersen	c Symonds b Clark	82	143	91	4	3
PD Collingwood	c Johnson b McGrath	43	76	70	2	0
A Flintoff	not out	47	62	38	5	0
PA Nixon	lbw Johnson	0	5	4	0	0
JWM Dalrymple	c Gilchrist b McGrath	2	8	8	0	0
J Lewis	c Ponting b Bracken	9	13	9	0	0
MS Panesar	not out	0	3	0	0	0
Extras	(b 1, lb 1, w 3, nb 1)	6				
Total	(8 wkts; 50 ov)	242				

DID NOT BAT: JM Anderson

FALL OF WICKETS: 1–20 (Strauss, 5.3 ov), 2–47 (Vaughan, 9.4 ov), 3–73 (Bell, 17.3 ov), 4–168 (Collingwood, 37.2 ov), 5–206 (Pietersen, 43.4 ov), 6–207 (Nixon, 44.5 ov), 7–211 (Dalrymple, 46.3 ov), 8–232 (Lewis, 49.2 ov)

BOWLING: McGrath 10–0–40–2; Bracken 9–0–46–3; Clark 10–0–58–1; Johnson 10–2–34–2; Clarke 8–0–35–0; White 3–0–27–0

Australia innings		R	M	B	4	6
AC Gilchrist	c Nixon b Dalrymple	60	69	61	7	1
ML Hayden	c Nixon b Panesar	28	82	42	4	0
RT Ponting	not out	82	120	96	8	0
MJ Clarke	not out	57	107	74	4	0
Extras	(b 1, lb 2, w 15, nb 1)	19				
Total	(2 wkts; 45.2 ov)	246				

DID NOT BAT: MEK Hussey, A Symonds, CL White, NW Bracken, SR Clark, MG Johnson, GD McGrath

FALL OF WICKETS: 1–101 (Gilchrist, 15.3 ov), 2–113 (Hayden, 18.1 ov)

BOWLING: Flintoff 6–0–48–0; Lewis 8.2–1–43–0; Anderson 7–0–47–0; Panesar 10–1–46–1; Dalrymple 10–1–38–1; Collingwood 4–0–21–0

GAME TWO
AUSTRALIA V NEW ZEALAND
Bellerive Oval, Hobart
14 January 2007 (50-over match)

Result: Australia won by 105 runs • Toss: Australia
Umpires: Asad Rauf (Pak) and DJ Harper • TV umpire: SJ Davis
Match referee: RS Madugalle (SL) • Player of the match: A Symonds (Aus)

Australia innings		R	M	B	4	6
AC Gilchrist	lbw Patel	61	78	58	8	2
ML Hayden	c McCullum b Gillespie	27	58	39	2	0
RT Ponting	c Fleming b Gillespie	10	41	22	2	0
MJ Clarke	c Astle b Bond	33	58	52	3	0
A Symonds	c McCullum b Bond	69	109	70	6	0
MEK Hussey	c sub (HJH Marshall) b McMillan	20	33	32	1	0
CL White	c McMillan b Bond	45	36	32	2	3
MG Johnson	not out	2	5	1	0	0
NW Bracken	b Bond	0	1	1	0	0
SR Clark	not out	1	1	1	0	0
Extras	(lb 7, w 6, nb 8)	21				
Total	(8 wkts; 50 ov)	289				

DID NOT BAT: BW Hilfenhaus

FALL OF WICKETS: 1–83 (Hayden, 13.2 ov), 2–104 (Gilchrist, 16.5 ov), 3–117 (Ponting, 21.5 ov), 4–164 (Clarke, 31.4 ov), 5–196 (Hussey, 40.2 ov), 6–286 (White, 49.2 ov), 7–286 (Symonds, 49.3 ov), 8–286 (Bracken, 49.4 ov)

BOWLING: Franklin 4–0–31–0; Bond 1–0–61–4; Gillespie 10–2–50–2; Patel 10–0–64–1; Vettori 10–1–48–0; Astle 4–0–18–0; McMillan 2–0–10–1

New Zealand innings		R	M	B	4	6
BB McCullum	lbw Hilfenhaus	5	15	16	1	0
NJ Astle	c Gilchrist b Bracken	0	8	3	0	0
SP Fleming	c Hussey b Johnson	29	73	47	1	1
RL Taylor	c Gilchrist b Johnson	84	114	82	10	3
PG Fulton	c Symonds b Clark	37	59	44	1	1
CD McMillan	run out	2	6	7	0	0
DL Vettori	c Hayden b Clark	1	14	5	0	0
JEC Franklin	c Clarke b White	6	18	13	0	0
SE Bond	b Symonds	2	5	5	0	0
MR Gillespie	not out	4	7	4	0	0
JS Patel	c Hilfenhaus b Symonds	4	4	5	1	0
Extras	(lb 3, w 7)	10				
Total	(all out; 38.3 ov)	184				

FALL OF WICKETS: 1–5 (Astle, 2.2 ov), 2–7 (McCullum, 3.6 ov), 3–80 (Fleming, 19.3 ov), 4–161 (Taylor, 31.1 ov), 5–165 (McMillan, 32.4 ov), 6–166 (Fulton, 33.2 ov), 7–171 (Vettori, 35.3 ov), 8–175 (Bond, 36.5 ov), 9–175 (Franklin, 37.1 ov), 10–184 (Patel, 38.3 ov)

BOWLING: Bracken 7–0–25–1; Hilfenhaus 7–1–26–1; Johnson 7–0–27–2; Clark 8–0–40–2; Symonds 6.3–0–41–2; White 3–0–22–1

GAME FOUR
AUSTRALIA V ENGLAND
The Gabba, Brisbane
19 January 2007 (50-over match)

Result: Australia won by four wickets • Toss: England
Umpires: DJ Harper and IL Howell (SA) • TV umpire: RL Parry
Match referee: RS Madugalle (SL) • Player of the match: MEK Hussey (Aus)

England innings		R	M	B	4	6
AJ Strauss	c Hodge b McGrath	18	56	37	0	1
MB Loye	c Hayden b Bracken	36	49	36	5	1
IR Bell	run out	10	32	15	1	0
EC Joyce	c Gilchrist b McGrath	5	19	15	1	0
PD Collingwood	c Gilchrist b McGrath	0	3	1	0	0
A Flintoff	c Hodge b Lee	27	65	38	3	0
PA Nixon	c Hayden b Lee	9	29	23	1	0
JWM Dalrymple	c Johnson b White	31	70	51	2	0
CT Tremlett	c Gilchrist b Bracken	8	20	19	1	0
J Lewis	c & b Bracken	1	6	4	0	0
JM Anderson	not out	4	11	13	0	0
Extras	(lb 3, w 3)	6				
Total	(all out; 42 ov)	155				

FALL OF WICKETS: 1–52 (Loye, 11.1 ov), 2–56 (Strauss, 12.4 ov), 3–70 (Joyce, 16.6 ov), 4–70 (Bell, 17.1 ov), 5–71 (Collingwood, 18.1 ov), 6–93 (Nixon, 24.6 ov), 7–118 (Flintoff, 30.6 ov), 8–141 (Tremlett, 36.5 ov), 9–145 (Lewis, 38.5 ov), 10–155 (Dalrymple, 41.6 ov)

BOWLING: Lee 10–0–53–2; Bracken 9–0–24–3; McGrath 8–1–24–3; Johnson 8–1–32–0; Symonds 5–1–14–0; White 2–1–5–1

Australia innings		R	M	B	4	6
AC Gilchrist	c Anderson b Lewis	8	24	16	1	0
ML Hayden	c Anderson b Lewis	19	45	37	2	0
BJ Hodge	c Dalrymple b Anderson	0	5	3	0	0
MJ Clarke	c Nixon b Lewis	36	91	62	3	0
A Symonds	c Nixon b Lewis	4	11	6	1	0
MEK Hussey	not out	46	135	73	5	1
CL White	lbw Anderson	5	19	9	1	0
B Lee	not out	20	47	30	2	0
Extras	(lb 5, w 9, nb 4)	18				
Total	(6 wkts; 38.4 ov)	156				

DID NOT BAT: GD McGrath, MG Johnson, NW Bracken

FALL OF WICKETS: 1–26 (Gilchrist, 6.2 ov), 2–30 (Hodge, 7.3 ov), 3–35 (Hayden, 10.5 ov), 4–48 (Symonds, 12.5 ov), 5–93 (Clarke, 26.2 ov), 6–108 (White, 29.4 ov)

BOWLING: Lewis 10–2–36–4; Anderson 10–3–29–2; Flintoff 9.4–0–45–0; Tremlett 9–0–41–0

GAME FIVE
AUSTRALIA V NEW ZEALAND
Sydney Cricket Ground
21 January 2007 (50-over match)

Result: Australia won by two wickets • Toss: New Zealand
Umpires: Asad Rauf (Pak) and SJA Taufel • TV umpire: RL Parry
Match referee: RS Madugalle (SL) • Player of the match: MJ Clarke (Aus)

New Zealand innings		R	M	B	4	6
SP Fleming	c Hussey b Clark	12	63	43	1	0
NJ Astle	c Gilchrist b Lee	0	13	4	0	0
HJH Marshall	c Gilchrist b Lee	0	7	3	0	0
RL Taylor	c Hussey b Clark	26	59	43	5	0
PG Fulton	c Hayden b Clark	19	59	39	1	0
CD McMillan	c & b McGrath	89	133	87	7	3
BB McCullum	lbw McGrath	15	32	24	0	1
DL Vettori	c Ponting b Clark	6	11	10	0	0
JEC Franklin	c Hayden b McGrath	18	34	18	1	0
MR Gillespie	not out	6	20	12	1	0
MJ Mason	b Bracken	4	10	7	0	0
Extras	(b 2, lb 12, w 5, nb 4)	23				
Total	(all out; 47.4 ov)	218				

FALL OF WICKETS: 1–5 (Astle, 2.4 ov), 2–7 (Marshall, 4.2 ov), 3–38 (Fleming, 13.1 ov), 4–53 (Taylor, 17.1 ov), 5–84 (Fulton, 26.4 ov), 6–126 (McCullum, 34.1 ov), 7–136 (Vettori, 36.5 ov), 8–193 (Franklin, 43.2 ov), 9–205 (McMillan, 45.2 ov), 10–218 (Mason, 47.4 ov)

BOWLING: Lee 10–1–43–2; Bracken 8.4–2–33–1; McGrath 10–1–24–3; Clark 10–1–54–4; Symonds 8–0–44–0; White 1–0–6–0

Australia innings		R	M	B	4	6
AC Gilchrist	c McCullum b Franklin	3	7	3	0	0
ML Hayden	c Taylor b Mason	0	13	10	0	0
MJ Clarke	c Taylor b Vettori	75	165	111	9	0
RT Ponting	lbw Mason	5	16	15	1	0
A Symonds	b Vettori	38	54	40	7	0
MEK Hussey	not out	65	147	73	6	1
CL White	c Fulton b Gillespie	5	14	15	0	0
B Lee	c Marshall b Gillespie	2	21	12	0	0
NW Bracken	c Taylor b McMillan	14	14	16	1	0
SR Clark	not out	1	5	3	0	0
Extras	(lb 6, w 4, nb 6)	16				
Total	(8 wkts; 48.4 ov)	224				

DID NOT BAT: GD McGrath

FALL OF WICKETS: 1–6 (Gilchrist, 1.2 ov), 2–6 (Hayden, 2.4 ov), 3–17 (Ponting, 6.5 ov), 4–77 (Symonds, 19.4 ov), 5–167 (Clarke, 37.1 ov), 6–175 (White, 40.3 ov), 7–198 (Lee, 44.3 ov), 8–217 (Bracken, 47.5 ov)

BOWLING: Mason 10–2–46–2; Franklin 10–1–47–1; Gillespie 10–2–34–2; Vettori 10–0–41–2; Astle 2.4–0–22–0; McMillan 6–0–28–1

GAME SEVEN
AUSTRALIA V ENGLAND
Adelaide Oval
26 January 2007 (50-over match)

Result: Australia won by nine wickets • Toss: England
Umpires: SJ Davis and IL Howell (SA) • TV umpire: DJ Harper
Match referee: RS Madugalle (SL) • Player of the match: MG Johnson (Aus)

England innings		R	M	B	4	6
AJ Strauss	c Gilchrist b Johnson	17	49	32	2	0
MB Loye	c Gilchrist b Lee	9	21	17	0	1
IR Bell	c Clarke b Clark	35	44	31	2	1
EC Joyce	c Johnson b Lee	11	31	25	2	0
PD Collingwood	c Clark b Symonds	3	20	17	0	0
A Flintoff	c Ponting b Johnson	16	33	28	1	0
JWM Dalrymple	c Gilchrist b Johnson	10	32	24	0	0
PA Nixon	c & b Hogg	4	29	19	0	0
LE Plunkett	c Clarke b Johnson	0	3	4	0	0
CT Tremlett	c White b Hogg	0	3	3	0	0
MS Panesar	not out	0	16	7	0	0
Extras	(w 5)	5				
Total	(all out; 34.3 ov)	110				

FALL OF WICKETS: 1–14 (Loye, 4.4 ov), 2–47 (Strauss, 11.1 ov), 3–72 (Bell, 15.4 ov), 4–79 (Joyce, 19.2 ov), 5–81 (Collingwood, 20.5 ov), 6–103 (Flintoff, 27.6 ov), 7–106 (Dalrymple, 29.2 ov), 8–106 (Plunkett, 29.6 ov), 9–107 (Tremlett, 30.5 ov), 10–110 (Nixon, 34.3 ov)

BOWLING: Lee 8–2–8–2; Johnson 10–2–45–4; Clark 5–0–21–1; Symonds 5–0–20–1; Hogg 6.3–0–16–2

Australia innings		R	M	B	4	6
AC Gilchrist	run out	23	29	19	4	0
ML Hayden	not out	30	101	68	2	0
RT Ponting	not out	51	71	61	6	0
Extras	(lb 2, w 4, nb 1)	7				
Total	(1 wkt; 24.3 ov)	111				

DID NOT BAT: MEK Hussey, A Symonds, MJ Clarke, CL White, GB Hogg, B Lee, SR Clark, MG Johnson

FALL OF WICKET: 1–32 (Gilchrist, 6.3 ov)

BOWLING: Plunkett 5–0–39–0; Tremlett 9.3–0–41–0; Flintoff 3–1–4–0; Panesar 5–0–19–0; Dalrymple 2–0–6–0

AUSTRALIA V NEW ZEALAND
Played at WACA Ground, Perth
28 January 2007 (50-over match)

Result: Australia won by eight runs • Toss: Australia
Umpires: Asad Rauf (Pak) and SJA Taufel • TV umpire: SJ Davis
Match referee: RS Madugalle (SL) • Player of the match: RT Ponting (Aus)

Australia innings		R	M	B	4	6
AC Gilchrist	c Patel b Mills	13	26	20	2	0
ML Hayden	b Vettori	117	171	111	15	0
RT Ponting	c Fulton b McMillan	111	170	122	8	1
MJ Clarke	c sub (HJH Marshall) b Patel	7	16	8	0	0
A Symonds	b Gillespie	24	24	13	0	2
MEK Hussey	not out	29	33	16	0	3
CL White	not out	20	22	12	1	1
Extras	(lb 2, w 18, nb 2)	22				
Total	(5 wkts; 50 ov)	343				

DID NOT BAT: B Lee, MG Johnson, NW Bracken, GD McGrath

FALL OF WICKETS: 1–28 (Gilchrist, 4.6 ov), 2–228 (Hayden, 38.4 ov), 3–254 (Clarke, 41.5 ov), 4–275 (Ponting, 44.1 ov), 5–293 (Symonds, 45.6 ov)

BOWLING: Mills 10–1–72–1; Gillespie 10–1–76–1; Oram 5–0–50–0; Vettori 10–0–34–1; JS Patel 10–0–67–1; McMillan 3–0–26–1; Taylor 2–0–16–0

New Zealand innings		R	M	B	4	6
L Vincent	lbw Clarke	66	105	82	8	1
SP Fleming	c Gilchrist b McGrath	28	39	27	6	0
PG Fulton	c Hayden b Johnson	23	37	26	4	0
RL Taylor	b Clarke	39	61	50	2	0
CD McMillan	run out	5	5	6	1	0
JDP Oram	not out	101	130	72	4	6
BB McCullum	not out	46	101	39	4	1
Extras	(b 2, lb 5, w 18, nb 2)	27				
Total	(5 wkts; 50 ov)	335				

DID NOT BAT: DL Vettori, MR Gillespie, KD Mills, JS Patel

FALL OF WICKETS: 1–47 (Fleming, 9.3 ov), 2–107 (Fulton, 18.3 ov), 3–142 (Vincent, 25.4 ov), 4–150 (McMillan, 27.2 ov), 5–198 (Taylor, 35.2 ov)

BOWLING: Lee 10–0–53–0; Bracken 10–1–75–0; McGrath 10–0–72–1; Johnson 6–0–48–1; Clarke 9–0–48–2; Symonds 5–0–32–0

GAME 10
AUSTRALIA V ENGLAND
Sydney Cricket Ground
2 February 2007 (50-over match)

Result: England won by 92 runs • Toss: England
Umpires: DJ Harper and IL Howell (SA) • TV umpire: RL Parry
Match referee: MJ Procter (SA) • Player of the match: EC Joyce (Eng)

England innings		R	M	B	4	6
EC Joyce	c Bracken b Tait	107	201	142	10	0
MB Loye	c Bracken b McGrath	29	52	33	3	1
IR Bell	c Gilchrist b McGrath	51	96	60	4	0
A Flintoff	lbw White	3	12	10	0	0
AJ Strauss	c Clark b Bracken	26	25	24	3	0
JWM Dalrymple	run out	30	27	18	3	1
PA Nixon	c Hodge b Tait	4	3	2	1	0
RS Bopara	not out	7	14	5	1	0
LE Plunkett	not out	10	8	7	1	0
Extras	(lb 5, w 19, nb 1)	25				
Total	(7 wkts; 50 ov)	292				

DID NOT BAT: SI Mahmood, MS Panesar

FALL OF WICKETS: 1–58 (Loye, 10.6 ov), 2–169 (Bell, 33.1 ov), 3–179 (Flintoff, 36.4 ov), 4–222 (Strauss, 42.3 ov), 5–256 (Joyce, 46.2 ov), 6–261 (Nixon, 46.6 ov), 7–274 (Dalrymple, 47.6 ov)

BOWLING: Tait 10–0–68–2; Bracken 9–1–53–1; SR Clark 10–0–55–0; McGrath 10–0–51–2; Clarke 4–0–18–0; Symonds 2–0–16–0; White 5–1–26–1

Australia innings		R	M	B	4	6
AC Gilchrist	b Plunkett	0	1	1	0	0
ML Hayden	c Dalrymple b Mahmood	51	103	62	7	1
BJ Hodge	b Mahmood	1	8	6	0	0
MJ Clarke	c Nixon b Plunkett	18	47	29	2	0
A Symonds	retired hurt	39	64	35	4	1
MEK Hussey	b Bopara	6	20	14	0	0
CL White	c Nixon b Flintoff	13	25	20	0	0
NW Bracken	b Panesar	21	34	26	3	0
SR Clark	not out	15	10	23	2	0
GD McGrath	lbw Plunkett	1	10	7	0	0
SW Tait	run out	11	6	10	1	1
Extras	(lb 8, w 16)	24				
Total	(all out; 38.5 ov)	200				

FALL OF WICKETS: 1–0 (Gilchrist, 0.1 ov), 2–4 (Hodge, 1.2 ov), 3–45 (Clarke, 12.2 ov), 4–116 (Hayden, 20.4 ov), 5–137 (Hussey, 24.4 ov), 6–160 (White, 30.1 ov), 7–180 (Bracken, 33.6 ov), 8–187 (McGrath, 36.3 ov), 9–200 (Tait, 38.5 ov)

BOWLING: Plunkett 9.5–1–24–3; Mahmood 7–0–38–2; A Flintoff 8–0–47–1; Panesar 10–0–64–1; RS Bopara 4–0–19–1

GAME 11
AUSTRALIA V NEW ZEALAND
Melbourne Cricket Ground

4 February 2007 (50-over match)

Result: Australia won by five wickets • Toss: New Zealand

Umpires: Asad Rauf (Pak) and SJ Davis • TV umpire: RL Parry

Match referee: MJ Procter (SA) • Player of the match: RT Ponting (Aus)

New Zealand innings		R	M	B	4	6
L Vincent	b Tait	90	160	113	6	1
SP Fleming	c Hussey b Lee	9	14	11	1	0
PG Fulton	lbw Clarke	60	134	81	4	0
RL Taylor	b Clarke	21	47	31	1	0
SB Styris	c Hussey b Clark	34	53	36	2	0
JDP Oram	c Hodge b Lee	15	13	9	1	1
BB McCullum	b Clark	19	27	14	1	0
DL Vettori	not out	3	9	4	0	0
JEC Franklin	not out	13	4	5	0	1
Extras	(b 2, lb 11, w 9, nb 4)	26				
Total	(7 wkts; 50 ov)	290				

DID NOT BAT: MR Gillespie, SE Bond

FALL OF WICKETS: 1–12 (Fleming, 2.5 ov), 2–163 (Fulton, 31.3 ov), 3–188 (Vincent, 36.5 ov), 4–212 (Taylor, 41.3 ov), 5–233 (Oram, 44.3 ov), 6–269 (Styris, 47.6 ov), 7–275 (McCullum, 49.1 ov)

BOWLING: Lee 10–0–71–2; Tait 10–1–26–1; Clark 10–1–61–2; MG Johnson 7–0–48–0; Clarke 9–0–45–2; White 4–0–26–0

Australia innings		R	M	B	4	6
AC Gilchrist	b Franklin	29	46	28	4	0
ML Hayden	c Taylor b Franklin	28	63	44	2	0
RT Ponting	c Vincent b Gillespie	104	171	113	6	1
MJ Clarke	c McCullum b Vettori	9	45	20	0	0
BJ Hodge	not out	99	123	86	7	1
MEK Hussey	run out	8	9	5	1	0
CL White	not out	1	5	1	0	0
Extras	(lb 1, w 3, nb 9)	13				
Total	(5 wkts; 48.2 ov)	291				

DID NOT BAT: SW Tait, SR Clark, B Lee, MG Johnson

FALL OF WICKETS: 1–56 (Gilchrist, 10.6 ov), 2–65 (Hayden, 12.6 ov), 3–112 (Clarke, 22.4 ov), 4–266 (Ponting, 46.1 ov), 5–279 (Hussey, 47.4 ov)

BOWLING: Franklin 10–0–56–2; Bond 9–0–64–0; Gillespie 8.2–0–45–1; Oram 5–0–44–0; Vettori 10–0–55–1; Styris 6–0–26–0

FIRST FINAL
AUSTRALIA V ENGLAND
Melbourne Cricket Ground
9 February 2007 (50-over match)

Result: England won by four wickets • Toss: Australia
Umpires: Asad Rauf (Pak) and DJ Harper • TV umpire: RL Parry
Match referee: MJ Procter (SA)

Australia innings		R	M	B	4	6
AC Gilchrist	c Flintoff b Mahmood	5	28	10	0	0
ML Hayden	c Mahmood b Dalrymple	82	152	102	7	0
RT Ponting	c Collingwood b Panesar	75	109	75	7	0
MJ Clarke	run out	33	51	39	0	1
BJ Hodge	lbw Panesar	5	12	10	0	0
MEK Hussey	c Nixon b Flintoff	17	29	19	1	0
SR Watson	c Bell b Mahmood	9	31	13	0	0
GB Hogg	c Bell b Flintoff	10	16	11	1	0
B Lee	run out	0	5	5	0	0
NW Bracken	not out	3	9	5	0	0
GD McGrath	b Flintoff	0	4	2	0	0
Extras	(lb 4, w 9)	13				
Total	(all out; 48.3 ov)	252				

FALL OF WICKETS: 1–32 (Gilchrist, 5.3 ov), 2–170 (Ponting, 30.1 ov), 3–180 (Hayden, 33.2 ov), 4–196 (Hodge, 36.5 ov), 5–229 (Clarke, 42.2 ov), 6–229 (Hussey, 42.3 ov), 7–248 (Hogg, 46.1 ov), 8–248 (Lee, 46.6 ov), 9–250 (Watson, 47.4 ov), 10–252 (McGrath, 48.3 ov)

BOWLING: Plunkett 10–0–56–0; Mahmood 8–0–45–2; Flintoff 9.3–1–41–3; Panesar 10–0–44–2; Collingwood 4–0–21–0; Dalrymple 7–0–41–1

England innings		R	M	B	4	6
EC Joyce	c McGrath b Lee	6	21	18	1	0
MB Loye	lbw Lee	0	9	6	0	0
IR Bell	b Lee	65	147	90	3	0
AJ Strauss	lbw Bracken	0	3	2	0	0
PD Collingwood	not out	120	222	133	7	1
A Flintoff	c Gilchrist b Watson	35	65	36	0	1
JWM Dalrymple	run out	3	6	5	0	0
PA Nixon	not out	11	19	10	0	0
Extras	(lb 3, w 7, nb 3)	13				
Total	(6 wkts; 49.3 ov)	253				

DID NOT BAT: LE Plunkett, SI Mahmood, MS Panesar

FALL OF WICKETS: 1–1 (Loye, 2.2 ov), 2–14 (Joyce, 4.6 ov), 3–15 (Strauss, 5.4 ov), 4–148 (Bell, 32.6 ov), 5–222 (Flintoff, 45.2 ov), 6–225 (Dalrymple, 46.1 ov)

BOWLING: Lee 10–0–41–3; Bracken 8.3–1–38–1; McGrath 10–0–53–0; Watson 8–0–51–1; GB Hogg 10–0–52–0; Clarke 3–0–15–0

SECOND FINAL
AUSTRALIA V ENGLAND
Sydney Cricket Ground
11 February 2007 (50-over match)

Result: England won by 34 runs (D/L method) • Toss: England
Umpires: SJ Davis and IL Howell (SA) • TV umpire: DJ Harper
Match referee: MJ Procter (SA)

Player of the finals: PD Collingwood (Eng)
Player of the series: RT Ponting (Aus)

England innings		R	M	B	4	6
EC Joyce	c Hodge b McGrath	15	37	27	3	0
MB Loye	run out	45	85	61	8	1
IR Bell	run out	26	84	45	1	0
AJ Strauss	c Gilchrist b Bracken	6	6	5	0	0
PD Collingwood	c Gilchrist b Bracken	70	119	90	2	0
A Flintoff	c & b Lee	42	71	50	3	0
JWM Dalrymple	run out	5	21	10	0	0
PA Nixon	c Hodge b McGrath	6	13	7	0	0
LE Plunkett	not out	8	9	10	0	0
Extras	(b 5, lb 4, w 9, nb 5)	23				
Total	(8 wkts; 50 ov)	246				

DID NOT BAT: SI Mahmood, MS Panesar

FALL OF WICKETS: 1–34 (Joyce, 8.1 ov), 2–79 (Loye, 18.3 ov), 3–86 (Strauss, 19.3 ov), 4–112 (Bell, 25.4 ov), 5–209 (Flintoff, 42.6 ov), 6–231 (Collingwood, 46.6 ov), 7–233 (Dalrymple, 47.3 ov), 8–246 (Nixon, 49.6 ov)

BOWLING: Lee 10–0–53–1; Bracken 10–1–38–2; McGrath 10–0–41–2; Watson 8–0–46–0; Hussey 2–0–12–0; Hogg 10–0–47–0

Australia innings		R	M	B	4	6
AC Gilchrist	b Plunkett	20	36	17	2	0
ML Hayden	c Collingwood b Mahmood	5	16	9	0	0
RT Ponting	c Strauss b Plunkett	7	6	6	1	0
MJ Clarke	c Nixon b Plunkett	0	17	9	0	0
BJ Hodge	c Bell b Dalrymple	49	85	46	5	1
MEK Hussey	c Strauss b Flintoff	0	18	10	0	0
SR Watson	c Dalrymple b Collingwood	37	37	44	4	1
GB Hogg	c Flintoff b Collingwood	10	17	14	1	0
B Lee	not out	10	15	7	2	0
NW Bracken	not out	3	5	3	0	0
Extras	(lb 2, w 6, nb 3)	11				
Total	(8 wkts; 27 ov)	152				

DID NOT BAT: GD McGrath

FALL OF WICKETS: 1–25 (Hayden, 3.1 ov), 2–33 (Ponting, 4.2 ov), 3–39 (Gilchrist, 6.1 ov), 4–40 (Clarke, 6.6 ov), 5–63 (Hussey, 11.2 ov), 6–109 (Watson, 20.6 ov), 7–132 (Hogg, 24.4 ov), 8–139 (Hodge, 25.3 ov)

BOWLING: LE Plunkett 6–0–43–3; Mahmood 6–0–31–1; Flintoff 5–1–10–1; MS Panesar 2–0–15–0; Dalrymple 4–0–25–1; Collingwood 4–0–26–2

COMMONWEALTH BANK SERIES — AUSTRALIAN AVERAGES

BATTING AND FIELDING

Batsman	ODI	Inn	NO	Runs	HS	Ave	100	50	Ct	St
RT Ponting	8	8	2	445	111	74.17	2	3	3	–
A Symonds	7	5	1	174	69	43.50	–	1	2	–
ML Hayden	10	10	1	387	117	43.00	1	2	8	–
BJ Hodge	5	5	1	154	99*	38.50	–	1	6	–
MEK Hussey	10	8	3	191	65*	38.20	–	1	6	–
MJ Clarke	10	9	1	268	75	33.50	–	2	3	–
SR Watson	2	2	0	46	37	23.00	–	–	–	–
CL White	8	6	2	89	45	22.25	–	–	1	–
AC Gilchrist	10	10	0	222	61	22.20	–	2	16	–
B Lee	7	4	2	32	20*	16.00	–	–	1	–
NW Bracken	8	5	2	41	21	13.67	–	–	3	–
SW Tait	2	1	0	11	11	11.00	–	–	–	–
GB Hogg	3	2	0	20	10	10.00	–	–	1	–
GD McGrath	7	2	0	1	1	0.50	–	–	2	–
SR Clark	6	3	3	17	15*	–	–	–	2	–
MG Johnson	6	1	1	2	2*	–	–	–	3	–
BW Hilfenhaus	1	0	–	–	–	–	–	–	1	–

BOWLING

Bowler	O	M	R	W	Ave	Best	4w
GD McGrath	68	2	305	13	23.46	3–24	–
BW Hilfenhaus	7	1	26	1	26.00	1–26	–
MG Johnson	48	5	234	9	26.00	4–45	1
B Lee	68	3	322	12	26.83	3–41	–
NW Bracken	71.1	6	332	12	27.67	3–24	–
SR Clark	53	2	289	10	28.90	4–54	1
SW Tait	20	1	94	3	31.33	2–68	–
CL White	18	2	112	3	37.33	1–5	–
MJ Clarke	33	0	161	4	40.25	2–45	–
A Symonds	31.3	1	167	3	55.67	2–41	–
GB Hogg	26.3	0	115	2	57.50	2–16	–
SR Watson	16	0	97	1	97.00	1–51	–
MEK Hussey	2	0	12	0	–	–	–

AUSTRALIAN CENTURIES

Ricky Ponting's 111 in game eight and 104 in game 11 were his 21st and 22nd centuries in one-day international cricket, in his 266th and 267th ODIs. Ponting became the fourth Australian, after Dean Jones, Geoff Marsh and Mark Waugh, to score centuries in consecutive ODIs.

Matthew Hayden's 117 in game eight was his sixth century in one-day international cricket, in his 127th ODI.

NOTABLE AUSTRALIAN LANDMARKS

Glenn McGrath took his 350th wicket in one-day international cricket during game five.

Andrew Symonds scored his 4000th run in one-day international cricket during game 10.

CHAPPELL–HADLEE TROPHY

GAME ONE
Westpac Stadium, Wellington
16 February 2007 (50-over match)

Result: New Zealand won by 10 wickets • Toss: New Zealand
Umpires: Aleem Dar (Pak) and BF Bowden • TV umpire: GA Baxter
Match referee: MJ Procter (SA) • Player of the match: SE Bond (NZ)

Australia innings		R	M	B	4	6
ML Hayden	c Fleming b Gillespie	14	77	39	2	0
PA Jaques	c Vettori b Bond	1	7	8	0	0
BJ Haddin	b Bond	6	8	5	1	0
MEK Hussey	c Taylor b McMillan	42	135	96	4	0
BJ Hodge	c Fleming b Vettori	22	62	49	2	0
CL White	c & b Bond	13	29	18	0	0
SR Watson	c Bond b Vettori	8	32	32	0	0
GB Hogg	b Bond	20	46	23	2	0
MG Johnson	c Oram b Gillespie	8	16	18	1	0
NW Bracken	b Bond	0	3	4	0	0
GD McGrath	not out	5	10	6	0	0
Extras	(b 1, lb 2, w 5, nb 1)	9				
Total	(all out; 49.3 ov)	148				

FALL OF WICKETS: 1–3 (Jaques, 1.4 ov), 2–16 (Haddin, 3.1 ov), 3–45 (Hayden, 17.2 ov), 4–86 (Hodge, 31.3 ov), 5–98 (Hussey, 34.3 ov), 6–108 (White, 39.1 ov), 7–120 (Watson, 42.6 ov), 8–133 (Johnson, 46.6 ov), 9–133 (Bracken, 47.4 ov), 10–148 (Hogg, 49.3 ov)

BOWLING: Tuffey 8–0–29–0; Bond 9.3–2–23–5; Oram 10–0–22–0; Gillespie 9–0–27–2; Vettori 9–1–26–2; Styris 2–0–15–0; McMillan 2–0–3–1

New Zealand innings		R	M	B	4	6
L Vincent	not out	73	117	87	8	2
SP Fleming	not out	70	117	76	8	2
Extras	(lb 3, w 2, nb 1)	6				
Total	(0 wkts; 27 ov)	149				

DID NOT BAT: RL Taylor, SB Styris, JDP Oram, CD McMillan, BB McCullum, DL Vettori, SE Bond, MR Gillespie, DR Tuffey

BOWLING: GD McGrath 6–1–23–0; Bracken 7–1–30–0; Johnson 8–0–49–0; Watson 4–0–28–0; Hogg 2–0–16–0

GAME TWO
Eden Park, Auckland
18 February 2007 (50-over match)

Result: New Zealand won by five wickets • Toss: New Zealand
Umpires: Aleem Dar (Pak) and AL Hill • TV umpire: BF Bowden
Match referee: MJ Procter (SA) • Player of the match: RL Taylor (NZ)

Australia innings		R	M	B	4	6
ML Hayden	c Vettori b Gillespie	24	58	36	5	0
PA Jaques	c Fleming b Bond	3	27	16	0	0
BJ Haddin	c & b Vettori	49	76	61	5	2
MEK Hussey	c Taylor b McMillan	105	123	84	8	6
BJ Hodge	not out	97	100	86	10	2
CL White	not out	42	32	19	3	3
Extras	(b 1, lb 5, w 8, nb 2)	16				
Total	(4 wkts; 50 ov)	336				

DID NOT BAT: SR Watson, GB Hogg, NW Bracken, GD McGrath, SW Tait

FALL OF WICKETS: 1–26 (Jaques, 5.5 ov), 2–52 (Hayden, 12.2 ov), 3–122 (Haddin, 25.4 ov), 4–252 (Hussey, 42.3 ov)

BOWLING: Tuffey 10–0–80–0; Bond 9–4–39–1; Gillespie 10–2–57–1; Vettori 10–0–54–1; Styris 4–0–34–0; McMillan 5–0–44–1; Vincent 2–0–22–0

New Zealand innings		R	M	B	4	6
L Vincent	c Jaques b Bracken	26	37	27	2	1
SP Fleming	c Haddin b Bracken	6	9	7	1	0
RL Taylor	c Hussey b Watson	117	157	127	16	1
SB Styris	c Hussey b Watson	17	49	25	2	0
PG Fulton	not out	76	136	65	5	2
CD McMillan	c Hussey b Watson	52	40	30	7	2
BB McCullum	not out	22	15	12	1	1
Extras	(b 1, lb 11, w 10, nb 2)	24				
Total	(5 wkts; 48.4 ov)	340				

DID NOT BAT: DL Vettori, MR Gillespie, SE Bond, DR Tuffey

FALL OF WICKETS: 1–9 (Fleming, 2.1 ov), 2–47 (Vincent, 8.5 ov), 3–113 (Styris, 19.4 ov), 4–228 (Taylor, 38.1 ov), 5–313 (McMillan, 45.5 ov)

BOWLING: NW Bracken 10–1–66–2; McGrath 9.4–0–53–0; Tait 9–0–64–0; Watson 10–0–58–3; Hogg 7–0–58–0; White 3–0–29–0

GAME THREE
Seddon Park, Hamilton
20 February 2007 (50-over match)

Result: New Zealand won by one wicket • Toss: Australia
Umpires: Aleem Dar (Pak) and GA Baxter • TV umpire: AL Hill
Match referee: MJ Procter (SA) • Player of the match: ML Hayden (Aus)

Australia innings		R	M	B	4	6
ML Hayden	not out	181	227	166	11	10
SR Watson	lbw Patel	68	104	69	8	0
BJ Haddin	c Vincent b Tuffey	38	65	31	4	1
BJ Hodge	b Patel	12	17	10	0	1
MEK Hussey	c McCullum b Gillespie	13	13	8	0	1
CL White	c Styris b Gillespie	13	8	8	0	2
AC Voges	not out	16	15	10	0	1
Extras	(b 1, lb 1, w 1, nb 2)	5				
Total	(5 wkts; 50 ov)	346				

DID NOT BAT: GB Hogg, NW Bracken, SW Tait, MG Johnson

FALL OF WICKETS: 1–122 (Watson, 25.4 ov), 2–210 (Haddin, 38.4 ov), 3–251 (Hodge, 41.5 ov), 4–279 (Hussey, 44.3 ov), 5–302 (White, 46.4 ov)

BOWLING: Tuffey 10–0–68–1; Franklin 10–0–43–0; Gillespie 10–0–83–2; Patel 10–0–70–2; Styris 8–0–52–0; McMillan 2–0–28–0

New Zealand innings		R	M	B	4	6
L Vincent	c Hogg b Tait	11	25	13	2	0
SP Fleming	c Hodge b Tait	9	15	11	2	0
RL Taylor	c & b Bracken	11	15	12	1	0
SB Styris	c Haddin b Johnson	0	18	7	0	0
PG Fulton	c Hussey b Watson	51	48	40	6	3
CD McMillan	b Watson	117	138	96	13	5
BB McCullum	not out	86	149	91	5	2
JEC Franklin	c Voges b Johnson	2	6	5	0	0
DR Tuffey	c Haddin b Johnson	8	11	8	1	0
MR Gillespie	run out	28	20	15	3	0
JS Patel	not out	0	4	0	0	0
Extras	(lb 4, w 22, nb 1)	27				
Total	(9 wkts; 49.3 ov)	350				

FALL OF WICKETS: 1–23 (Fleming, 3.2 ov), 2–34 (Vincent, 5.3 ov), 3–38 (Taylor, 6.3 ov), 4–41 (Styris, 9.1 ov), 5–116 (Fulton, 16.5 ov), 6–281 (McMillan, 41.2 ov), 7–285 (Franklin, 42.2 ov), 8–303 (Tuffey, 44.5 ov), 9–339 (Gillespie, 48.5 ov)

BOWLING: Bracken 9.3–0–44–1; Tait 10–0–60–2; Johnson 10–0–81–3; Watson 10–0–88–2; Hogg 7–0–40–0; Voges 3–0–33–0

CHAPPELL-HADLEE TROPHY — AUSTRALIAN AVERAGES

BATTING AND FIELDING

Batsman	ODI	Inn	NO	Runs	HS	Ave	100	50	Ct	St
ML Hayden	3	3	1	219	181*	109.50	1	–	–	–
BJ Hodge	3	3	1	131	97*	65.50	–	1	1	–
MEK Hussey	3	3	0	160	105	53.33	1	–	4	–
SR Watson	3	2	0	76	68	38.00	–	1	–	–
CL White	3	3	1	68	42*	34.00	–	–	–	–
BJ Haddin	3	3	0	93	49	31.00	–	–	3	–
GB Hogg	3	1	0	20	20	20.00	–	–	1	–
MG Johnson	2	1	0	8	8	8.00	–	–	–	–
PA Jaques	2	2	0	4	3	2.00	–	–	1	–
NW Bracken	3	1	0	0	0	0.00	–	–	1	–
AC Voges	1	1	1	16	16*	–	–	–	1	–
GD McGrath	2	1	1	5	5*	–	–	–	–	–
SW Tait	2	0	–	–	–	–	–	–	–	–

BOWLING

Bowler	O	M	R	W	Ave	Best	4w
SR Watson	24	0	174	5	34.80	3–58	–
MG Johnson	18	0	130	3	43.33	3–81	–
NW Bracken	26.3	2	140	3	46.67	2–66	–
SW Tait	19	0	124	2	62.00	2–60	–
CL White	3	0	29	0	–	–	–
AC Voges	3	0	33	0	–	–	–
GD McGrath	15.4	1	76	0	–	–	–
GB Hogg	16	0	114	0	–	–	–

AUSTRALIAN CENTURIES

Mike Hussey's 105 in game two was his second century in one-day international cricket, in his 60th ODI.

Matthew Hayden's 181 not out in game three was his seventh century in one-day international cricket, in his 134th ODI.

NOTABLE AUSTRALIAN LANDMARKS

Matthew Hayden's 181 not out at Hamilton is the highest score made by an Australian in ODI cricket, beating Mark Waugh's 173 made against the West Indies at the MCG in 2000-01. It is also the highest score made by a batsman on the losing team in a ODI.

New Zealand's 3–0 series win meant that Australia had lost five consecutive ODIs, following their 2–0 loss to England in the Commonwealth Bank Series finals. This sequence of five straight defeats equalled Australia's longest losing run in one-day internationals, previously suffered in 1983, 1987, 1996, 1996–97 and 1997–98.

ICC WORLD CUP 2007
In the West Indies, March 14–April 28, 2007

1. GROUP MATCHES

The 16 competing teams were divided into four groups of four, with the top two teams in each group to progress to the second stage of the competition, the 'Super Eights'.

GROUP A: BASSETERRE, ST KITTS & NEVIS

March 14: Australia v Scotland

Australia 6–334 (50 overs: RT Ponting 113, ML Hayden 60, AC Gilchrist 46, GB Hogg 40*) defeated Scotland 131 (40.1 overs: CJO Smith 51; GD McGrath 3–14) by 203 runs

March 16: South Africa v Netherlands

South Africa 3–353 (40 overs: JH Kallis 128*, MV Boucher 75*, HH Gibbs 72, GC Smith 67) defeated Netherlands 9–132 (40 overs: RN ten Doeschate 57) by 221 runs

March 18: Australia v Netherlands

Australia 5–358 (50 overs: BJ Hodge 123, MJ Clarke 93*, AC Gilchrist 57) defeated Netherlands 129 (26.5 overs: GB Hogg 4–27) by 229 runs

March 20: South Africa v Scotland

Scotland 8–186 (50 overs: DR Brown 45*; AJ Hall 3–48) lost to South Africa 3–188 (23.2 overs: GC Smith 91, AB de Villiers 62) by seven wickets

March 22: Netherlands v Scotland

Scotland 136 (34.1 overs: WF Stelling 3–12) lost to Netherlands 2–140 (23.5 overs: RN ten Doeschate 70*, B Zuiderent 43*) by eight wickets

March 24: Australia v South Africa

Australia 6–377 (50 overs: ML Hayden 101, RT Ponting 91, MJ Clarke 92, AC Gilchrist 42) defeated South Africa 294 (48 overs: AB de Villiers 92, GC Smith 74, JH Kallis 48; GB Hogg 3–61) by 83 runs

GROUP A

Team	P	W	L	NR	T	Pts	NRR
Australia	3	3	0	0	0	6	+3.433
South Africa	3	2	1	0	0	4	+2.403
Netherlands	3	1	2	0	0	2	-2.527
Scotland	3	0	3	0	0	0	-3.793

GROUP B: PORT OF SPAIN, TRINIDAD

March 15: Sri Lanka v Bermuda

Sri Lanka 6–321 (50 overs: DPMD Jayawardene 85, KC Sangakkara 76, LPC Silva 55*) defeated Bermuda 78 (24.4 overs: MF Maharoof 4–23, SL Malinga 3–10) by 243 runs

March 17: Bangladesh v India

India 191 (49.3 overs: SC Ganguly 66, Yuvraj Singh 47; Mashrafe Mortaza 4–38, Abdur Razzak 3–38) lost to Bangladesh 5–192 (Saqibul Hasan 53, Mushfiqur Rahim 56*, Tamim Iqbal 51) by five wickets

March 19: India v Bermuda

India 5–413 (50 overs: V Sehwag 114, SC Ganguly 89, Yuvraj Singh 83, SR Tendulkar 57*) defeated Bermuda 156 (43.1 overs: DL Hemp 76*; AB Agarkar 3–38, A Kumble 3–38) by 257 runs

March 21: Sri Lanka v Bangladesh

Sri Lanka 4–318 (50 overs: ST Jayasuriya 109, KC Sangakkara 56, LPC Silva 52*, DPMD Jayawardene 46) defeated Bangladesh 112 (37 overs: Mohammad Ashraful 45*; SL Malinga 3–27) by 198 runs (D/L method)

March 23: Sri Lanka v India

Sri Lanka 6–254 (50 overs: WU Tharanga 64, LPC Silva 59) defeated India 185 (43.3 overs: R Dravid 60, V Sehwag 48; M Muralitharan 3–41) by 69 runs

March 25: Bangladesh v Bermuda

Bermuda 9–94 (21 overs: Abdur Razzak 3–20) lost to Bangladesh 3–96 (17.3 overs: S Mukuddem 3–19) by seven wickets (D/L method)

GROUP B

Team	P	W	L	NR	T	Pts	NRR
Sri Lanka	3	3	0	0	0	6	+3.493
Bangladesh	3	2	1	0	0	4	-1.523
India	3	1	2	0	0	2	+1.206
Bermuda	3	0	3	0	0	0	-4.345

GROUP C: GROS ISLET, ST LUCIA

March 14: Kenya v Canada

Canada 199 (50 overs: GEF Barnett 41) lost to Kenya 3–203 (43.2 overs: SO Tikolo 72*, MA Ouma 58) by seven wickets

March 16: New Zealand v England

England 7–209 (50 overs: KP Pietersen 60, PA Nixon 42*) lost to New Zealand 4–210 (41 overs: SB Styris 87*, JDP Oram 63*) by six wickets

March 18: England v Canada

England 6–279 (50 overs: EC Joyce 66, PD Collingwood 62*, MP Vaughan 45; S Dhaniram 3–41) defeated Canada 7–228 (50 overs: AA Mulla 58) by 51 runs

March 20: New Zealand v Kenya

New Zealand 7–331 (50 overs: RL Taylor 85, CD McMillan 71, SB Styris 63, SP Fleming 60) defeated Kenya 183 (49.2 overs: RD Shah 71, TM Odoyo 42) by 148 runs

March 22: New Zealand v Canada

New Zealand 5–363 (50 overs: L Vincent 101, SP Fleming 66, BB McCullum 52*, PG Fulton 47) defeated Canada 249 (49.2 overs: JM Davison 52, IS Billcliff 52, GEF Barnett 40; JS Patel 3–25, DL Vettori 3–57) by 114 runs

March 24: England v Kenya

Kenya 177 (43 overs: SO Tikolo 76) lost to England 3–178 (33 overs: EC Joyce 75, KP Pietersen 56*) by seven wickets

GROUP C

Team	P	W	L	NR	T	Pts	NRR
New Zealand	3	3	0	0	0	6	+2.138
England	3	2	1	0	0	4	+0.418
Kenya	3	1	2	0	0	2	-1.194
Canada	3	0	3	0	0	0	-1.389

GROUP D: KINGSTON, JAMAICA

March 13: West Indies v Pakistan

West Indies 9–241 (50 overs: MN Samuels 63, RR Sarwan 49; Iftikhar Anjum 3–44) defeated Pakistan 187 (47.2 overs: Shoaib Malik 62; DR Smith 3–36, DJ Bravo 3–42) by 54 runs

March 15: Ireland v Zimbabwe

Ireland 9–221 (50 overs: JP Bray 115*) tied with Zimbabwe 221 (50 overs: S Matsikenyeri 73*, V Sibanda 67)

March 17: Ireland v Pakistan

Pakistan 132 (45.4 overs: WB Rankin 3–32) lost to Ireland 7–133 (41.4 overs: NJ O'Brien 72) by three wickets

March 19: West Indies v Zimbabwe

Zimbabwe 5–202 (50 overs: SC Williams 70*, BRM Taylor 50) lost to West Indies 4–204 (47.5 overs: BC Lara 44*, CH Gayle 40) by six wickets

March 21: Pakistan v Zimbabwe

Pakistan 349 (49.5 overs: Imran Nazir 160; E Chigumbura 3–50, GB Brent 3–68) defeated Zimbabwe 99 (19.1 overs: Shahid Afridi 3–20) by 93 runs (D/L method)

March 23: West Indies v Ireland

Ireland 8–183 (48 overs: JP Bray 41) lost to West Indies 2–190 (38.1 overs: S Chanderpaul 102*) by eight wickets

GROUP D

Team	P	W	L	NR	T	Pts	NRR
West Indies	3	3	0	0	0	6	+0.764
Ireland	3	1	1	1	0	3	-0.092
Pakistan	3	1	2	0	0	2	+0.089
Zimbabwe	3	0	2	1	0	1	-0.886

2. SUPER EIGHTS

March 27: Australia v West Indies at St John's (North Sound), Antigua

Australia 6–322 (50 overs: ML Hayden 158, MJ Clarke 41) defeated West Indies 219 (45.3 overs: BC Lara 77; GD McGrath 3–31, GB Hogg 3–56) by 103 runs

March 28: South Africa v Sri Lanka at Georgetown (Providence), Guyana

Sri Lanka 209 (49.3 overs: TM Dilshan 58, RP Arnold 50; CK Langeveldt 5–39) lost to South Africa 9–212 (48.2 overs: JH Kallis 86, GC Smith 59; SL Malinga 4–54, M Muralitharan 3–34) by one wicket

March 29: New Zealand v West Indies at St John's (North Sound), Antigua

West Indies 177 (44.4 overs: CH Gayle 44; JDP Oram 3–23, SE Bond 3–31, DL Vettori 3–39) lost to New Zealand 3–179 (39.2 overs: SB Styris 80*, SP Fleming 45) by seven wickets

March 30: England v Ireland at Georgetown (Providence), Guyana

England 7–266 (50 overs: PD Collingwood 90, KP Pietersen 48, A Flintoff 43) defeated Ireland 218 (48.1 overs: NJ O'Brien 63, A Flintoff 4–43) by 48 runs

March 31: Australia v Bangladesh at St John's (North Sound), Antigua

Bangladesh 6–104 (22 overs: GD McGrath 3–16) lost to Australia 0–106 (13.5 overs: AC Gilchrist 59*, ML Hayden 47*) by 10 wickets

April 1: Sri Lanka v West Indies at Georgetown (Providence), Guyana

Sri Lanka 5–303 (50 overs: ST Jayasuriya 115, DPMD Jayawardene 82) defeated West Indies 190 (44.3 overs: S Chanderpaul 76, RR Sarwan 44; ST Jayasuriya 3–38) by 113 runs

April 2: New Zealand v Bangladesh at St John's (North Sound), Antigua

Bangladesh 174 (48.3 overs: SB Styris 4–43) lost to New Zealand 1–178 (29.2 overs: SP Fleming 102*, HJH Marshall 50*) by nine wickets

April 3: South Africa v Ireland at Georgetown (Providence), Guyana

Ireland 8–152 (35 overs: CK Langeveldt 3–41) lost to South Africa 3–165 (31.3 overs: JH Kallis 66*, AG Prince 47*, GC Smith 41) by seven wickets (D/L method)

April 4: Sri Lanka v England at St John's (North Sound), Antigua

Sri Lanka 235 (50 overs: WU Tharanga 62, DPMD Jayawardene 56; SI Mahmood 4–50, A Flintoff 3–35) defeated England 8–233 (50 overs: KP Pietersen 58, RS Bopara 52, IR Bell 47; CRD Fernando 3–41) by two runs

April 7: Bangladesh v South Africa at Georgetown (Providence), Guyana

Bangladesh 8–251 (50 overs: Mohammad Ashraful 87; A Nel 5–45) defeated South Africa 184 (48.4 overs: HH Gibbs 56*; Abdur Razzak 3–25) by 67 runs

April 8: Australia v England at St John's (North Sound), Antigua

England 247 (49.5 overs: KP Pietersen 104, IR Bell 77; NW Bracken 3–33, SW Tait 3–41, GD McGrath 3–62) lost to Australia 3–248 (47.2 overs: RT Ponting 86, MJ Clarke 55*, ML Hayden 41) by seven wickets

April 9: New Zealand v Ireland at Georgetown (Providence), Guyana

New Zealand 8–263 (50 overs: PG Fulton 83, BB McCullum 47) defeated Ireland 134 (37.4 overs: KJ O'Brien 49; DL Vettori 4–23) by 129 runs

April 10: South Africa v West Indies at St George's, Grenada

South Africa 4–356 (50 overs: AB de Villiers 146, JH Kallis 81, HH Gibbs 61*, MV Boucher 52) defeated West Indies 9–289 (50 overs: RR Sarwan 92, DB Powell 48*) by 67 runs

April 11: England v Bangladesh at Bridgetown

Bangladesh 143 (37.2 overs: Saqibul Hasan 57*; SI Mahmood 3–27, MS Panesar 3–25) lost to England 6–147 (44.5 overs) by four wickets

April 12: Sri Lanka v New Zealand at St George's, Grenada

New Zealand 7–219 (50 overs: SB Styris 111*; WPUJC Vaas 3–33, M Muralitharan 3–32) lost to Sri Lanka 4–222 (45.1 overs: ST Jayasuriya 64, KC Sangakkara 69*) by six wickets

April 13: Australia v Ireland at Bridgetown, Barbados

Ireland 91 (30 overs: GD McGrath 3–17, SW Tait 3–39) lost to Australia 1–92 (12.2 overs) by nine wickets

April 14: New Zealand v South Africa at St George's, Grenada

South Africa 7–193 (50 overs: HH Gibbs 60; CD McMillan 3–23) lost to New Zealand 5–196 (48.2 overs: SB Styris 56, SP Fleming 50) by five wickets

April 15: Ireland v Bangladesh at Bridgetown, Barbados

Ireland 7–243 (50 overs: WTS Porterfield 85, KJ O'Brien 48) defeated Bangladesh 169 (41.2 overs) by 74 runs

April 16: Australia v Sri Lanka at St George's, Grenada

Sri Lanka 226 (49.4 overs: DPMD Jayawardene 72, LPC Silva 64; NW Bracken 4–19) lost to Australia 3–232 (42.4 overs: RT Ponting 66*, Symonds 63*, ML Hayden 41) by seven wickets

April 17: South Africa v England at Bridgetown, Barbados

England 154 (48 overs: AJ Strauss 46; AJ Hall 5–18, A Nel 3–35) lost to South Africa 1–157 (19.2 overs: GC Smith 89*, AB de Villiers 42) by nine wickets

April 18: Sri Lanka v Ireland at St George's, Grenada

Ireland 77 (27.4 overs: M Muralitharan 4–19, MF Maharoof 4–25) lost to Sri Lanka 2–81 (10 overs) by eight wickets

April 19: West Indies v Bangladesh at Bridgetown, Barbados

West Indies 5–230 (50 overs: RR Sarwan 91*, S Chanderpaul 50) defeated Bangladesh 131 (43.5 overs: DB Powell 3–38) by 99 runs

April 20: Australia v New Zealand at St George's, Grenada

Australia 6–348 (50 overs: ML Hayden 103, RT Ponting 66, SR Watson 65*, MJ Clarke 49) defeated New Zealand 133 (25.5 overs: PG Fulton 62; GB Hogg 4–29, SW Tait 3–32) by 215 runs

April 21: England v West Indies at Bridgetown, Barbados

West Indies 300 (49.5 overs: CH Gayle 79, DS Smith 61, MN Samuels 51; MP Vaughan 3–39) lost to England 9–301 (49.5 overs: KP Pietersen 100, MP Vaughan 79) by one wicket

SUPER EIGHTS POINTS TABLE

Team	P	W	L	NR	T	Pts	NRR
Australia	7	7	0	0	0	14	+2.400
Sri Lanka	7	5	2	0	0	10	+1.483
New Zealand	7	5	2	0	0	10	+0.253
South Africa	7	4	3	0	0	8	+0.313
England	7	3	4	0	0	6	-0.394
West Indies	7	2	5	0	0	4	-0.566
Bangladesh	7	1	6	0	0	2	-1.514
Ireland	7	1	6	0	0	2	-1.730

Points won from the game against the other qualifier in a team's group were carried forward. For example, Australia carried into the Super Eights the two points they received for beating South Africa in their Group A match. All teams, therefore, started the Super Eights having played one game.

3. SEMI-FINALS

April 24: Sri Lanka v New Zealand at Kingston, Jamaica

Sri Lanka 5–289 (50 overs: DPMD Jayawardene 115*, WU Tharanga 73) defeated New Zealand 208 (41.4 overs: PG Fulton 46; M Muralitharan 4–31) by 81 runs

April 25: Australia v South Africa at Gros Islet, St Lucia

South Africa 149 (43.5 overs: JM Kemp 49*; SW Tait 4–39, GD McGrath 3–18) lost to Australia 3–153 (31.3 overs: MJ Clarke 60*, ML Hayden 41) by seven wickets

4. FINAL

April 28: Australia v Sri Lanka at Bridgetown, Barbados

Australia 4–281 (38 overs: AC Gilchrist 149) defeated Sri Lanka 8–215 (36 overs: ST Jayasuriya 63, KC Sangakkara 54) by 53 runs (D/L method)

GROUP A
AUSTRALIA V SCOTLAND
Warner Park, Basseterre, St Kitts
14 March 2007 (50-over match)

Result: Australia won by 203 runs • Toss: Scotland
Umpires: SA Bucknor and EAR de Silva (SL) • TV umpire: AL Hill (NZ)
Match referee: J Srinath (India) • Player of the match: RT Ponting (Aus)

Australia innings		R	M	B	4	6
AC Gilchrist	lbw b Brown	46	71	55	7	0
ML Hayden	lbw b Haq	60	114	73	6	1
RT Ponting	b Wright	113	144	93	9	5
MJ Clarke	b Haq	15	29	20	1	0
BJ Hodge	c Hoffmann b Rogers	29	62	28	3	0
MEK Hussey	st Smith b Hoffmann	4	19	6	0	0
SR Watson	not out	18	23	11	3	0
GB Hogg	not out	40	15	15	3	3
Extras	(b 1, lb 2, w 5, nb 1)	9				
Total	(6 wkts; 50 ov)	334				

DID NOT BAT: NW Bracken, SW Tait, GD McGrath

FALL OF WICKETS: 1–91 (Gilchrist, 16.6 ov), 2–139 (Hayden, 26.5 ov), 3–193 (Clarke, 34.3 ov), 4–256 (Hodge, 43.1 ov), 5–274 (Ponting, 45.2 ov), 6–276 (Hussey, 46.1 ov)

BOWLING: Hoffmann 10–0–57–1; Blain 4–0–29–0; Wright 10–0–58–1; Brown 9–0–86–1; Rogers 10–0–52–1; Haq 7–0–49–2

Scotland innings		R	M	B	4	6
DF Watts	b McGrath	9	40	25	0	0
RM Haq	run out	16	23	22	2	0
NS Poonia	b Tait	1	4	4	0	0
RR Watson	c Bracken b McGrath	6	21	20	0	0
GM Hamilton	c Gilchrist b McGrath	3	23	18	0	0
DR Brown	c Watson b Hodge	19	55	37	3	0
CJO Smith	b Hogg	51	93	76	7	0
CM Wright	lbw b Tait	4	12	21	0	0
GA Rogers	run out	6	29	19	0	0
PJC Hoffmann	not out	0	1	0	0	0
JAR Blain	absent hurt	–				
Extras	(lb 9, w 6, nb 1)	16				
Total	(all out; 40.1 ov)	131				

FALL OF WICKETS: 1–21 (Haq, 5.5 ov), 2–27 (Poonia, 7.4 ov), 3–32 (Watts, 9.3 ov), 4–37 (Watson, 13.3 ov), 5–42 (Hamilton, 15.3 ov), 6–89 (Brown, 27.4 ov), 7–104 (Wright, 32.5 ov), 8–131 (Rogers, 39.6 ov), 9–131 (Smith, 40.1 ov)

BOWLING: Bracken 6–1–12–0; Tait 8–0–45–2; McGrath 6–1–14–3; Watson 7–1–18–0; Hogg 7.1–1–16–1; Hodge 6–0–17–1

GROUP A
AUSTRALIA V NETHERLANDS
Warner Park, Basseterre, St Kitts
18 March 2007 (50-over match)

Result: Australia won by 229 runs • Toss: Australia
Umpires: SA Bucknor and AL Hill (NZ) • TV umpire: EAR de Silva (SL)
Match referee: J Srinath (India) • Player of the match: BJ Hodge (Aus)

Australia innings		R	M	B	4	6
AC Gilchrist	c van Troost b de Leede	57	80	64	11	0
ML Hayden	c Borren b de Leede	29	47	34	4	1
RT Ponting	c & b ten Doeschate	23	33	22	4	1
MJ Clarke	not out	93	124	85	6	3
BJ Hodge	b Borren	123	108	89	8	7
MEK Hussey	c sub (Kashif) b ten Doeschate	2	4	4	0	0
SR Watson	not out	12	5	4	1	1
Extras	(lb 9, w 8, nb 2)	19				
Total	(5 wickets; 50 ov)	358				

DID NOT BAT: GB Hogg, NW Bracken, SW Tait, GD McGrath

FALL OF WICKETS: 1–73 (Hayden, 11.5 ov), 2–116 (Gilchrist, 19.4 ov), 3–116 (Ponting, 20.1 ov), 4–320 (Hodge, 47.3 ov), 5–325 (Hussey, 48.4 ov)

BOWLING: Jonkman 6.1–1–35–0; Reekers 6–1–48–0; de Leede 10–1–40–2; ten Doeschate 10–0–76–2; Adeel Raja 7.5–0–61–0; Borren 10–0–89–1;

Netherlands innings		R	M	B	4	6
B Zuiderent	run out	9	53	29	1	0
DJ Reekers	c Clarke b Bracken	25	28	19	5	0
AN Kervezee	lbw b Bracken	0	2	2	0	0
RN ten Doeschate	lbw b Tait	1	4	6	0	0
LP van Troost	lbw b McGrath	0	6	4	0	0
DLS van Bunge	lbw b McGrath	33	49	33	4	1
TBM de Leede	c Hayden b Hogg	14	35	22	2	0
PW Borren	c Hussey b Hogg	24	30	18	4	1
J Smits	lbw b Hogg	3	8	12	0	0
Adeel Raja	not out	8	16	14	1	0
MBS Jonkman	st Gilchrist b Hogg	0	2	2	0	0
Extras	(b 4, lb 3, w 5)	12				
Total	(all out; 26.5 ov; 125 mins)	129				

FALL OF WICKETS: 1–36 (Reekers, 6.3 ov), 2–36 (Kervezee, 6.5 ov), 3–38 (ten Doeschate, 7.5 ov), 4–40 (van Troost, 9.2 ov), 5–46 (Zuiderent, 10.6 ov), 6–87 (de Leede, 18.4 ov), 7–97 (van Bunge, 19.4 ov), 8–106 (Smits, 22.3 ov), 9–129 (Borren, 26.3 ov), 10–129 (Jonkman, 26.5 ov)

BOWLING: Bracken 7–1–33–2; Tait 7–0–29–1; McGrath 8–0–33–2; Hogg 4.5–0–27–4

GROUP A
AUSTRALIA V SOUTH AFRICA
Warner Park, Basseterre, St Kitts
24 March 2007 (50-over match)

Result: Australia won by 83 runs • Toss: South Africa
Umpires: MR Benson (Eng) and SA Bucknor • TV umpire: AL Hill (NZ)
Match referee: RS Madugalle (SL) • Player of the match: ML Hayden (Aus)

Australia innings		R	M	B	4	6
AC Gilchrist	c Gibbs b Langeveldt	42	65	42	6	1
ML Hayden	c Gibbs b Kallis	101	107	68	14	4
RT Ponting	c de Villiers b Ntini	91	136	91	8	2
MJ Clarke	run out	92	103	75	7	4
A Symonds	b Hall	18	25	13	2	0
MEK Hussey	c Kallis b Hall	5	5	3	1	0
SR Watson	not out	14	12	9	2	0
Extras	(lb 4, w 9, nb 1)	14				
Total	(6 wkts; 50 ov)	377				

DID NOT BAT: GB Hogg, NW Bracken, SW Tait, GD McGrath

FALL OF WICKETS: 1–106 (Gilchrist, 14.5 ov), 2–167 (Hayden, 23.3 ov), 3–328 (Ponting, 45.1 ov), 4–347 (Clarke, 46.4 ov), 5–353 (Hussey, 47.2 ov), 6–377 (Symonds, 49.6 ov)

BOWLING: Pollock 10–0–83–0; Ntini 9–0–68–1; Langeveldt 10–0–82–1; Hall 10–0–60–2; Smith 2–0–14–0; Kallis 9–0–66–1

South Africa innings		R	M	B	4	6
GC Smith	c Gilchrist b Hogg	74	128	69	9	2
AB de Villiers	run out	92	194	70	14	2
JH Kallis	c Clarke b Hogg	48	114	63	5	0
HH Gibbs	st Gilchrist b Hogg	17	30	19	1	1
AG Prince	c Hayden b McGrath	1	6	3	0	0
MV Boucher	b Tait	22	26	26	1	1
JM Kemp	lbw b Tait	1	9	6	0	0
SM Pollock	b Watson	7	15	7	1	0
AJ Hall	not out	8	23	12	0	0
CK Langeveldt	b Bracken	0	8	6	0	0
M Ntini	b Bracken	7	11	8	1	0
Extras	(w 11, nb 1, pen 5)	17				
Total	(all out; 48 ov)	294				

FALL OF WICKETS: 1–160 (de Villiers, 20.6 ov), 2–220 (Gibbs, 31.3 ov), 3–223 (Prince, 32.2 ov), 4–256 (Boucher, 38.5 ov), 5–264 (Kemp, 40.5 ov), 6–267 (Smith, 41.3 ov), 7–277 (Kallis, 43.1 ov), 8–279 (Pollock, 44.1 ov), 9–280 (Langeveldt, 45.2 ov), 10–294 (Ntini, 47.6 ov)

BOWLING: Bracken 9–0–40–2; Tait 10–0–61–2; McGrath 9–0–62–1; Watson 8–1–46–1; Hogg 10–0–61–3; Symonds 2–0–19–0

SUPER EIGHTS
AUSTRALIA V WEST INDIES
Sir Vivian Richards Stadium, North Sound, Antigua
27–28 March 2007 (50-over match)

Result: Australia won by 103 runs • Toss: West Indies
Umpires: Aleem Dar (Pak) and Asad Rauf (Pak) • TV umpire: BF Bowden (NZ)
Match referee: BC Broad (Eng) • Player of the match: ML Hayden (Aus)

Australia innings		R	M	B	4	6
AC Gilchrist	c Ramdin b Powell	7	21	9	0	0
ML Hayden	c Samuels b Bravo	158	216	143	14	4
RT Ponting	run out	35	46	36	4	1
MJ Clarke	lbw b Bravo	41	71	47	4	0
A Symonds	c Ramdin b Samuels	13	22	18	1	0
MEK Hussey	b Powell	9	20	18	1	0
SR Watson	not out	33	45	26	3	1
GB Hogg	not out	5	13	6	0	0
Extras	(b 1, lb 9, w 8, nb 3)	21				
Total	(6 wkts; 50 ov)	322				

DID NOT BAT: NW Bracken, SW Tait, GD McGrath

FALL OF WICKETS: 1–10 (Gilchrist, 4.1 ov), 2–76 (Ponting, 14.4 ov), 3–174 (Clarke, 30.5 ov), 4–208 (Symonds, 35.6 ov), 5–234 (Hussey, 40.5 ov), 6–297 (Hayden, 47.1 ov)

BOWLING: Powell 10–2–53–2; Taylor 10–0–67–0; Collymore 10–0–56–0; Gayle 4–0–29–0; Bravo 7–0–49–2; Samuels 9–0–58–1

West Indies innings		R	M	B	4	6
CH Gayle	c Watson b McGrath	2	37	23	0	0
S Chanderpaul	lbw b Tait	5	20	12	0	0
RR Sarwan	c Ponting b Hogg	29	101	58	1	0
MN Samuels	c Symonds b McGrath	4	9	8	1	0
BC Lara	lbw b Hogg	77	118	83	8	1
DJ Bravo	c Ponting b McGrath	9	13	10	1	0
D Ramdin	c Gilchrist b Bracken	52	56	43	6	0
DR Smith	lbw b Hogg	9	5	7	0	1
JE Taylor	lbw b Symonds	10	13	18	1	0
DB Powell	b Tait	5	10	9	0	0
CD Collymore	not out	1	3	2	0	0
Extras	(b 1, w 15)	16				
Total	(all out; 45.3 ov)	219				

FALL OF WICKETS: 1–11 (Chanderpaul, 3.5 ov), 2–16 (Gayle, 7.2 ov), 3–20 (Samuels, 9.4 ov), 4–91 (Sarwan, 25.2 ov), 5–107 (Bravo, 28.3 ov), 6–156 (Lara, 35.3 ov), 7–172 (Smith, 37.4 ov), 8–199 (Taylor, 42.4 ov), 9–217 (Ramdin, 44.2 ov), 10–219 (Powell, 45.3 ov)

BOWLING: Bracken 9–1–25–1; Tait 7.3–0–43–2; McGrath 8–1–31–3; Watson 7–0–31–0; Hogg 10–0–56–3; Symonds 4–0–32–1

SUPER EIGHTS
AUSTRALIA V BANGLADESH
Sir Vivian Richards Stadium, North Sound, Antigua
31 March 2007 (50-over match; reduced to 22 overs per side)

Result: Australia won by 10 wickets • Toss: Australia
Umpires: Aleem Dar (Pak) and BF Bowden (NZ) • TV umpire: RE Koertzen (SA)
Match referee: BC Broad (Eng) • Player of the match: GD McGrath (Aus)

Bangladesh innings		R	M	B	4	6
Tamim Iqbal	c Hogg b Bracken	3	11	14	0	0
Shahriar Nafees	b McGrath	1	15	4	0	0
Aftab Ahmed	c Bracken b McGrath	11	14	7	1	0
Saqibul Hasan	c Gilchrist b Tait	25	50	36	0	1
Mohammad Ashraful	c Ponting b McGrath	6	11	8	1	0
Habibul Bashar	c Ponting b Bracken	24	48	43	0	0
Mashrafe Mortaza	not out	25	21	17	2	1
Mushfiqur Rahim	not out	2	2	3	0	0
Extras	(w 7)	7				
Total	(6 wkts; 22 ov)	104				

DID NOT BAT: Mohammad Rafique, Abdur Razzak, Tapash Baisya

FALL OF WICKETS: 1–4 (Tamim Iqbal, 2.4 ov), 2–8 (Shahriar Nafees, 3.3 ov), 3–25 (Aftab Ahmed, 5.3 ov), 4–37 (Mohammad Ashraful, 7.5 ov), 5–65 (Saqibul Hasan, 16.2 ov), 6–97 (Habibul Bashar, 21.1 ov)

BOWLING: Bracken 4–0–20–2; McGrath 5–0–16–3; Tait 4–0–28–1; Watson 1.4–0–4–0; Hogg 5–0–20–0; Symonds 2.2–0–16–0

Australia innings		R	M	B	4	6
AC Gilchrist	not out	59	56	44	8	1
ML Hayden	not out	47	56	39	3	3
Extras		0				
Total	(0 wkts; 13.5 ov)	106				

DID NOT BAT: RT Ponting, MJ Clarke, A Symonds, MEK Hussey, SR Watson, GB Hogg, NW Bracken, SW Tait, GD McGrath

BOWLING: Mashrafe Mortaza 4–0–20–0; Tapash Baisya 2.5–0–35–0; Aftab Ahmed 0.1–0–1–0; Abdur Razzak 3–0–15–0; Mohammad Rafique 3–0–21–0; Saqibul Hasan 0.5–0–14–0

SUPER EIGHTS
AUSTRALIA V ENGLAND
Sir Vivian Richards Stadium, North Sound, Antigua
8 April 2007 (50-over match)

Result: Australia won by seven wickets • Toss: England
Umpires: BF Bowden (NZ) and RE Koertzen (SA) • TV umpire: Asad Rauf (Pak)
Match referee: MJ Procter (SA) • Player of the match: SW Tait (Aus)

England innings		R	M	B	4	6
IR Bell	c Hussey b McGrath	77	126	90	9	0
MP Vaughan	b Tait	5	12	8	1	0
AJ Strauss	b Tait	7	11	10	0	0
KP Pietersen	c Clarke b Bracken	104	182	122	6	1
PD Collingwood	c Gilchrist b Tait	2	3	5	0	0
A Flintoff	st Gilchrist b Hogg	4	20	19	0	0
RS Bopara	c Hussey b Bracken	21	43	36	2	0
PA Nixon	c Hodge b McGrath	8	14	6	0	1
SI Mahmood	c Hodge b Bracken	0	2	2	0	0
MS Panesar	not out	1	3	2	0	0
JM Anderson	lbw b McGrath	0	2	1	0	0
Extras	(b 4, lb 4, w 7, nb 3)	18				
Total	(all out; 49.5 ov)	247				

FALL OF WICKETS: 1–10 (Vaughan, 3.2 ov), 2–24 (Strauss, 5.6 ov), 3–164 (Bell, 29.3 ov), 4–167 (Collingwood, 30.3 ov), 5–179 (Flintoff, 35.3 ov), 6–230 (Bopara, 46.2 ov), 7–240 (Pietersen, 48.4 ov), 8–240 (Mahmood, 48.6 ov), 9–246 (Nixon, 49.2 ov), 10–247 (Anderson, 49.5 ov)

BOWLING: Bracken 10–1–33–3; Tait 10–0–41–3; McGrath 9.5–0–62–3; Clarke 4–0–27–0; Hogg 10–0–36–1; Symonds 6–0–40–0

Australia innings		R	M	B	4	6
AC Gilchrist	c Collingwood b Flintoff	27	51	37	5	0
ML Hayden	b Collingwood	41	91	50	6	0
RT Ponting	run out	86	133	106	11	0
MJ Clarke	not out	55	130	63	2	0
A Symonds	not out	28	33	28	4	1
Extras	(b 1, lb 5, w 5)	11				
Total	(3 wkts; 47.2 ov)	248				

DID NOT BAT: MEK Hussey, BJ Hodge, GB Hogg, NW Bracken, SW Tait, GD McGrath

FALL OF WICKETS: 1–57 (Gilchrist, 10.6 ov), 2–89 (Hayden, 19.1 ov), 3–201 (Ponting, 40.1 ov)

BOWLING: Anderson 10–1–4–0; Mahmood 9.2–1–60–0; Flintoff 10–1–35–1; Panesar 9–0–48–0; Collingwood 9–0–50–1

SUPER EIGHTS
AUSTRALIA V IRELAND
Kensington Oval, Bridgetown, Barbados
13 April 2007 (50-over match)

Result: Australia won by nine wickets • Toss: Australia
Umpires: BF Bowden (NZ) and RE Koertzen (SA) • TV umpire: SA Bucknor
Match referee: RS Madugalle (SL)

Reserve umpire SJA Taufel (Aus) • Player of the match: GD McGrath (Aus)

Ireland innings		R	M	B	4	6
JP Bray	b McGrath	1	3	2	0	0
WTS Porterfield	lbw b Tait	1	14	11	0	0
EJG Morgan	c Hayden b McGrath	0	19	9	0	0
NJ O'Brien	b Tait	0	1	1	0	0
KJ O'Brien	c Hodge b Clark	16	51	25	3	0
AR White	c Hogg b McGrath	6	30	20	0	0
DT Johnston	b Tait	17	30	25	2	0
WK McCallan	c Tait b Symonds	5	32	18	0	0
JF Mooney	run out	23	53	44	2	0
D Langford-Smith	c Ponting b Hogg	2	8	7	0	0
WB Rankin	not out	4	25	19	0	0
Extras	(w 15, nb 1)	16				
Total	(all out; 30 ov)	91				

FALL OF WICKETS: 1–2 (Bray, 0.6 ov), 2–2 (Porterfield, 3.1 ov), 3–2 (NJ O'Brien, 3.2 ov), 4–12 (Morgan, 4.3 ov), 5–32 (White, 10.3 ov), 6–42 (KJ O'Brien, 13.2 ov), 7–54 (Johnston, 16.3 ov), 8–72 (McCallan, 20.6 ov), 9–80 (Langford-Smith, 23.1 ov), 10–91 (Mooney, 29.6 ov)

BOWLING: McGrath 7–1–17–3; Tait 6–1–39–3; Clark 8–1–19–1; Hogg 6–2–9–1; Symonds 3–1–7–1

Australia innings		R	M	B	4	6
AC Gilchrist	b Johnston	34	38	25	4	0
MEK Hussey	not out	30	57	41	3	1
A Symonds	not out	15	17	9	1	1
Extras	(lb 4, w 8, nb 1)	13				
Total	(1 wkt; 12.2 ov)	92				

DID NOT BAT: ML Hayden, RT Ponting, MJ Clarke, BJ Hodge, GB Hogg, SR Clark, SW Tait, GD McGrath

FALL OF WICKETS: 1–62 (Gilchrist, 8.5 ov)

BOWLING: Langford-Smith 3–0–27–0; Rankin 4.2–0–24–0; Johnston 3–0–18–1; Mooney 1–0–14–0; McCallan 1–0–5–0

SUPER EIGHTS
AUSTRALIA V SRI LANKA
National Cricket Stadium, St George's, Grenada
16 April 2007 (50-over match)

Result: Australia won by seven wickets • Toss: Sri Lanka
Umpires: Aleem Dar (Pak) and BR Doctrove • TV umpire: MR Benson (Eng)
Match referee: MJ Procter (SA) • Player of the match: NW Bracken (Aus)

Sri Lanka innings		R	M	B	4	6
WU Tharanga	c Hayden b Bracken	6	33	22	0	0
ST Jayasuriya	lbw b Bracken	12	21	12	2	0
KC Sangakkara	lbw b McGrath	0	6	4	0	0
DPMD Jayawardene	st Gilchrist b Hogg	72	133	88	5	1
LPC Silva	c Clarke b Hogg	64	119	107	6	0
TM Dilshan	c Hodge b Tait	7	13	12	0	0
RP Arnold	b Tait	3	15	10	0	0
MF Maharoof	c Symonds b Bracken	25	40	22	4	0
KMDN Kulasekara	c Hayden b Bracken	1	5	5	0	0
CM Bandara	c Hogg b McGrath	17	23	19	0	2
CRD Fernando	not out	0	4	0	0	0
Extras	(lb 5, w 11, nb 3)	19				
Total	(all out; 49.4 ov)	226				

FALL OF WICKETS: 1–26 (Jayasuriya, 4.3 ov), 2–27 (Sangakkara, 5.3 ov), 3–27 (Tharanga, 6.4 ov), 4–167 (Silva, 37.2 ov), 5–174 (Jayawardene, 39.4 ov), 6–178 (Dilshan, 40.6 ov), 7–183 (Arnold, 42.4 ov), 8–184 (Kulasekara, 43.3 ov), 9–218 (Bandara, 48.6 ov), 10–226 (Maharoof, 49.4 ov)

BOWLING: Bracken 9.4–3–19–4; Tait 10–0–68–2; McGrath 9–1–48–2; Hogg 10–0–35–2; Symonds 3–0–15–0; Clarke 8–0–36–0

Australia innings		R	M	B	4	6
AC Gilchrist	lbw b Arnold	30	65	49	4	0
ML Hayden	c Dilshan b Arnold	41	56	30	5	2
RT Ponting	not out	66	116	80	4	1
MJ Clarke	c Dilshan b Bandara	23	38	31	4	0
A Symonds	not out	63	66	71	5	2
Extras	(w 4, nb 5)	9				
Total	(3 wickets; 42.4 ov)	232				

DID NOT BAT: MEK Hussey, BJ Hodge, GB Hogg, NW Bracken, SW Tait, GD McGrath

FALL OF WICKETS: 1–76 (Hayden, 11.5 ov), 2–79 (Gilchrist, 13.3 ov), 3–126 (Clarke, 23.1 ov)

BOWLING: Fernando 6–1–36–0; Maharoof 7–0–52–0; Kulasekara 4–0–20–0; Arnold 4–0–20–2; Bandara 9.4–0–53–1; Jayasuriya 6–0–32–0; Dilshan 6–0–19–0

SUPER EIGHTS
AUSTRALIA V NEW ZEALAND
National Cricket Stadium, St George's, Grenada
20 April 2007 (50-over match)

Result: Australia won by 215 runs • Toss: Australia
Umpires: Aleem Dar (Pak) and Asad Rauf (Pak) • TV umpire: BR Doctrove
Match referee: MJ Procter (SA) • Player of the match: ML Hayden (Aus)

Australia innings		R	M	B	4	6
AC Gilchrist	c Gillespie b Franklin	1	7	2	0	0
ML Hayden	c & b Styris	103	150	100	10	2
RT Ponting	c Taylor b Patel	66	96	70	7	0
MJ Clarke	b Franklin	49	59	46	7	0
MEK Hussey	c Styris b Franklin	37	75	44	2	0
A Symonds	c Mason b Patel	11	20	16	1	0
SR Watson	not out	65	44	32	4	4
GB Hogg	not out	0	3	0	0	0
Extras	(lb 1, w 5, nb 10)	16				
Total	(6 wickets; 50 ov)	348				

DID NOT BAT: NW Bracken, SW Tait, GD McGrath

FALL OF WICKETS: 1–7 (Gilchrist, 1.1 ov), 2–144 (Ponting, 22.6 ov), 3–216 (Hayden, 32.4 ov), 4–233 (Clarke, 35.3 ov), 5–257 (Symonds, 40.1 ov), 6–334 (Hussey, 49.3 ov)

BOWLING: Mason 3–0–27–0; Franklin 8–0–74–3; Patel 10–0–48–2; Vettori 10–0–60–0; Styris 10–0–50–1; Gillespie 6–0–67–0; McMillan 3–0–21–0

New Zealand innings		R	M	B	4	6
PG Fulton	b Hogg	62	127	72	5	0
SP Fleming	c Ponting b Tait	12	18	9	1	1
RL Taylor	c Hussey b McGrath	3	8	6	0	0
SB Styris	c Hayden b McGrath	27	30	22	5	0
CD McMillan	lbw b Tait	1	6	5	0	0
JEC Franklin	b Watson	6	11	9	0	0
BB McCullum	c Hussey b Hogg	7	19	16	0	0
DL Vettori	c Symonds b Hogg	4	7	4	1	0
MR Gillespie	c McGrath b Hogg	2	9	8	0	0
MJ Mason	c Gilchrist b Tait	0	6	5	0	0
JS Patel	not out	0	3	1	0	0
Extras	(w 7, nb 2)	9				
Total	(all out; 25.5 ov)	133				

FALL OF WICKETS: 1–21 (Fleming, 3.3 ov), 2–29 (Taylor, 5.1 ov), 3–77 (Styris, 11.1 ov), 4–80 (McMillan, 12.3 ov), 5–89 (Franklin, 14.3 ov), 6–111 (McCullum, 19.3 ov), 7–117 (Vettori, 21.1 ov), 8–127 (Gillespie, 23.5 ov), 9–133 (Mason, 24.5 ov), 10–133 (Fulton, 25.5 ov)

BOWLING: Bracken 4–0–27–0; Tait 6–0–32–3; McGrath 4–0–25–2; Hogg 6.5–1–29–4; Watson 5–0–20–1

SECOND SEMI FINAL
AUSTRALIA V SOUTH AFRICA
Beausejour Cricket Ground, Gros Islet, St Lucia
25 April 2007 (50-over match)

Result: Australia won by seven wickets • Toss: South Africa
Umpires: Aleem Dar (Pak) and SA Bucknor • TV umpire: BF Bowden (NZ)
Match referee: JJ Crowe (NZ) • Player of the match: GD McGrath (Aus)

South Africa innings		R	M	B	4	6
GC Smith	b Bracken	2	10	5	0	0
AB de Villiers	c Gilchrist b Tait	15	39	34	3	0
JH Kallis	b McGrath	5	12	9	1	0
HH Gibbs	c Gilchrist b Tait	39	77	49	6	0
AG Prince	c Gilchrist b McGrath	0	4	2	0	0
MV Boucher	c Hayden b McGrath	0	1	1	0	0
JM Kemp	not out	49	151	91	4	1
AJ Hall	c Gilchrist b Tait	3	14	8	0	0
SM Pollock	c & b Hogg	5	15	13	1	0
A Nel	c Clarke b Tait	8	45	41	1	0
CK Langeveldt	b Watson	6	18	10	1	0
Extras	(lb 4, w 13)	17				
Total	(all out; 43.5 ov)	149				

FALL OF WICKETS: 1–7 (Smith, 2.3 ov), 2–12 (Kallis, 5.3 ov), 3–26 (de Villiers, 8.5 ov),
4–27 (Prince, 9.4 ov), 5–27 (Boucher, 9.5 ov), 6–87 (Gibbs, 22.5 ov), 7–93 (Hall, 26.1 ov),
8–103 (Pollock, 29.4 ov), 9–130 (Nel, 40.1 ov), 10–149 (Langeveldt, 43.5 ov)

BOWLING: NW Bracken 7–2–15–1; McGrath 8–1–18–3; Tait 10–0–39–4; Watson
8.5–0–49–1; Hogg 10–2–24–1

Australia innings		R	M	B	4	6
AC Gilchrist	b Langeveldt	1	4	5	0	0
ML Hayden	c Smith b Pollock	41	115	60	4	0
RT Ponting	b Nel	22	38	25	5	0
MJ Clarke	not out	60	109	86	8	0
A Symonds	not out	18	29	16	3	0
Extras	(lb 5, w 3, nb 3)	11				
Total	(3 wkts; 31.3 ov)	153				

DID NOT BAT: MEK Hussey, SR Watson, GB Hogg, NW Bracken, SW Tait, GD McGrath

FALL OF WICKETS: 1–1 (Gilchrist, 1.1 ov), 2–44 (Ponting, 8.6 ov), 3–110 (Hayden, 24.4 ov)

BOWLING: Pollock 5–1–16–1; Langeveldt 6–0–34–1; Kallis 5–1–20–0; Nel 7–1–31–1; Hall
6.3–0–43–0; Kemp 2–0–4–0

FINAL
AUSTRALIA V SRI LANKA
Kensington Oval, Bridgetown, Barbados
28 April 2007 (50-over match, reduced to 38 overs per side)

Result: Australia won by 53 runs (D/L method) • Toss: Australia
Umpires: Aleem Dar (Pak) and SA Bucknor • TV umpire: RE Koertzen (SA)
Match referee: JJ Crowe (NZ) • Player of the match: AC Gilchrist (Aus)
Player of the series: GD McGrath (Aus)

Australia innings		R	M	B	4	6
AC Gilchrist	c Silva b Fernando	149	129	104	13	8
ML Hayden	c Jayawardene b Malinga	38	100	55	3	1
RT Ponting	run out	37	53	42	1	1
A Symonds	not out	23	39	21	2	0
SR Watson	b Malinga	3	3	3	0	0
MJ Clarke	not out	8	10	6	1	0
Extras	(lb 4, w 16, nb 3)	23				
Total	(4 wkts; 38 ov)	281				

DID NOT BAT: MEK Hussey, GB Hogg, NW Bracken, SW Tait, GD McGrath

FALL OF WICKETS: 1–172 (Hayden, 22.5 ov), 2–224 (Gilchrist, 30.3 ov), 3–261 (Ponting, 35.4 ov), 4–266 (Watson, 36.2 ov)

BOWLING: Vaas 8–0–54–0, Malinga 8–1–49–2; Fernando 8–0–74–1; Muralitharan 7–0–44–0; Dilshan 2–0–23–0; Jayasuriya 5–0–33–0

Sri Lanka innings		R	M	B	4	6
WU Tharanga	c Gilchrist b Bracken	6	11	8	1	0
ST Jayasuriya	b Clarke	63	108	67	9	0
KC Sangakkara	c Ponting b Hogg	54	72	52	6	1
DPMD Jayawardene	lbw b Watson	19	31	19	1	0
LPC Silva	b Clarke	21	41	22	1	1
TM Dilshan	run out	14	20	13	2	0
RP Arnold	c Gilchrist b McGrath	1	9	2	0	0
WPUJC Vaas	not out	11	20	21	0	0
SL Malinga	st Gilchrist b Symonds	10	6	6	0	1
CRD Fernando	not out	1	6	6	0	0
Extras	(lb 1, w 14)	15				
Total	(8 wkts; 36 ov)	215				

DID NOT BAT: M Muralitharan

FALL OF WICKETS: 1–7 (Tharanga, 2.1 ov), 2–123 (Sangakkara, 19.5 ov), 3–145 (Jayasuriya, 22.6 ov), 4–156 (Jayawardene, 25.5 ov), 5–188 (Dilshan, 29.6 ov), 6–190 (Silva, 30.1 ov), 7–194 (Arnold, 31.5 ov), 8–211 (Malinga, 33.6 ov)

BOWLING: Bracken 6–1–34–1; Tait 6–0–42–0; McGrath 7–0–31–1; Watson 7–0–49–1; Hogg 3–0–19–1; Clarke 5–0–33–2; Symonds 2–0–6–1

ICC WORLD CUP — AUSTRALIAN AVERAGES

BATTING AND FIELDING

Batsman	ODI	Inn	NO	Runs	HS	Ave	100	50	Ct	St
SR Watson	8	6	5	145	65*	145.00	0	1	2	–
MJ Clarke	11	9	4	436	93*	87.20	0	4	5	–
BJ Hodge	5	2	0	152	123	76.00	1	0	4	–
ML Hayden	11	10	1	659	158	73.22	3	1	7	–
RT Ponting	11	9	1	539	113	67.38	1	4	7	–
A Symonds	9	8	5	189	63*	63.00	0	1	3	–
AC Gilchrist	11	11	1	453	149	45.30	1	2	12	5
MEK Hussey	11	6	1	87	37	17.40	0	0	5	–
GB Hogg	11	3	3	45	40*	–	0	0	4	–
NW Bracken	10	–	–	–	–	–	–	–	2	–
SR Clark	1	–	–	–	–	–	–	–	–	–
GD McGrath	11	–	–	–	–	–	–	–	1	–
SW Tait	11	–	–	–	–	–	–	–	1	–

BOWLING

Bowler	O	M	R	W	Ave	Best	4w
GD McGrath	80.5	5	357	26	13.73	3–14	0
GB Hogg	82.5	6	332	21	15.81	4–27	2
NW Bracken	71.4	10	258	16	16.13	4–19	1
BJ Hodge	6.0	0	17	1	17.00	1–17	0
SR Clark	8.0	1	19	1	19.00	1–19	0
SW Tait	84.3	1	467	23	20.30	4–39	1
A Symonds	22.2	1	135	3	45.00	1–6	0
MJ Clarke	17.0	0	96	2	48.00	2–33	0
SR Watson	44.3	2	217	4	54.25	1–20	0

AUSTRALIAN CENTURIES

Ricky Ponting's 113 in the game against Scotland was his 23rd century in one-day international cricket, in his 270th ODI.

Brad Hodge's 123 in the game against the Netherlands was his first century in one-day international cricket, in his 15th ODI.

Matthew Hayden's 101 in the Group A game against South Africa was his eighth century in one-day international cricket, in his 137th ODI.

Matthew Hayden's 158 in the game against the West Indies was his ninth century in one-day international cricket, in his 138th ODI.

Matthew Hayden's 103 in the game against New Zealand was his 10th century in one-day international cricket, in his 143rd ODI.

Adam Gilchrist's 149 in the final against Sri Lanka was his 15th century in one-day international cricket, in his 268th ODI.

NOTABLE AUSTRALIAN LANDMARKS

A number of players passed landmarks in the Group A game against South Africa. Ricky Ponting scored his 10,000th ODI run, Matthew Hayden his 5000th ODI run, and Michael Clarke his 3000th ODI run, and Nathan Bracken took his 100th ODI wicket.

Matthew Hayden became the fifth Australian to score centuries in consecutive ODIs. His 158 is the highest score made by an Australian in a World Cup match.

Adam Gilchrist became the fifth batsman and second Australian to score a century in a World Cup final, after Clive Lloyd (102 v Australia in 1975), Viv Richards (138 not out v England in 1979), Aravinda de Silva (107 not out v Australia in 1996) and Ricky Ponting (140 not out v India in 2003). His 149 was his first century in his 31st World Cup match, and his third 50-plus score in a World Cup final, following scores of 54 at Lord's in 1999 and 57 at Johannesburg in 2003.

Gilchrist scored his 9000th run in ODI cricket in the final. Earlier in the tournament, in the Super Eights game against Sri Lanka, he completed his 50th stumping in ODI cricket. In the final, he became the first keeper to complete 50 dismissals in World Cup matches.

Ricky Ponting went into the final having scored exactly 1500 runs in World Cup matches. He finished the tournament with 1537 career World Cup runs, at 48.03. The only man to have scored more World Cup runs is Sachin Tendulkar, with 1796 runs at 57.94. Adam Gilchrist became the second Australia to have scored 1000 runs in World Cup games during his century in the final.

The fourth-wicket partnership of 204 between Michael Clarke and Brad Hodge in the game against the Netherlands was the highest stand for any wicket during the tournament.

Glenn McGrath's 26 wickets are the most taken by any bowler in a single World Cup. McGrath's total World Cup wicket tally of 71, achieved between 1996 and 2007, is the most by any bowler. Next best is Pakistan's Wasim Akram, with 55. Next best Australian is Brad Hogg, with 34, then Shane Warne, with 32.

Ponting and McGrath have each appeared in 39 World Cup matches, most by any player.

Ponting's 25 catches is the most taken by a non-wicketkeeper in World Cup matches. Next best is 18 by Sri Lanka's Sanath Jayasuriya.

Matthew Hayden's tournament runs aggregate of 659 from 10 innings is the second highest achieved at a World Cup, behind Sachin Tendulkar's 673 from 11 innings in 2003.

Australia became the first team to appear in six World Cup finals (1975, 1987, 1996, 1999, 2003 and 2007; next best is West Indies and England, each with three), and the first to win four World Cups (1987, 1999, 2003 and 2007; next best is West Indies, with two).

Australia extended its unbeaten run in World Cup matches to 29, stretching back to the group matches at the 1999 World Cup. This sequence includes the 1999 semi-final in which Australia tied with South Africa, Australia going through to the final. Australia has won its last 23 World Cup matches. Ricky Ponting and Glenn McGrath played in all 29 of these matches, Adam Gilchrist in 28 (missing only the game against the Netherlands at the 2003 World Cup).

Ricky Ponting has led Australia in 22 World Cup matches, for 22 victories. In all, he has led his country to 116 ODI victories, the most by any captain (next best is another Australian, Allan Border, with 107 wins as captain).

Glenn McGrath did not bat in the tournament, giving him a career World Cup batting record of 39 matches, four innings, three not outs, three runs, highest score of 3 not out, average 3.00. He faced no deliveries in the 1996 and 2007 World Cups, three in 1999 and two in 2003. The 2007 final was McGrath's last game in international cricket, and he retired as Australia's leading wicket-taker in ODI matches. Where he and other prominent players from the 2006–07 one-day season rank in the lists of Australia's leading one-day run-scorers and wicket-takers is as follows:

MOST ODI RUNS (AS AT SEPTEMBER 1, 2007)

Rank	Player	ODIs	Inn	NO	Runs	HS	Ave	100	50
1.	RT Ponting	280	272	32	10395	164	43.31	23	62
2.	AC Gilchrist	268	261	10	9038	172	36.01	15	50
3.	ME Waugh	244	236	20	8500	173	39.35	18	50
4.	SR Waugh	325	288	58	7569	120	32.91	3	45
5.	MG Bevan	232	196	67	6912	108	53.58	6	46
9.	ML Hayden	145	140	15	5499	181	43.99	10	30
10.	DR Martyn	208	182	51	5346	144	40.81	5	37
12.	A Symonds	170	136	29	4226	156	39.50	5	22
14.	MJ Clarke	112	98	25	3326	105	45.56	2	25
19.	MEK Hussey	72	54	23	1826	109*	58.90	2	10

MOST ODI WICKETS (AS AT SEPTEMBER 1, 2007)

Rank	Player	ODIs	Balls	Mdns	Runs	Wkts	Avg	Best	4w
1.	GD McGrath	250	12970	279	8389	381	22.02	7–15	16
2.	SK Warne	194	10642	110	7541	293	25.74	5–33	13
3.	B Lee	150	7729	101	6048	267	22.65	5–22	17
4.	CJ McDermott	138	7461	101	5018	203	24.72	5–44	5
5.	SR Waugh	325	8883	56	6761	195	34.67	4–33	3
8.	GB Hogg	106	4814	28	3605	133	27.11	5–32	4
9.	A Symonds	170	5588	29	4659	124	37.57	5–18	3
10.	NW Bracken	67	3303	56	2393	112	21.37	5–67	4

* * *

AUSTRALIA'S ODI RECORD FOR 2006–07

Tournament	Played	Won	Lost	NR	Tied
DLF Cup	5	3	1	1	–
Champions Trophy	5	4	1	–	–
Commonwealth Bank Series	10	7	3	–	–
Chappell–Hadlee Trophy	3	–	3	–	–
World Cup	11	11	–	–	–
Total	*34*	*25*	*8*	*1*	–

AUSTRALIAN ONE-DAY TEAM AVERAGES 2006–07

BATTING AND FIELDING

Batsman	ODI	Inn	NO	Runs	HS	Ave	100	50	Ct	St
ML Hayden	26	25	3	1368	181*	62.18	5	4	15	–
BJ Hodge	13	10	2	437	123	54.63	1	2	11	–
DR Martyn	8	8	2	316	78	52.67	–	3	4	–
RT Ponting	28	26	3	1185	113	51.52	3	10	20	–
MJ Clarke	30	25	6	936	93*	49.26	0	8	9	–
MEK Hussey	32	23	7	670	109*	41.88	2	1	22	–
A Symonds	24	20	7	529	69	40.69	0	4	7	–
BJ Haddin	8	8	1	267	70	38.14	–	1	15	–
AC Gilchrist	26	26	1	805	149	32.20	1	5	40	6
SR Watson	22	20	6	494	79	35.29	–	5	3	–
CL White	11	9	3	157	45	26.17	–	–	1	–
GB Hogg	21	9	3	145	40*	24.17	0	0	8	–
SM Katich	4	4	0	92	36	23.00	–	–	1	–
MJ Cosgrove	2	2	0	38	34	19.00	–	–	–	–
SR Clark	10	5	3	26	15*	13.00	–	–	3	–
NW Bracken	29	9	4	60	21	12.00	–	–	7	–
SW Tait	15	1	–	11	11	11.00	–	–	1	–
MG Johnson	13	4	1	29	15	9.67	–	–	3	–
B Lee	15	8	3	45	20*	9.00	–	–	1	–
PA Jaques	4	4	0	31	25	7.75	–	–	3	–
GD McGrath	29	8	6	11	5*	5.50	–	–	3	–
AC Voges	1	1	1	16	16*	–	–	–	1	–
DJ Cullen	2	1	1	2	2*	–	–	–	–	–
BW Hilfenhaus	1	0	–	–	–	–	–	–	1	–

BOWLING

Bowler	O	M	R	W	Ave	Best	4w
MJ Cosgrove	1	0	1	1	1.00	1–1	–
BJ Hodge	6.0	0	17	1	17.00	1–17	0
GD McGrath	234.3	19	967	50	19.34	3–14	–
B Lee	137.5	8	634	30	21.13	5–38	2
NW Bracken	233	24	1016	16	21.62	4–19	1
MG Johnson	103	5	551	23	23.96	4–11	2
SW Tait	123.3	1	685	28	24.46	4–39	1
GB Hogg	142.2	7	637	26	24.50	4–27	2
BW Hilfenhaus	7	1	26	1	26.00	1–26	–
SR Watson	142.3	2	739	25	29.56	4–43	1
SR Clark	77	3	445	13	34.23	4–54	1
MJ Clarke	59	0	288	7	41.14	2–33	–
CL White	21	2	141	3	47.00	1–5	–
A Symonds	94.1	2	511	10	51.10	2–41	–
MEK Hussey	2	0	12	0	–	–	–
AC Voges	3	0	33	0	–	–	–
DJ Cullen	8	1	49	0	–	–	–

PHOTOGRAPHS

All the photographs that appear in *Captain's Diary 2007* come from the resources of Getty Images. We are very grateful for the support of all the staff at Getty, especially Georgina Turner, and for the brilliant work by their photographers who follow the Australian team throughout the year. The photographers responsible for the images in this book are as follows:

SECTION ONE

Page 1 — Top and middle: Hamish Blair. Bottom: AFP.

Page 2 — All pics: Hamish Blair.

Page 3 — Top left, top right and bottom: Hamish Blair. Middle: Julian Herbert.

Page 4 — Top: Clive Mason. Middle: Ezra Shaw. Bottom: Quinn Rooney.

Page 5 — Top: Hamish Blair. Bottom: Cameron Spencer.

Page 6 — Top left: Hamish Blair. Top right: Jonathan Wood. Bottom left and right: Bradley Kanaris.

Page 7 — Both pics: Hamish Blair.

Page 8 — Top left: Quinn Rooney. Top right: Tom Shaw. Bottom left and right: Hamish Blair.

SECTION TWO

Page 1 — Top: Hamish Blair. Bottom: Mark Dadswell.

Page 2 — Top: James Knowler. Bottom left and right: Hamish Blair.

Page 3 — Top left: Cameron Spencer. Top right and bottom: Paul Kane.

Page 4 — Top and middle: Hamish Blair. Bottom left: Ezra Shaw. Bottom right: Paul Kane.

Page 5 — Top and bottom left: Hamish Blair. Bottom right: Mark Dadswell.

Page 6 — Top Left: Robert Cianflone. Top right: Tom Shaw. Bottom left: Quinn Rooney. Bottom right: Mark Dadswell.

Page 7 — Top and bottom: Ezra Shaw. Middle: Hamish Blair.

Page 8 — Top and bottom: Tom Shaw. Middle: Cameron Spencer.

SECTION THREE

Page 1 — All pics: Hamish Blair.

Page 2 — Top Left: Paul Kane. Top right: Quinn Rooney. Bottom left: Simon Ferguson. Bottom right: Clive Rose.

Page 3 — Both pics: Hamish Blair.

Page 4 — Top, middle left and middle right: Hamish Blair. Bottom: Shaun Botterill.

Page 5 — Top and bottom: Hamish Blair. Middle: Duif du Toit.

Page 6 — Top left and bottom: Hamish Blair. Top right: Tom Shaw.

Page 7 — Top: Clive Mason. Middle left: Hamish Blair. Middle right: Shaun Botterill. Bottom: Tom Shaw.

Page 8 — Top: Clive Mason. Middle left and bottom: Hamish Blair. Middle right: Tom Shaw.